Norihiro Yagi won the 32nd
Akatsuka Award for his
debut work, *UNDEADMAN*,
which appeared in *Monthly
Shonen Jump* magazine and
produced two sequels. His
first serialized manga was
his comedy *Angel Densetsu*
(Angel Legend), which appeared
in *Monthly Shonen Jump*
from 1992 to 2000. His epic
saga, *Claymore*, is running
in *Monthly Jump Square*
magazine.

In his spare time, Yagi enjoys
things like the Japanese
comedic duo Downtown, martial
arts, games, driving, and hard
rock music, but he doesn't
consider these actual hobbies.

CLAYMORE VOL. 25
SHONEN JUMP ADVANCED Manga Edition

STORY AND ART BY
NORIHIRO YAGI

English Adaptation & Translation/John Werry
Touch-up Art & Lettering/Sabrina Heep
Design/Stacie Yamaki
Editor/Megan Bates

Printed in the U.S.A.

Published by VIZ Media, LLC
P.O. Box 77010
San Francisco, CA 94107

10 9 8 7 6 5 4 3 2 1
First printing, November 2014

SHONEN JUMP ADVANCED Manga Edition

Claymore
クレイモア

Vol. 25
Sword of the Dark Deep

Story and Art by Norihiro Yagi

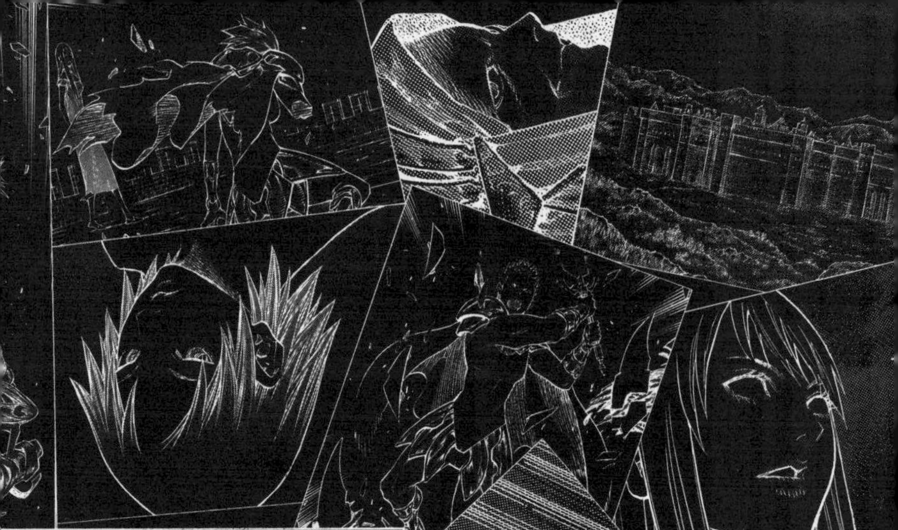

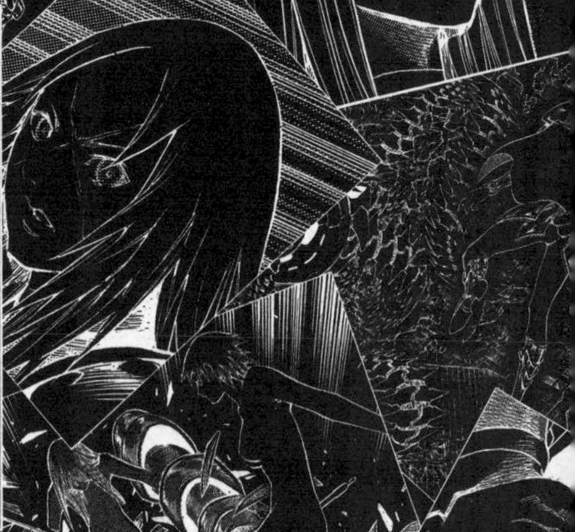

The Abyssal One Cassandra advances on the Holy City of Rabona. Side by side with Awakened Beings, Clare and the others try to prevent her attack. Meanwhile, a change occurs in the battle between Priscilla and the one who surpasses an Abyssal One...

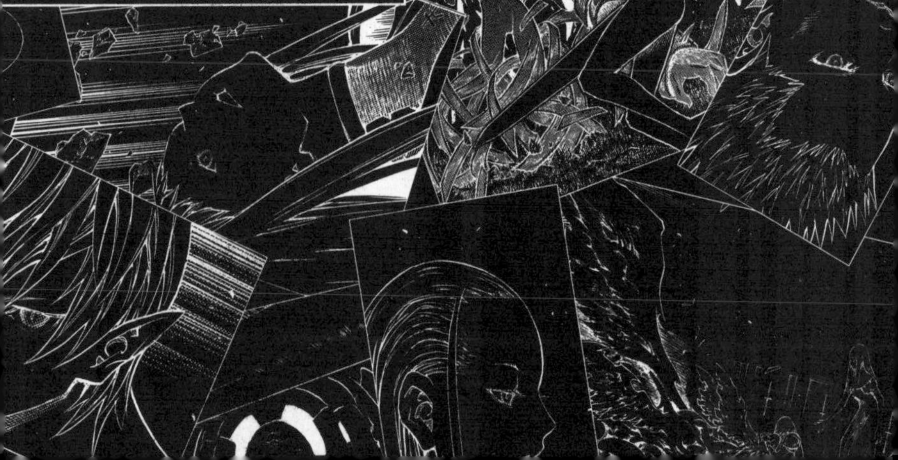

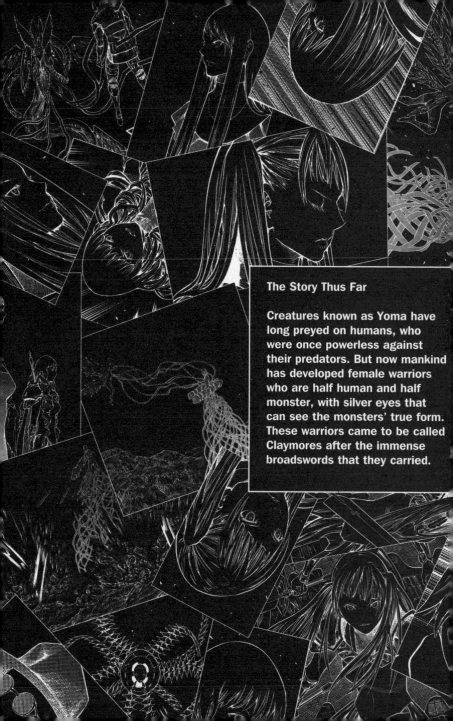

The Story Thus Far

Creatures known as Yoma have long preyed on humans, who were once powerless against their predators. But now mankind has developed female warriors who are half human and half monster, with silver eyes that can see the monsters' true form. These warriors came to be called Claymores after the immense broadswords that they carried.

Claymore
クレイエア

Vol. 25

CONTENTS

Scene 138: Army of the Underworld, Part 6

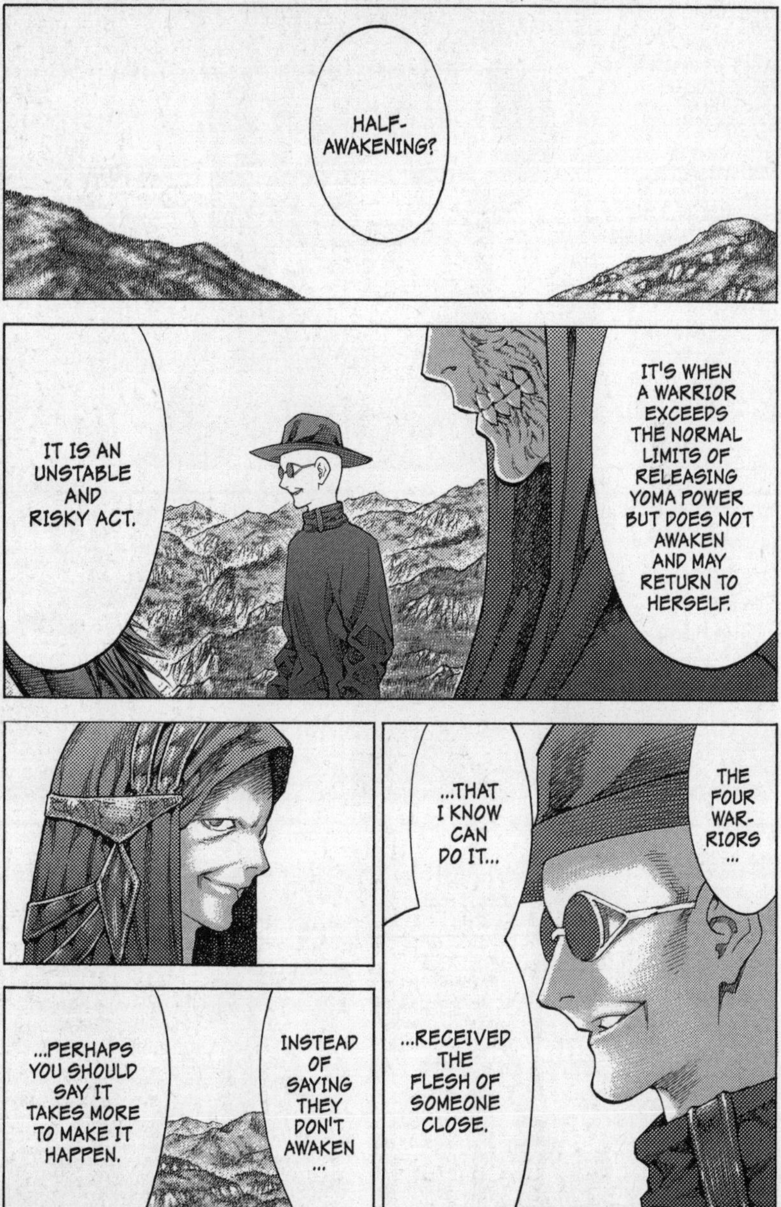
HALF-AWAKENING?
IT'S WHEN A WARRIOR EXCEEDS THE NORMAL LIMITS OF RELEASING YOMA POWER BUT DOES NOT AWAKEN AND MAY RETURN TO HERSELF.
IT IS AN UNSTABLE AND RISKY ACT.
THE FOUR WARRIORS ...
...THAT I KNOW CAN DO IT...
...RECEIVED THE FLESH OF SOMEONE CLOSE.
INSTEAD OF SAYING THEY DON'T AWAKEN ...
...PERHAPS YOU SHOULD SAY IT TAKES MORE TO MAKE IT HAPPEN.

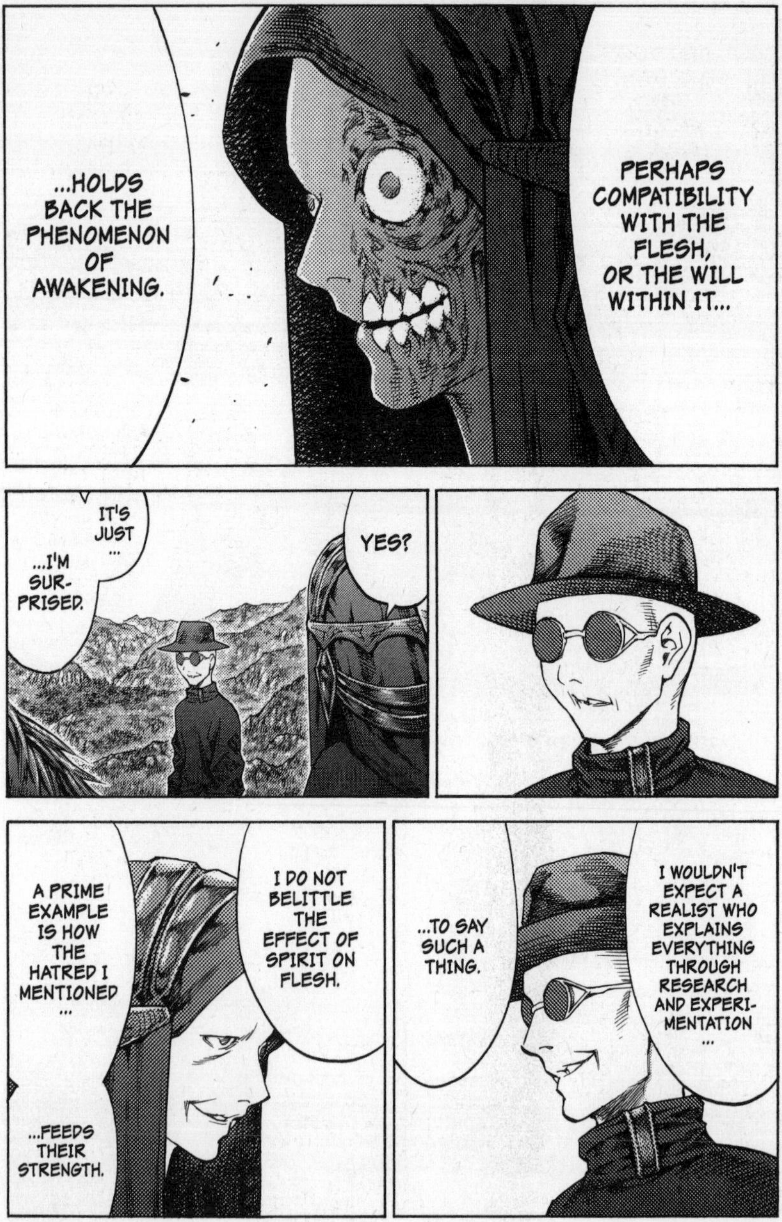
PERHAPS COMPATIBILITY WITH THE FLESH, OR THE WILL WITHIN IT...
...HOLDS BACK THE PHENOMENON OF AWAKENING.
YES?
IT'S JUST ...
...I'M SUR-PRISED.
I WOULDN'T EXPECT A REALIST WHO EXPLAINS EVERYTHING THROUGH RESEARCH AND EXPERI-MENTATION ...
...TO SAY SUCH A THING.
I DO NOT BELITTLE THE EFFECT OF SPIRIT ON FLESH.
A PRIME EXAMPLE IS HOW THE HATRED I MENTIONED ...
...FEEDS THEIR STRENGTH.

READ THIS WAY

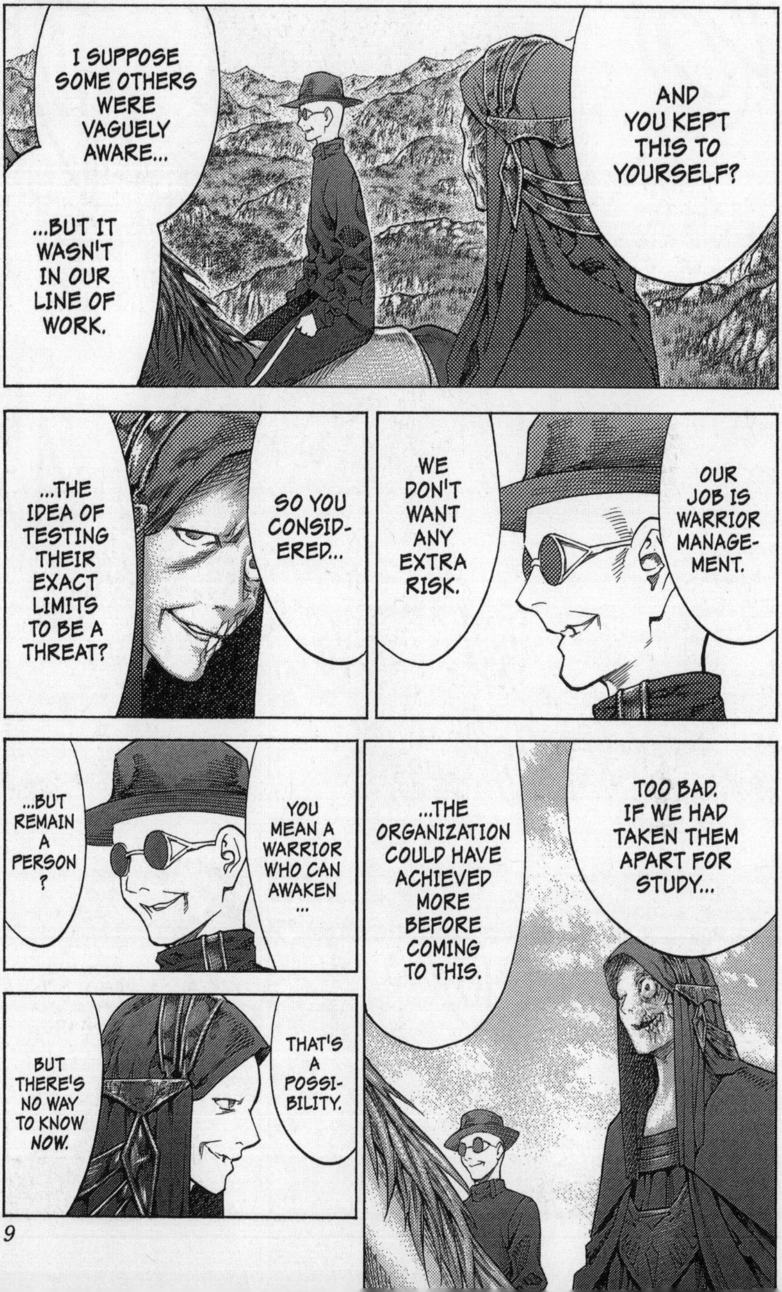
AND YOU KEPT THIS TO YOURSELF?
I SUPPOSE SOME OTHERS WERE VAGUELY AWARE...
...BUT IT WASN'T IN OUR LINE OF WORK.
OUR JOB IS WARRIOR MANAGE-MENT.
WE DON'T WANT ANY EXTRA RISK.
SO YOU CONSID-ERED...
...THE IDEA OF TESTING THEIR EXACT LIMITS TO BE A THREAT?
TOO BAD. IF WE HAD TAKEN THEM APART FOR STUDY...
...THE ORGANIZATION COULD HAVE ACHIEVED MORE BEFORE COMING TO THIS.
YOU MEAN A WARRIOR WHO CAN AWAKEN...
...BUT REMAIN A PERSON?
THAT'S A POSSI-BILITY.
BUT THERE'S NO WAY TO KNOW NOW.

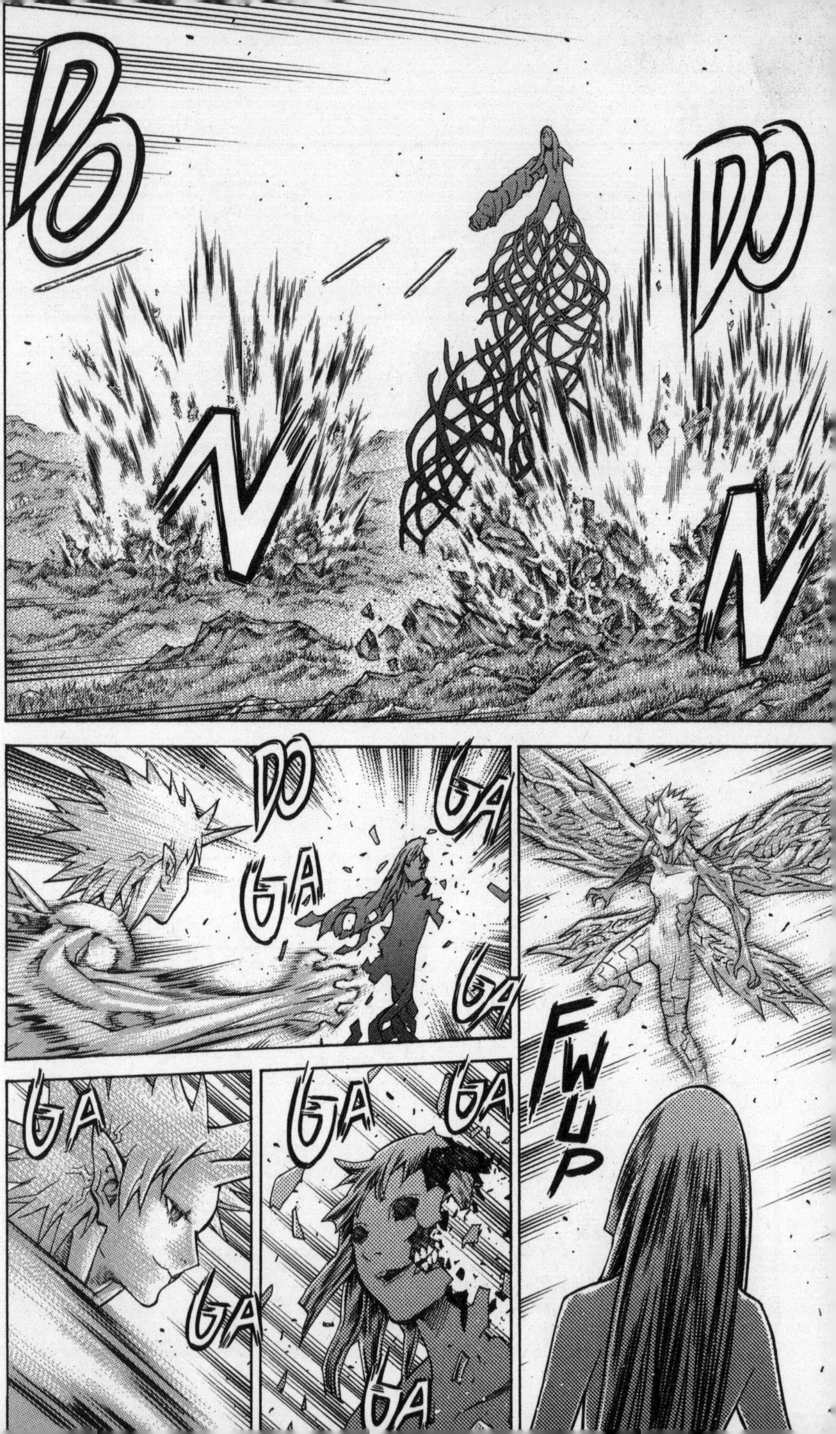

DO
N
DO
N
FWUP
DO
GA
GA
GA
GA
GA
GA
GA
GA

READ THIS WAY

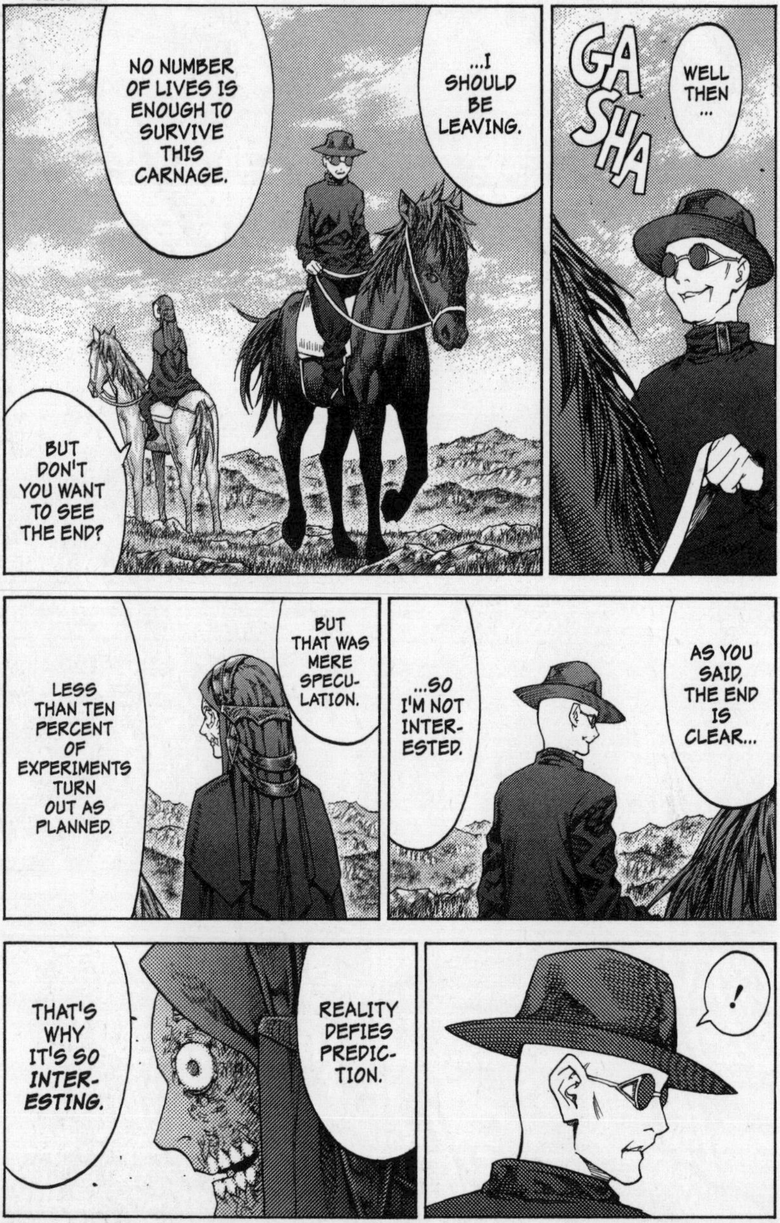
WELL THEN...
GASHA
...I SHOULD BE LEAVING.
NO NUMBER OF LIVES IS ENOUGH TO SURVIVE THIS CARNAGE.
BUT DON'T YOU WANT TO SEE THE END?
AS YOU SAID, THE END IS CLEAR...
...SO I'M NOT INTERESTED.
BUT THAT WAS MERE SPECULATION.
LESS THAN TEN PERCENT OF EXPERIMENTS TURN OUT AS PLANNED.
!
REALITY DEFIES PREDICTION.
THAT'S WHY IT'S SO INTERESTING.

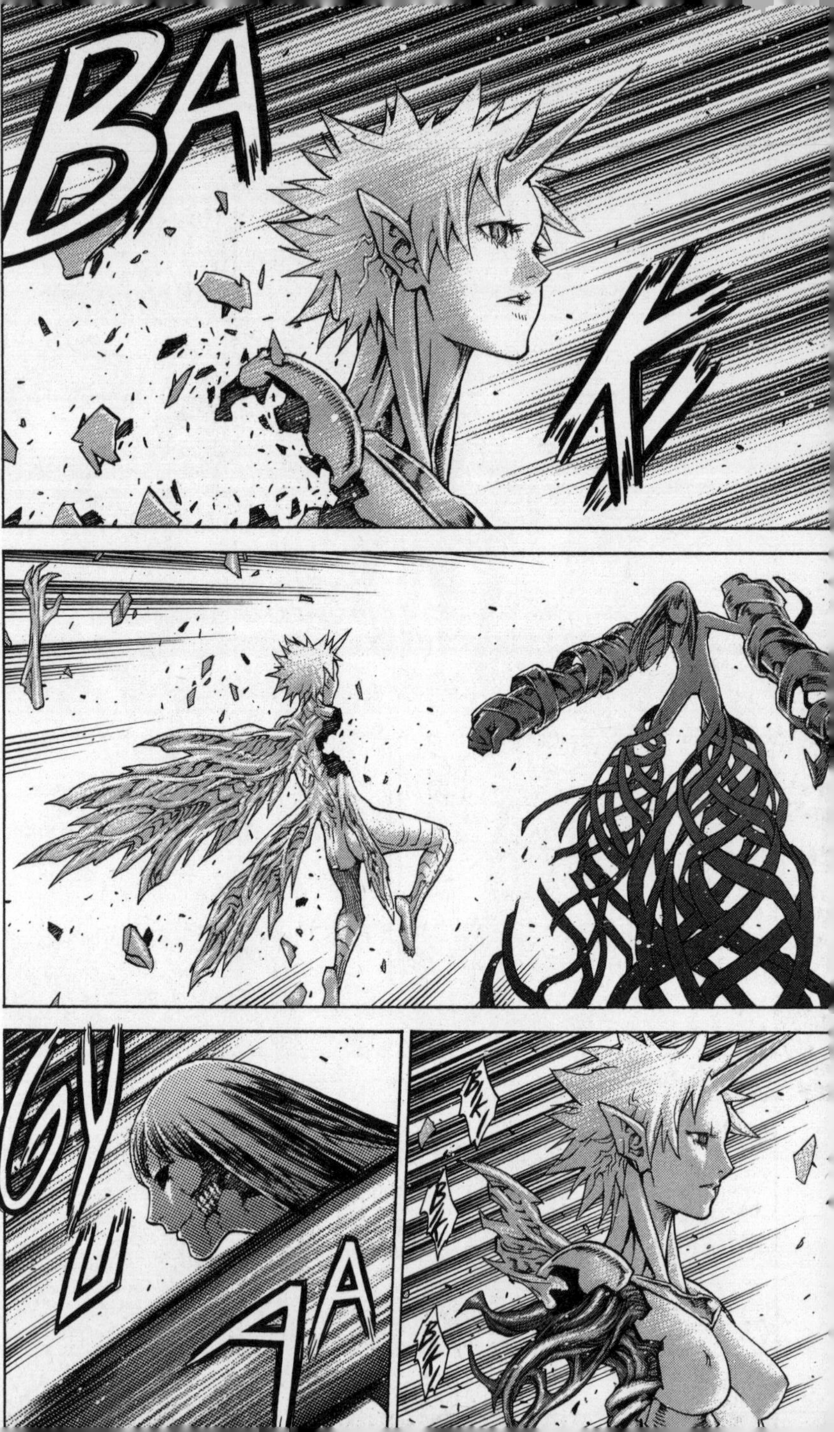
BA
BIK
BIK
BIK
GYU
AA

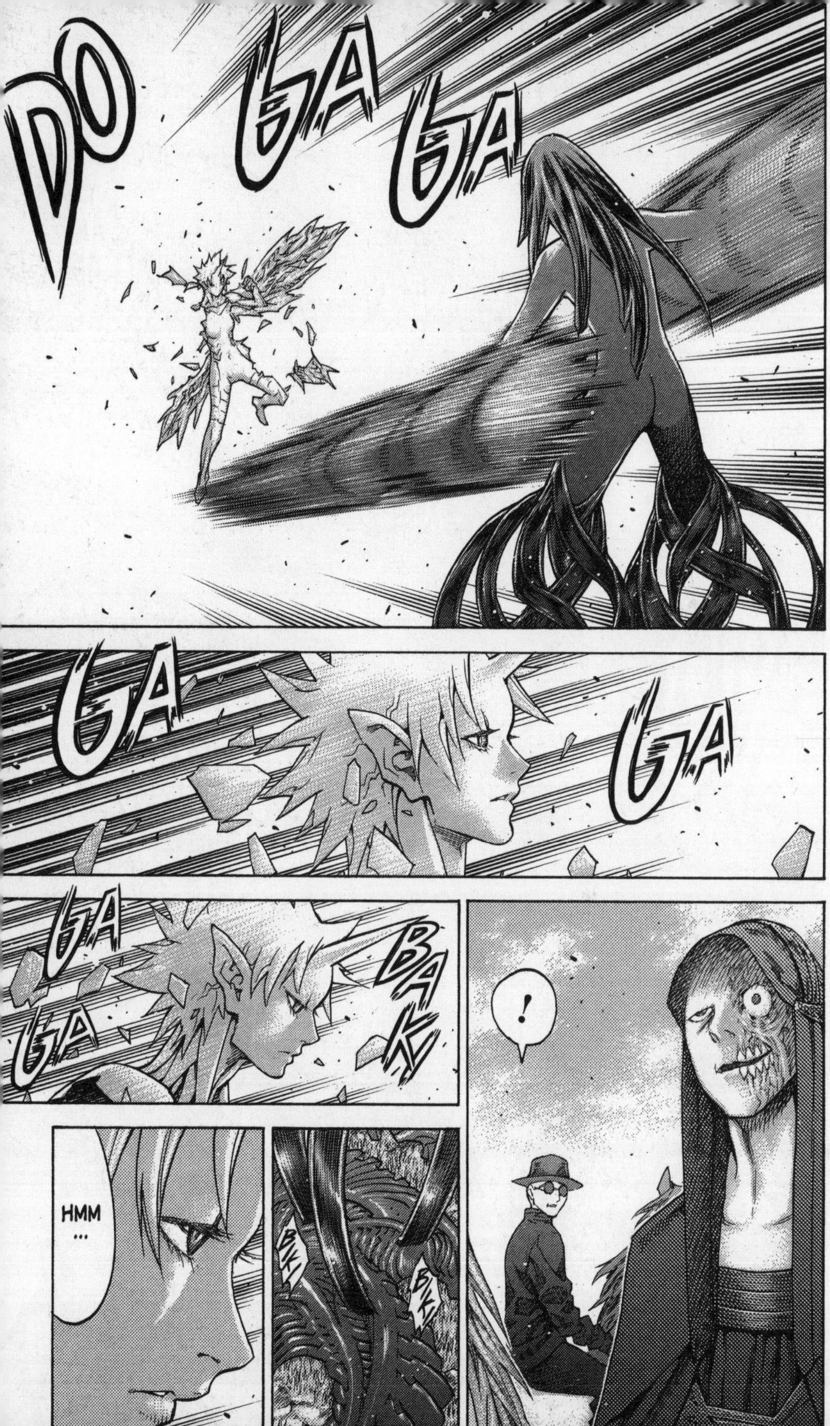
DO GA GA
GA
GA
!
BAKI
GA GA
BKI
BKI
HMM...

COULD IT BE...

...YOU ABSORBED THE ONE I VOMITED?

DO GA AA

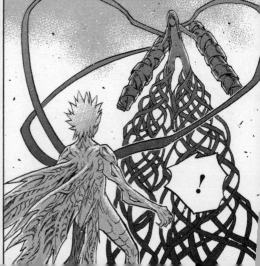

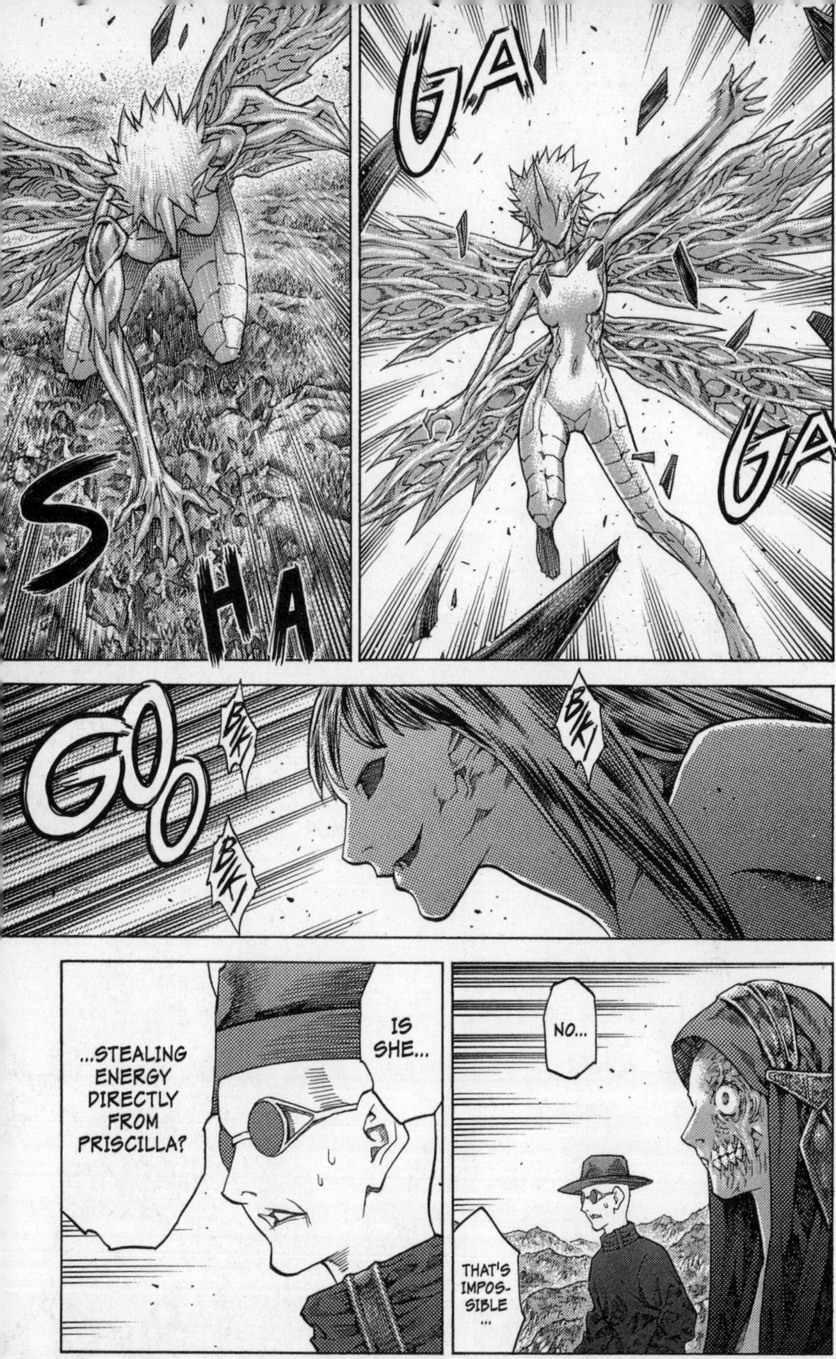

GA
GA
SHA
GOOO
BIKI
BIKI
BIKI
NO...
THAT'S IMPOSSIBLE...
IS SHE...
...STEALING ENERGY DIRECTLY FROM PRISCILLA?

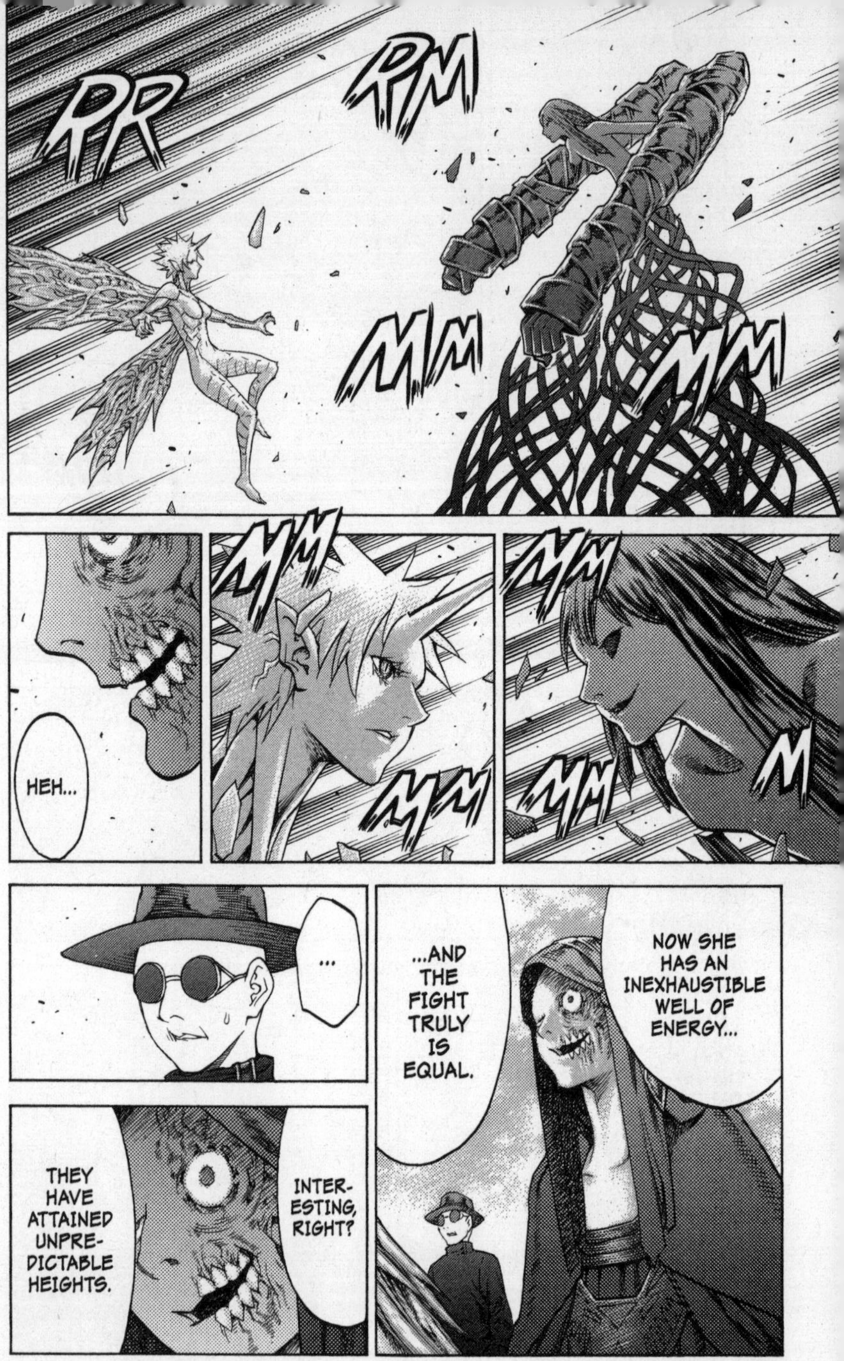
RR
RM
MM
MM
MM
MM
M
MM
MM
HEH...
NOW SHE HAS AN INEXHAUSTIBLE WELL OF ENERGY...
...AND THE FIGHT TRULY IS EQUAL.
...
INTER-ESTING, RIGHT?
THEY HAVE ATTAINED UNPRE-DICTABLE HEIGHTS.

READ THIS WAY

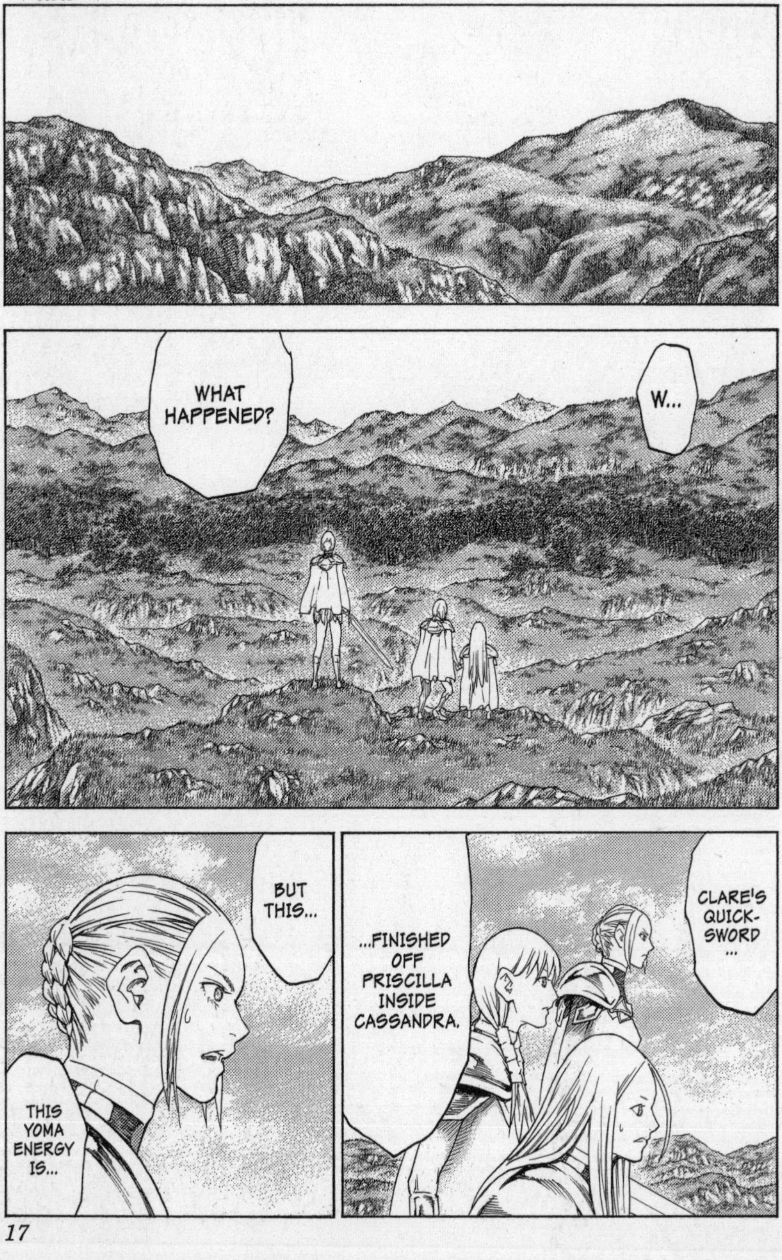
W...
WHAT HAPPENED?
CLARE'S QUICK-SWORD ...
...FINISHED OFF PRISCILLA INSIDE CASSANDRA.
BUT THIS...
THIS YOMA ENERGY IS...

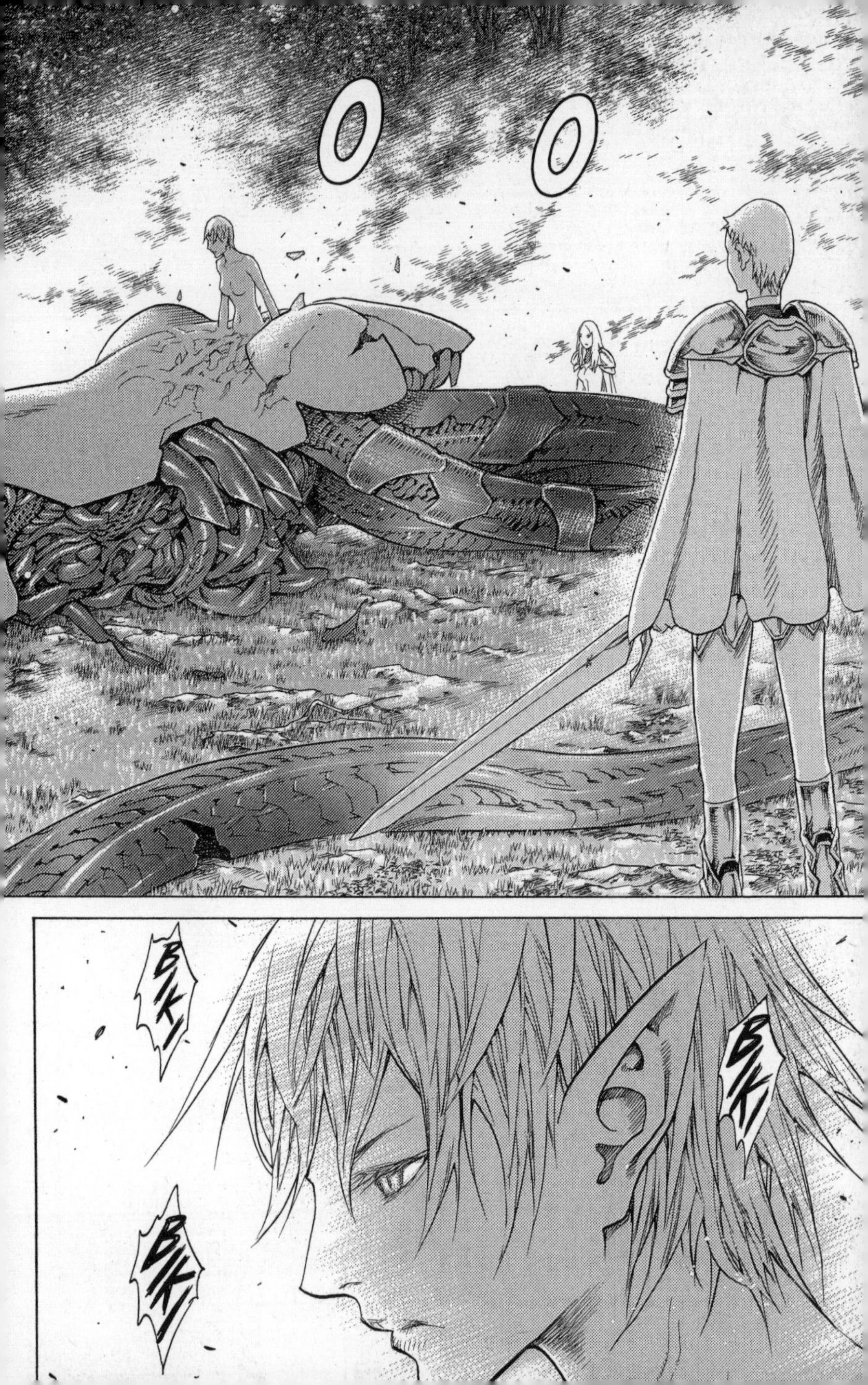
BIKI
BIKI
BIKI

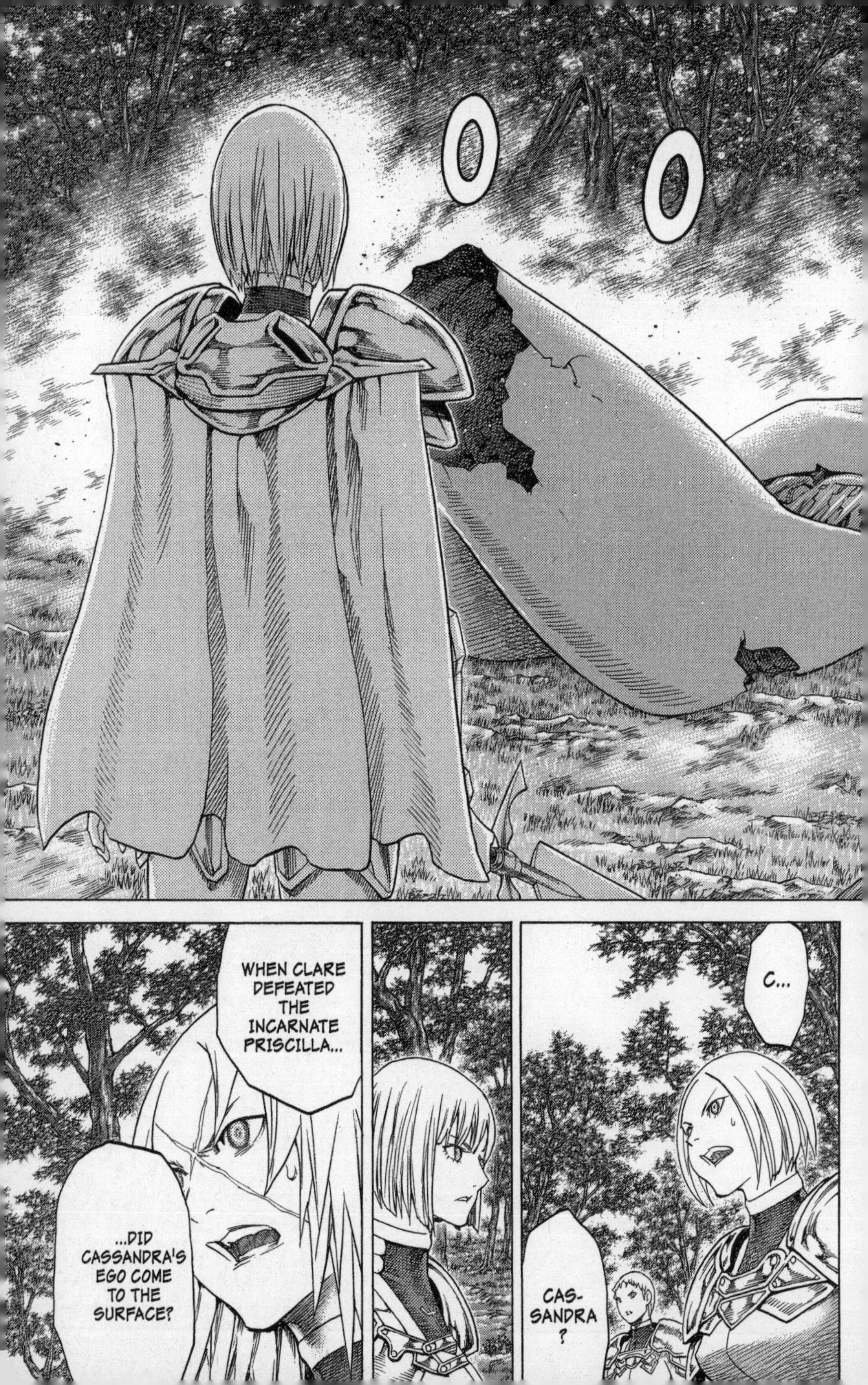
C...
CAS-SANDRA?
WHEN CLARE DEFEATED THE INCARNATE PRISCILLA...
...DID CASSANDRA'S EGO COME TO THE SURFACE?

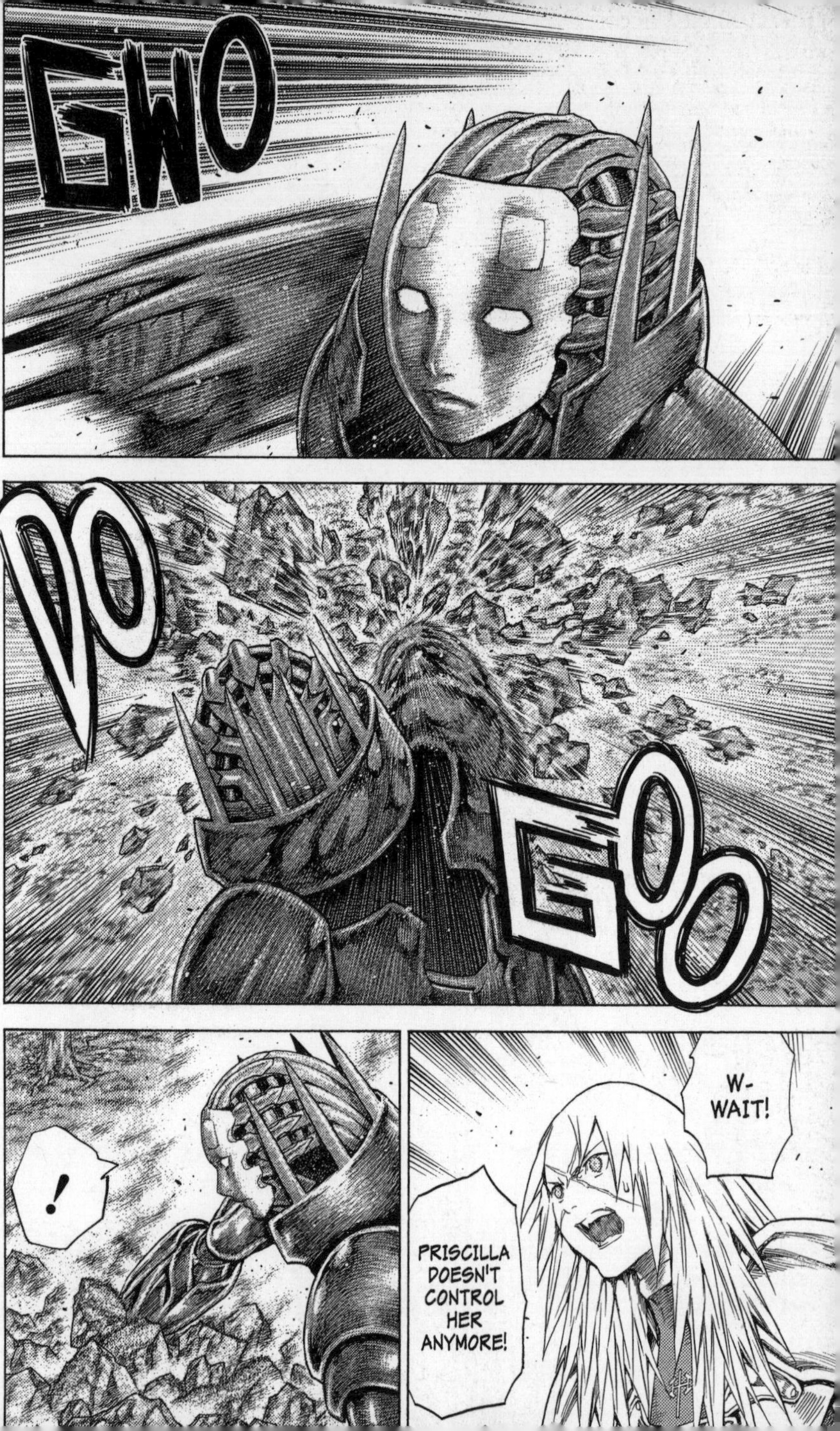
GWO
GOO
DO
W-WAIT!
PRISCILLA DOESN'T CONTROL HER ANYMORE!
!

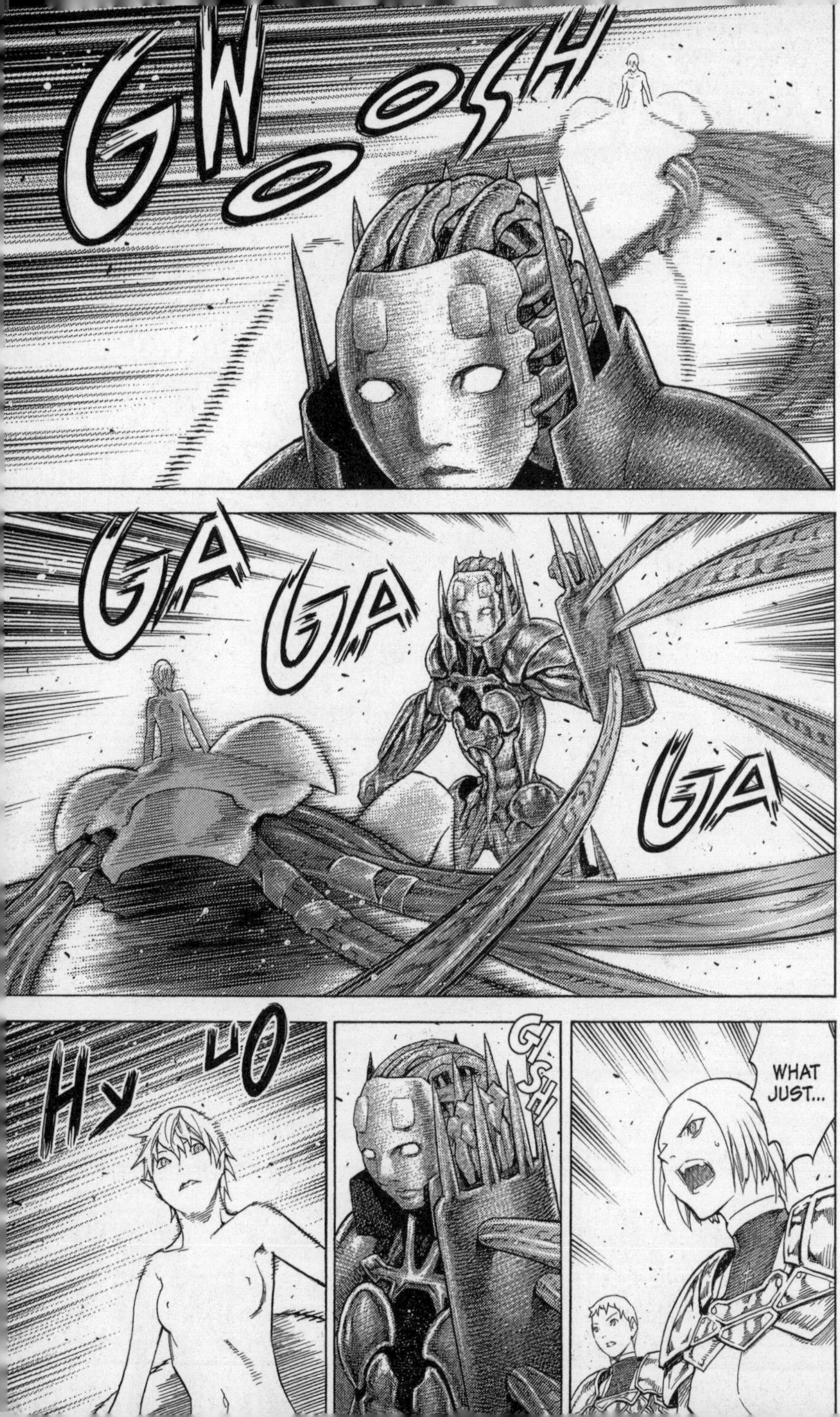
GWOOSH
GA
GA
GA
WHAT JUST...
GISH
HYUO

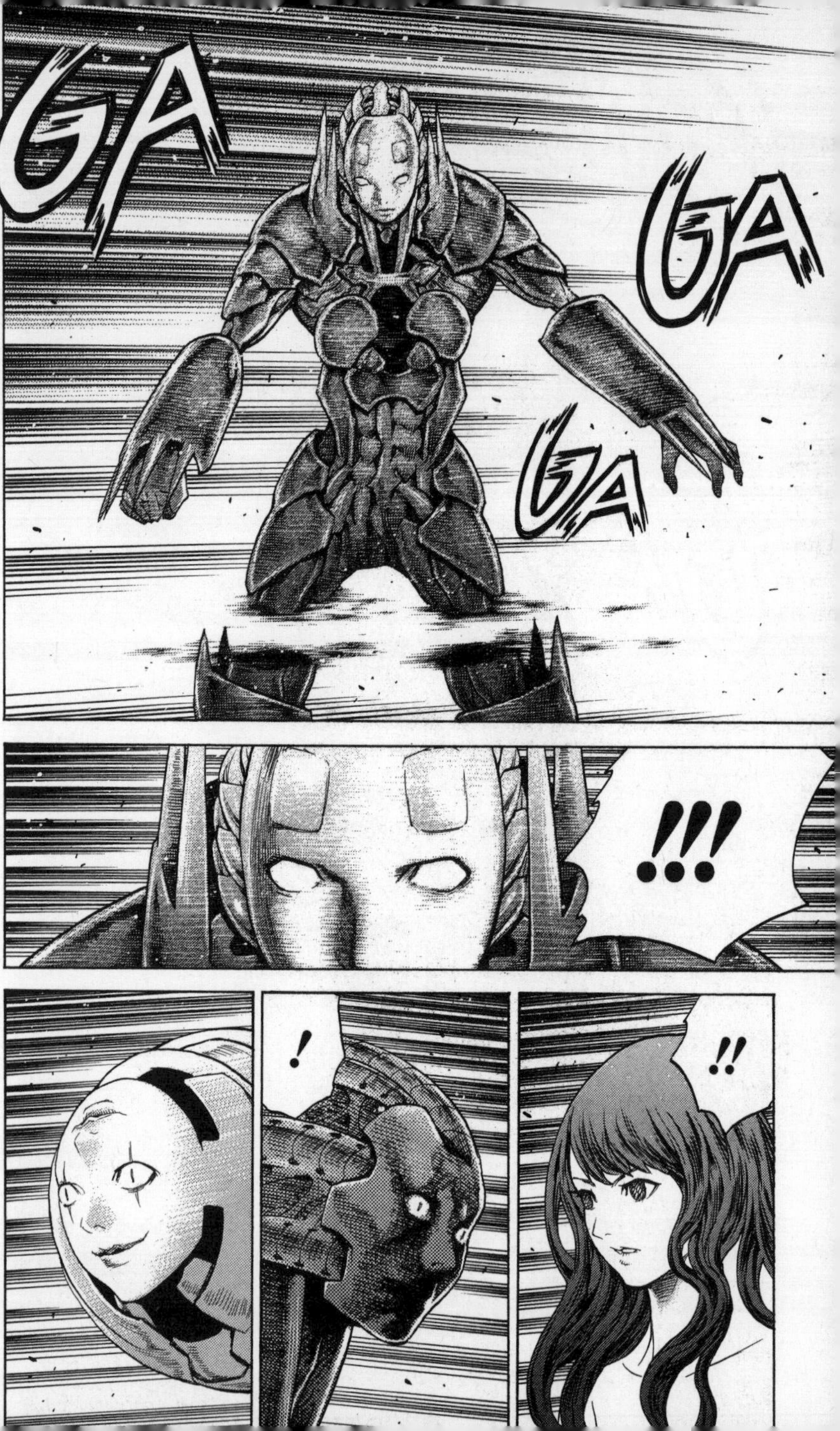
GA
GA
GA
!!!
!!
!

READ THIS WAY

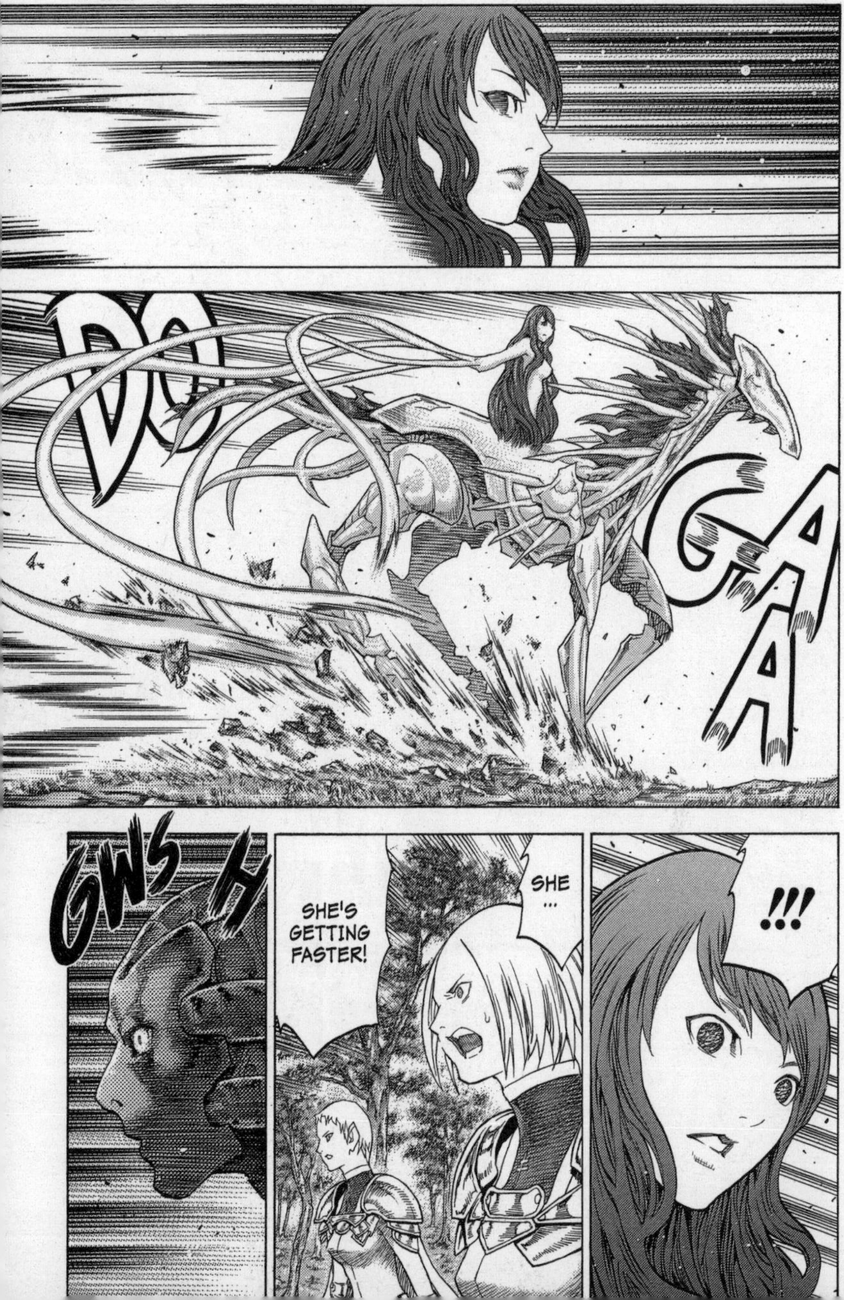
DO
GAGA
!!!
SHE ...
SHE'S GETTING FASTER!
GWSH

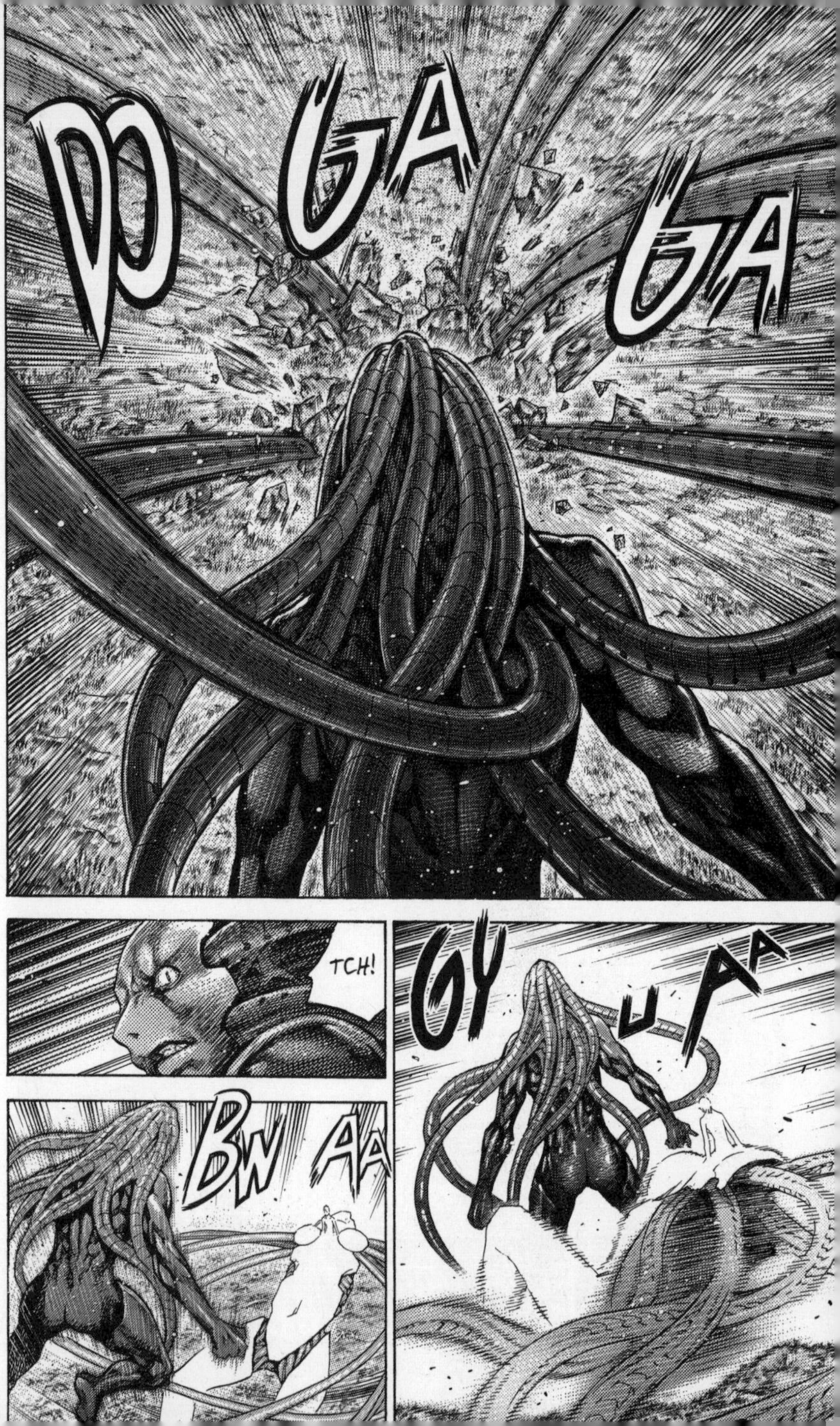
DOGAGA
GYUAA
TCH!
BWAA

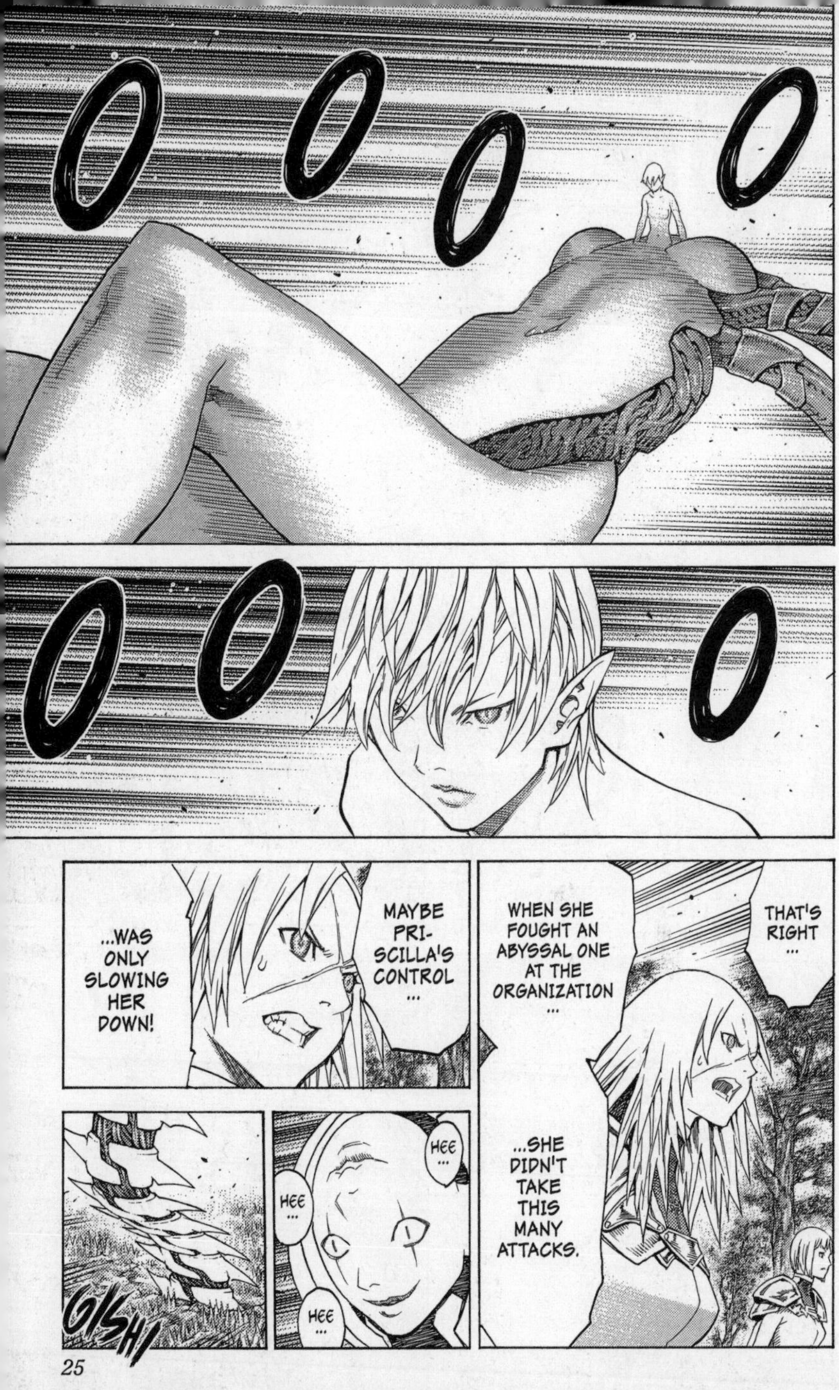

THAT'S RIGHT ...
WHEN SHE FOUGHT AN ABYSSAL ONE AT THE ORGANIZATION ...
...SHE DIDN'T TAKE THIS MANY ATTACKS.
MAYBE PRI-SCILLA'S CONTROL ...
...WAS ONLY SLOWING HER DOWN!
HEE ...
HEE ...
HEE ...
GISHI

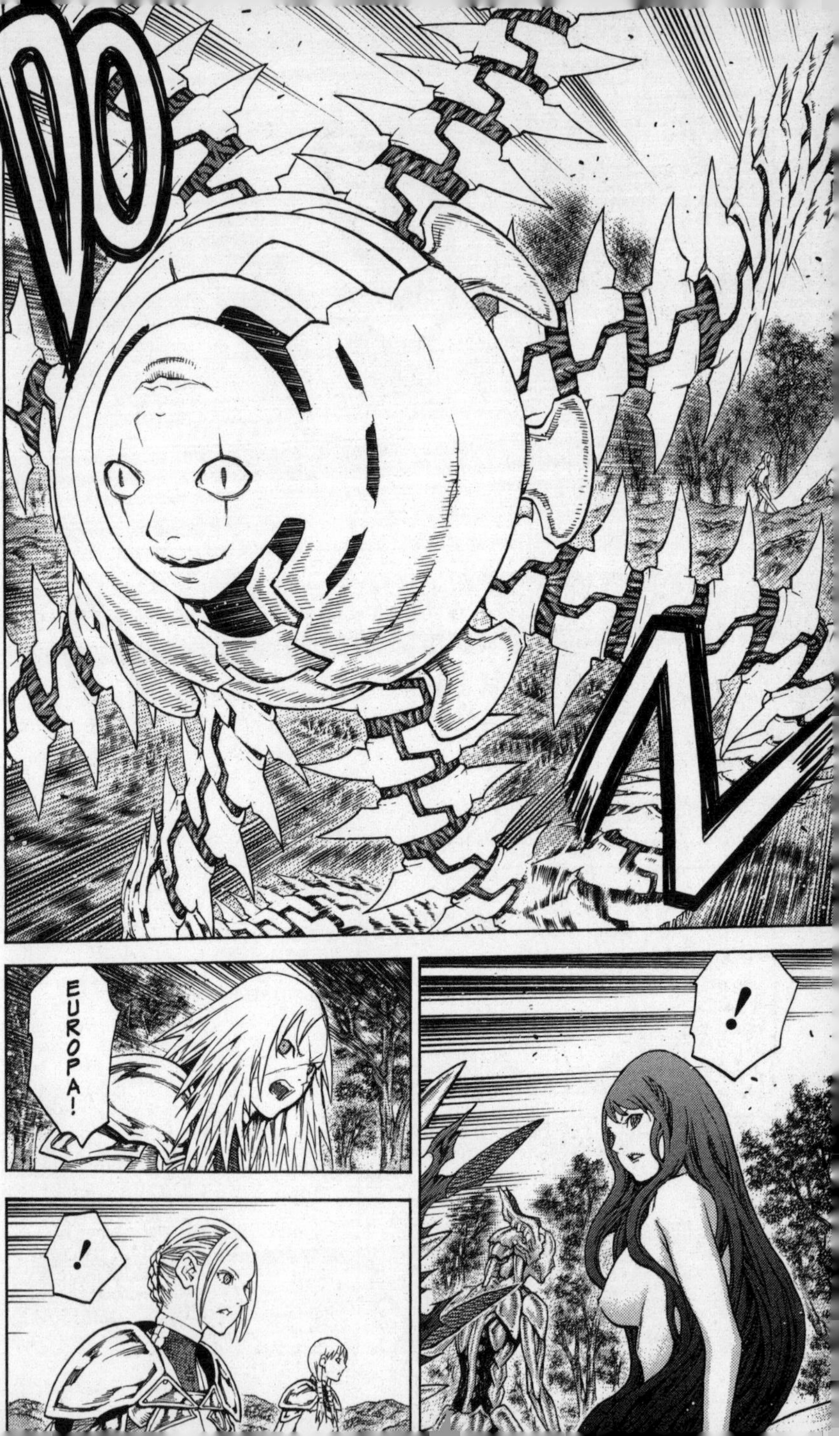
DO
N
!
EUROPA!
!

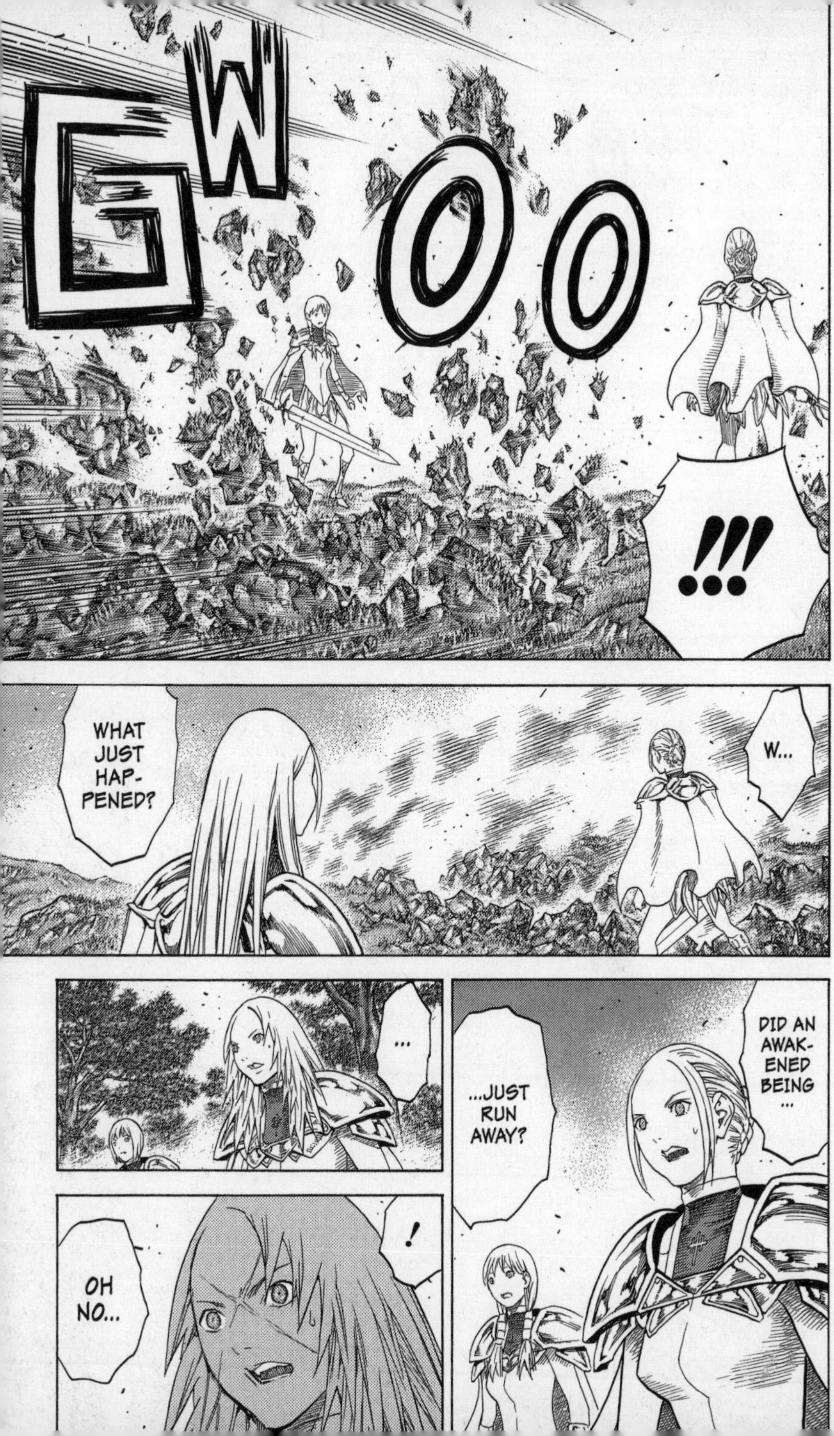
GWOOO
!!!
W...
WHAT JUST HAP-PENED?
DID AN AWAK-ENED BEING...
...JUST RUN AWAY?
...
!
OH NO...

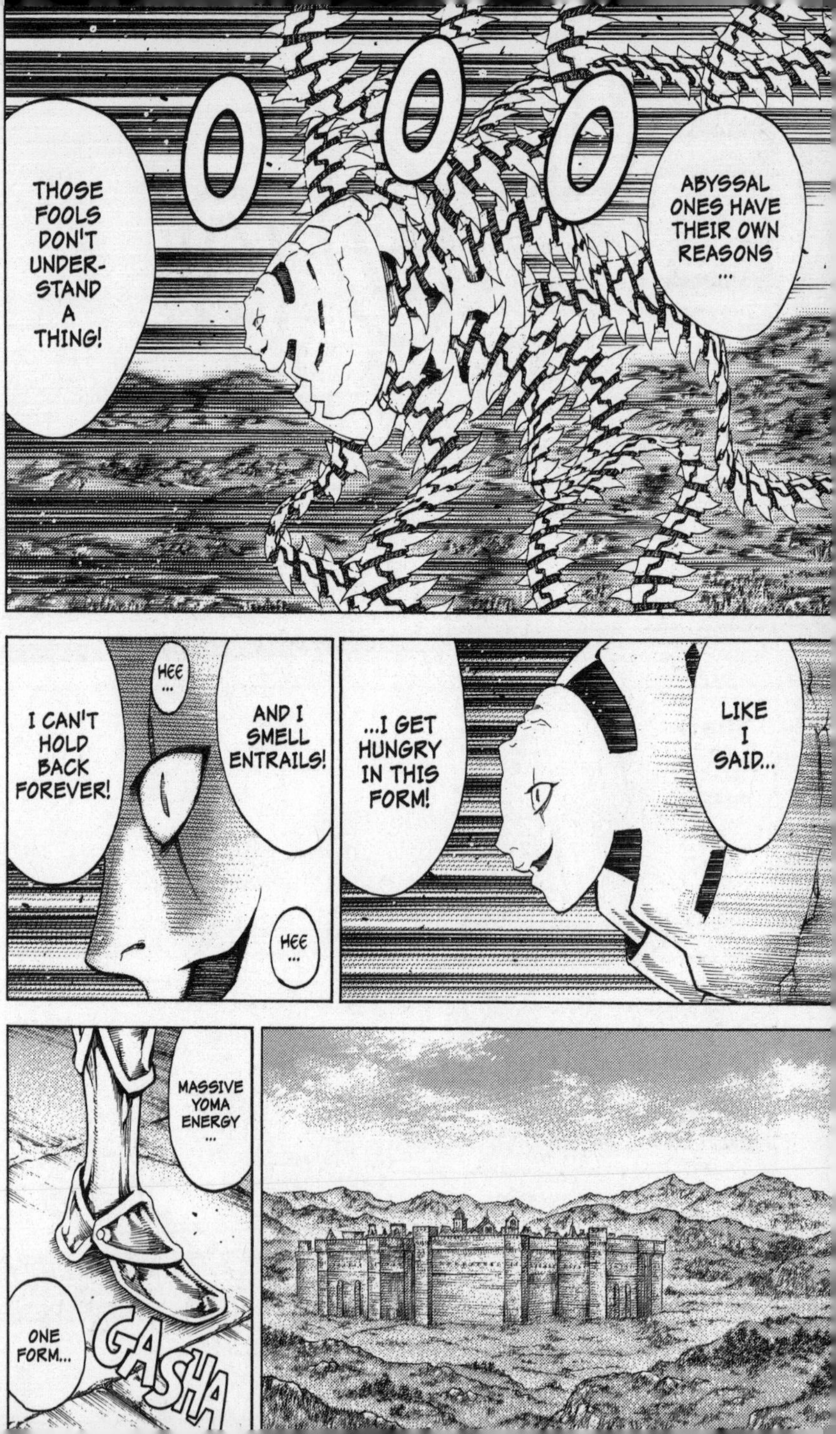
ABYSSAL ONES HAVE THEIR OWN REASONS ...
THOSE FOOLS DON'T UNDER-STAND A THING!
LIKE I SAID...
...I GET HUNGRY IN THIS FORM!
AND I SMELL ENTRAILS!
HEE ...
I CAN'T HOLD BACK FOREVER!
HEE ...
MASSIVE YOMA ENERGY ...
ONE FORM...
GASHA

READ THIS WAY

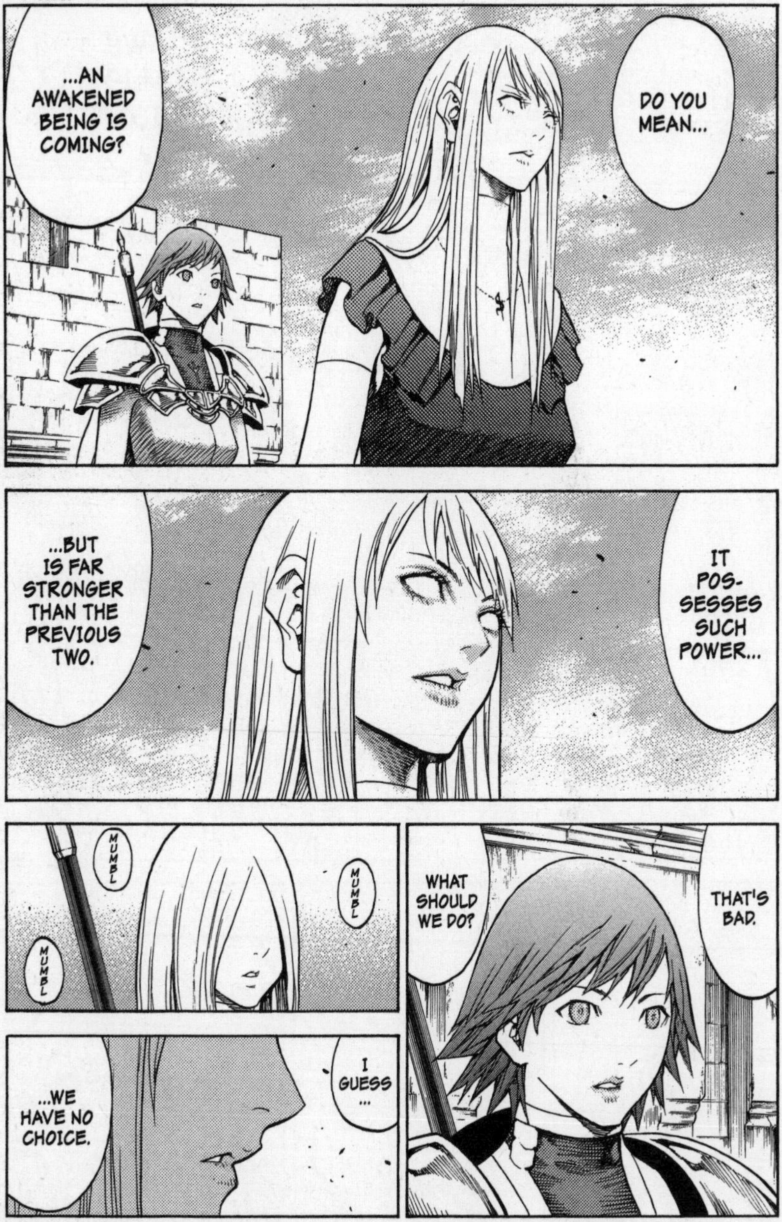

DO YOU MEAN...
...AN AWAKENED BEING IS COMING?
IT POS-SESSES SUCH POWER...
...BUT IS FAR STRONGER THAN THE PREVIOUS TWO.
THAT'S BAD.
WHAT SHOULD WE DO?
MUMBL
MUMBL
MUMBL
I GUESS...
...WE HAVE NO CHOICE.

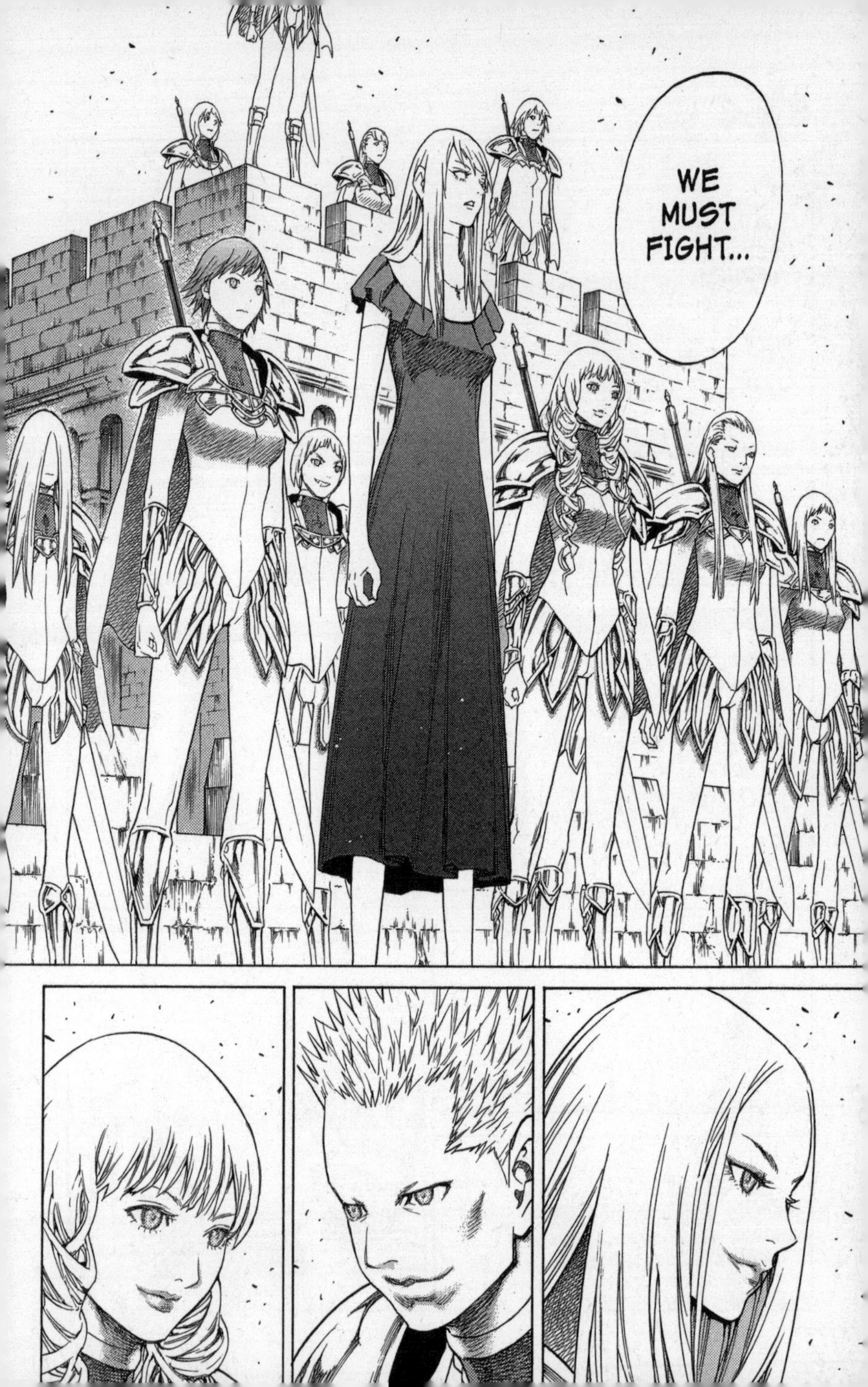
WE MUST FIGHT...

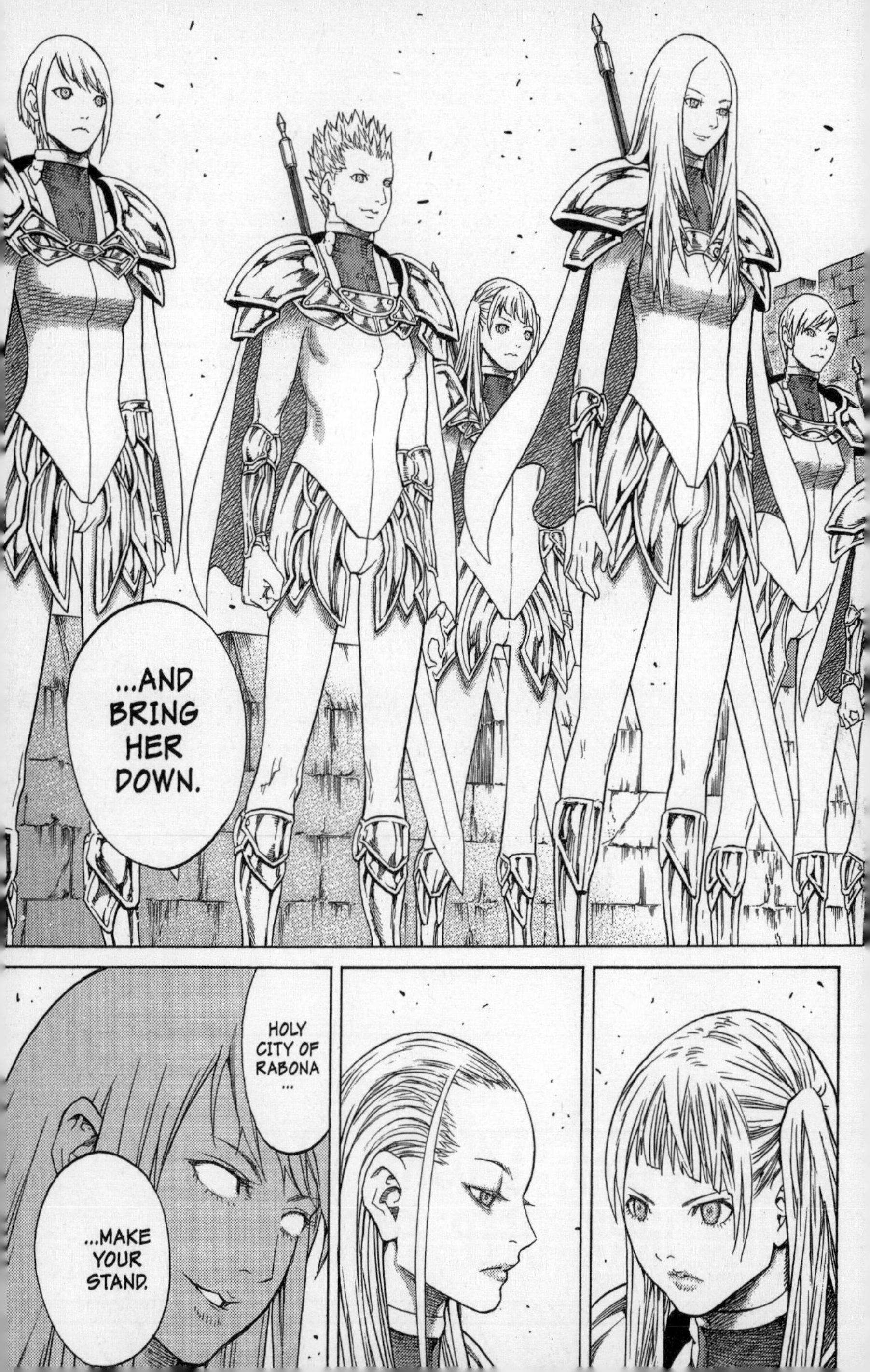
...AND BRING HER DOWN.
HOLY CITY OF RABONA ...
...MAKE YOUR STAND.

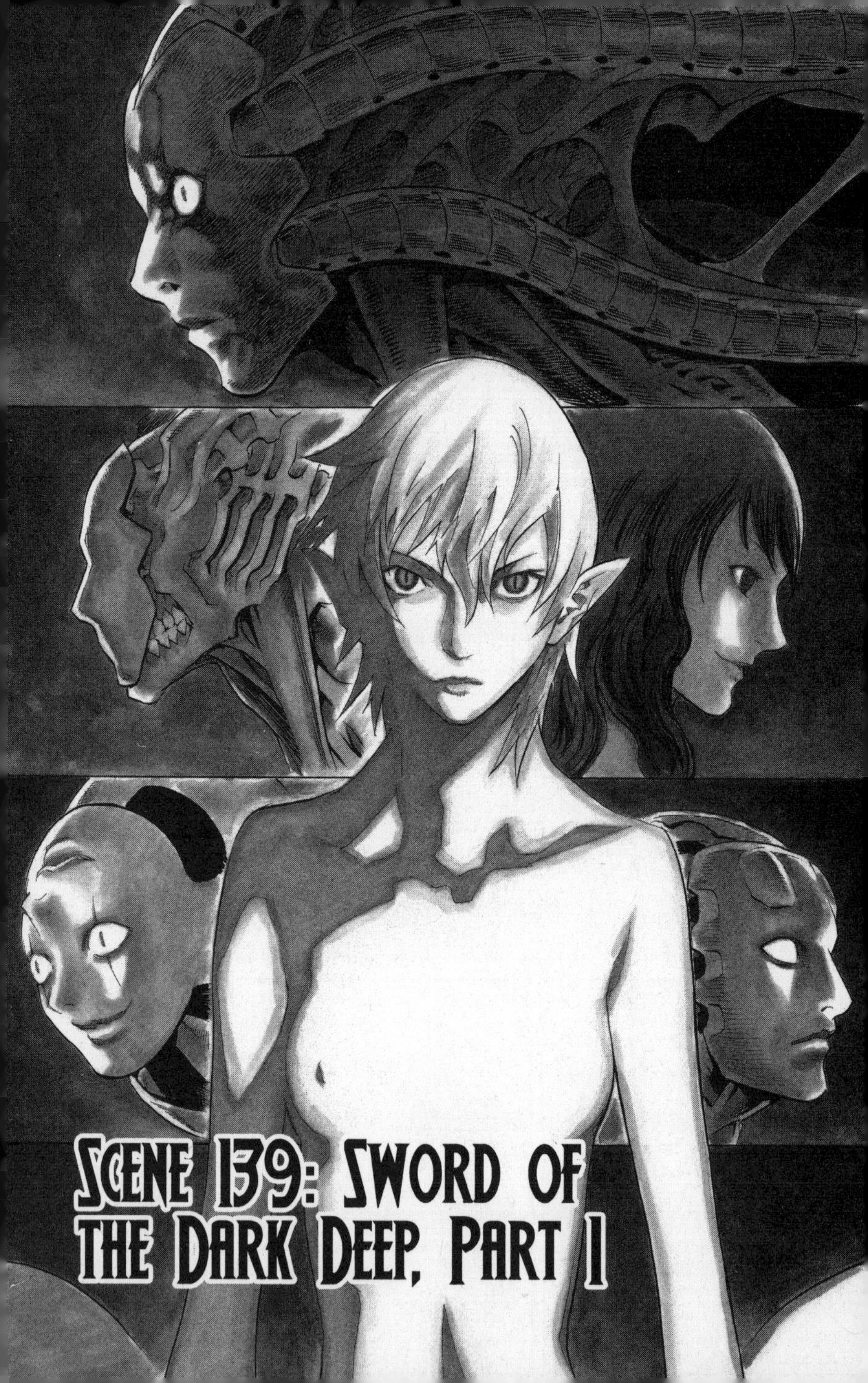
SCENE 139: SWORD OF THE DARK DEEP, PART 1

READ THIS WAY

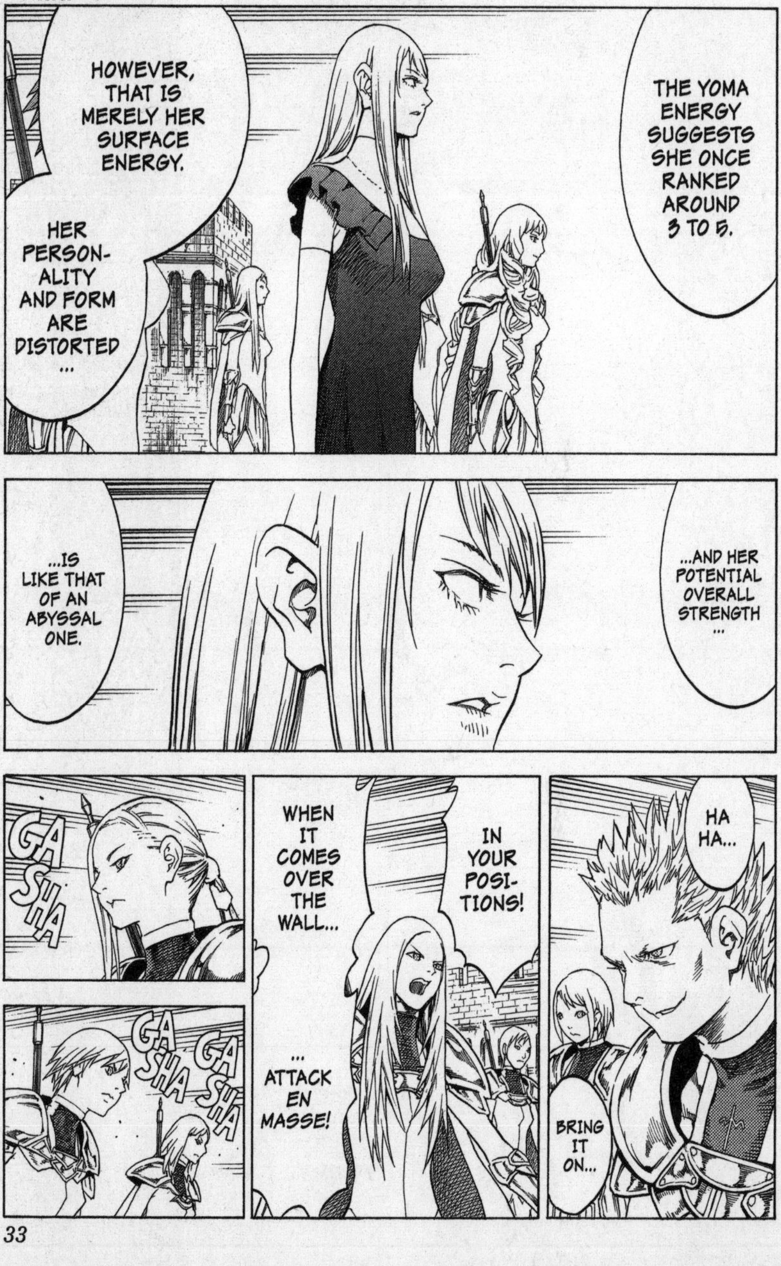
THE YOMA ENERGY SUGGESTS SHE ONCE RANKED AROUND 3 TO 5.
HOWEVER, THAT IS MERELY HER SURFACE ENERGY.
HER PERSON-ALITY AND FORM ARE DISTORTED ...
...AND HER POTENTIAL OVERALL STRENGTH ...
...IS LIKE THAT OF AN ABYSSAL ONE.
HA HA...
BRING IT ON...
IN YOUR POSI-TIONS!
WHEN IT COMES OVER THE WALL...
... ATTACK EN MASSE!
GA SHA
GA SHA GA SHA

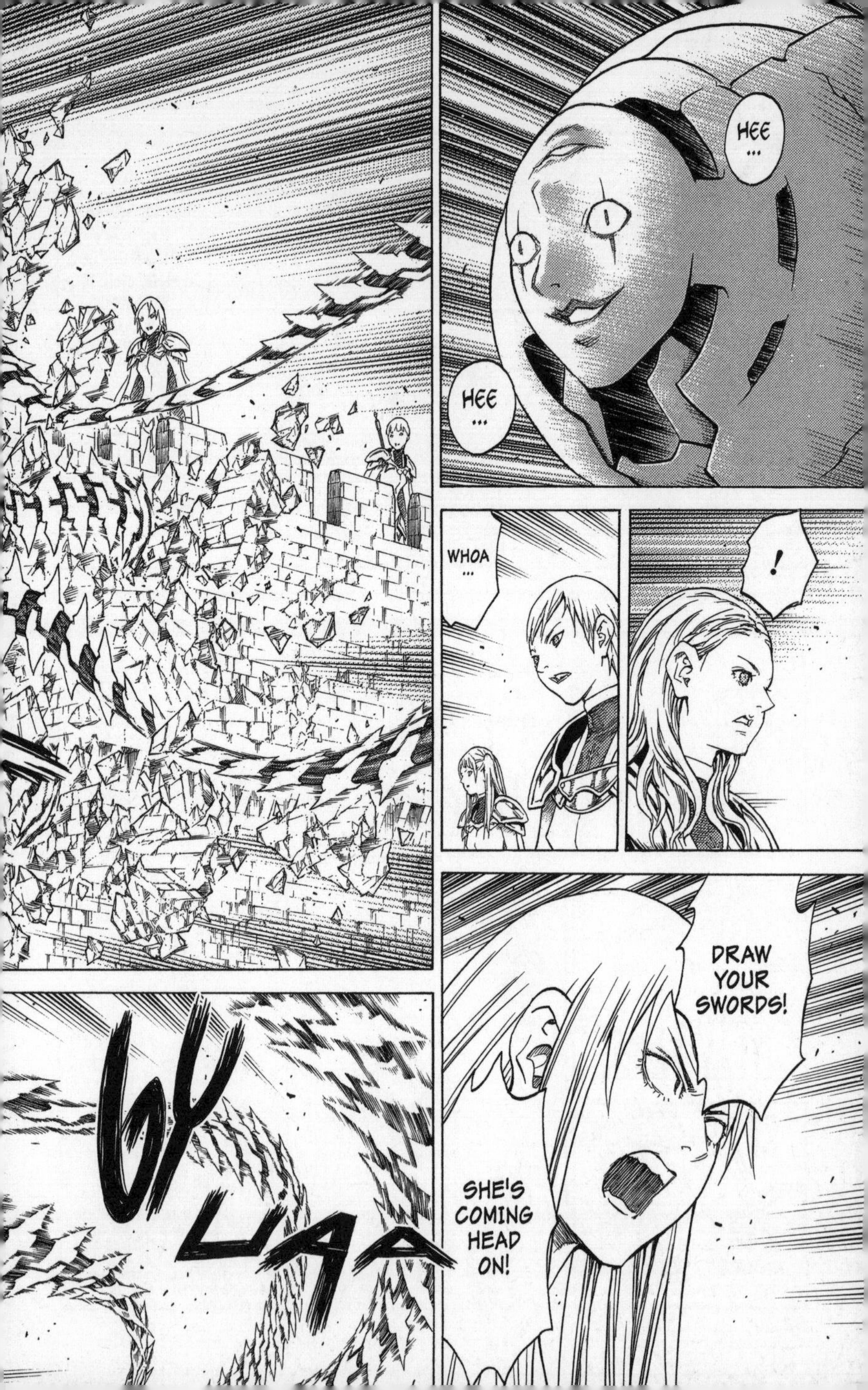
HEE ...
HEE ...
!
WHOA ...
DRAW YOUR SWORDS!
SHE'S COMING HEAD ON!

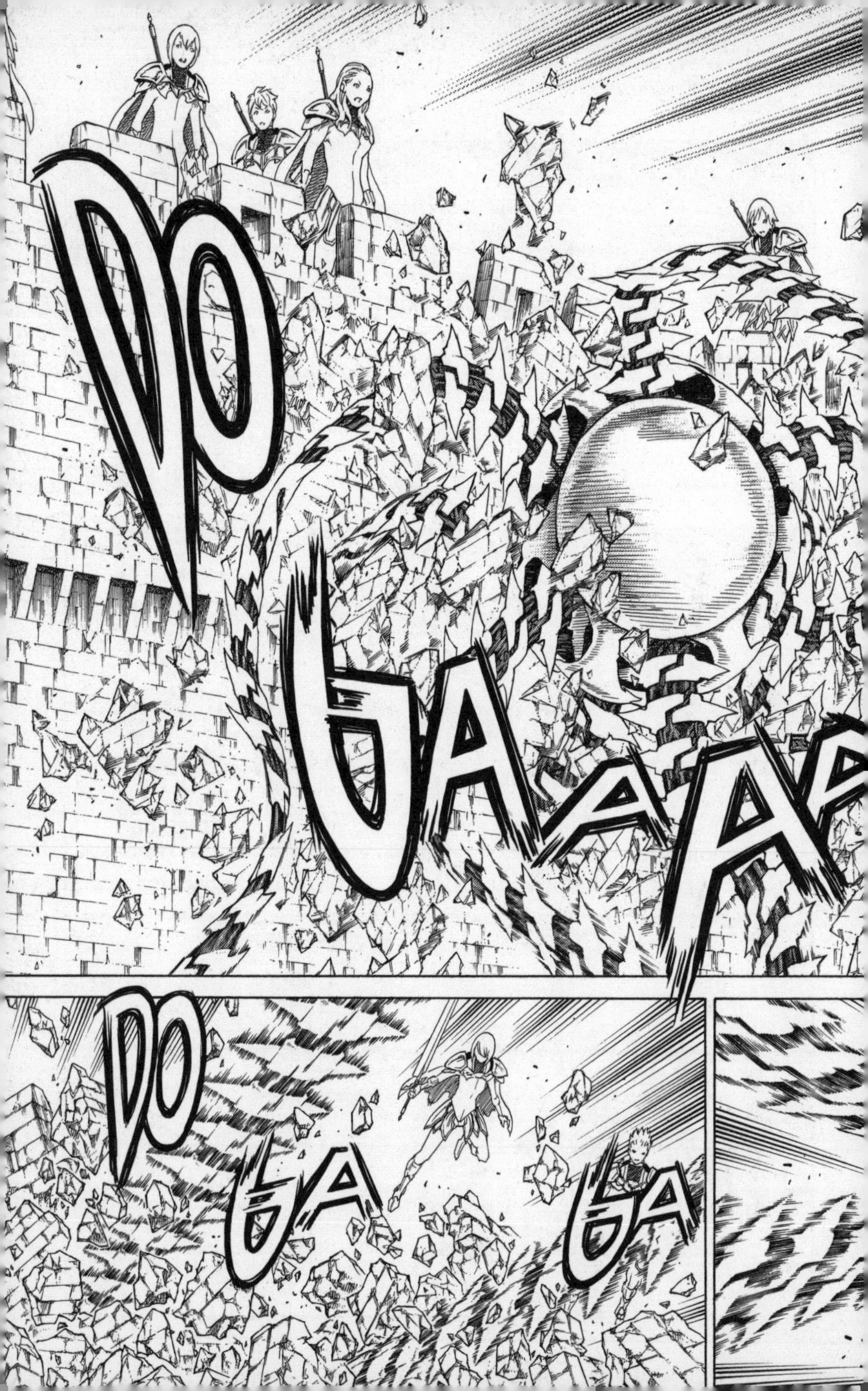
DOGAAAA
DO
GA
GA

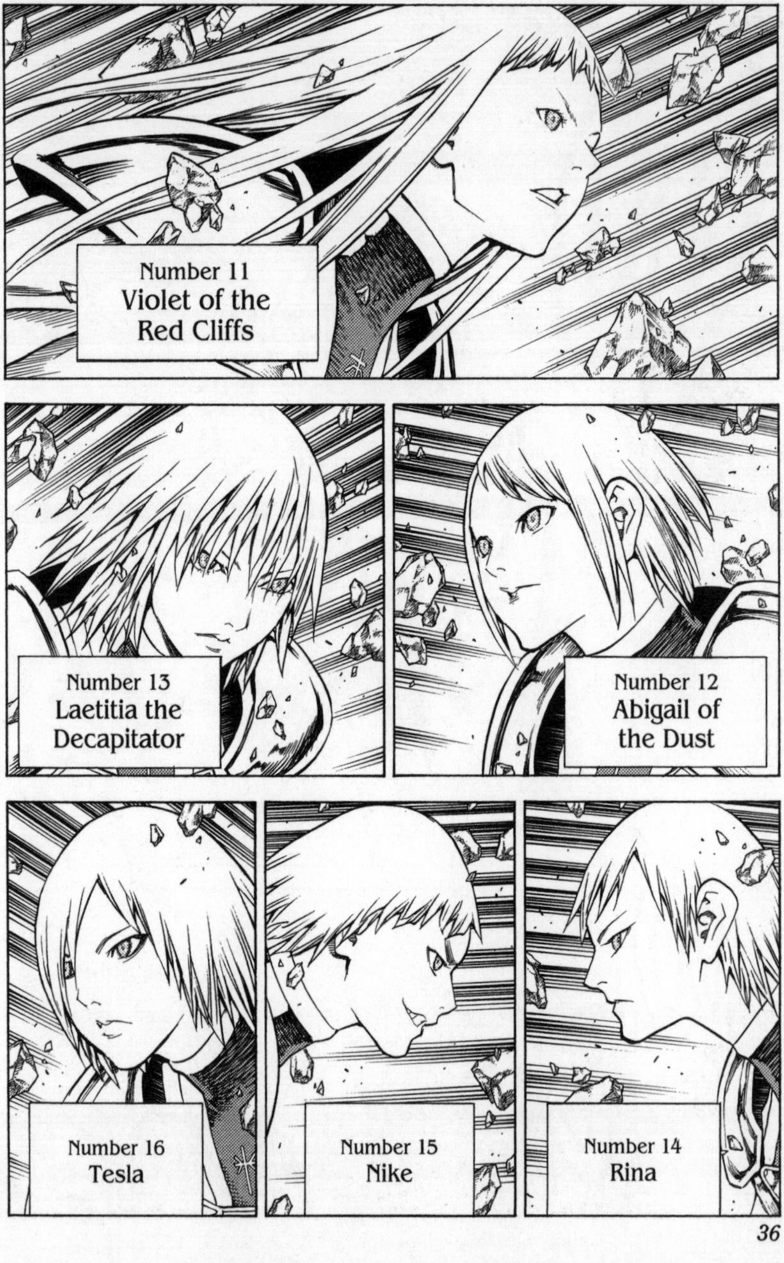
Number 11
Violet of the Red Cliffs
Number 12
Abigail of the Dust
Number 13
Laetitia the Decapitator
Number 14
Rina
Number 15
Nike
Number 16
Tesla

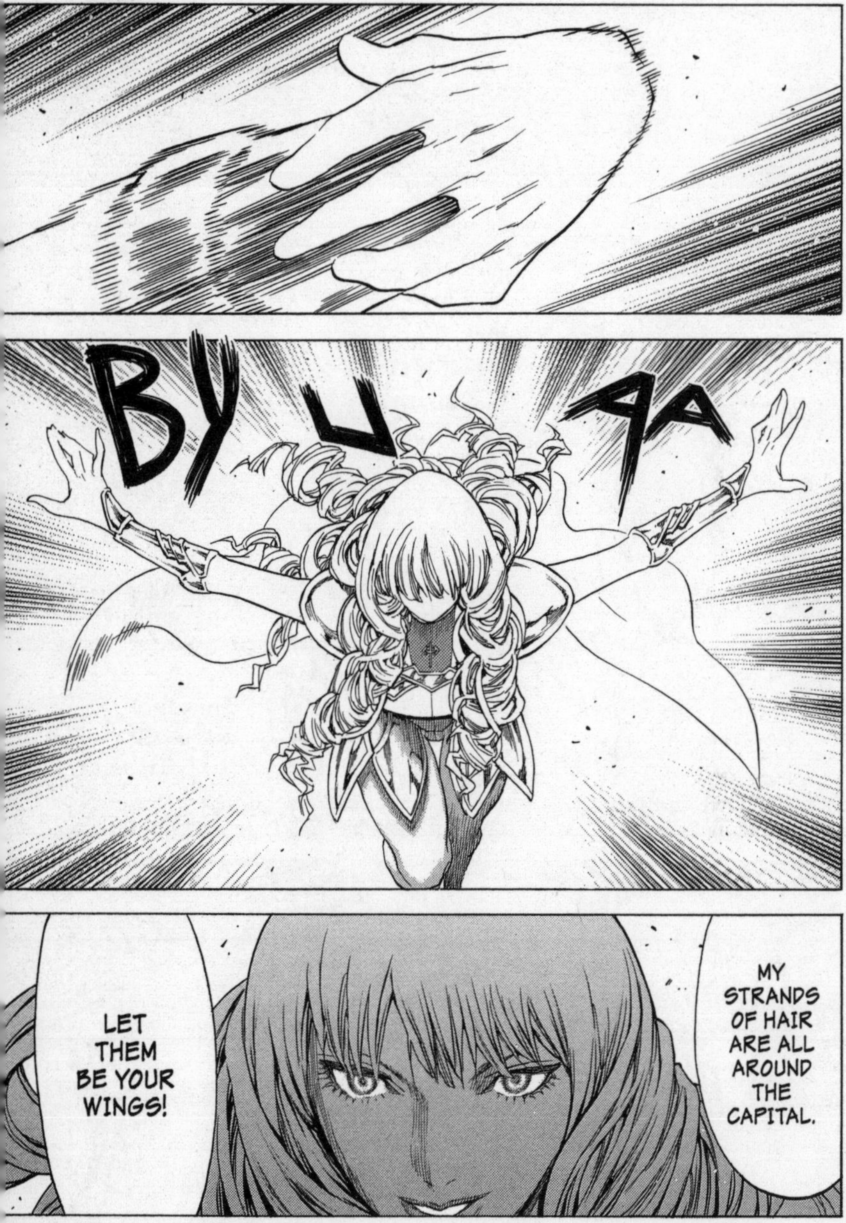
BYUAA
MY STRANDS OF HAIR ARE ALL AROUND THE CAPITAL.
LET THEM BE YOUR WINGS!

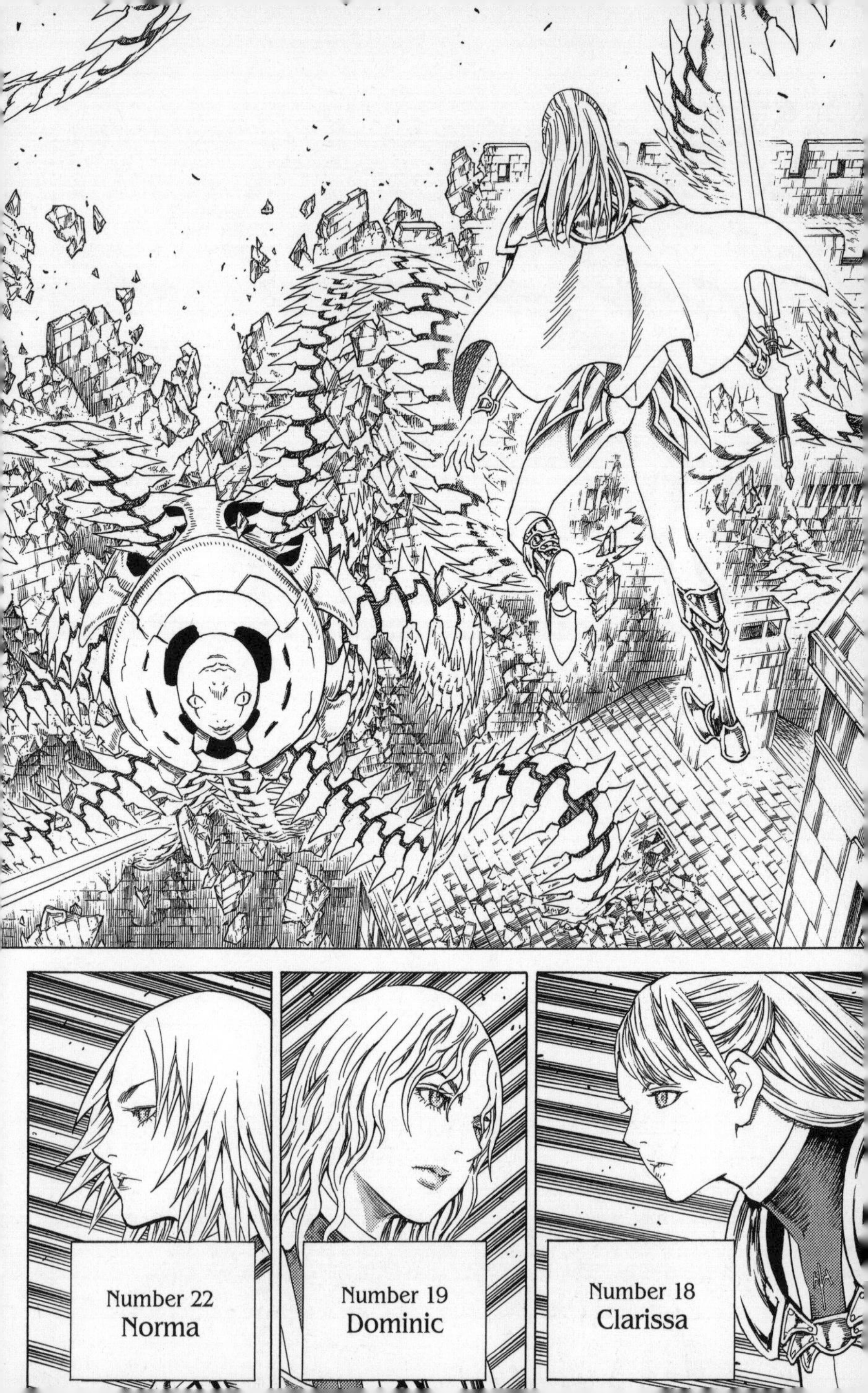
Number 18
Clarissa
Number 19
Dominic
Number 22
Norma

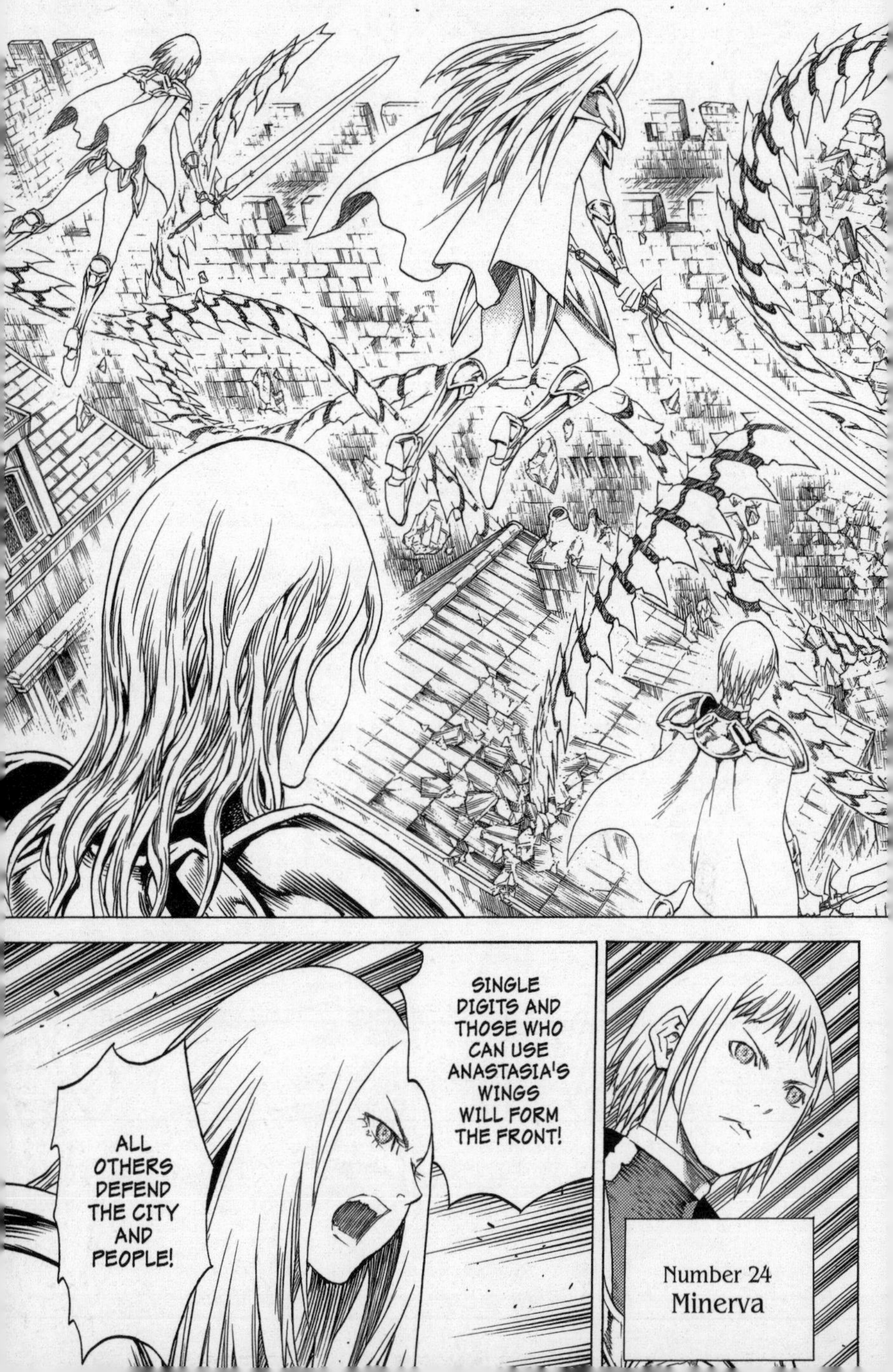
Number 24
Minerva
SINGLE DIGITS AND THOSE WHO CAN USE ANASTASIA'S WINGS WILL FORM THE FRONT!
ALL OTHERS DEFEND THE CITY AND PEOPLE!

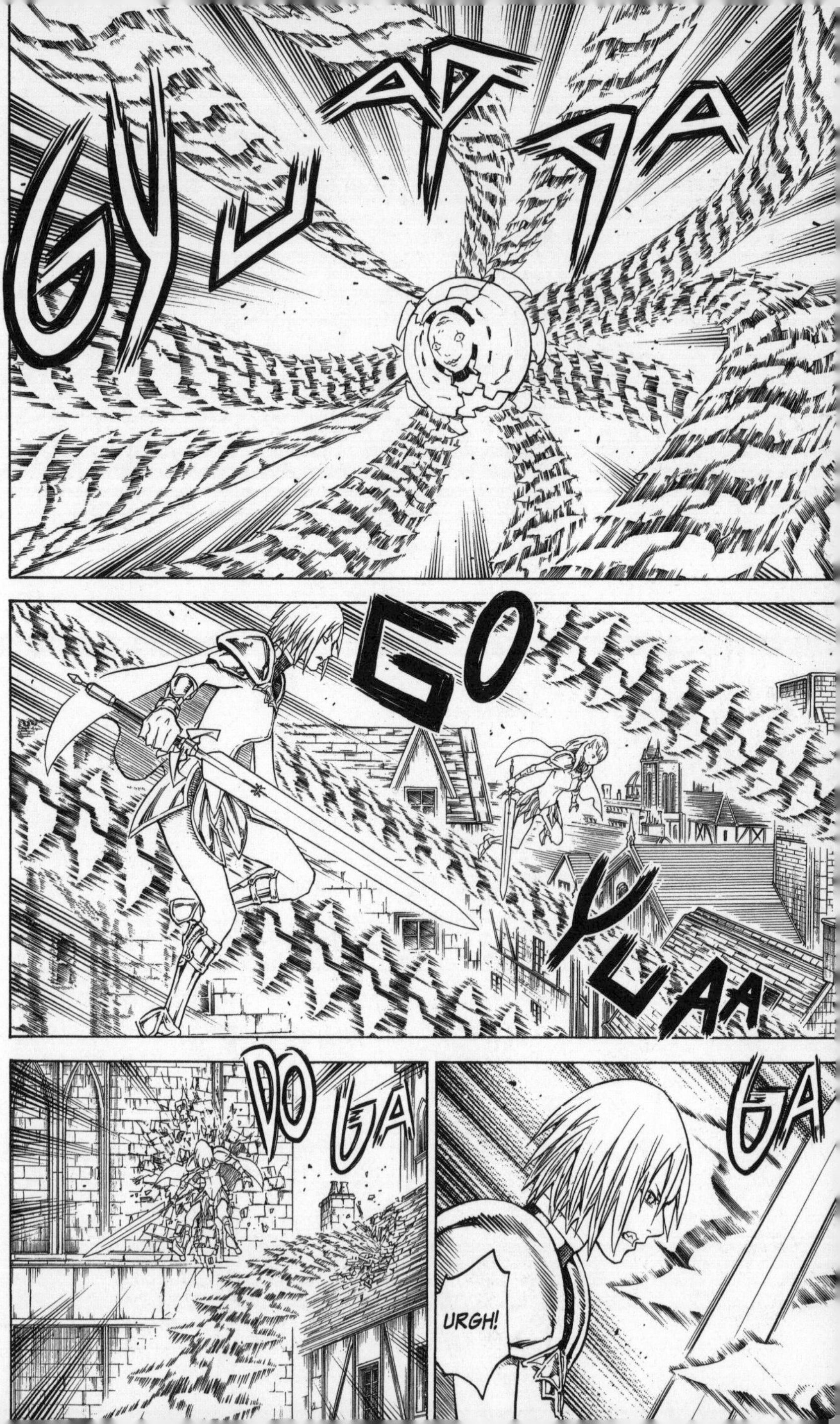
GYU AA AA
GO
YUAA
GA
URGH!
DO GA

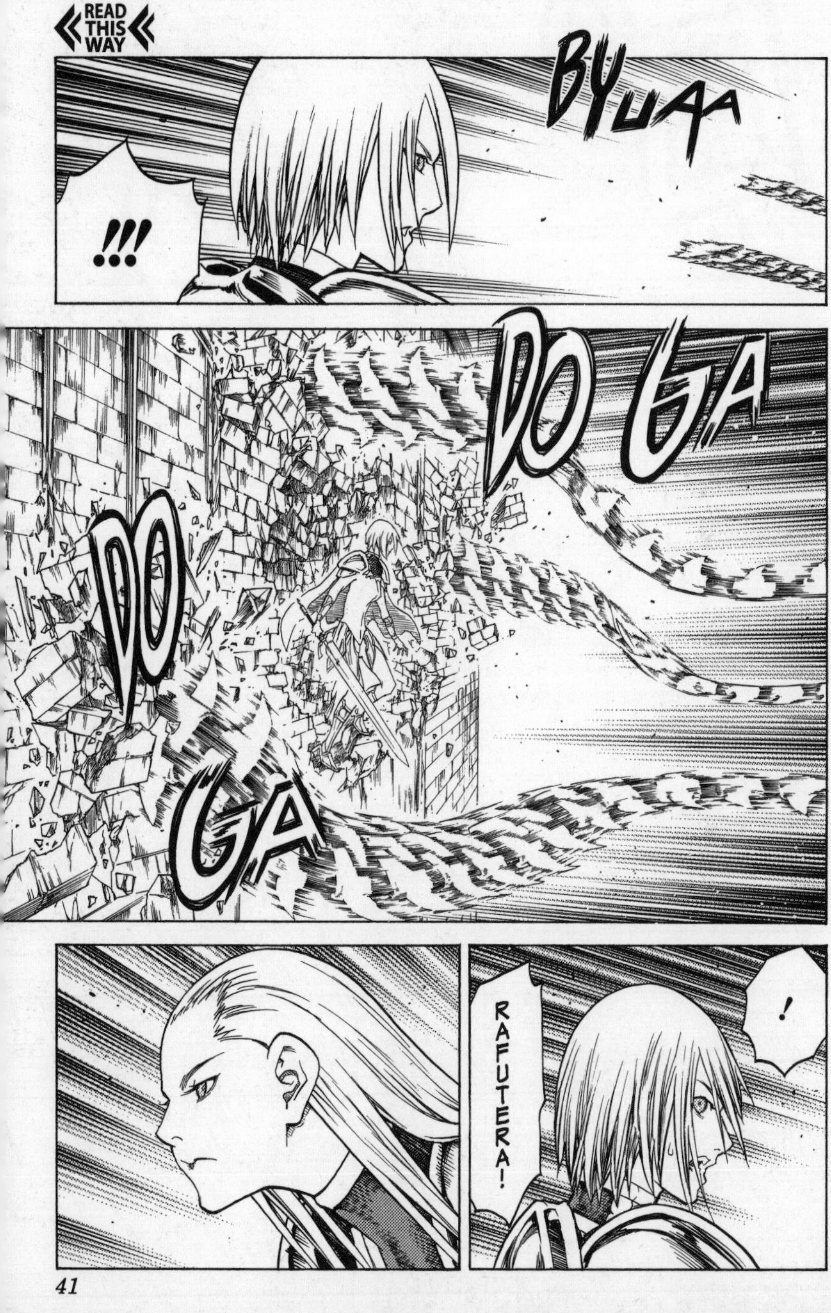
READ THIS WAY
BYUAA
!!!
DO GA
DO GA
!
RAFUTERA!

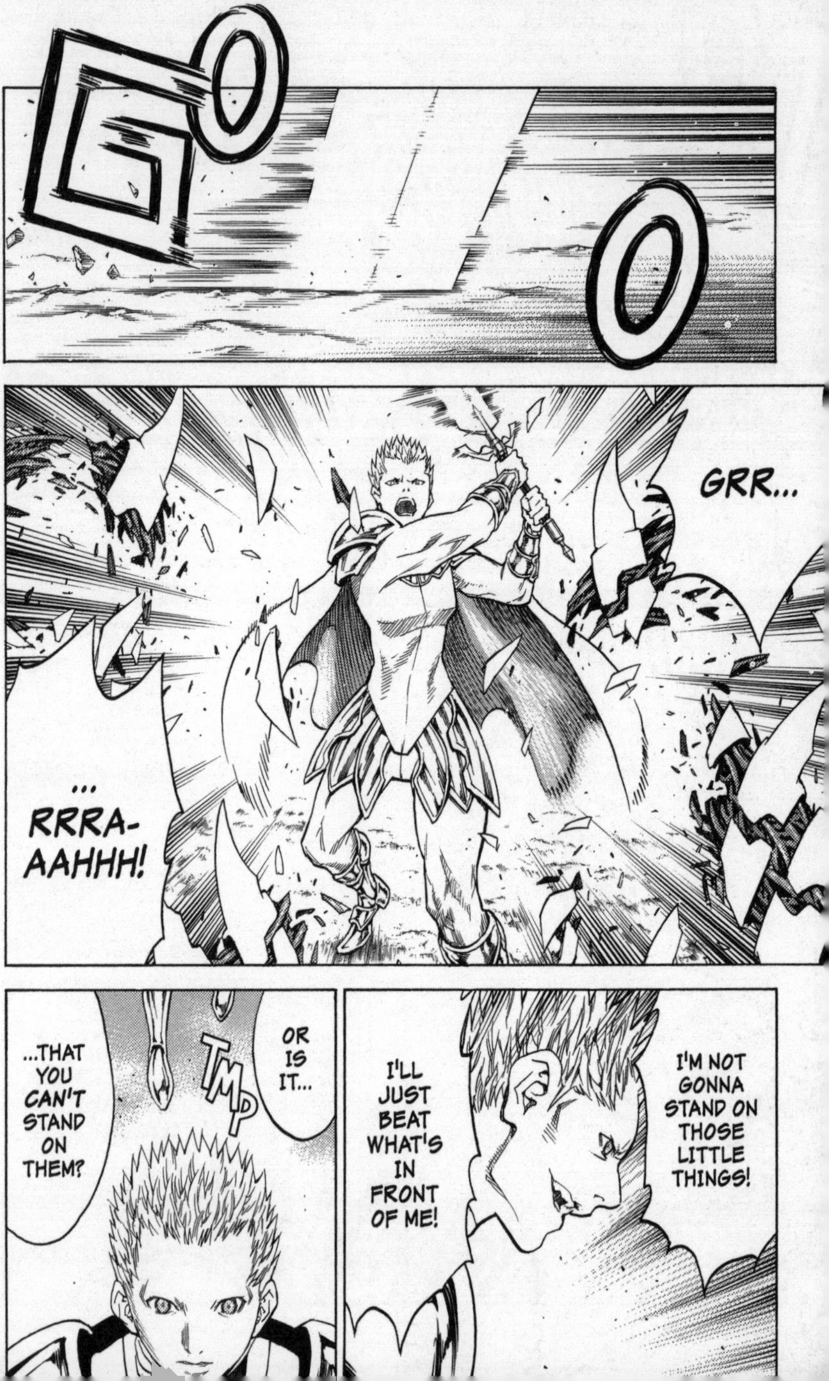
GOO
GRR...
...RRRA-AAHHH!
I'M NOT GONNA STAND ON THOSE LITTLE THINGS!
I'LL JUST BEAT WHAT'S IN FRONT OF ME!
OR IS IT...
TMP
...THAT YOU CAN'T STAND ON THEM?

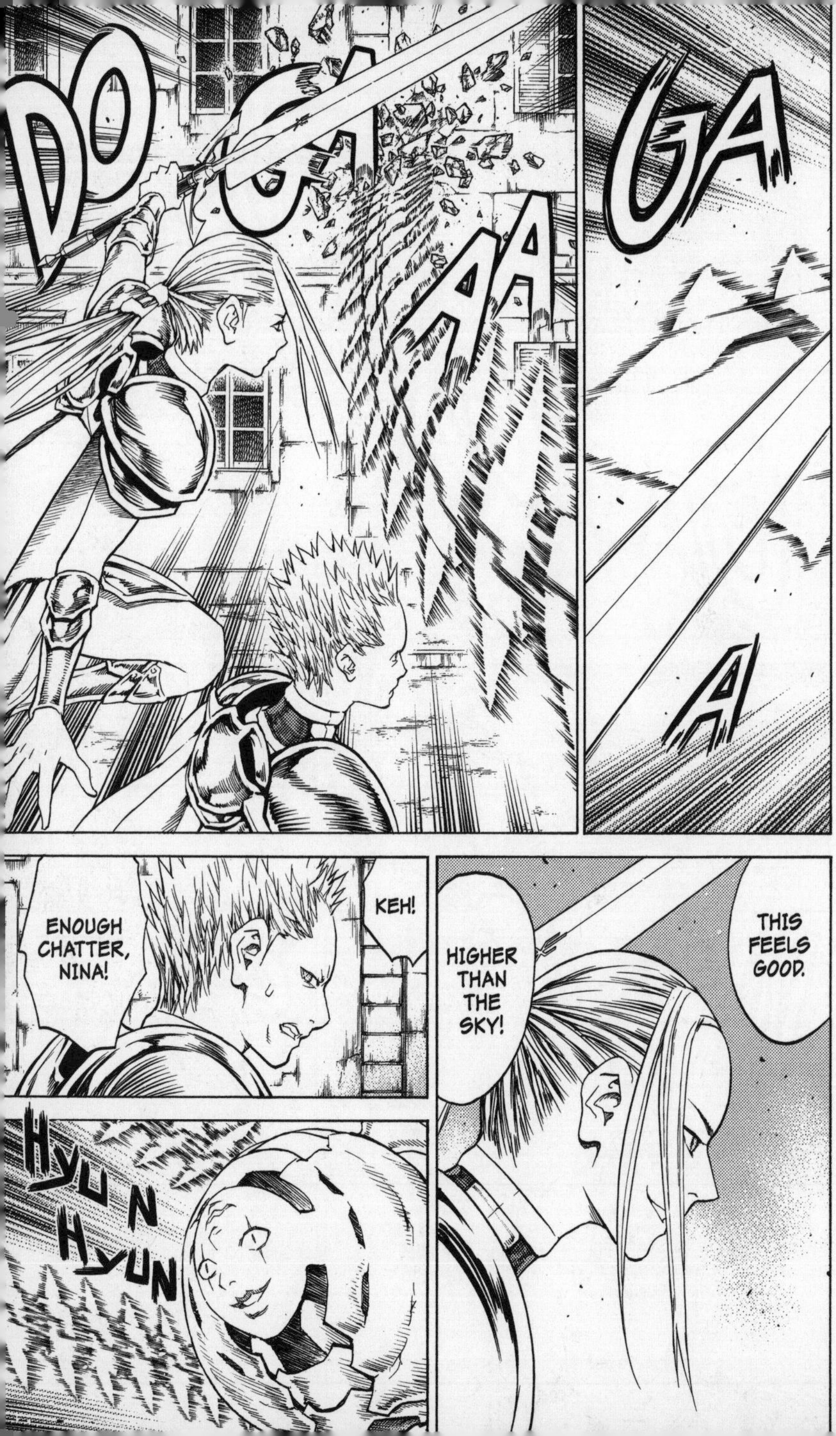
GA
A
DO
GA
AA
THIS FEELS GOOD.
HIGHER THAN THE SKY!
KEH!
ENOUGH CHATTER, NINA!
HYUN
HYUN

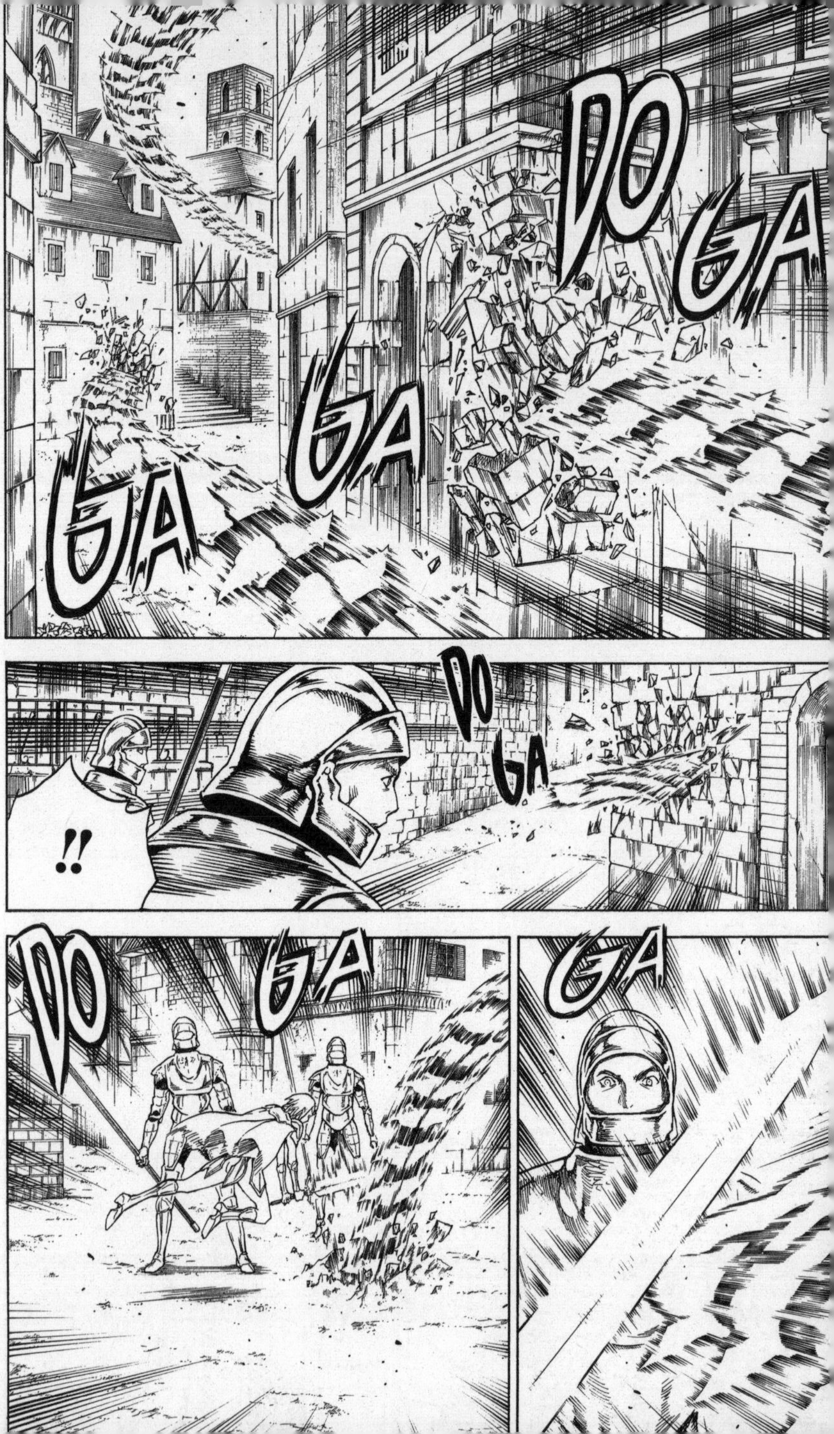
DO GA
GA
GA
DO GA
!!
GA
DO GA

READ THIS WAY

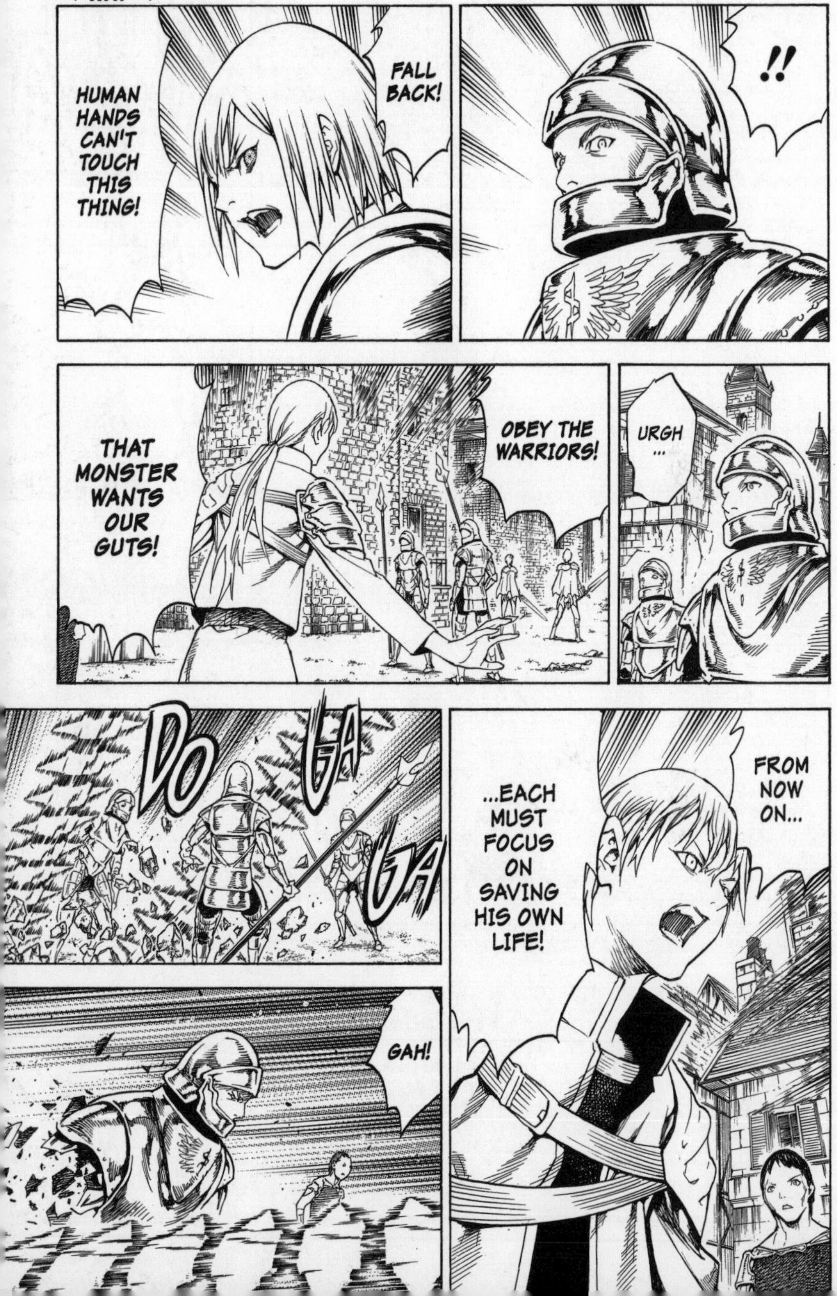
!!
FALL BACK!
HUMAN HANDS CAN'T TOUCH THIS THING!
URGH ...
OBEY THE WARRIORS!
THAT MONSTER WANTS OUR GUTS!
FROM NOW ON...
...EACH MUST FOCUS ON SAVING HIS OWN LIFE!
DO
GA
GA
GAH!

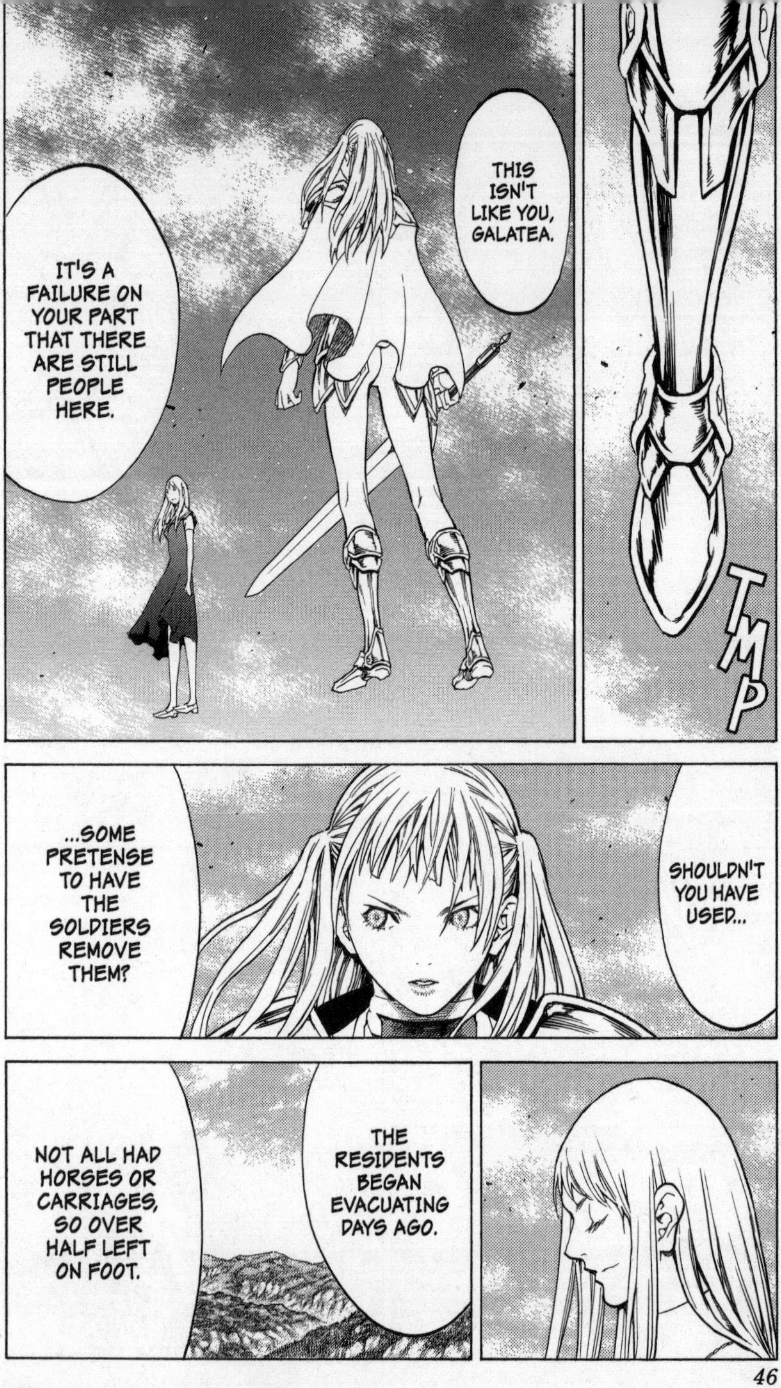
TMP
THIS ISN'T LIKE YOU, GALATEA.
IT'S A FAILURE ON YOUR PART THAT THERE ARE STILL PEOPLE HERE.
SHOULDN'T YOU HAVE USED...
...SOME PRETENSE TO HAVE THE SOLDIERS REMOVE THEM?
THE RESIDENTS BEGAN EVACUATING DAYS AGO.
NOT ALL HAD HORSES OR CARRIAGES, SO OVER HALF LEFT ON FOOT.

READ THIS WAY

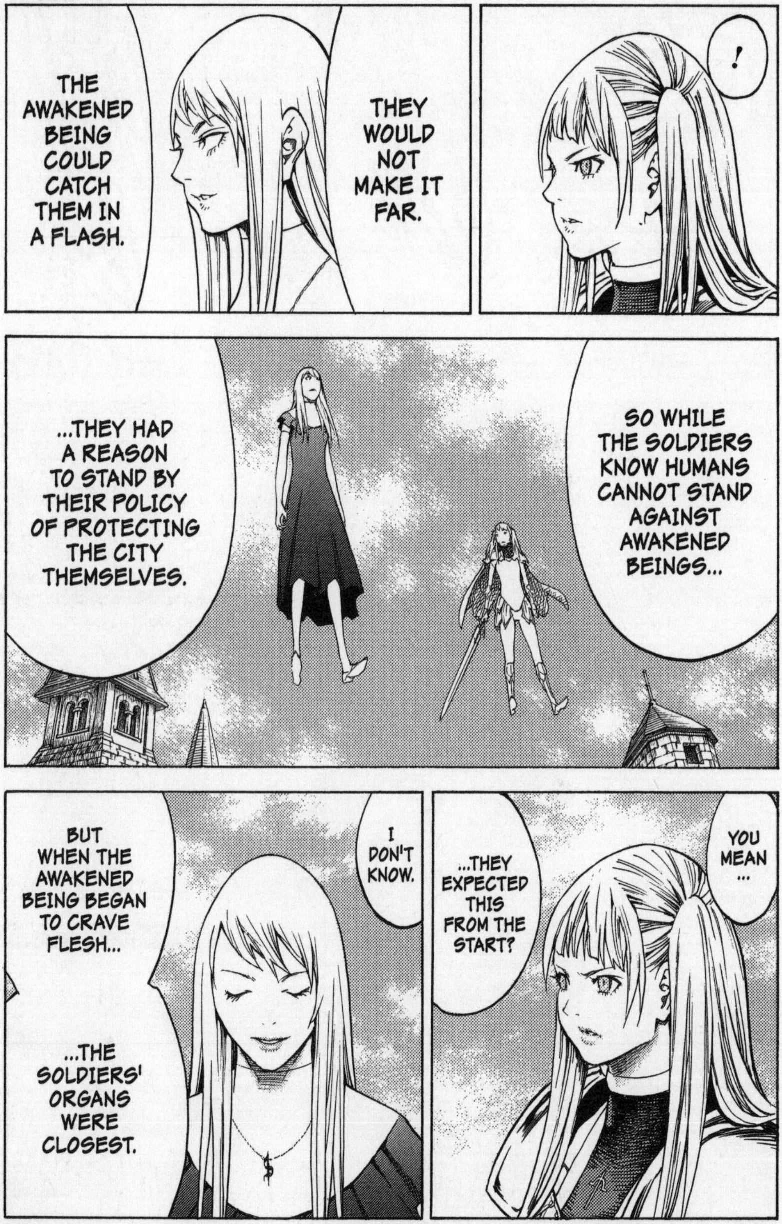
!
THEY WOULD NOT MAKE IT FAR.
THE AWAKENED BEING COULD CATCH THEM IN A FLASH.
SO WHILE THE SOLDIERS KNOW HUMANS CANNOT STAND AGAINST AWAKENED BEINGS...
...THEY HAD A REASON TO STAND BY THEIR POLICY OF PROTECTING THE CITY THEMSELVES.
YOU MEAN ...
...THEY EXPECTED THIS FROM THE START?
I DON'T KNOW.
BUT WHEN THE AWAKENED BEING BEGAN TO CRAVE FLESH...
...THE SOLDIERS' ORGANS WERE CLOSEST.

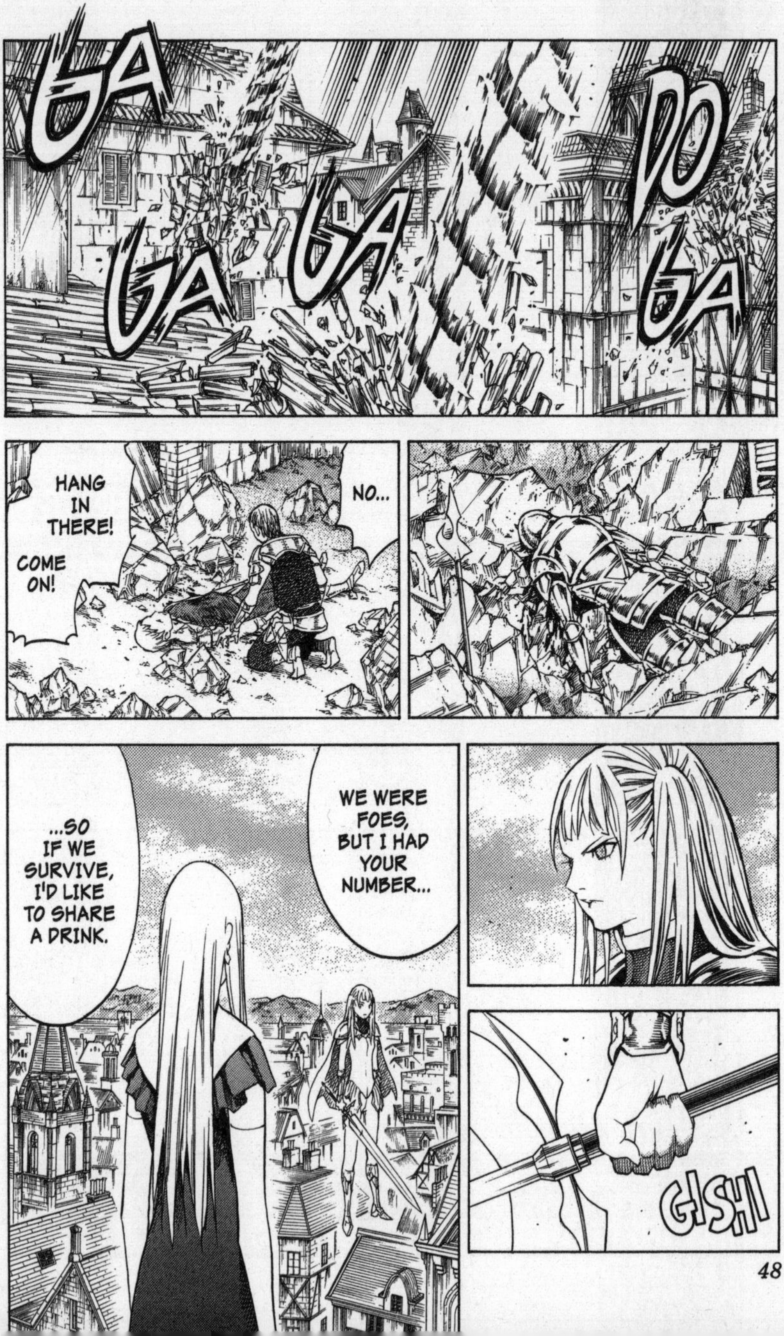
DO GA
GA
GA GA
NO...
HANG IN THERE!
COME ON!
GISHI
WE WERE FOES, BUT I HAD YOUR NUMBER...
...SO IF WE SURVIVE, I'D LIKE TO SHARE A DRINK.

READ THIS WAY

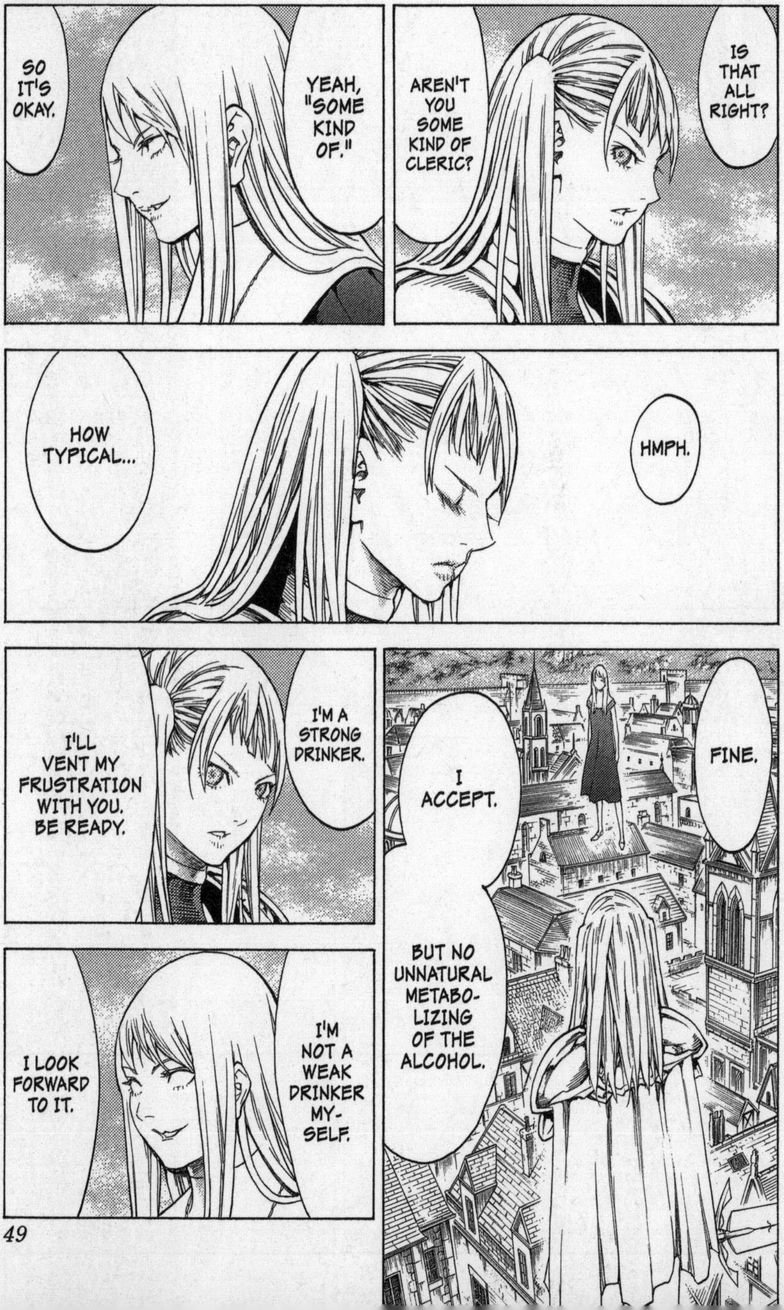

IS THAT ALL RIGHT?
AREN'T YOU SOME KIND OF CLERIC?
YEAH, "SOME KIND OF."
SO IT'S OKAY.
HMPH.
HOW TYPICAL...
FINE.
I ACCEPT.
BUT NO UNNATURAL METABO-LIZING OF THE ALCOHOL.
I'M A STRONG DRINKER.
I'LL VENT MY FRUSTRATION WITH YOU. BE READY.
I'M NOT A WEAK DRINKER MY-SELF.
I LOOK FORWARD TO IT.

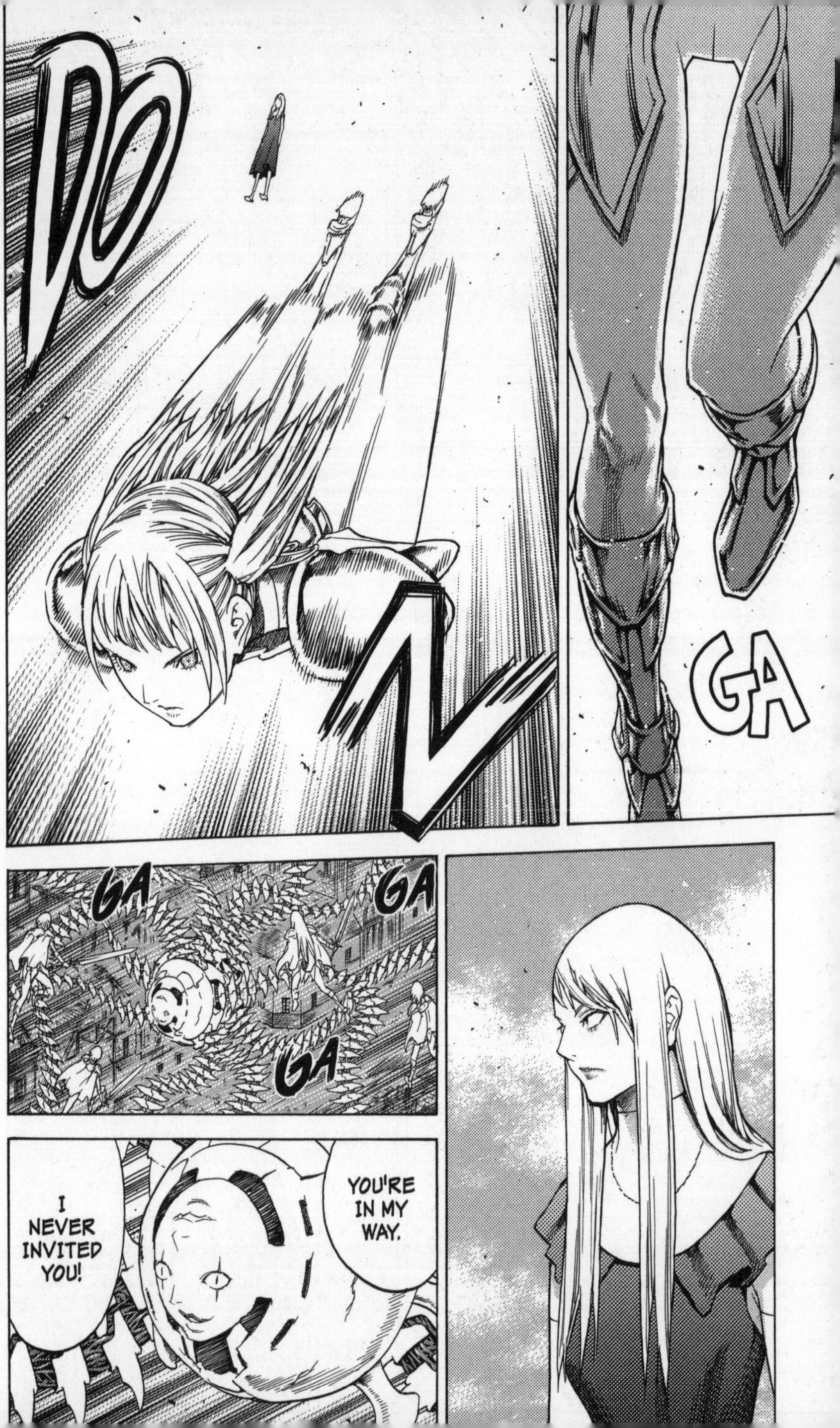
GA
DO
N
GA
GA
GA
YOU'RE IN MY WAY.
I NEVER INVITED YOU!

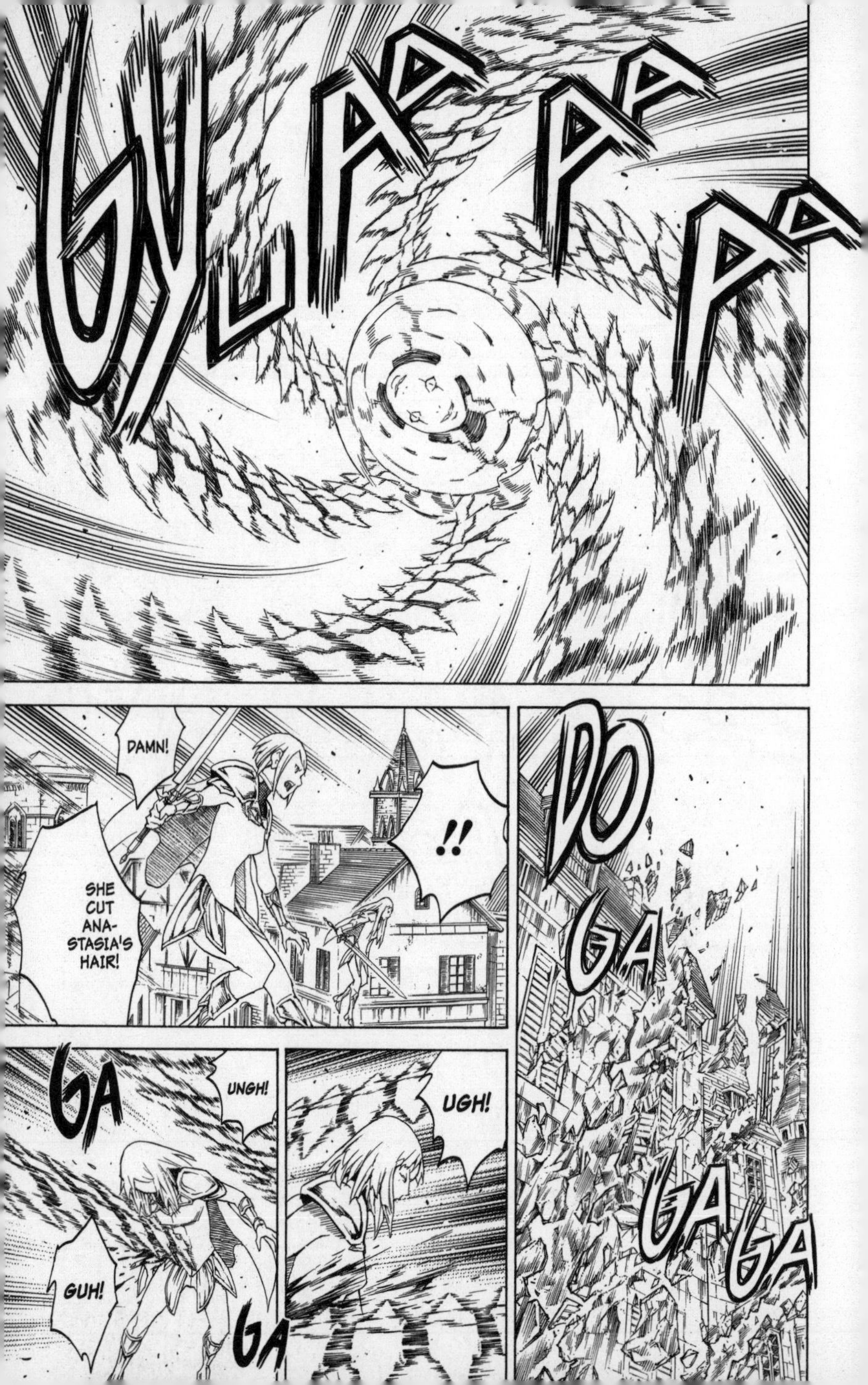
GYUAAA
DO
GA
GAGA
!!
DAMN!
SHE CUT ANA-STASIA'S HAIR!
UGH!
GA
UNGH!
GA
GUH!

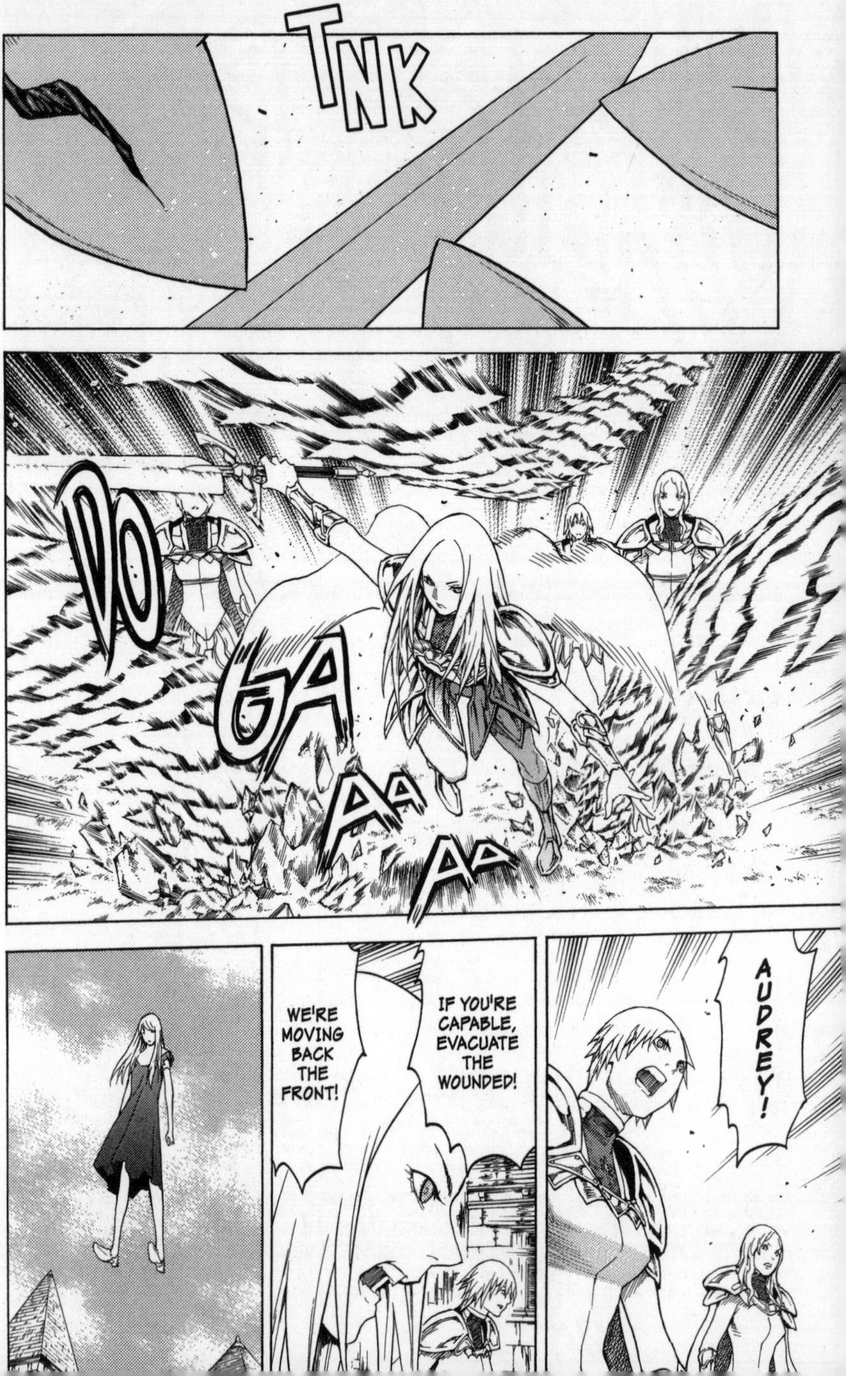
TNK
DOGAAAA
AUDREY!
IF YOU'RE CAPABLE, EVACUATE THE WOUNDED!
WE'RE MOVING BACK THE FRONT!

READ THIS WAY

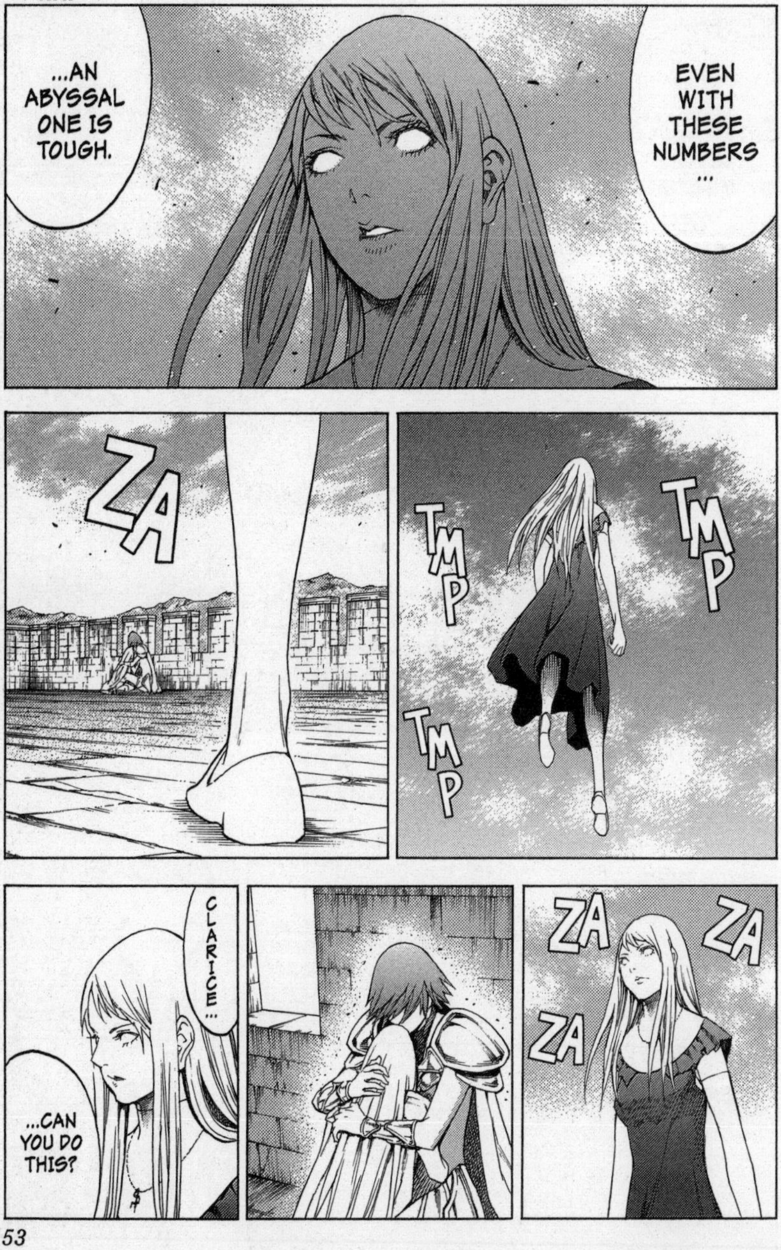
EVEN WITH THESE NUMBERS ...
...AN ABYSSAL ONE IS TOUGH.
TMP
TMP
TMP
TMP
ZA
ZA
ZA
ZA
CLARICE...
...CAN YOU DO THIS?

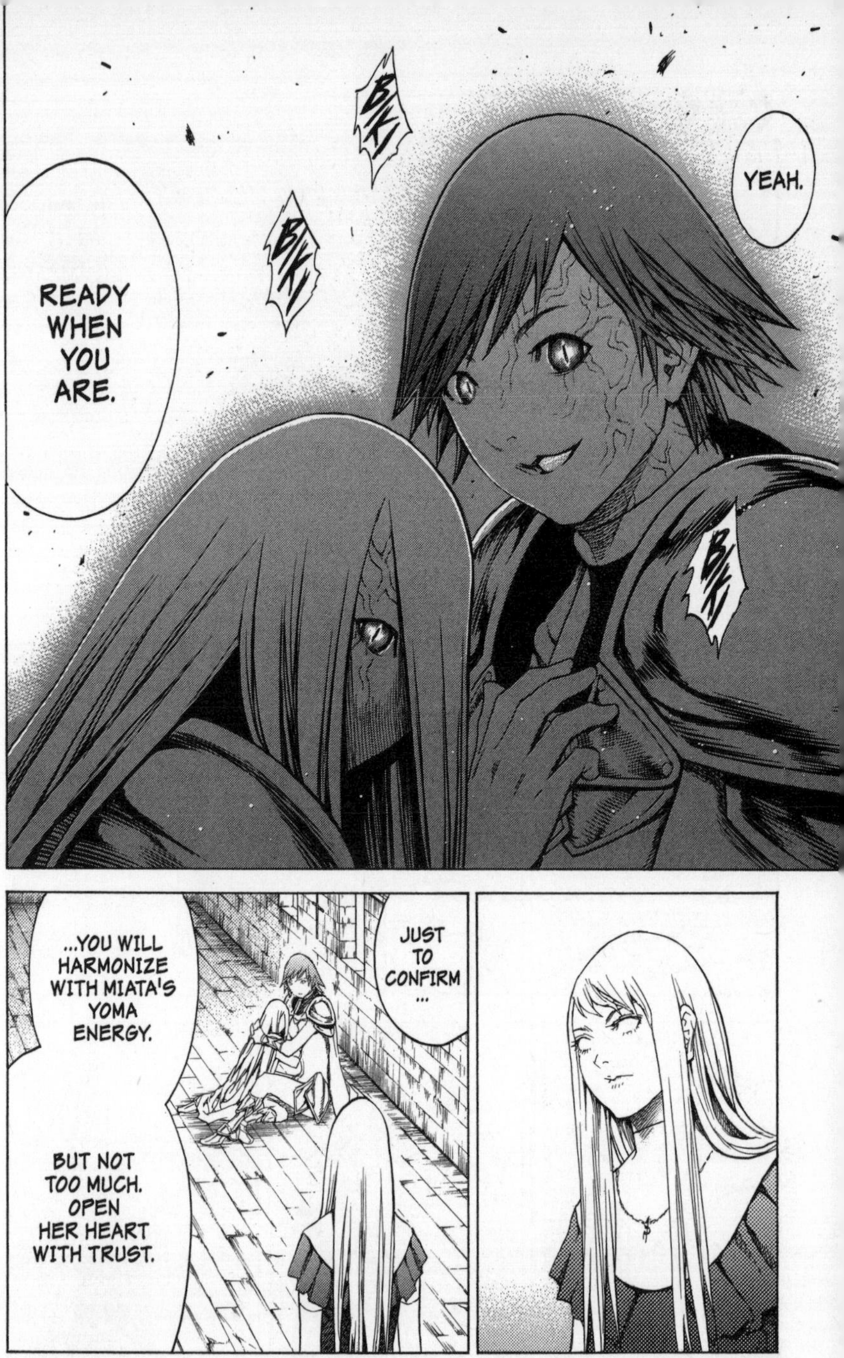
YEAH.
BIKI
BIKI
READY WHEN YOU ARE.
BIKI
JUST TO CONFIRM ...
...YOU WILL HARMONIZE WITH MIATA'S YOMA ENERGY.
BUT NOT TOO MUCH. OPEN HER HEART WITH TRUST.

READ THIS WAY

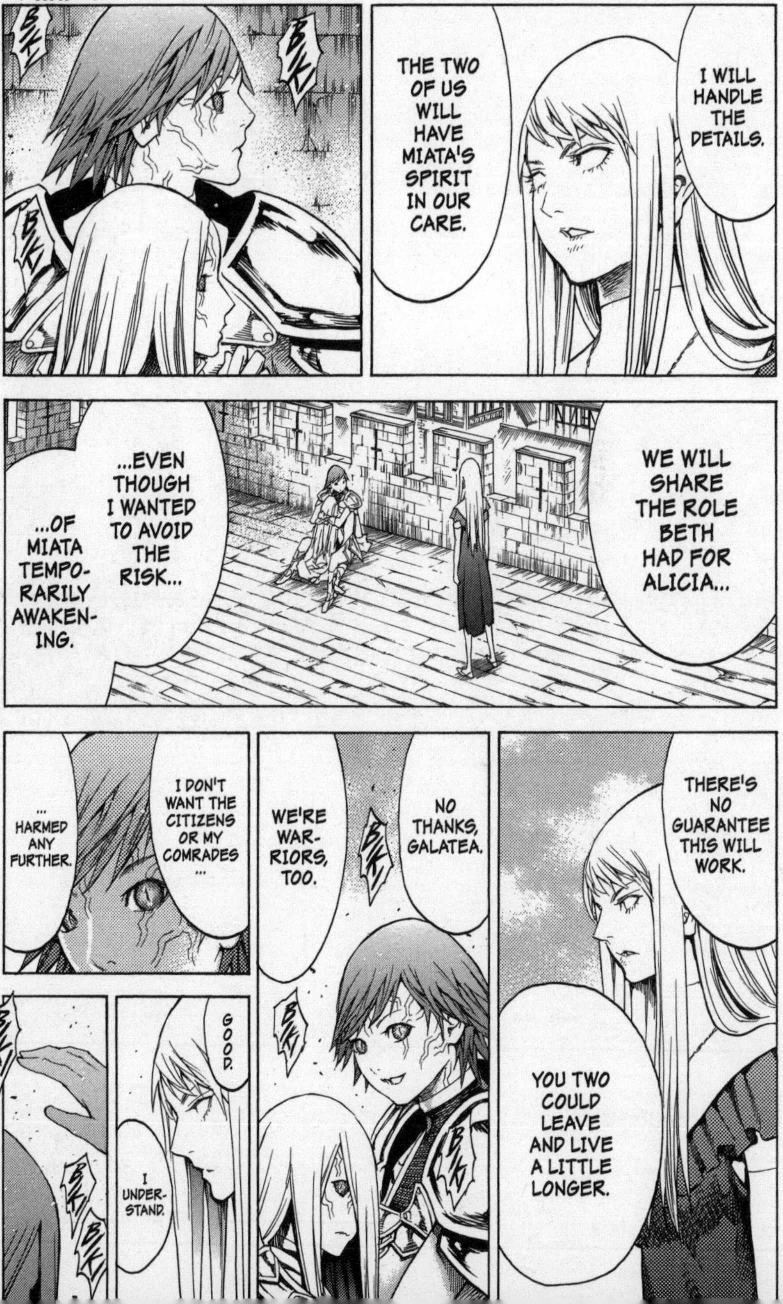
I WILL HANDLE THE DETAILS.
THE TWO OF US WILL HAVE MIATA'S SPIRIT IN OUR CARE.
BIK
BIK
BIK
WE WILL SHARE THE ROLE BETH HAD FOR ALICIA...
...EVEN THOUGH I WANTED TO AVOID THE RISK...
...OF MIATA TEMPORARILY AWAKENING.
THERE'S NO GUARANTEE THIS WILL WORK.
YOU TWO COULD LEAVE AND LIVE A LITTLE LONGER.
NO THANKS, GALATEA.
WE'RE WARRIORS, TOO.
BIK
BIK
BIK
I DON'T WANT THE CITIZENS OR MY COMRADES ...
... HARMED ANY FURTHER.
GOOD.
I UNDERSTAND.
BIK
BIK
BIK

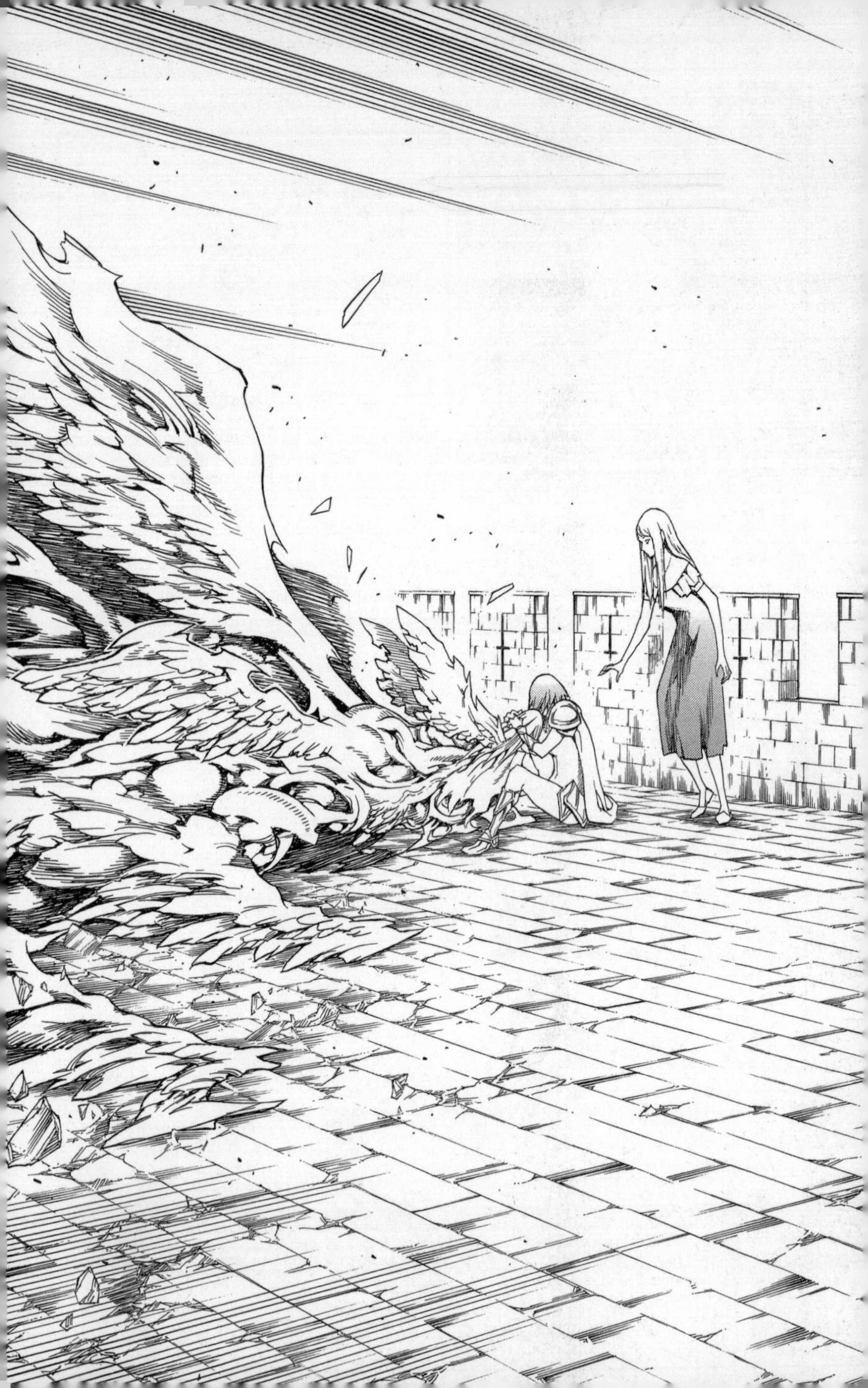

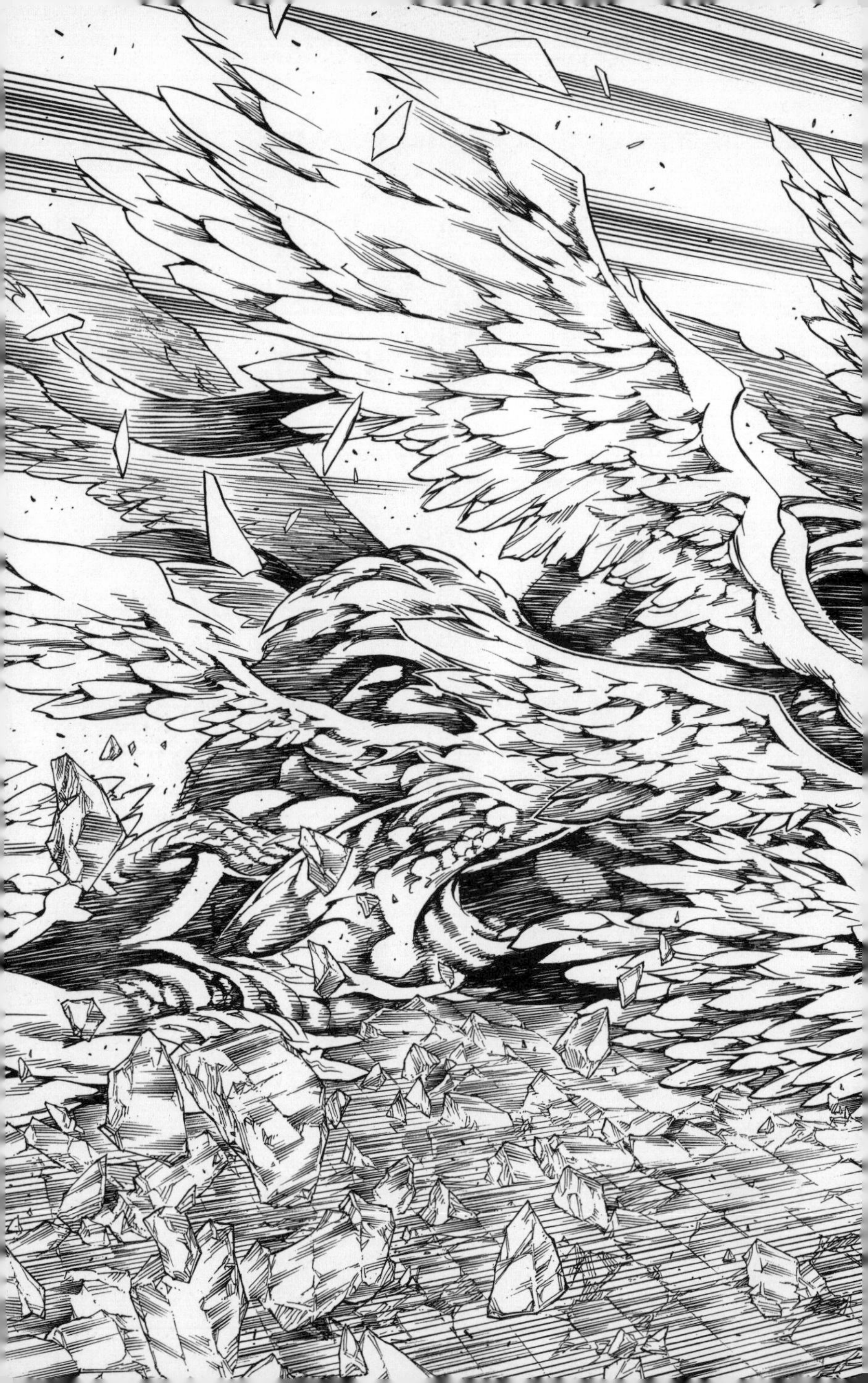

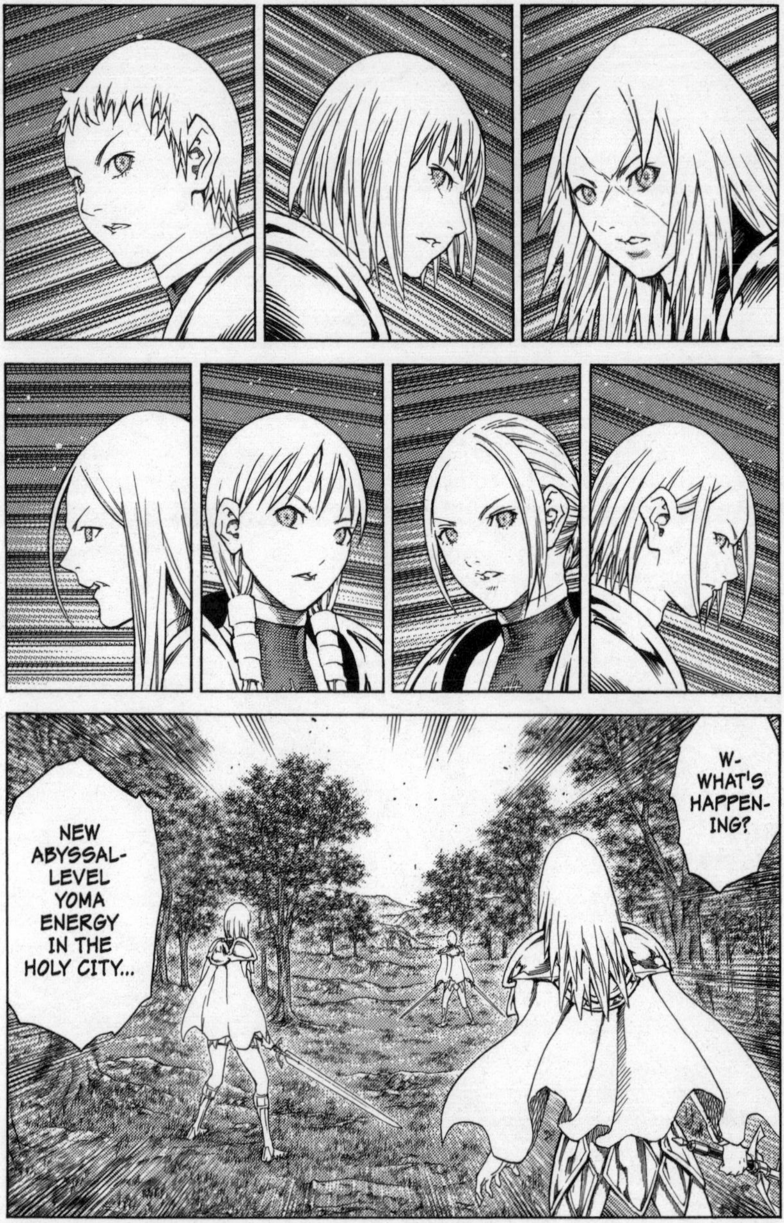
W- WHAT'S HAPPEN- ING?
NEW ABYSSAL- LEVEL YOMA ENERGY IN THE HOLY CITY...

READ THIS WAY

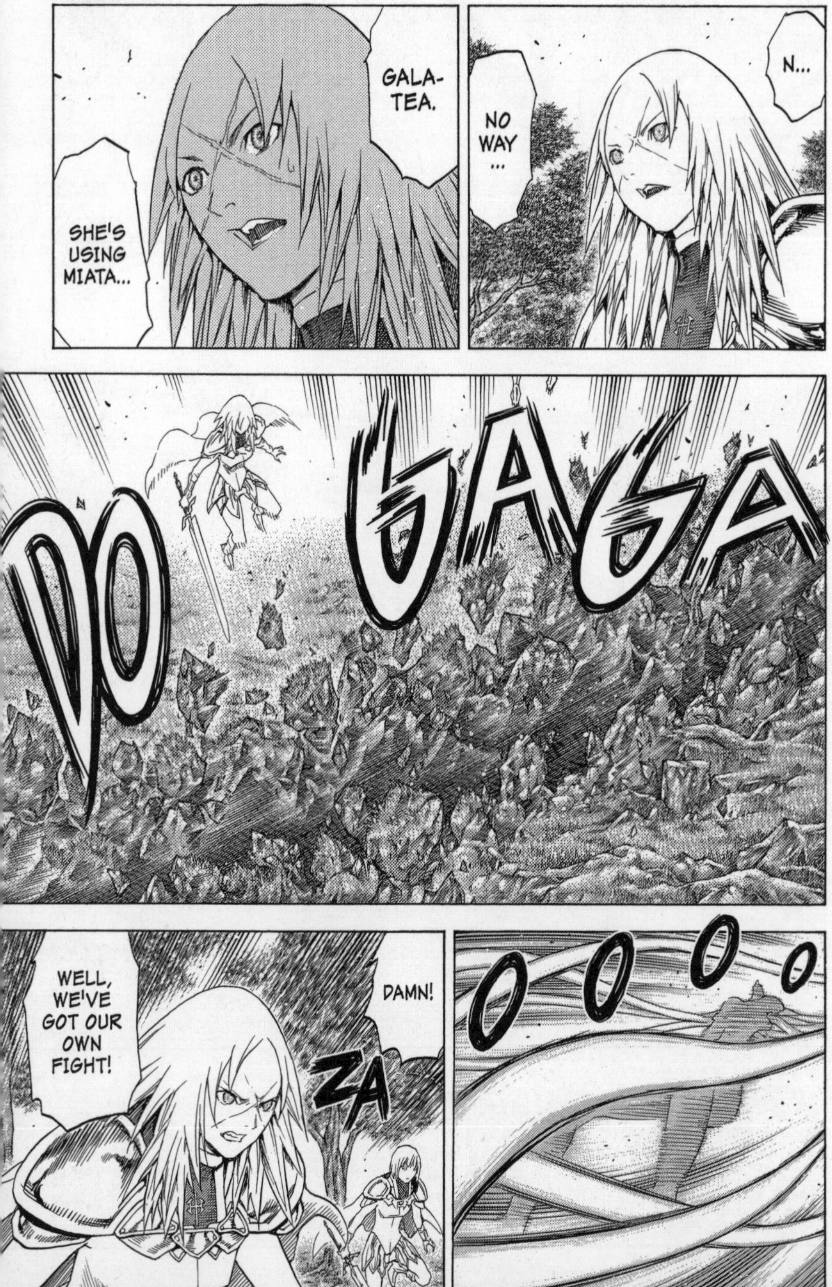
N...
NO WAY ...
GALA-TEA.
SHE'S USING MIATA...
DO GAGA
OOOOO
DAMN!
WELL, WE'VE GOT OUR OWN FIGHT!
ZA

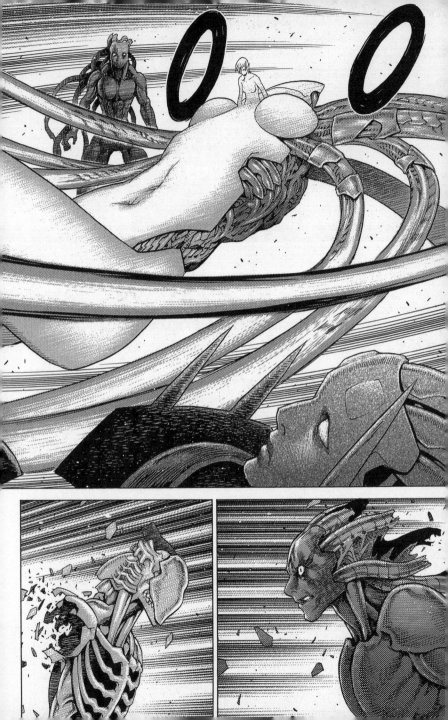

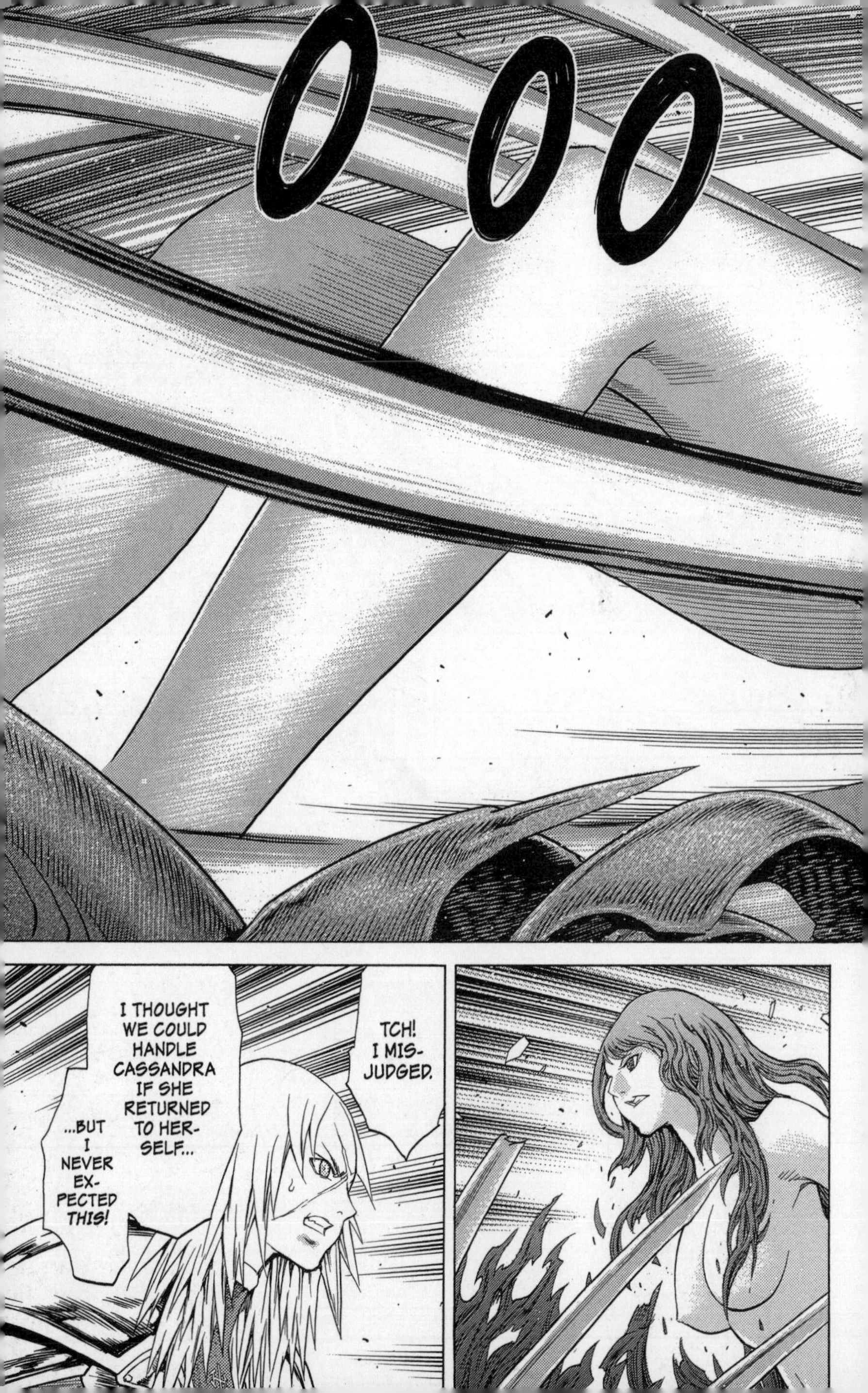
TCH! I MIS-JUDGED.
I THOUGHT WE COULD HANDLE CASSANDRA IF SHE RETURNED TO HER-SELF...
...BUT I NEVER EX-PECTED THIS!

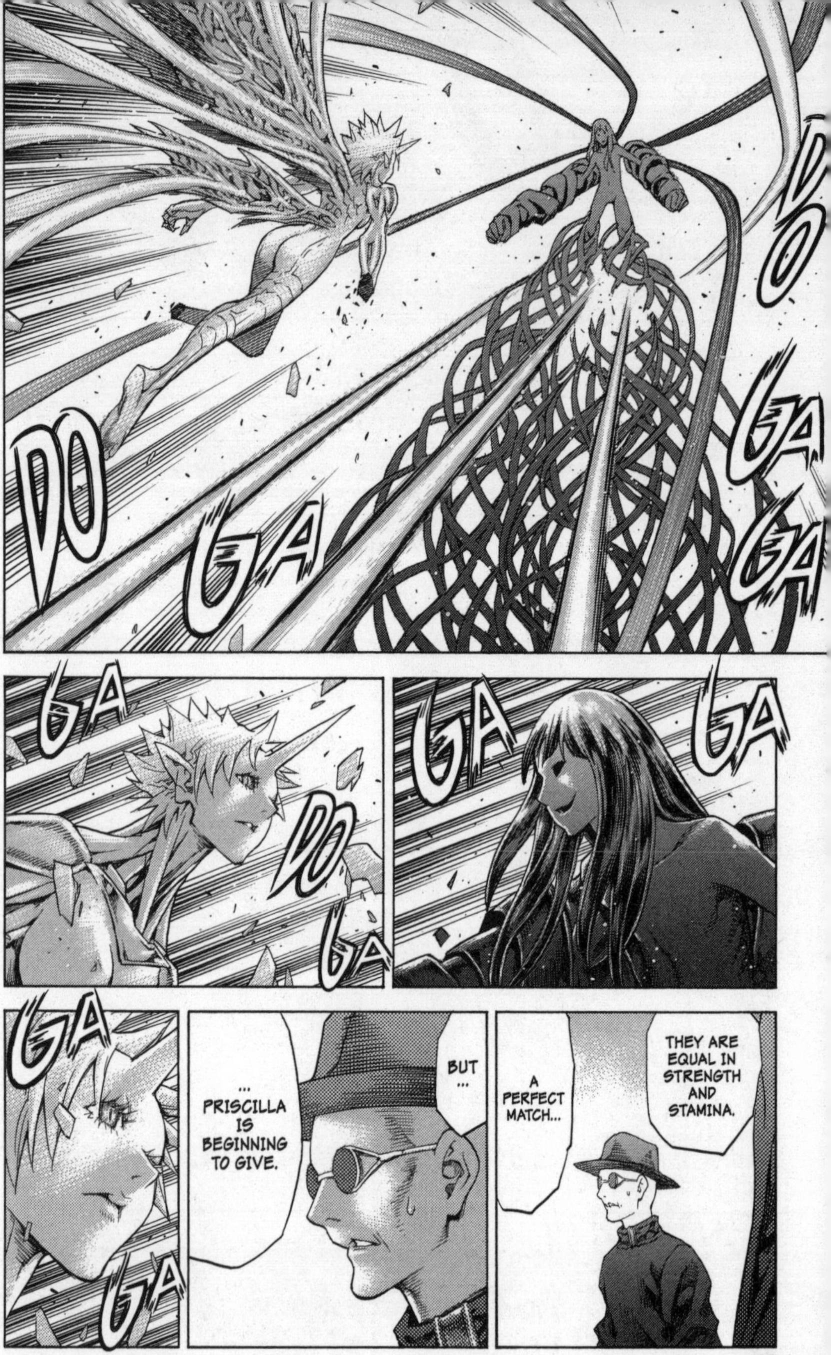
DO
GA
GA
DO
GA
GA
GA
GA
DO
GA
THEY ARE EQUAL IN STRENGTH AND STAMINA.
A PERFECT MATCH...
BUT ...
... PRISCILLA IS BEGINNING TO GIVE.
GA
GA

READ THIS WAY

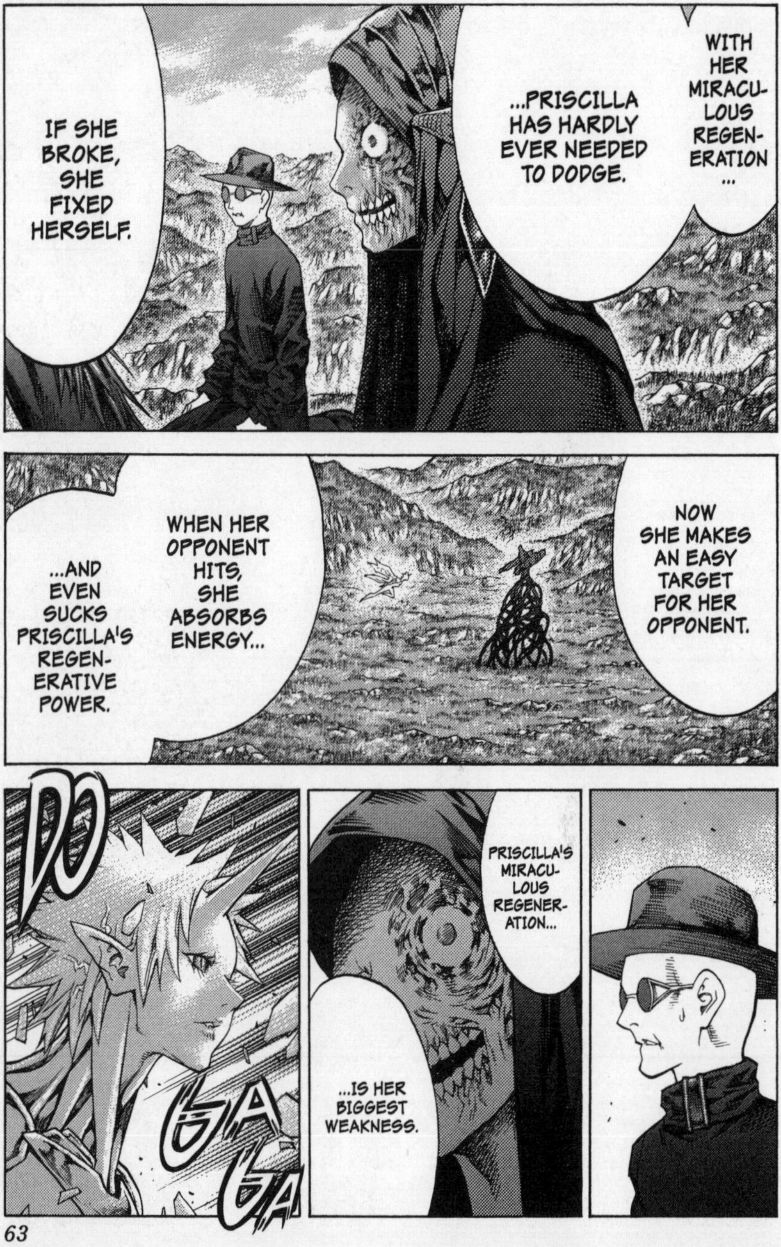
WITH HER MIRACU-LOUS REGEN-ERATION...
...PRISCILLA HAS HARDLY EVER NEEDED TO DODGE.
IF SHE BROKE, SHE FIXED HERSELF.
NOW SHE MAKES AN EASY TARGET FOR HER OPPONENT.
WHEN HER OPPONENT HITS, SHE ABSORBS ENERGY...
...AND EVEN SUCKS PRISCILLA'S REGEN-ERATIVE POWER.
PRISCILLA'S MIRACU-LOUS REGENER-ATION...
...IS HER BIGGEST WEAKNESS.
DO
GA
GA

クレイモア
Claymore

Scene 140: Sword of the Dark Deep, Part 2

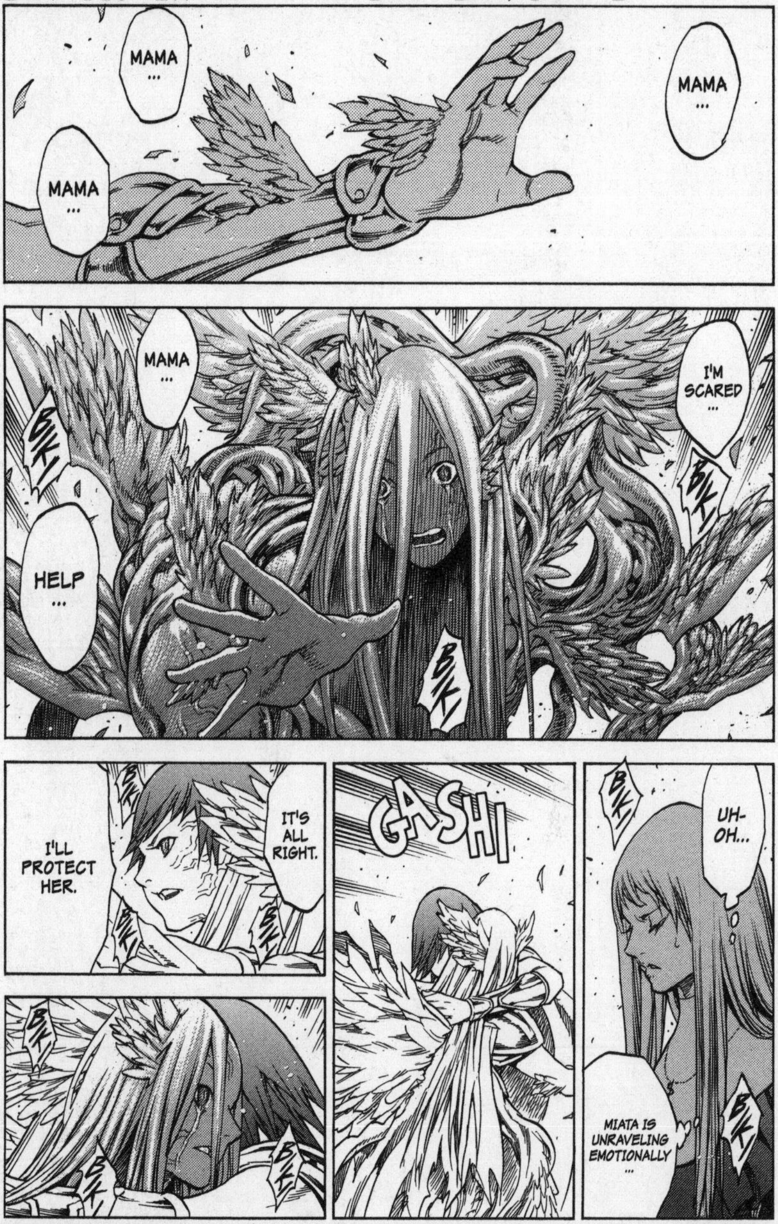
MAMA ...
MAMA ...
MAMA ...
I'M SCARED ...
BIKI
MAMA ...
BIKI
HELP ...
BIKI
UH-OH...
BIKI
MIATA IS UNRAVELING EMOTIONALLY ...
BIKI
GASHI
IT'S ALL RIGHT.
BIKI
I'LL PROTECT HER.
BIKI
BIKI
BIKI
BIKI

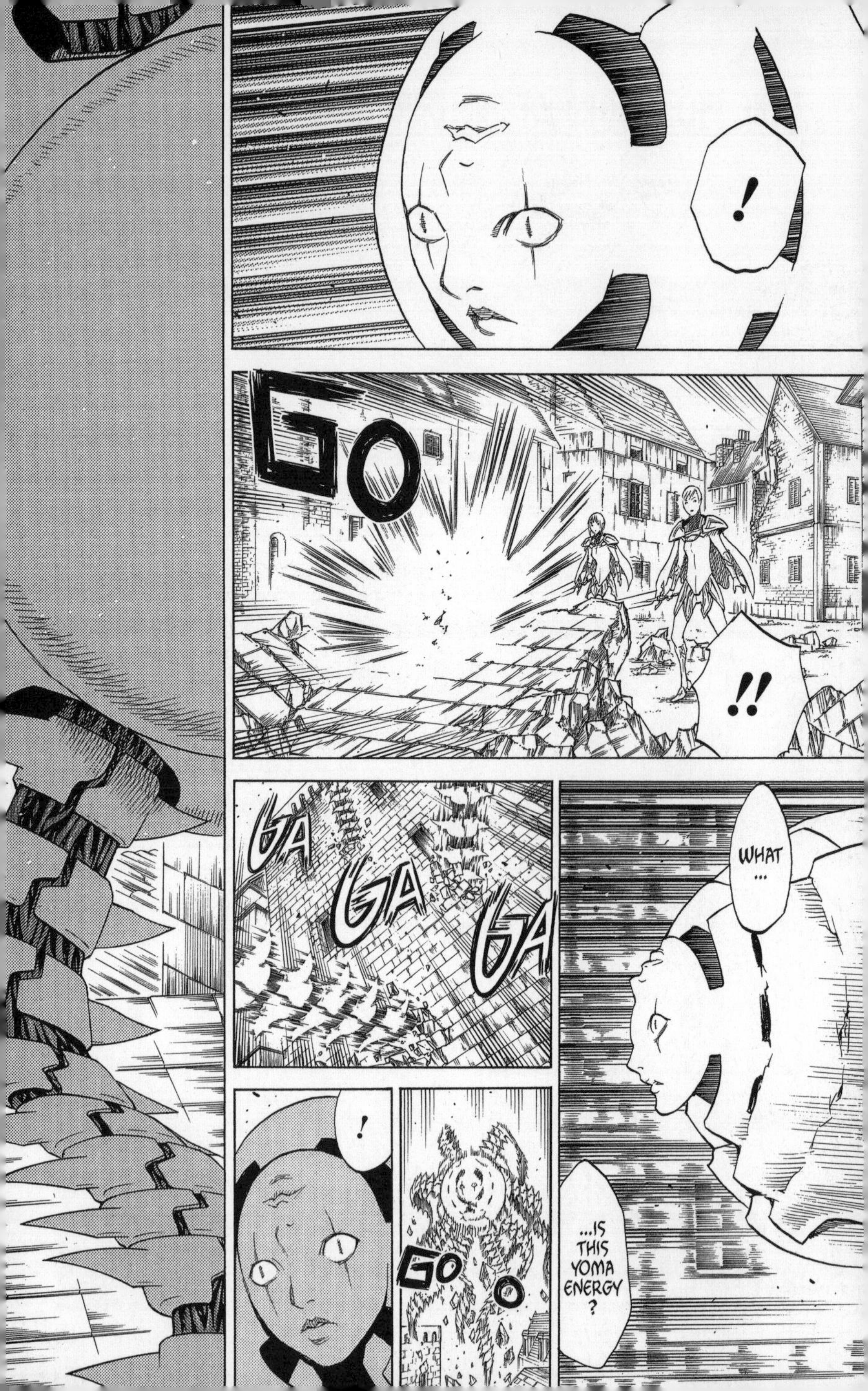

!
GO
O
!!
WHAT ...
...IS THIS YOMA ENERGY ?
GA
GA
GA
GO
O
!

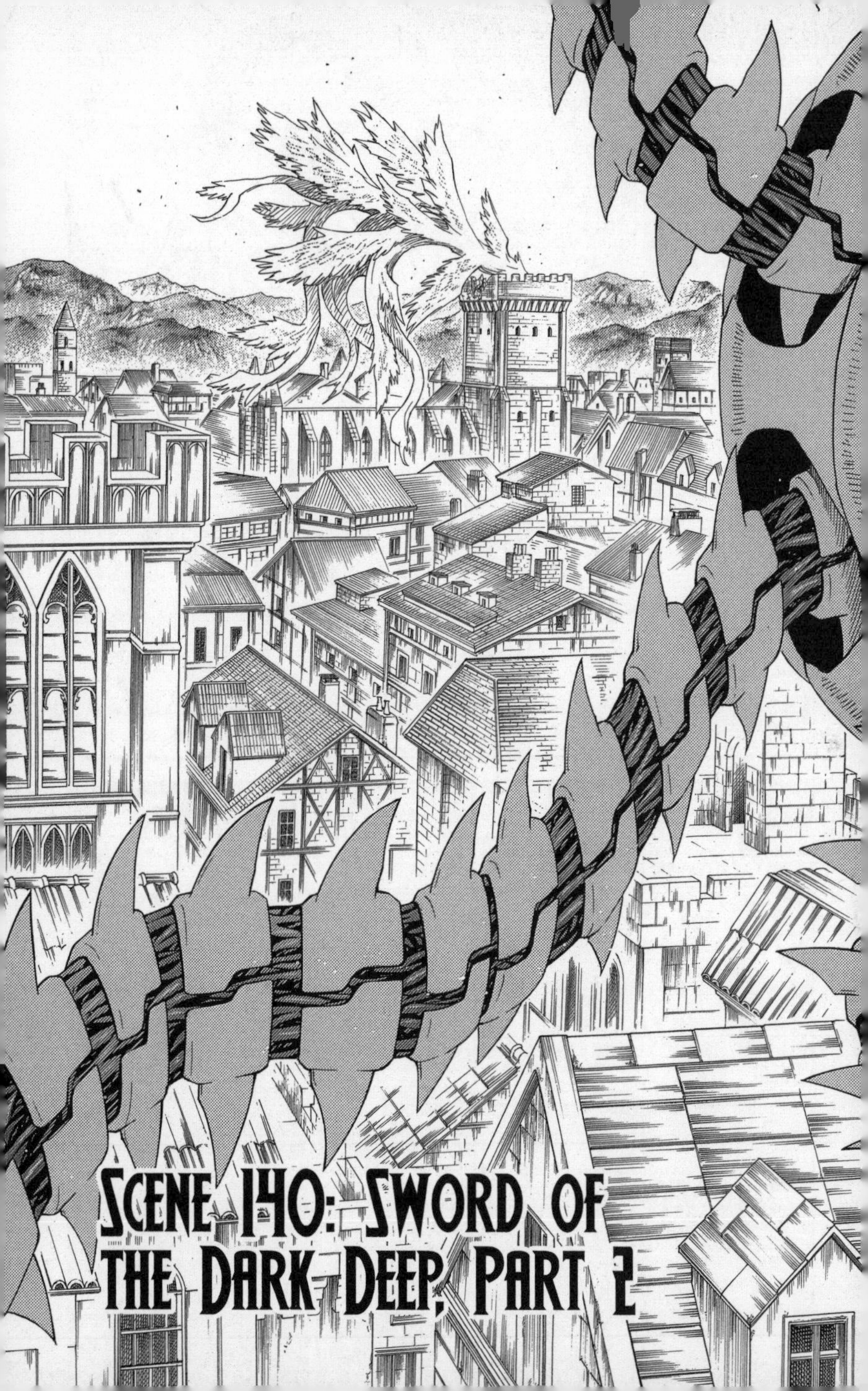
SCENE 140: SWORD OF THE DARK DEEP, PART 2

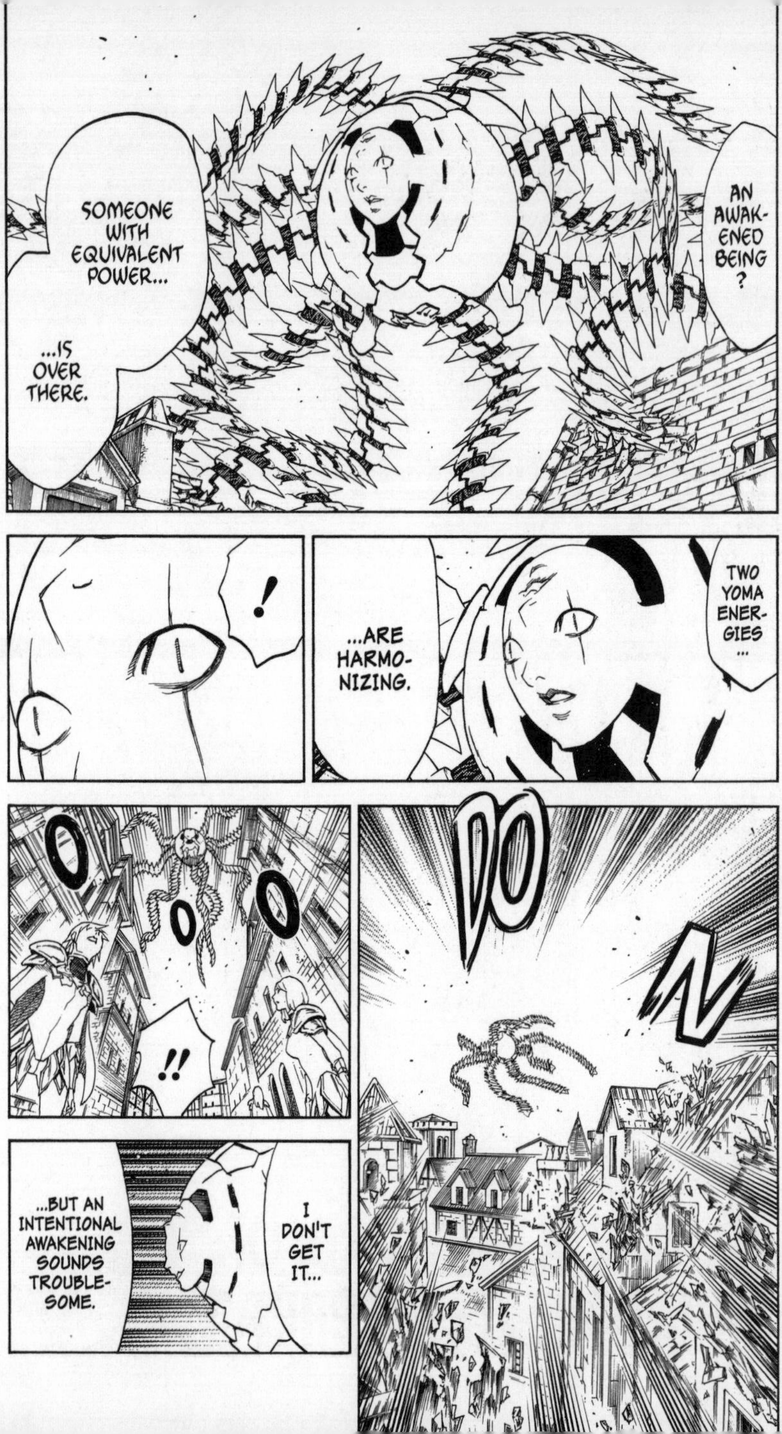

AN AWAKENED BEING?
SOMEONE WITH EQUIVALENT POWER...
...IS OVER THERE.
TWO YOMA ENERGIES...
...ARE HARMONIZING.
!
DON
OOO
!!
I DON'T GET IT...
...BUT AN INTENTIONAL AWAKENING SOUNDS TROUBLESOME.

READ THIS WAY

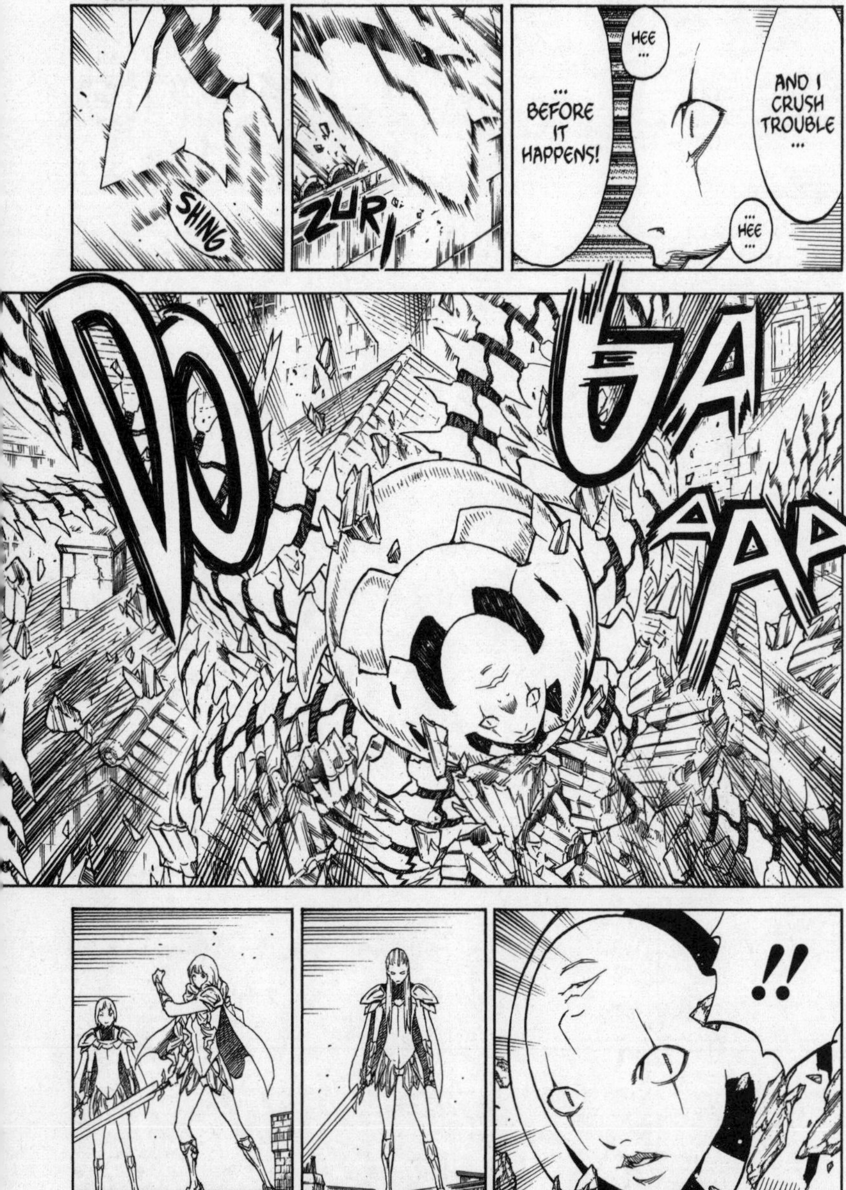
AND I CRUSH TROUBLE ...
HEE ...
... BEFORE IT HAPPENS!
... HEE ...
ZURI
SHING
DO
GAAAA
!!

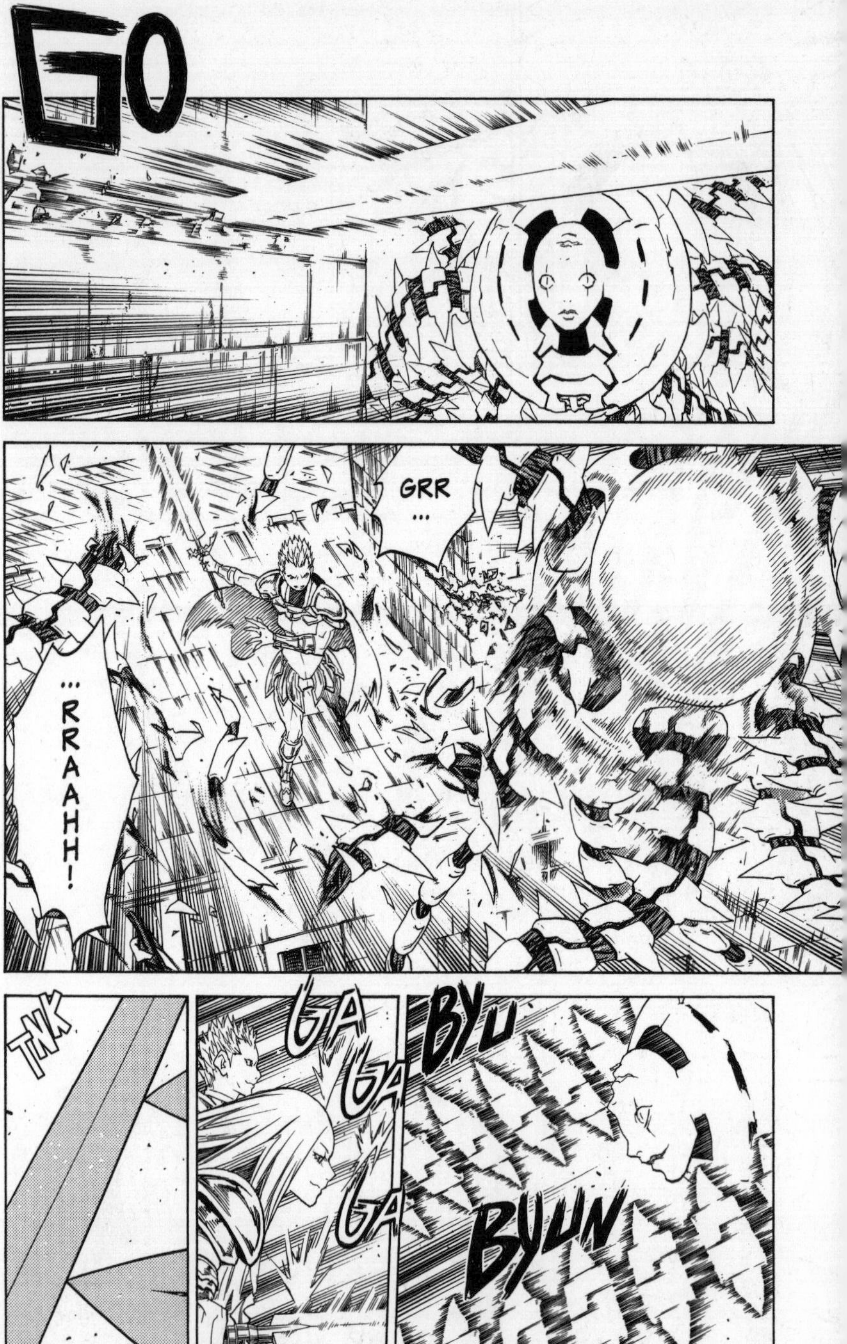
GO
GRR ...
... RRAAHH!
BYU
GA
GA
GA
BYUN
TNK

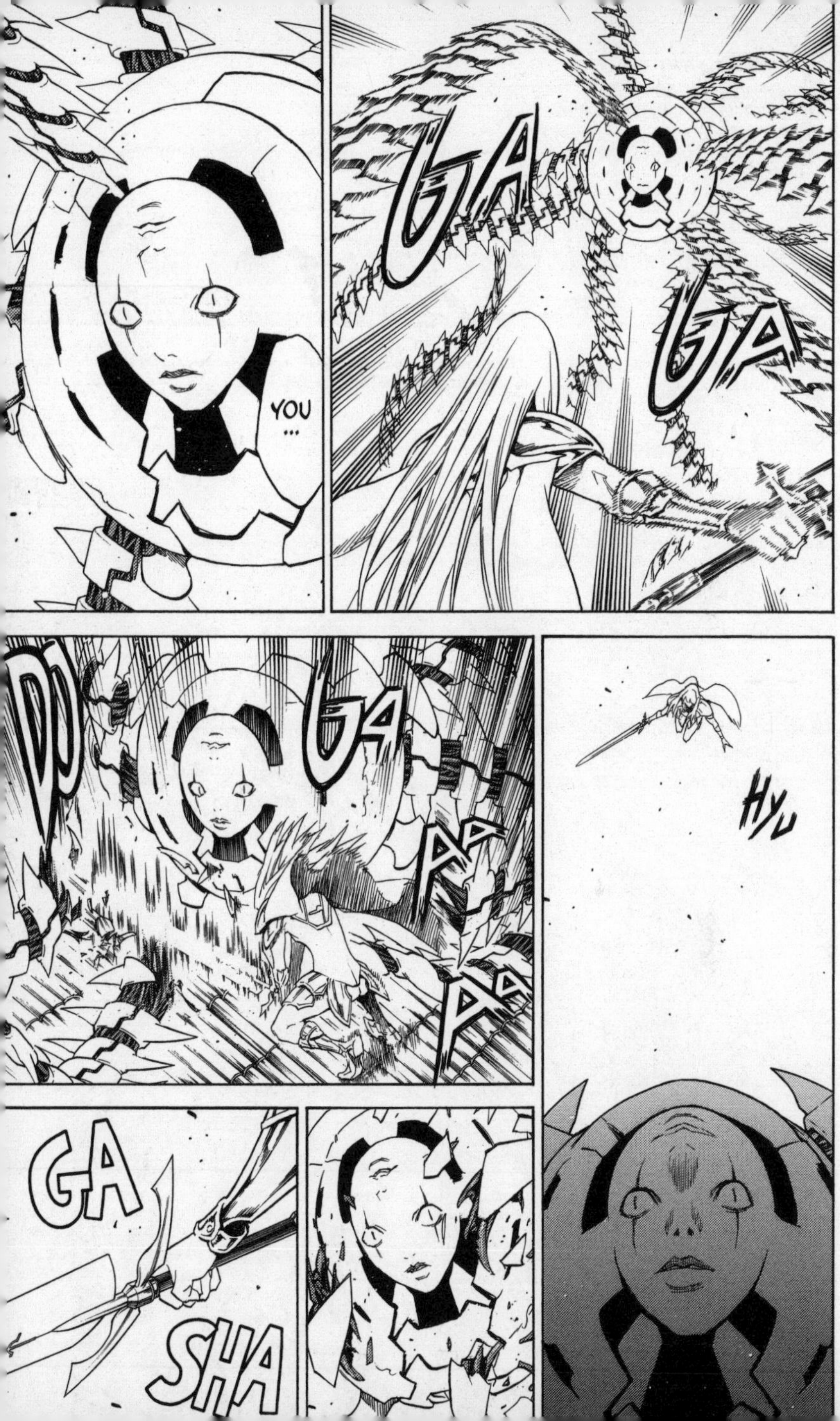
GA
GA
YOU ...
HYU
DO
GA
PA
PA
GA
SHA

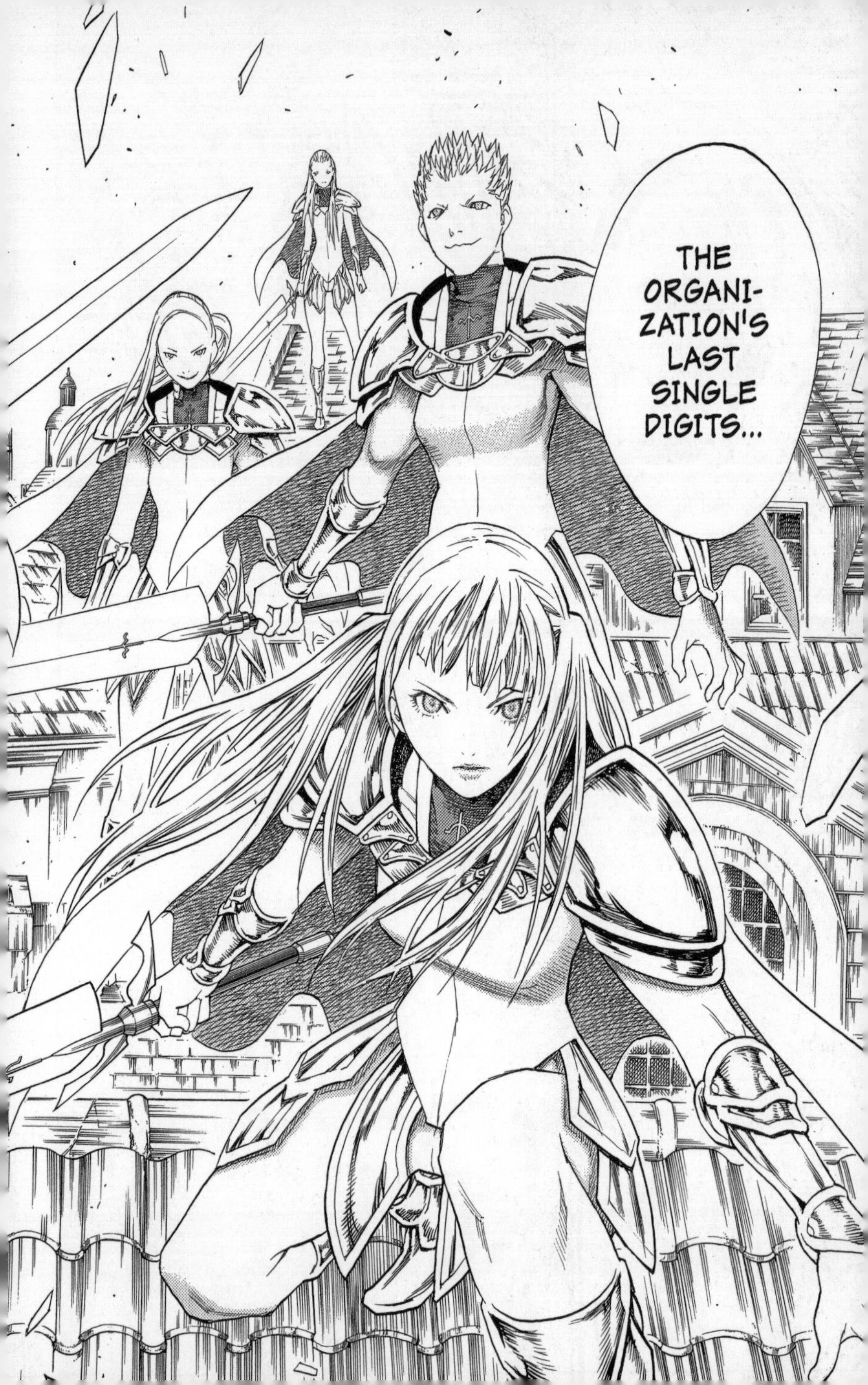
THE ORGANI-ZATION'S LAST SINGLE DIGITS...

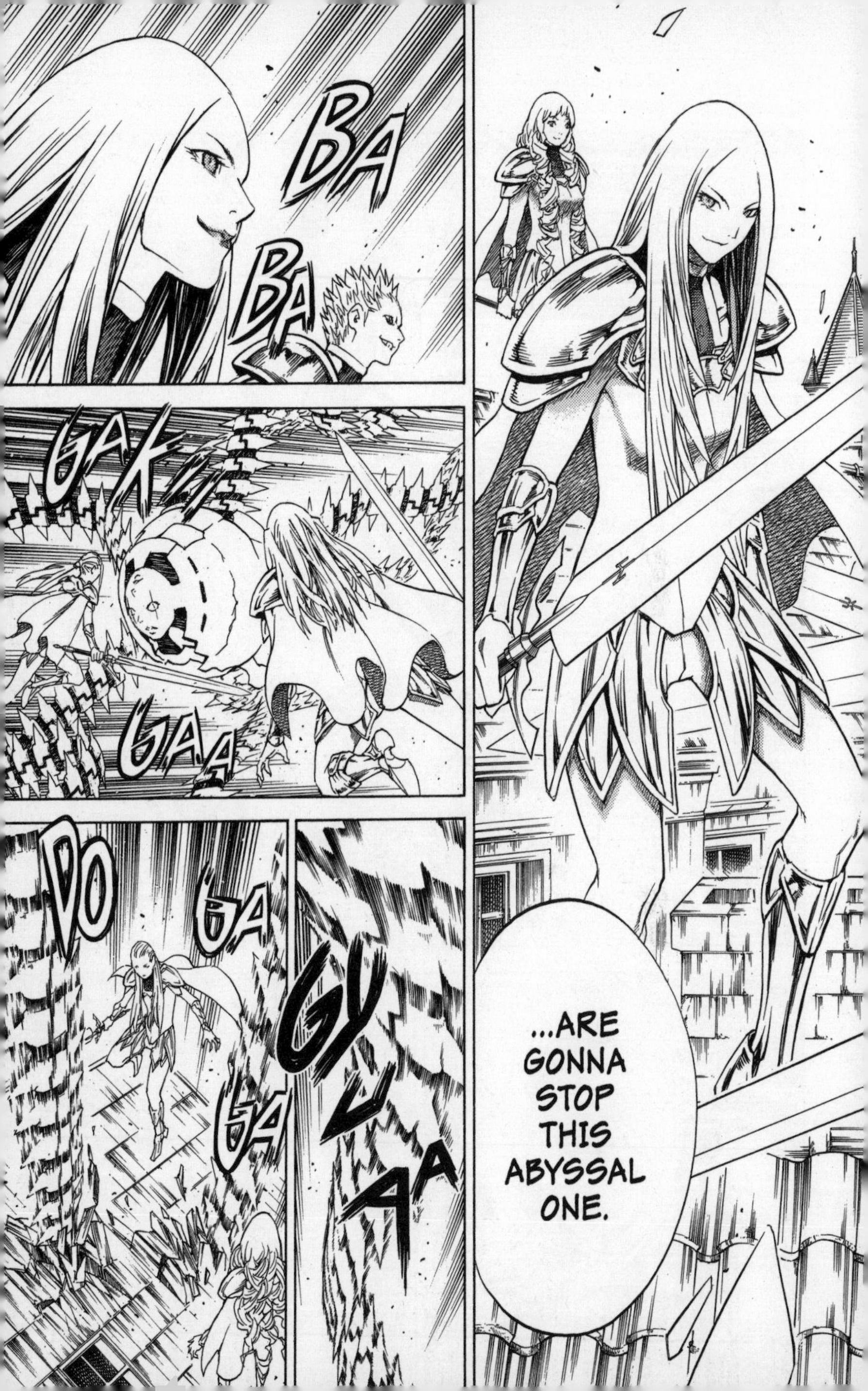
...ARE GONNA STOP THIS ABYSSAL ONE.
BA
BA
BA
GAK
GAA
GYU
AA
DO
GA
GA

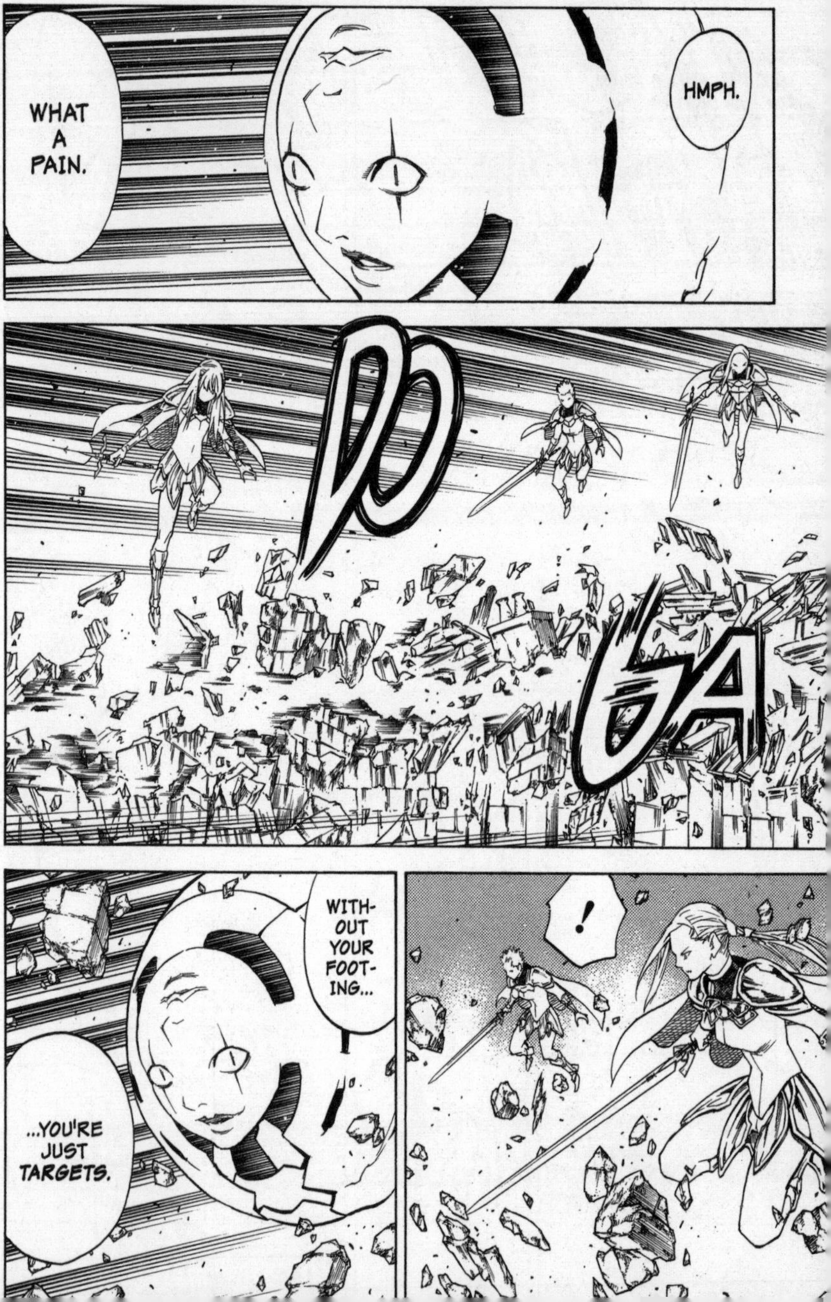
HMPH.
WHAT A PAIN.
DO
GA
!
WITH-OUT YOUR FOOT-ING...
...YOU'RE JUST TARGETS.

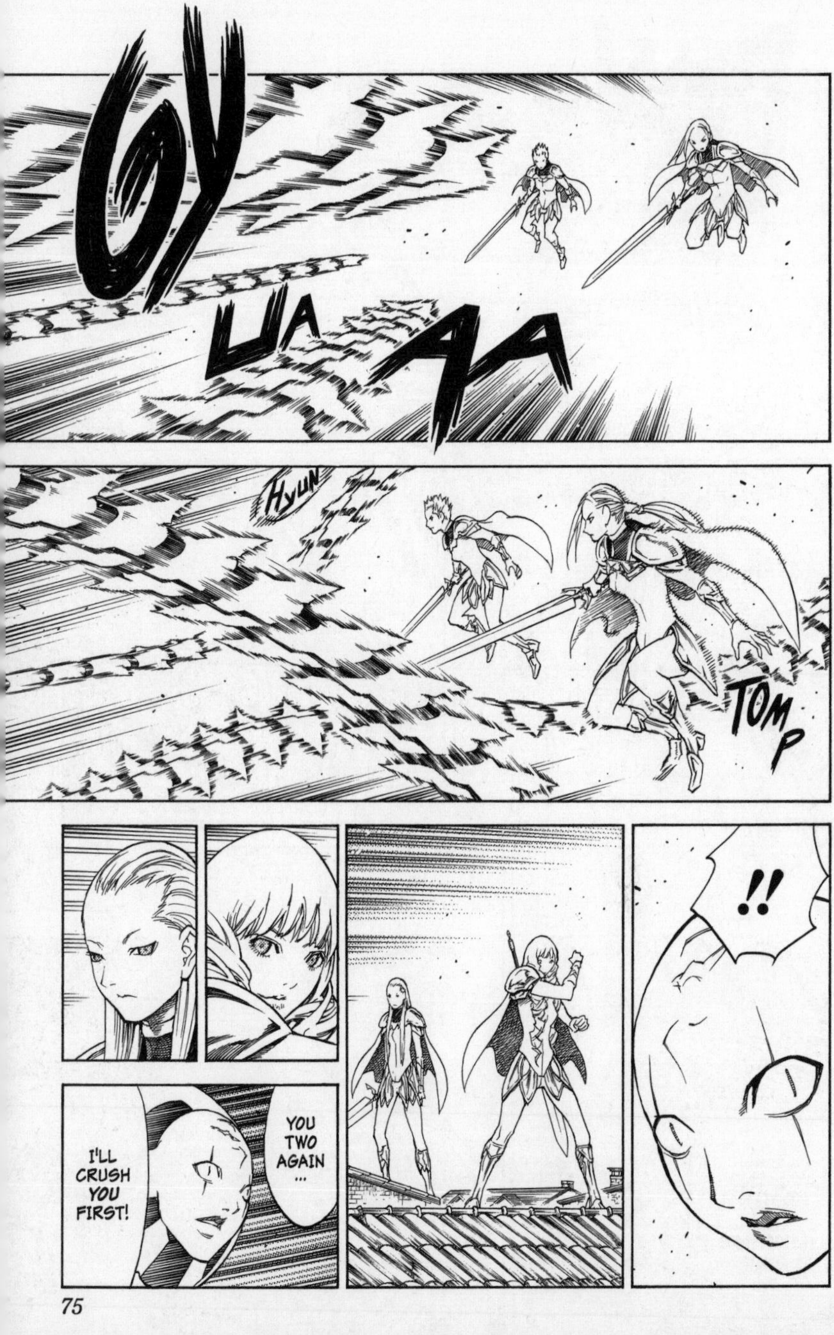
OY
UAAA
HYUN
TOMP
!!
YOU TWO AGAIN ...
I'LL CRUSH YOU FIRST!

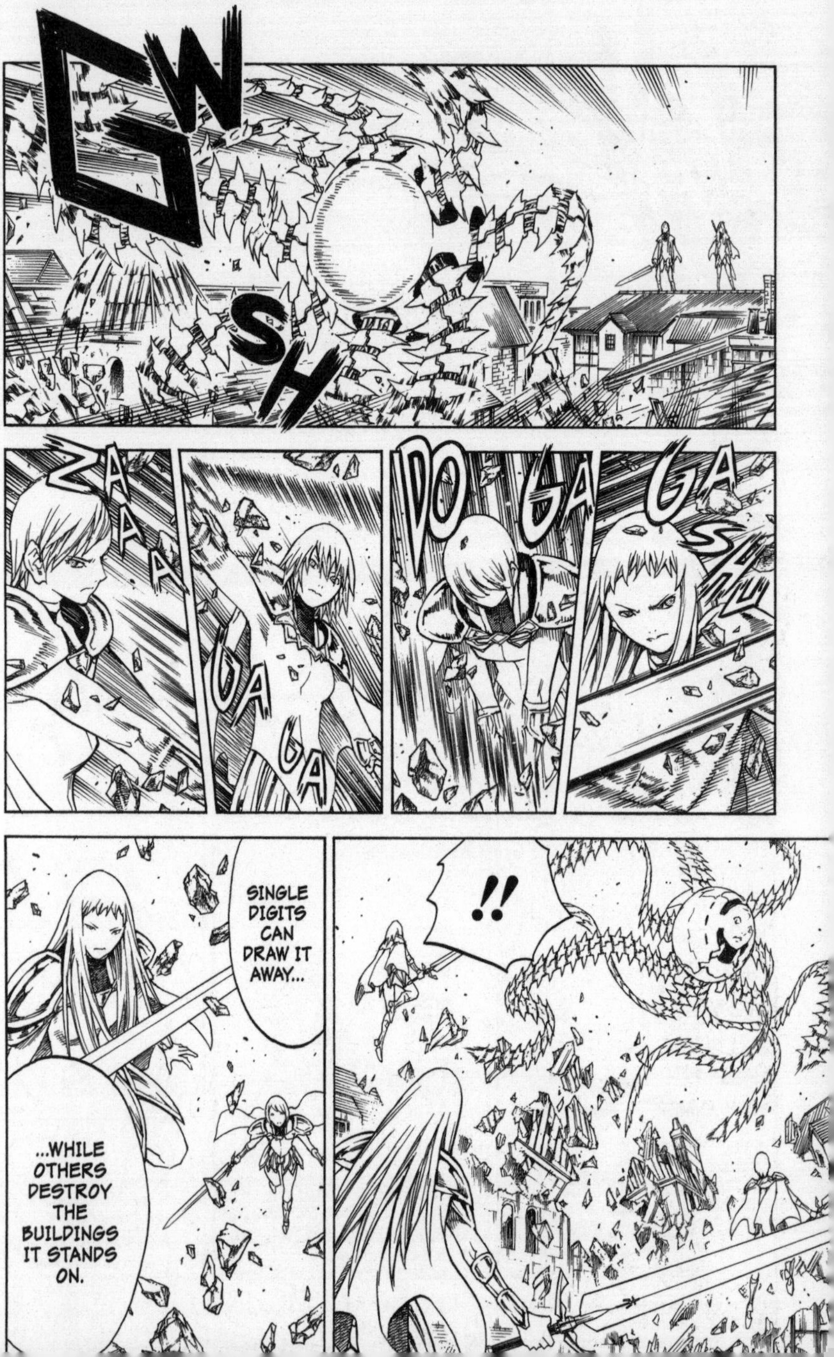
GASH
ZAAA
!!
SINGLE DIGITS CAN DRAW IT AWAY...
...WHILE OTHERS DESTROY THE BUILDINGS IT STANDS ON.

READ THIS WAY

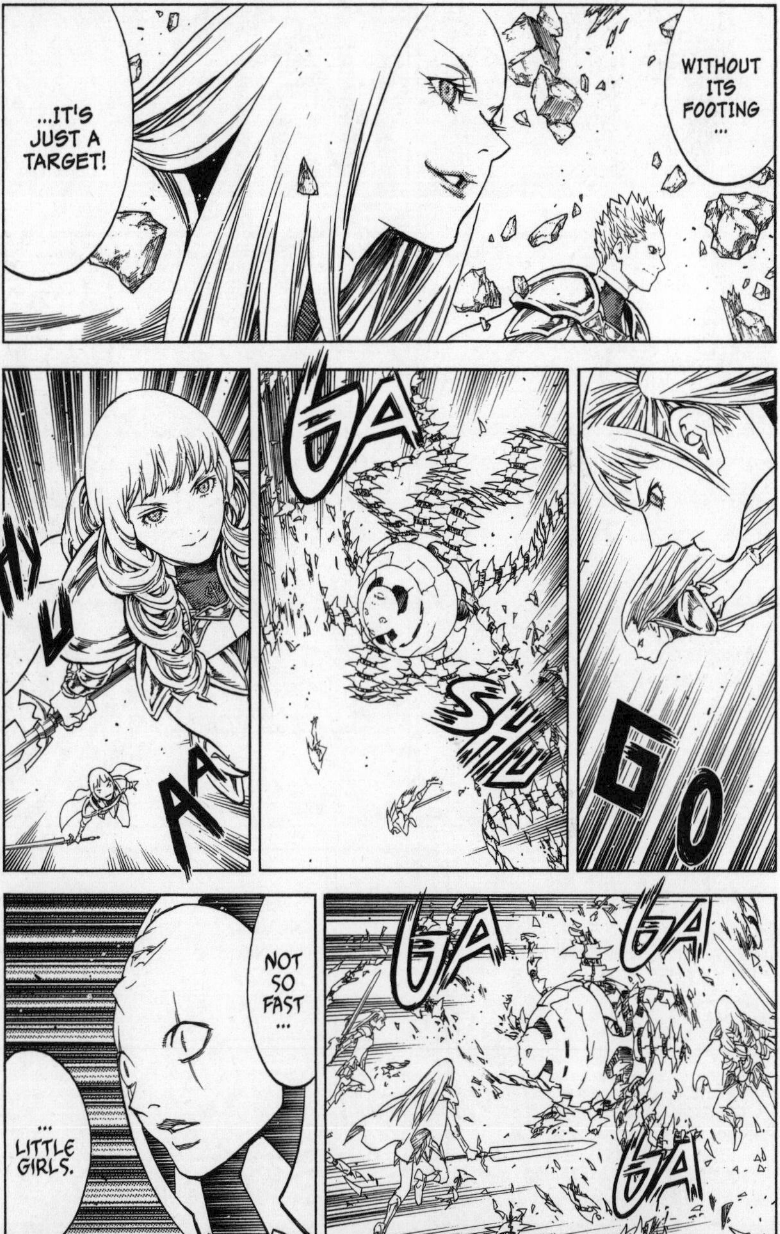
WITHOUT ITS FOOTING...
...IT'S JUST A TARGET!
GO
GA
SHU
HYU
AA
GA
GA
GA
NOT SO FAST...
...LITTLE GIRLS.

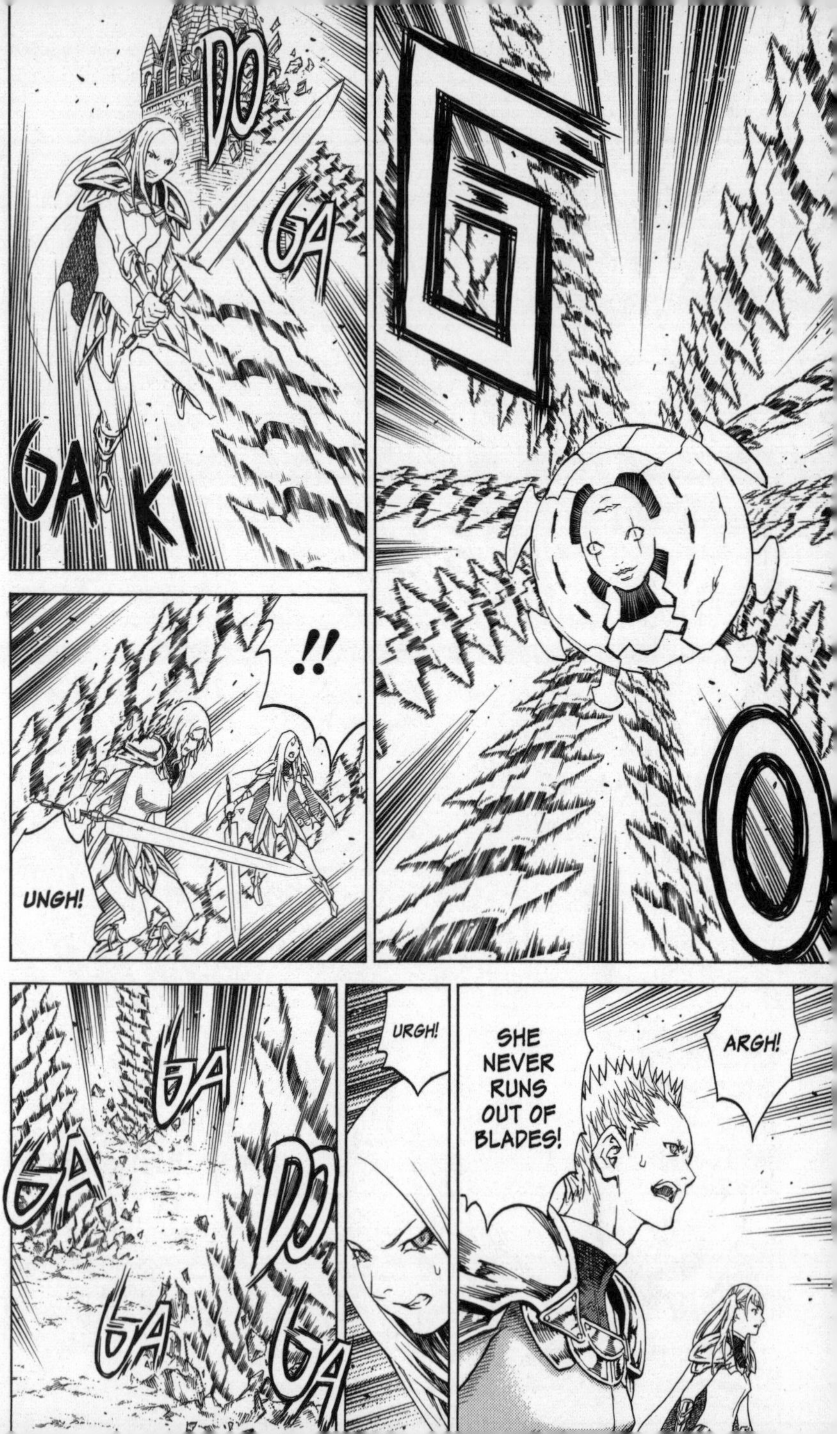
GO
DO
GA
GA KI
!!
UNGH!
ARGH!
SHE NEVER RUNS OUT OF BLADES!
URGH!
GA
GA
DO
GA
GA

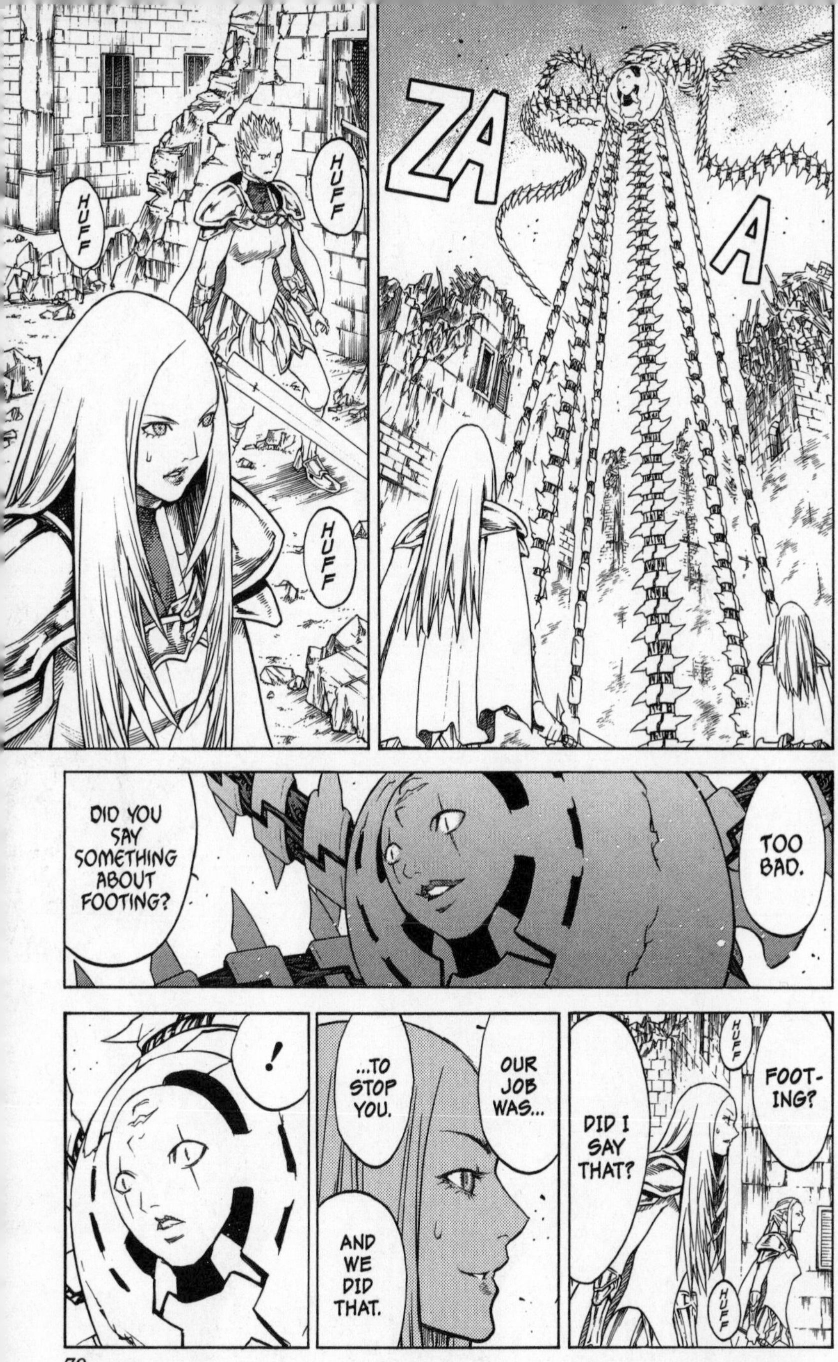
ZA
A
HUFF
HUFF
HUFF
TOO BAD.
DID YOU SAY SOMETHING ABOUT FOOTING?
HUFF
FOOT-ING?
DID I SAY THAT?
HUFF
OUR JOB WAS...
...TO STOP YOU.
AND WE DID THAT.
!

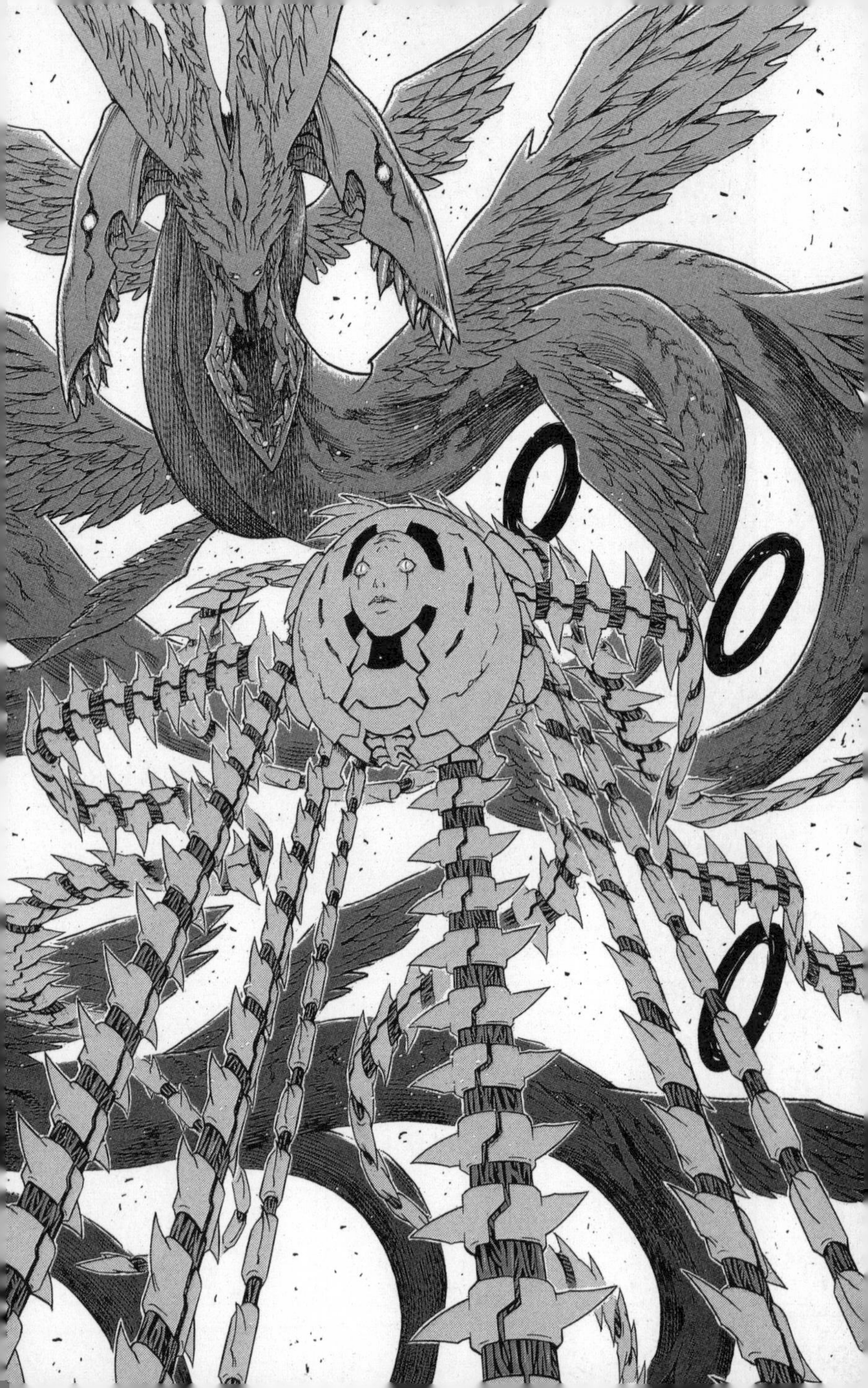

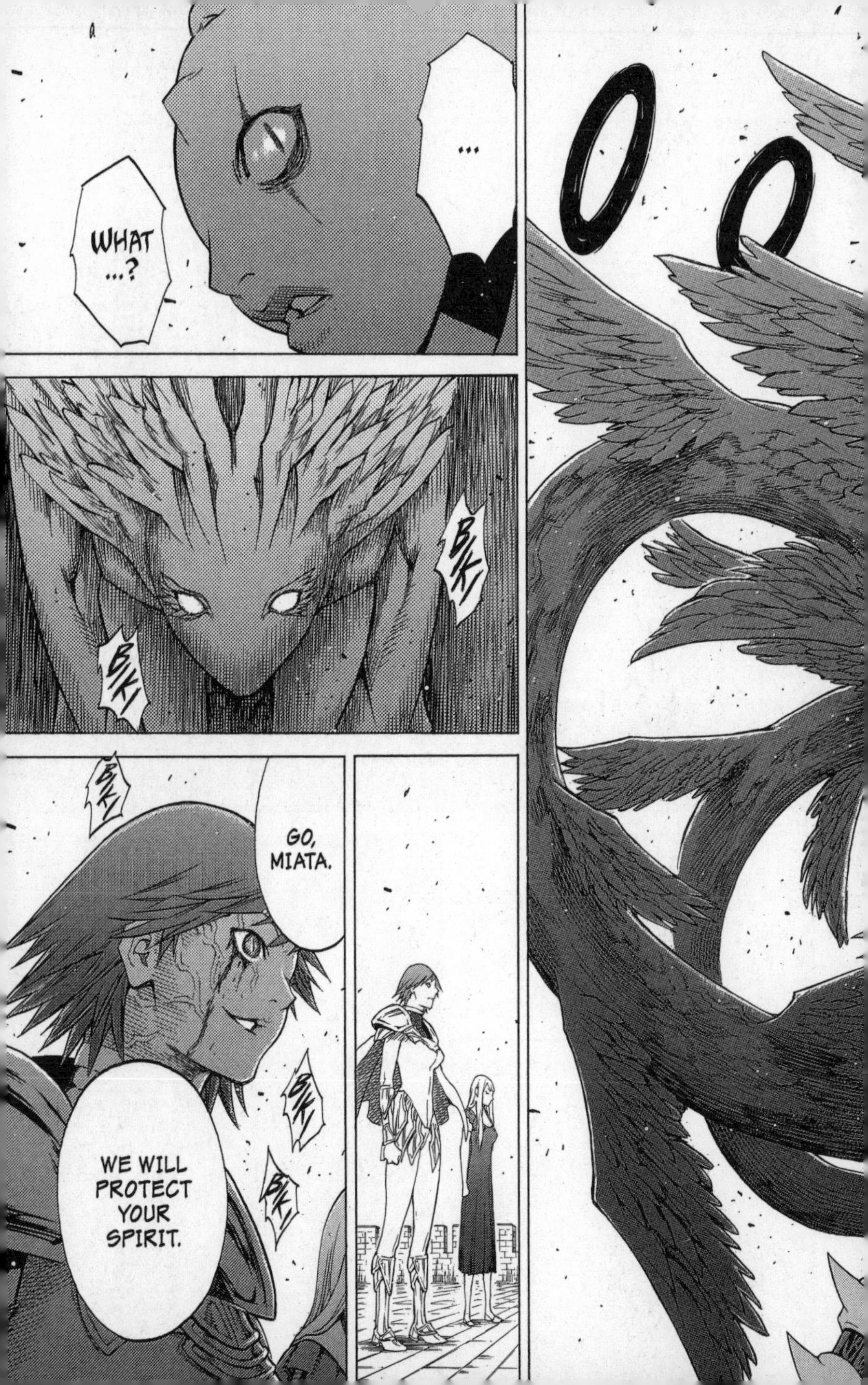
...
WHAT ...?
BIKI
BIKI
GO, MIATA.
BIKI
WE WILL PROTECT YOUR SPIRIT.
BIKI
BIKI

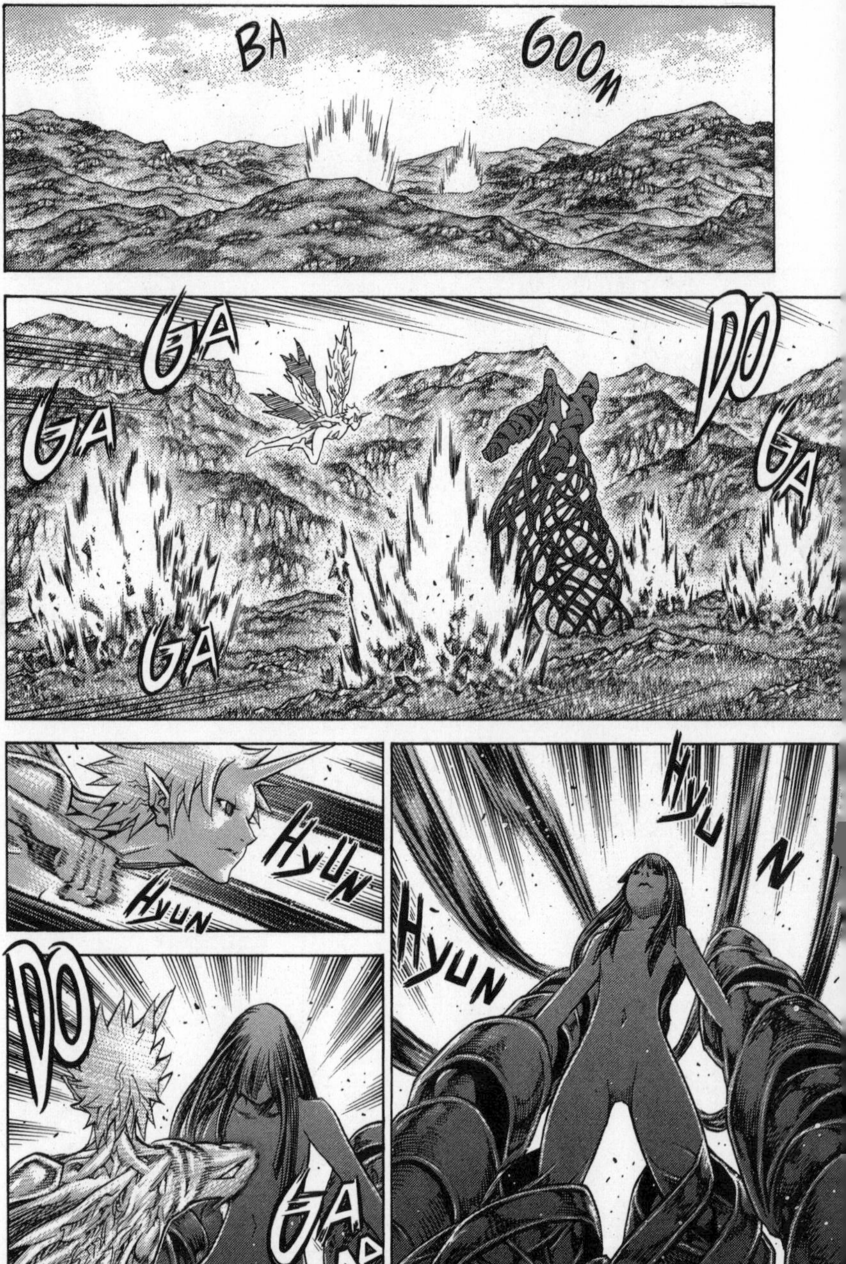

BA
GOOM
DOGA
GA
GA
GA
HYUN
HYUN
HYUN
HYUN
DO
GAA

READ THIS WAY

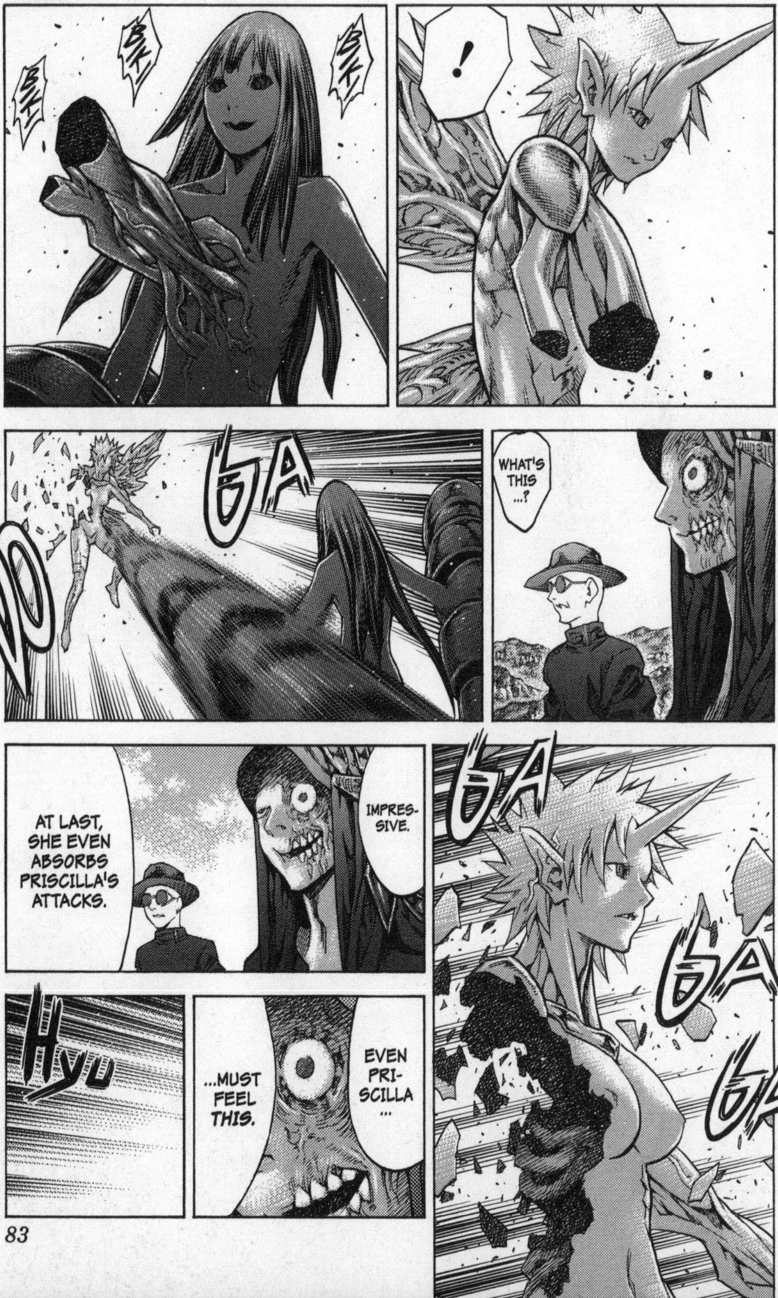
!
BIKI
BIKI
BIKI
WHAT'S THIS ...?
GA
DO
GA
GA
GA
GA
IMPRES-SIVE.
AT LAST, SHE EVEN ABSORBS PRISCILLA'S ATTACKS.
EVEN PRI-SCILLA ...
...MUST FEEL THIS.
Hyu

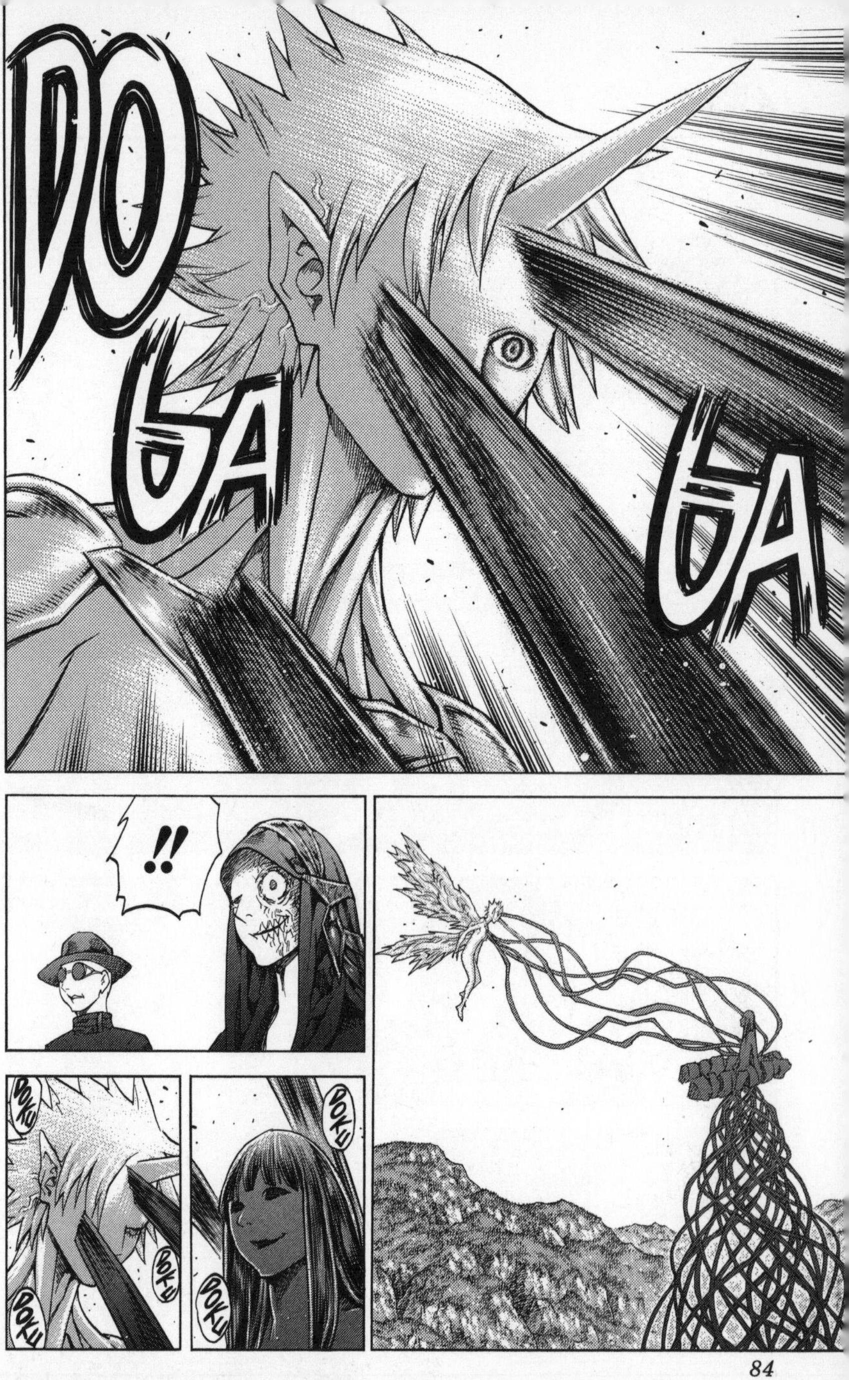
DO
GA
GA
!!
DOKU
DOKU
DOKU
DOKU
DOKU

READ THIS WAY

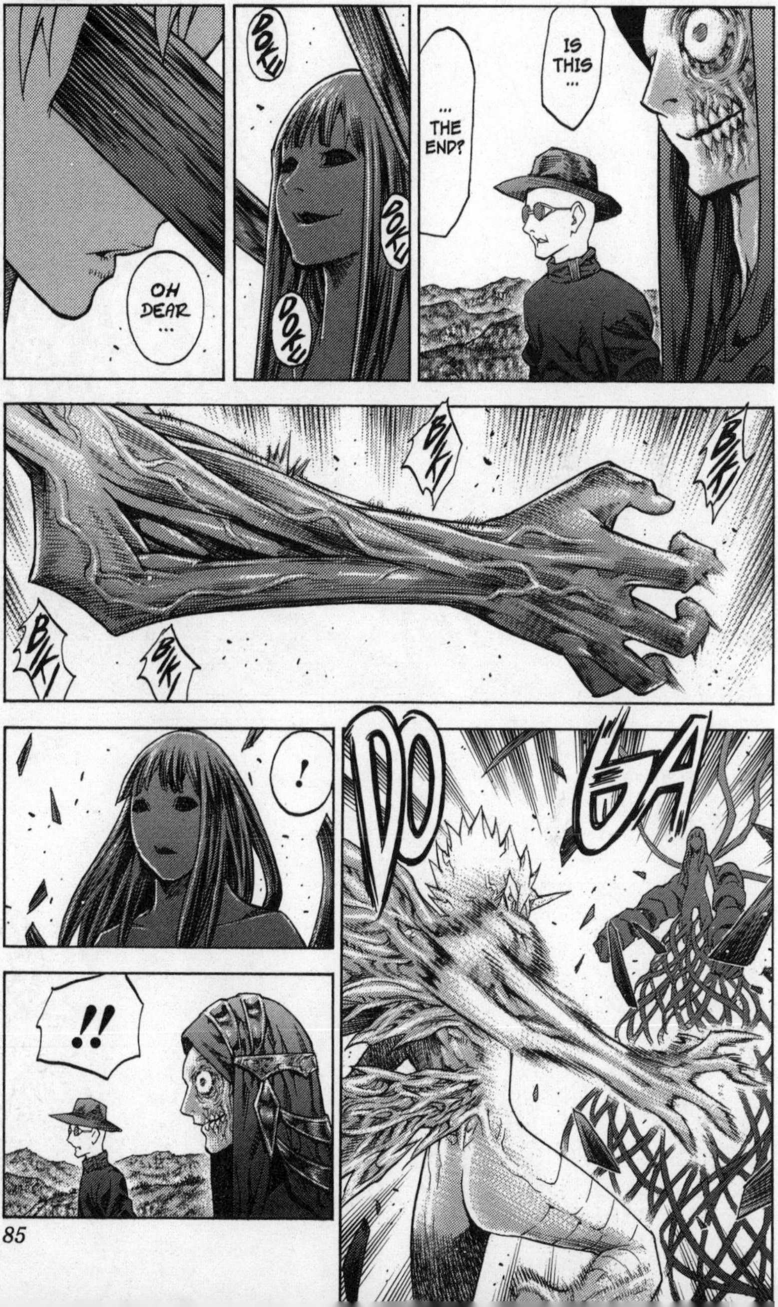

IS THIS ...
... THE END?
DOKU
DOKU
DOKU
OH DEAR ...
BIKI
BIKI
BIKI
BIKI
DO
GA
!
!!

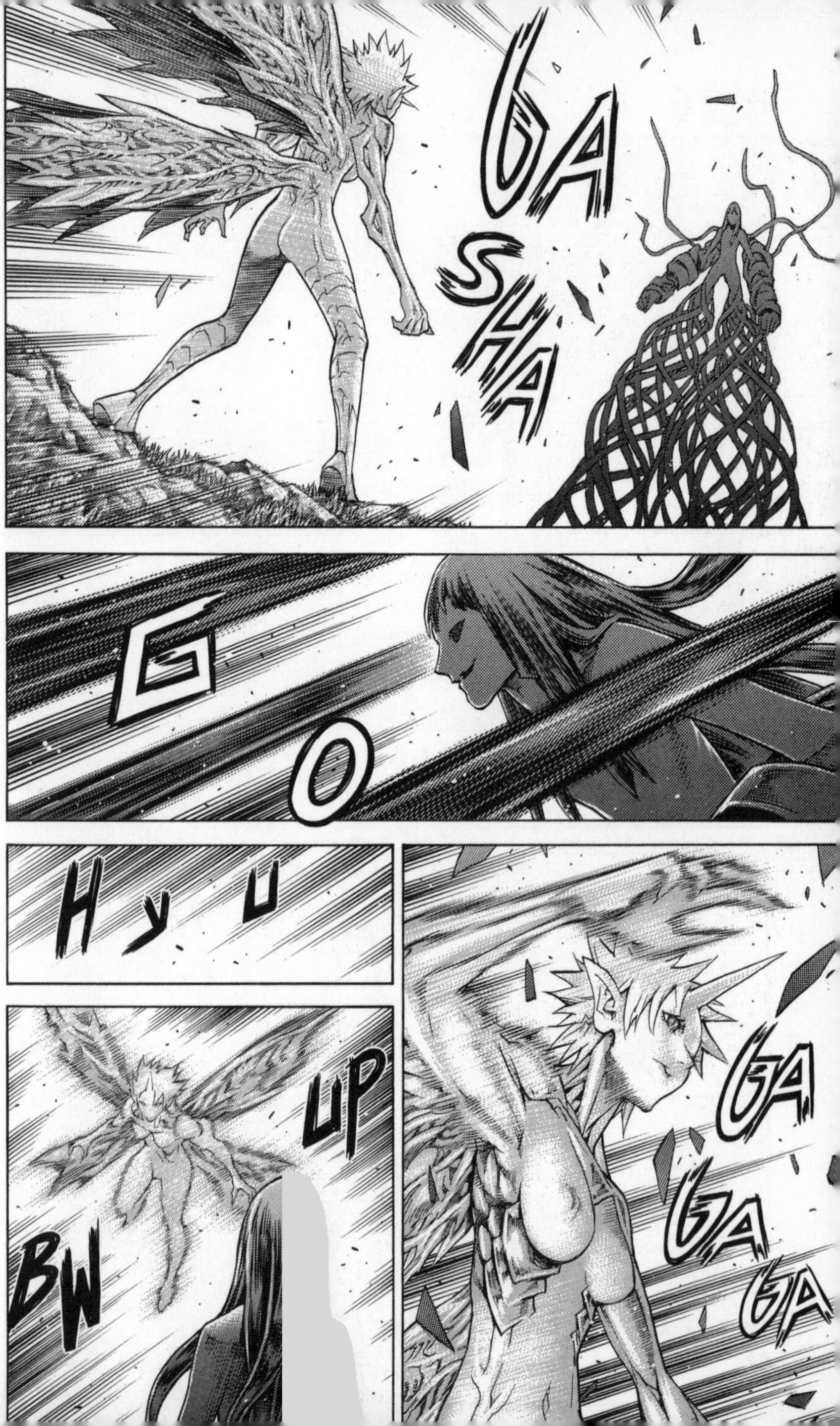
GASHA
GO
GA GA GA
Hyu
BWUP

READ THIS WAY

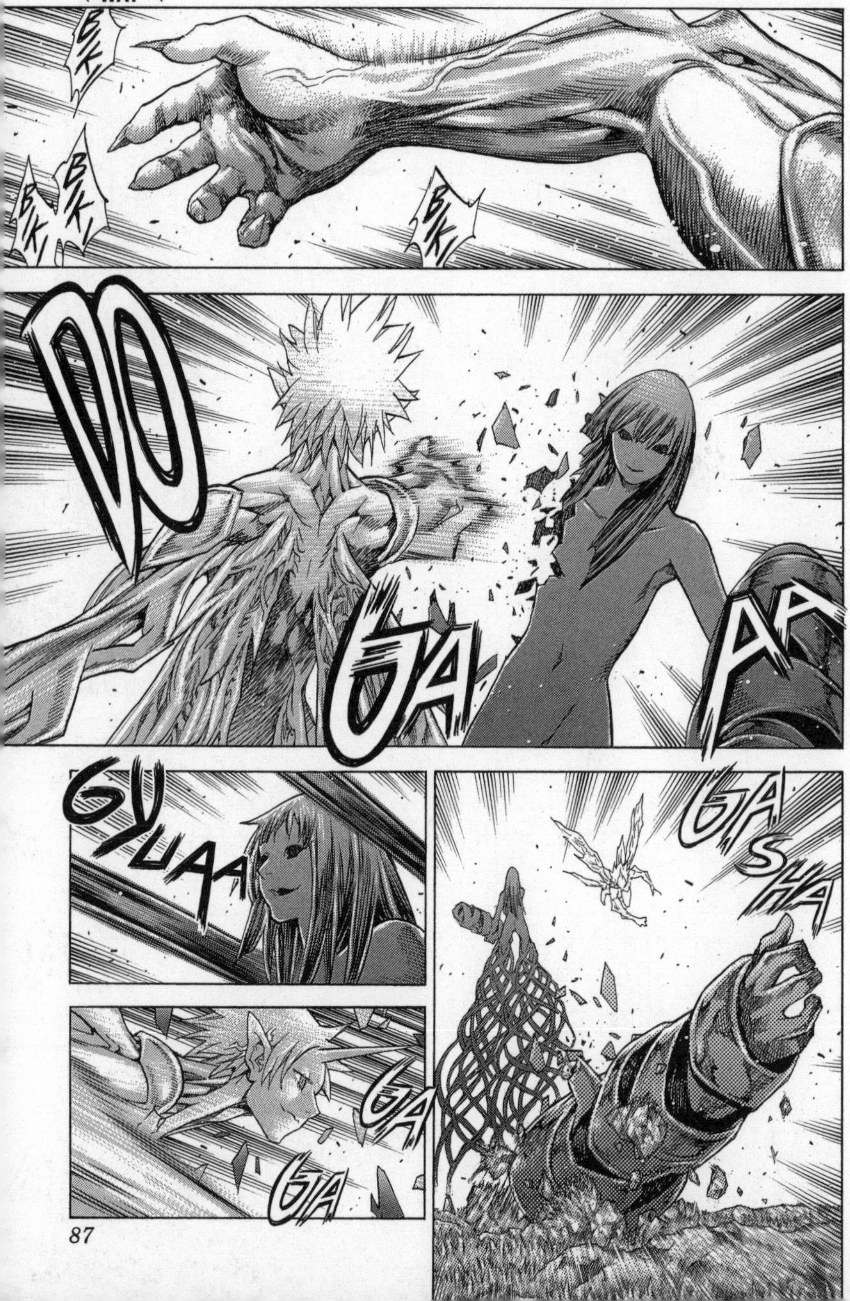
BIKI
BIKI
BIKI
BIKI
DO
GA
AA
GASHA
GYUAA
GA
GA

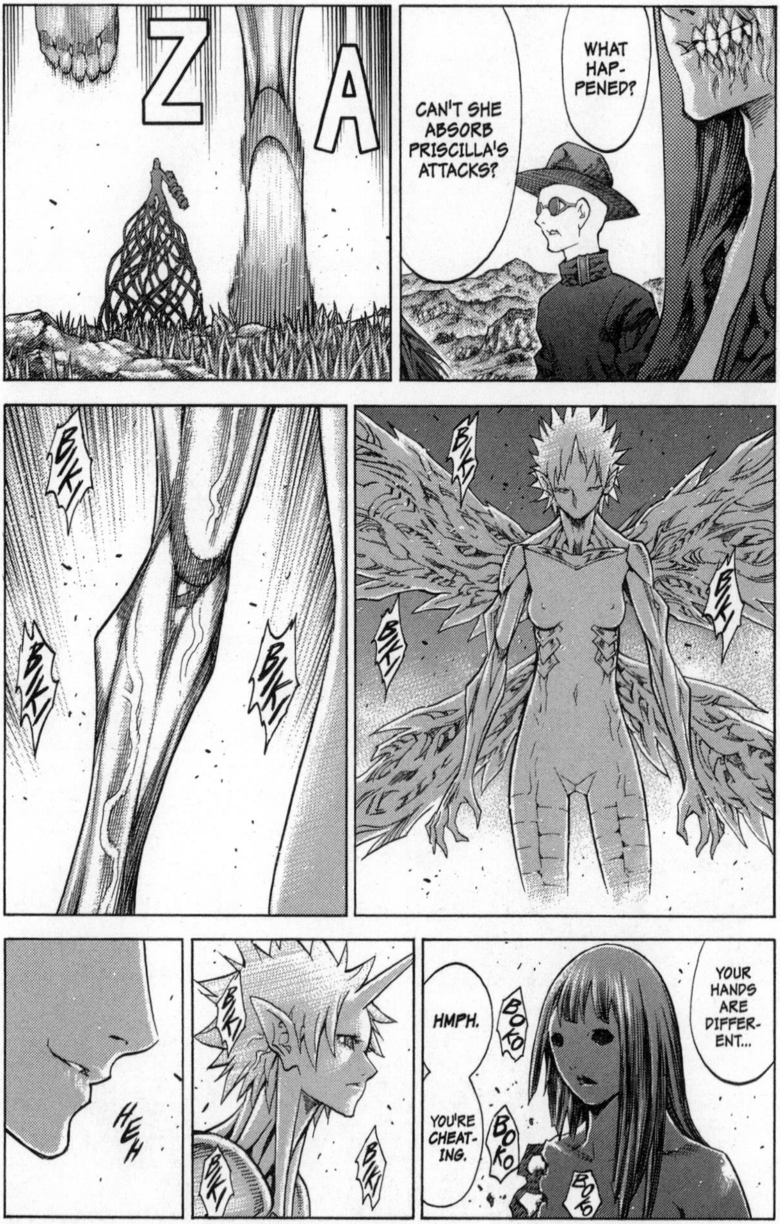
WHAT HAP-PENED?
CAN'T SHE ABSORB PRISCILLA'S ATTACKS?
ZA
BIKI
BIKI
BIKI
BIKI
BIKI
YOUR HANDS ARE DIFFER-ENT...
HMPH.
BOKO
YOU'RE CHEAT-ING.
BOKO
BOKO
BIKI
BIKI
BIKI
HEH

READ THIS WAY

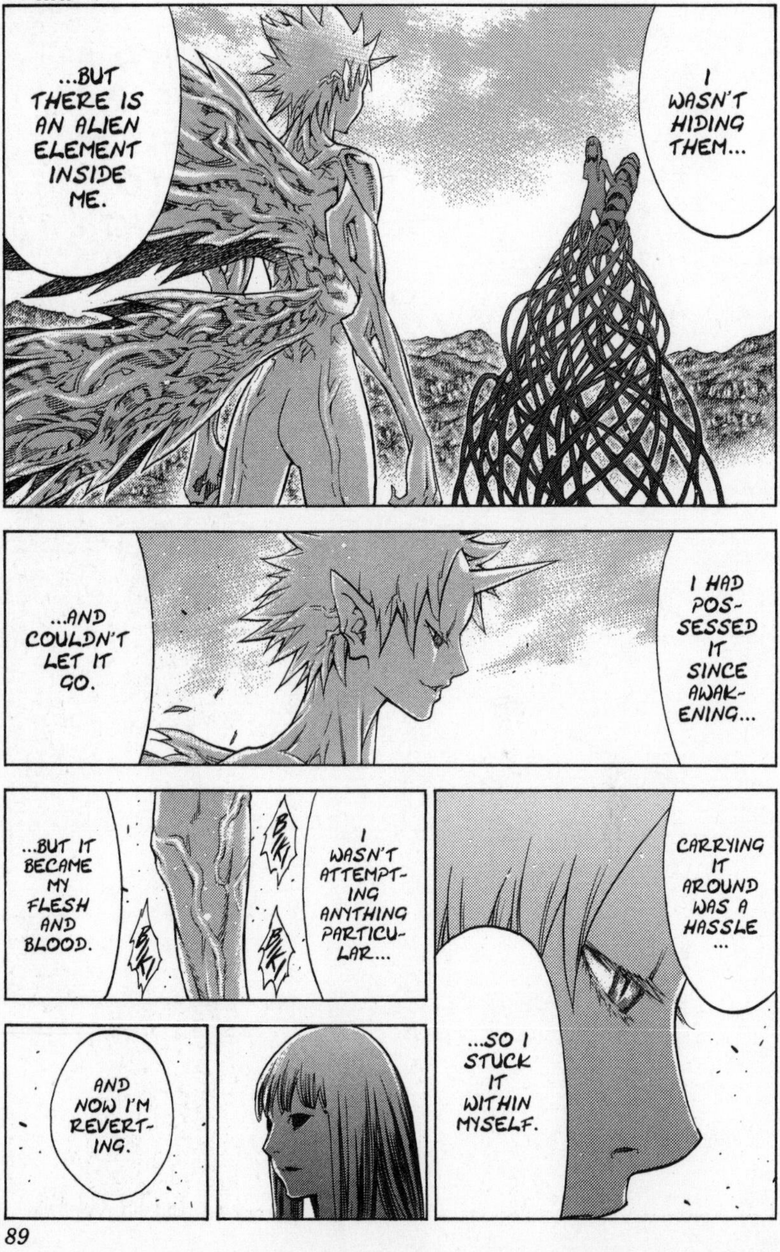

I WASN'T HIDING THEM...
...BUT THERE IS AN ALIEN ELEMENT INSIDE ME.
I HAD POSSESSED IT SINCE AWAKENING...
...AND COULDN'T LET IT GO.
CARRYING IT AROUND WAS A HASSLE...
...SO I STUCK IT WITHIN MYSELF.
I WASN'T ATTEMPTING ANYTHING PARTICULAR...
BIKI
BIKI
BIKI
...BUT IT BECAME MY FLESH AND BLOOD.
AND NOW I'M REVERTING.

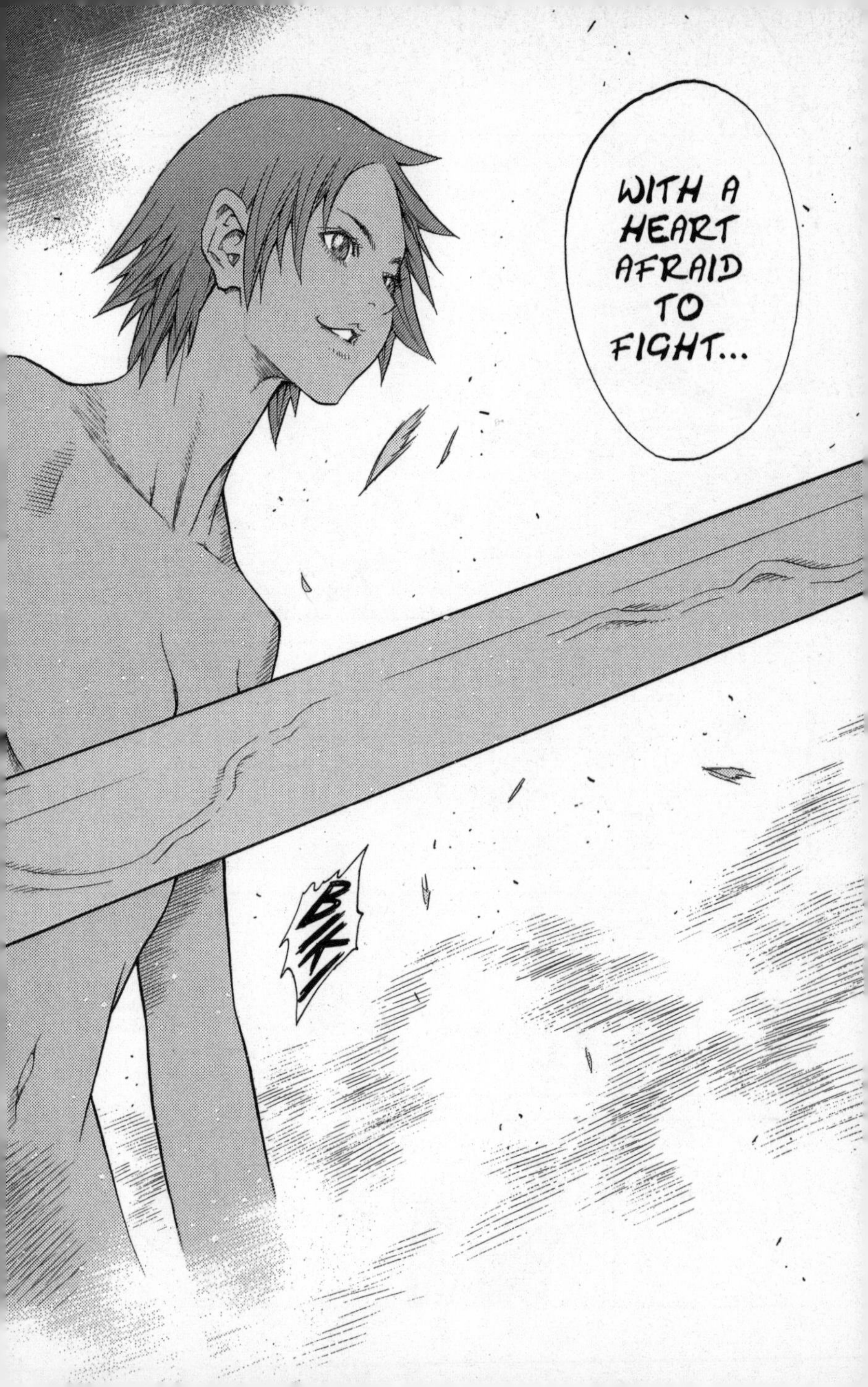
WITH A HEART AFRAID TO FIGHT...
BIK!

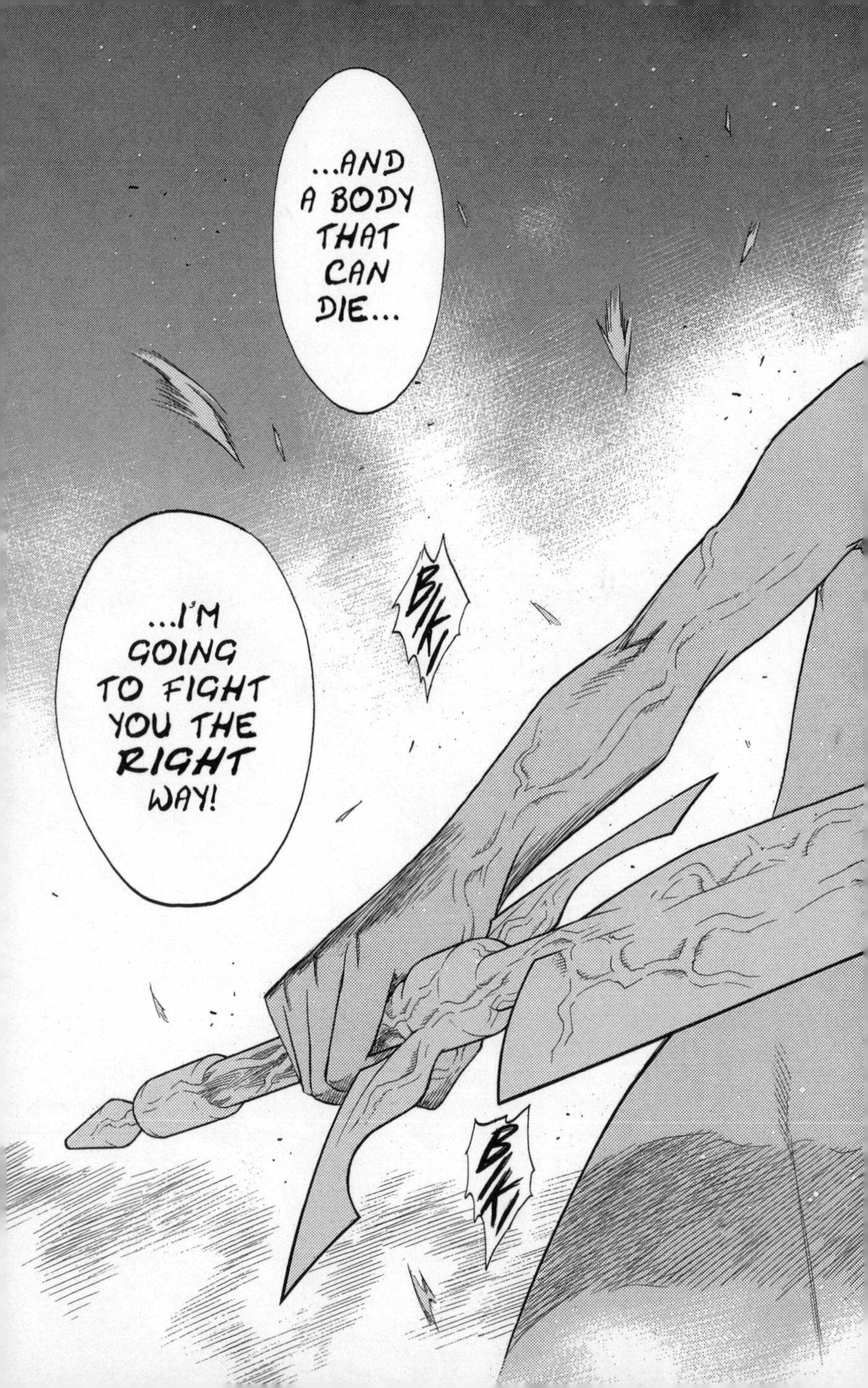
...AND A BODY THAT CAN DIE...
...I'M GOING TO FIGHT YOU THE **RIGHT** WAY!
BIKI
BIKI

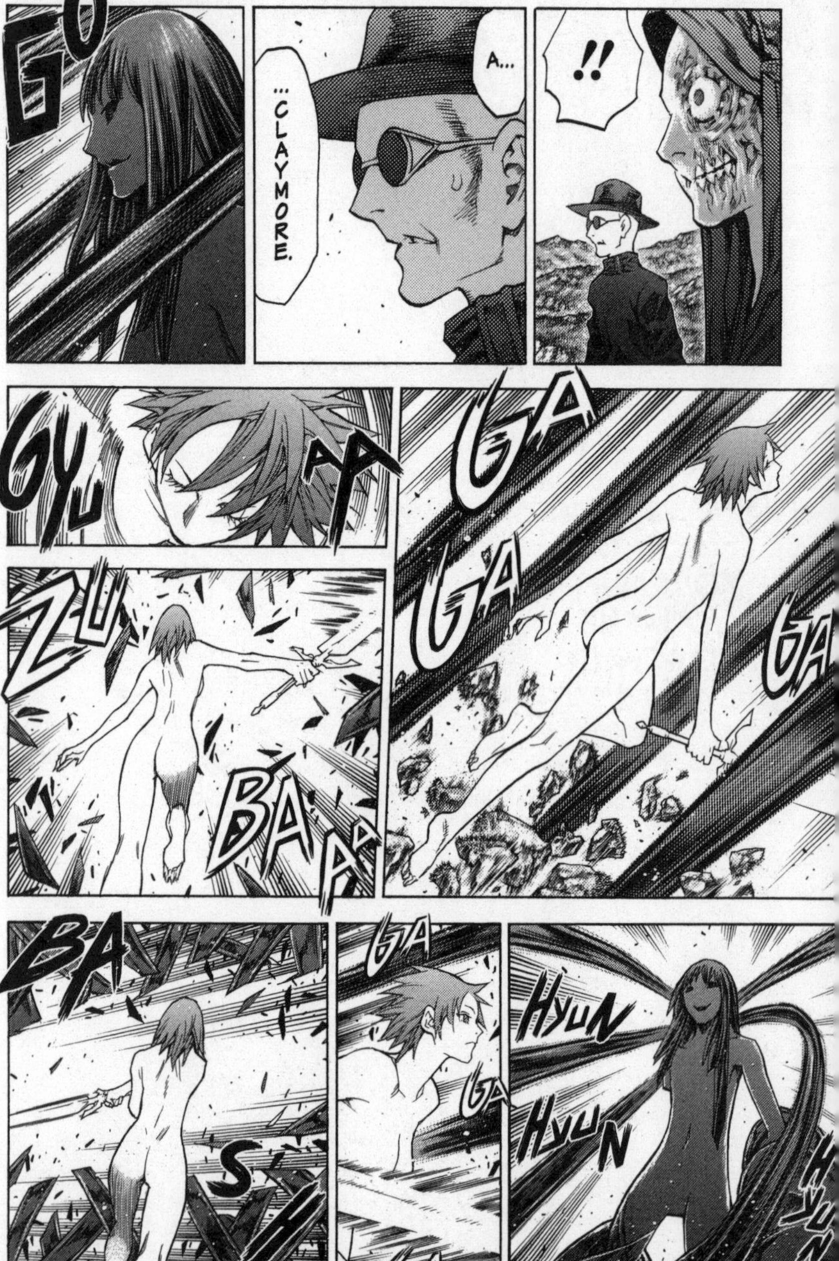
!!
A...
...CLAYMORE.
GO
GA
GA
GA
GA
GYU
AA
ZU
BA
A
A
HYUN
HYUN
HYUN
GA
GA
GA
BA
SH

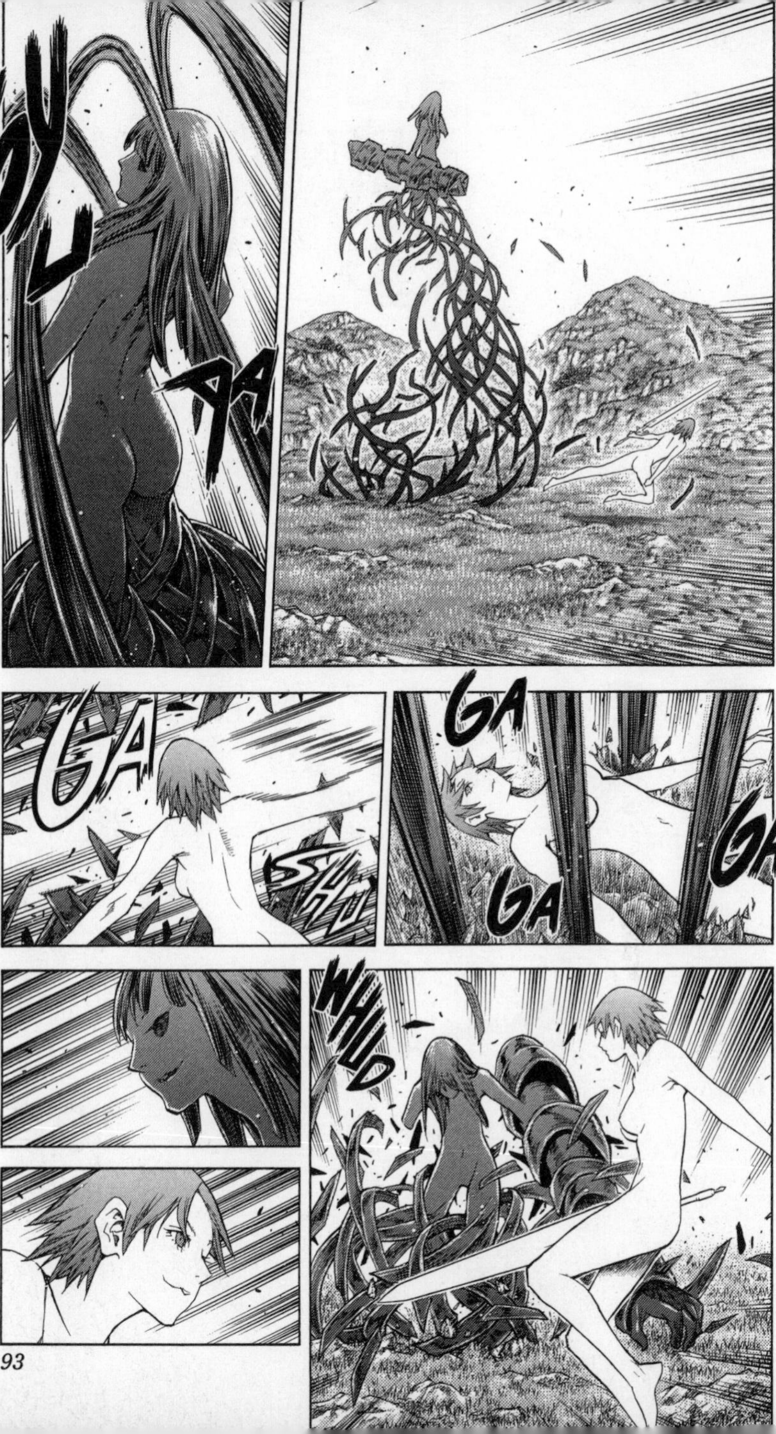
GYU
AA
GA
GA
GA
GA
SHU
WHUD

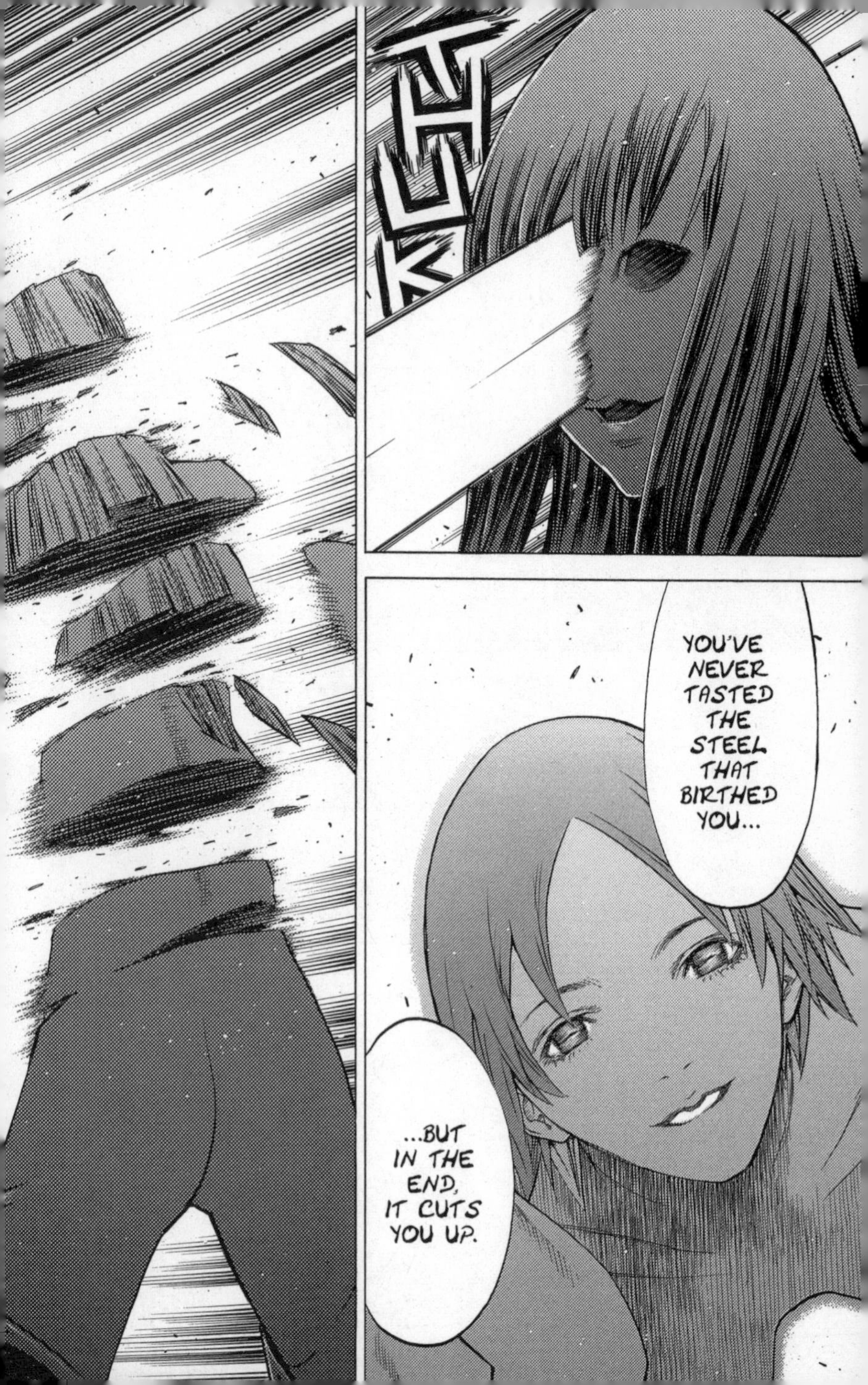
THUK
YOU'VE NEVER TASTED THE STEEL THAT BIRTHED YOU...
...BUT IN THE END, IT CUTS YOU UP.

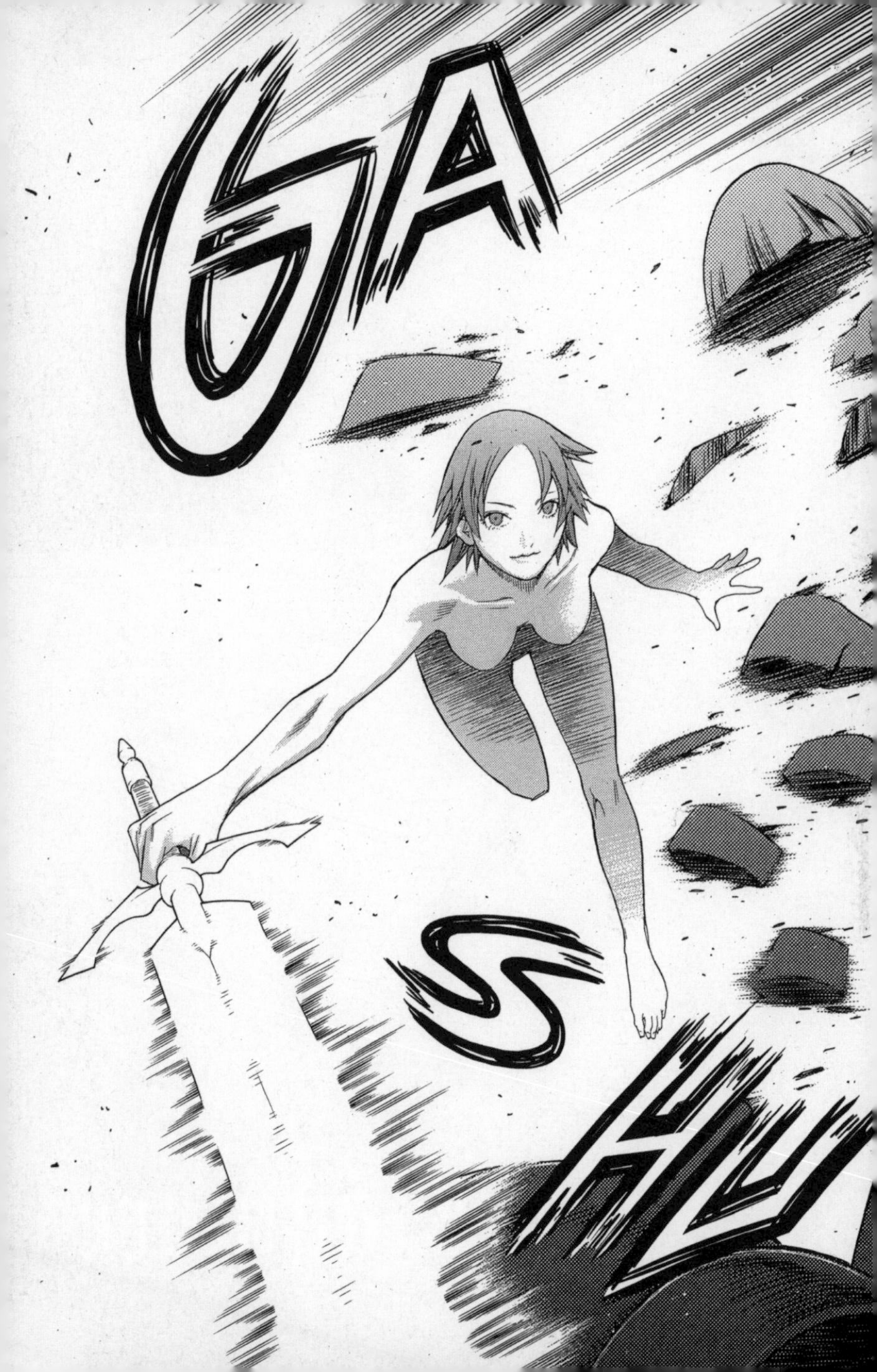
GA
S
HU

クレイモア
Claymore

Scene 141: Sword of the Dark Deep, Part 3

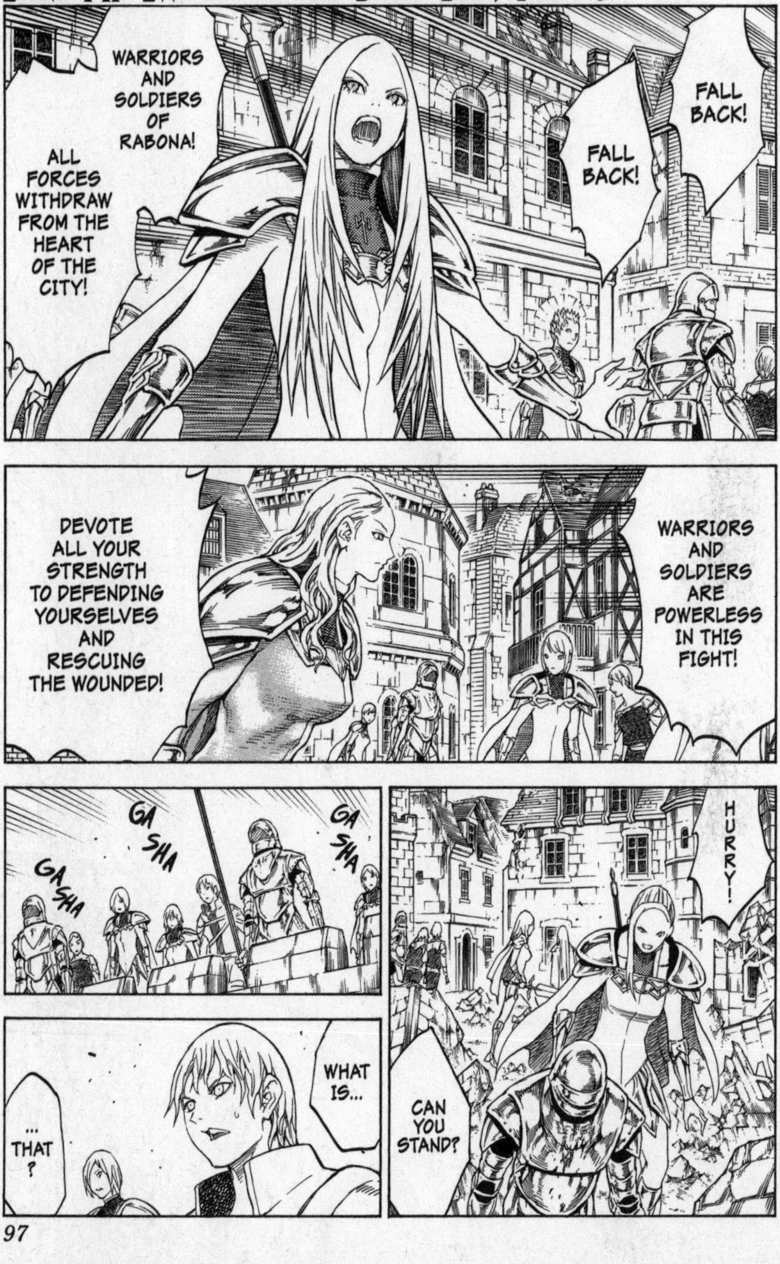
FALL BACK!
FALL BACK!
WARRIORS AND SOLDIERS OF RABONA!
ALL FORCES WITHDRAW FROM THE HEART OF THE CITY!
WARRIORS AND SOLDIERS ARE POWERLESS IN THIS FIGHT!
DEVOTE ALL YOUR STRENGTH TO DEFENDING YOURSELVES AND RESCUING THE WOUNDED!
HURRY!
CAN YOU STAND?
GA SHA
GA SHA
GA SHA
WHAT IS...
...THAT?

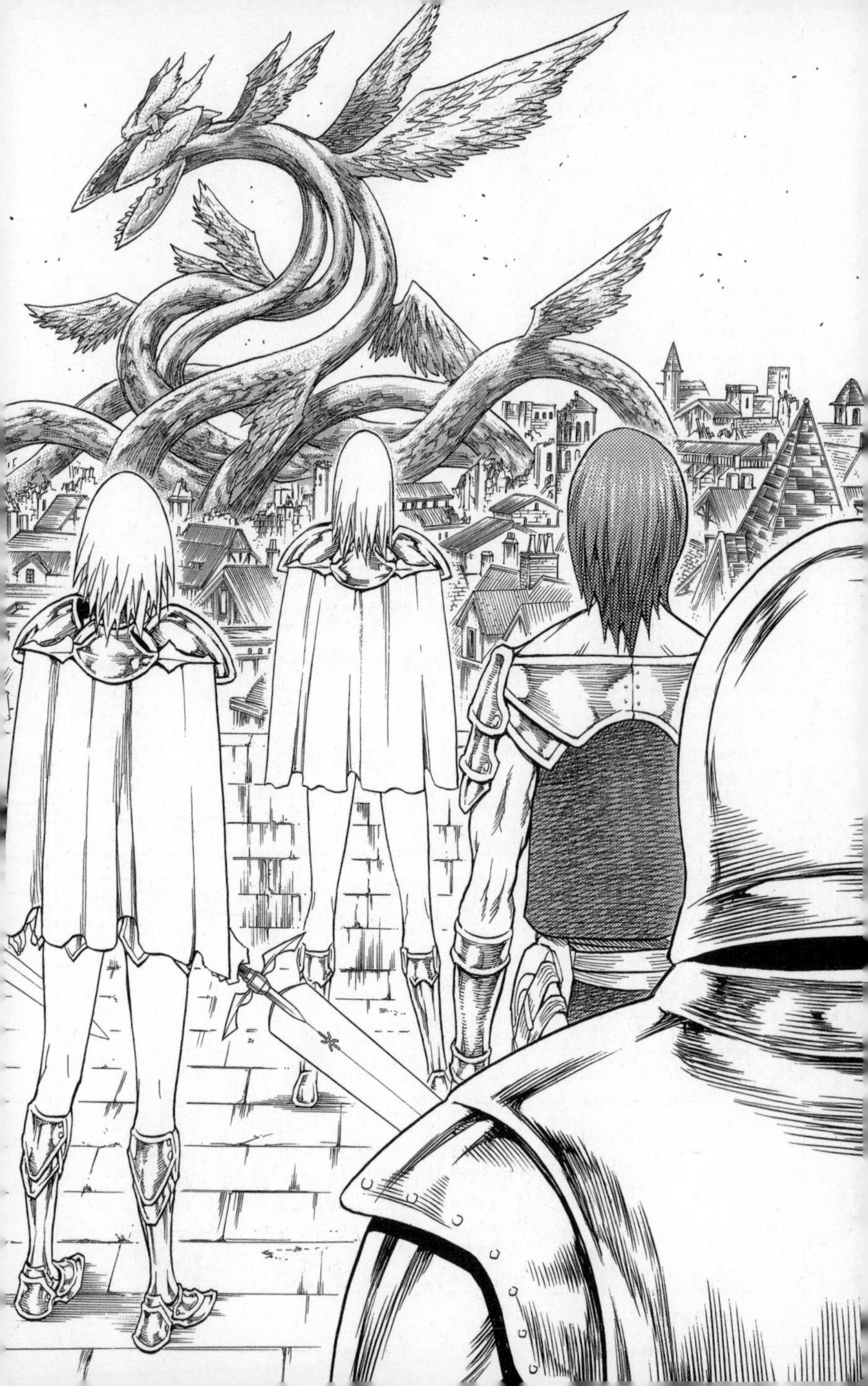

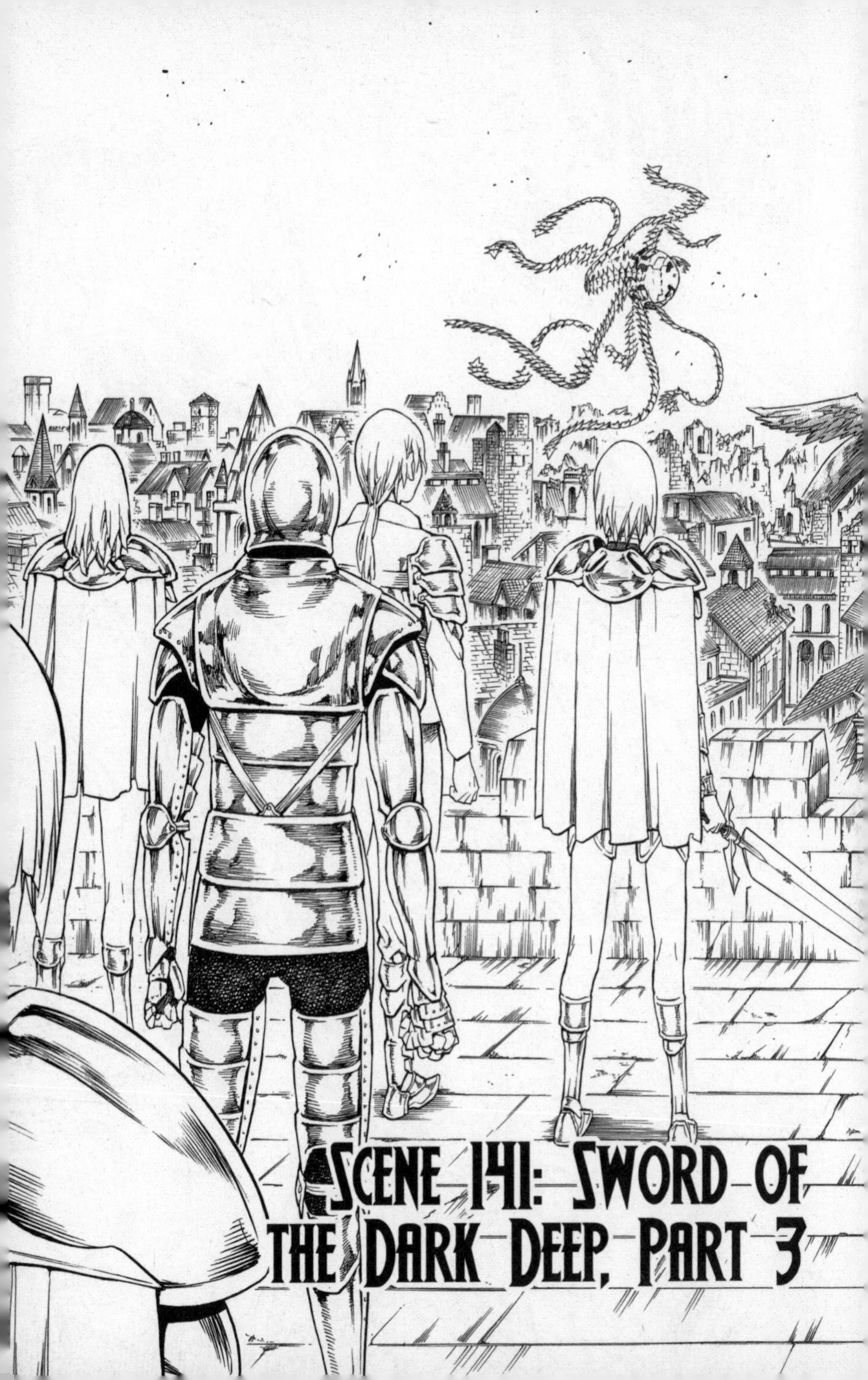
SCENE 141: SWORD OF THE DARK DEEP, PART 3

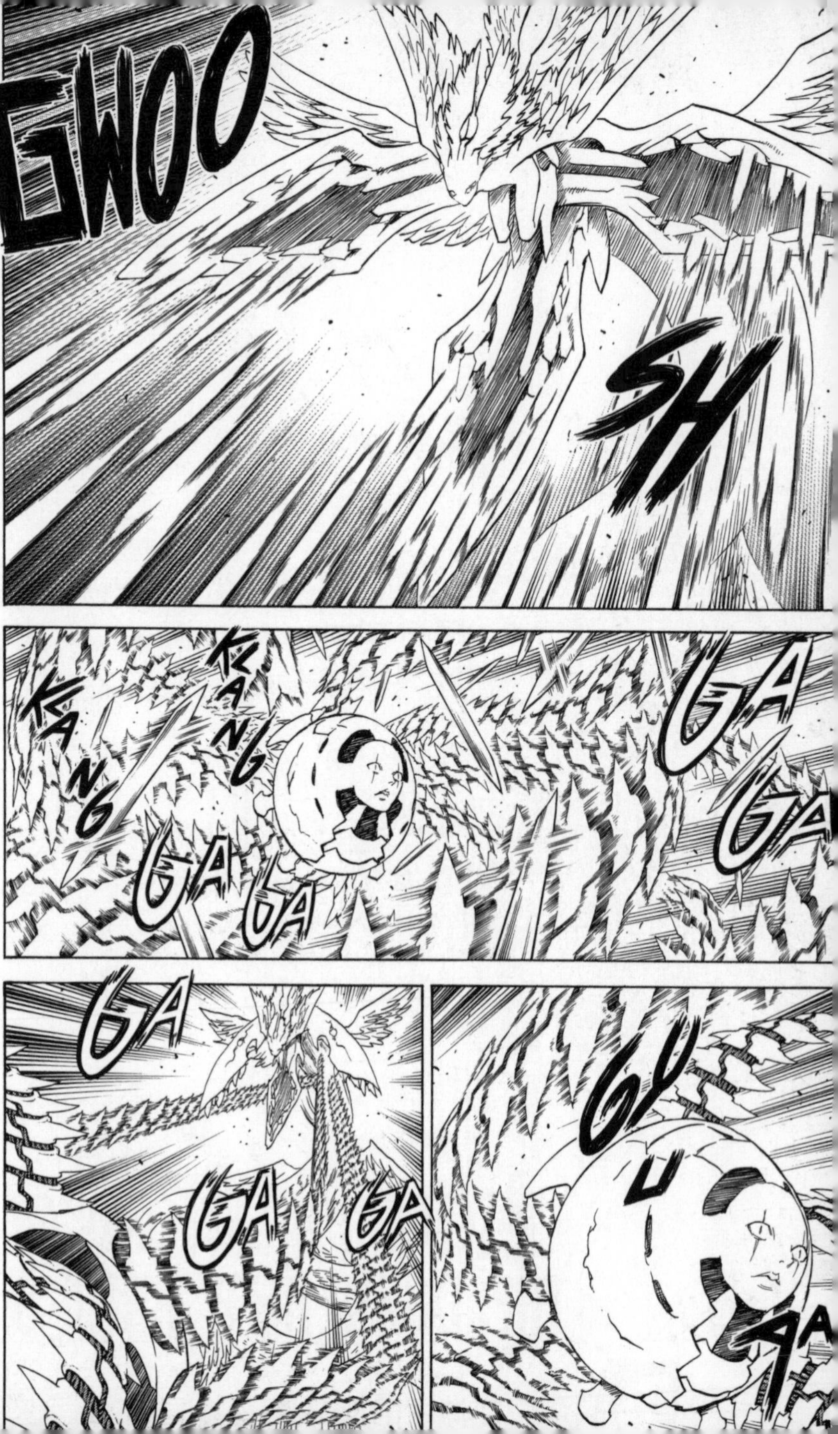
GWOO
SH
GA GA
KLANG
KANG
GA GA
GU
GA
GA
GA GA

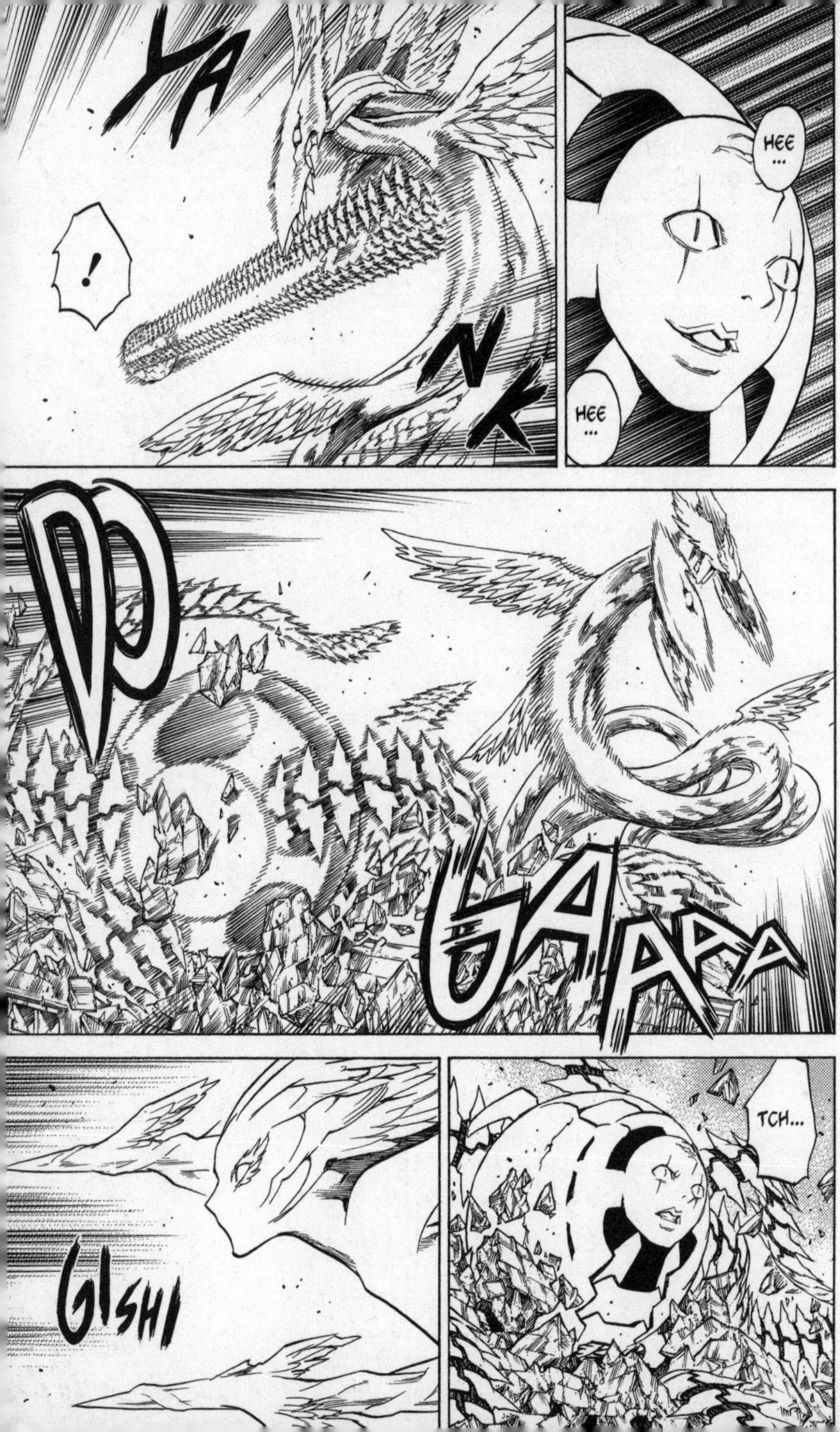
HEE ...
HEE ...
YA
!
NK
DO
GAAAA
TCH...
GISHI

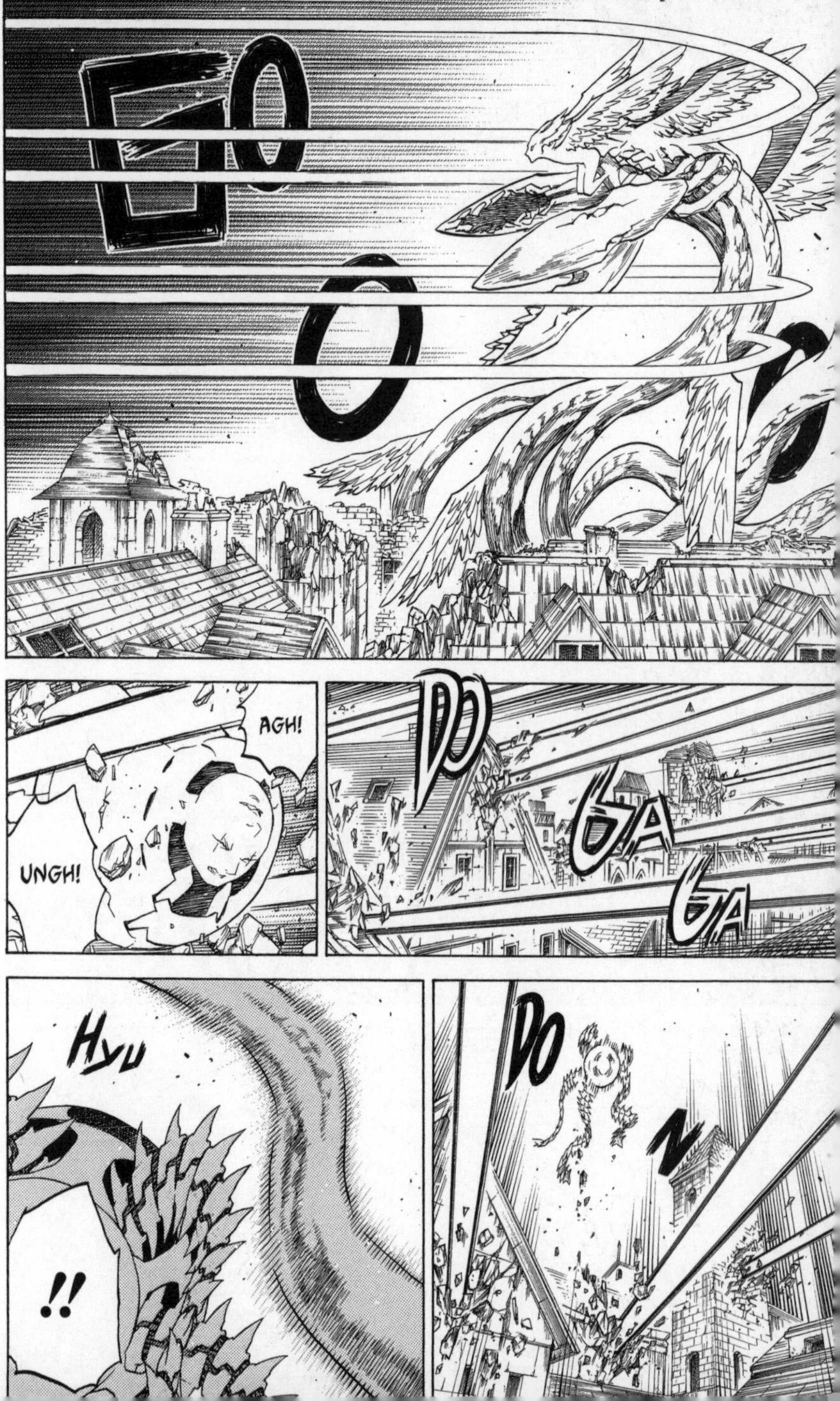
GO
O
DO
GA
GA
AGH!
UNGH!
DO
N
HYU
!!

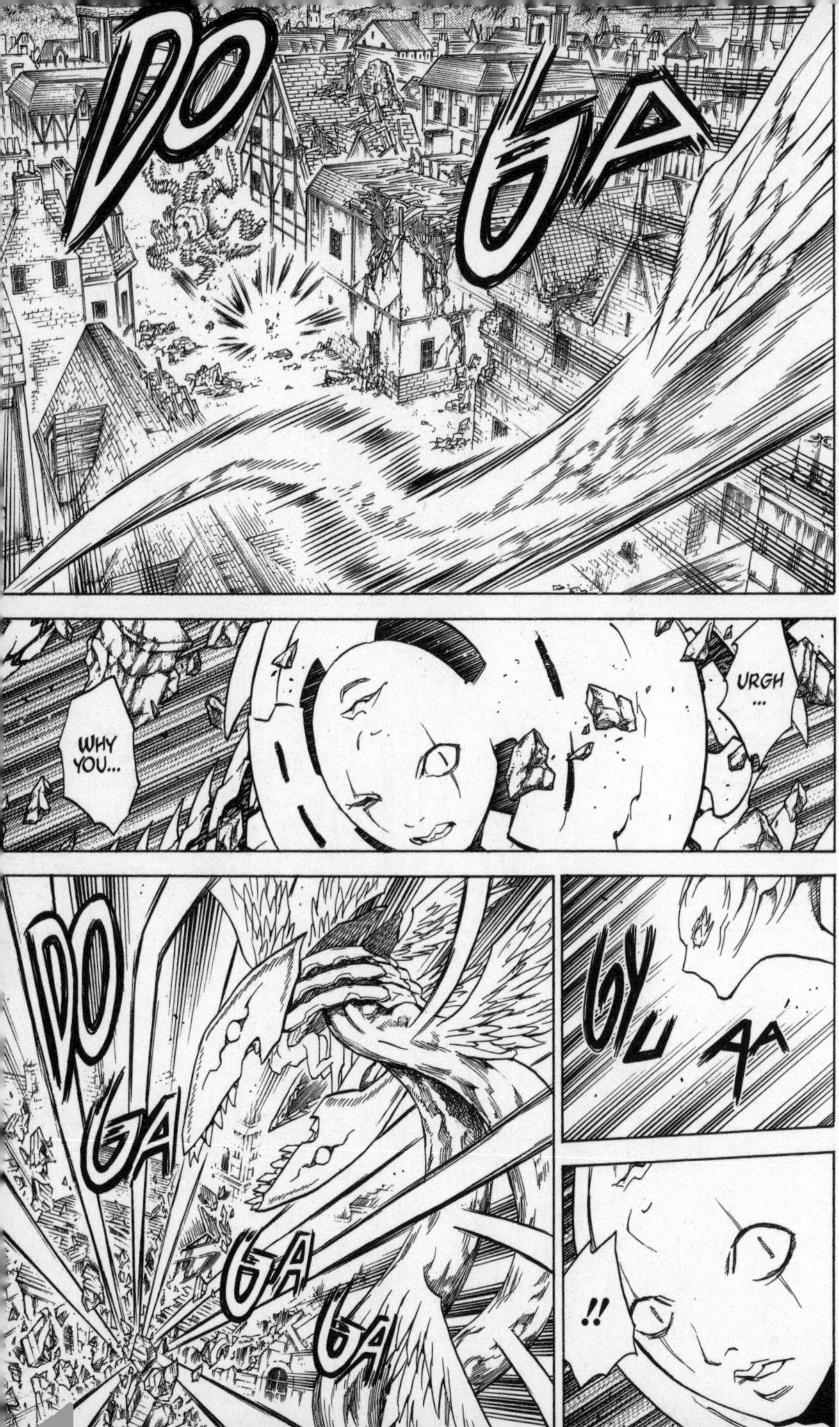
DO GA
URGH...
WHY YOU...
GYU AA
!!
DO GA
GA
GA

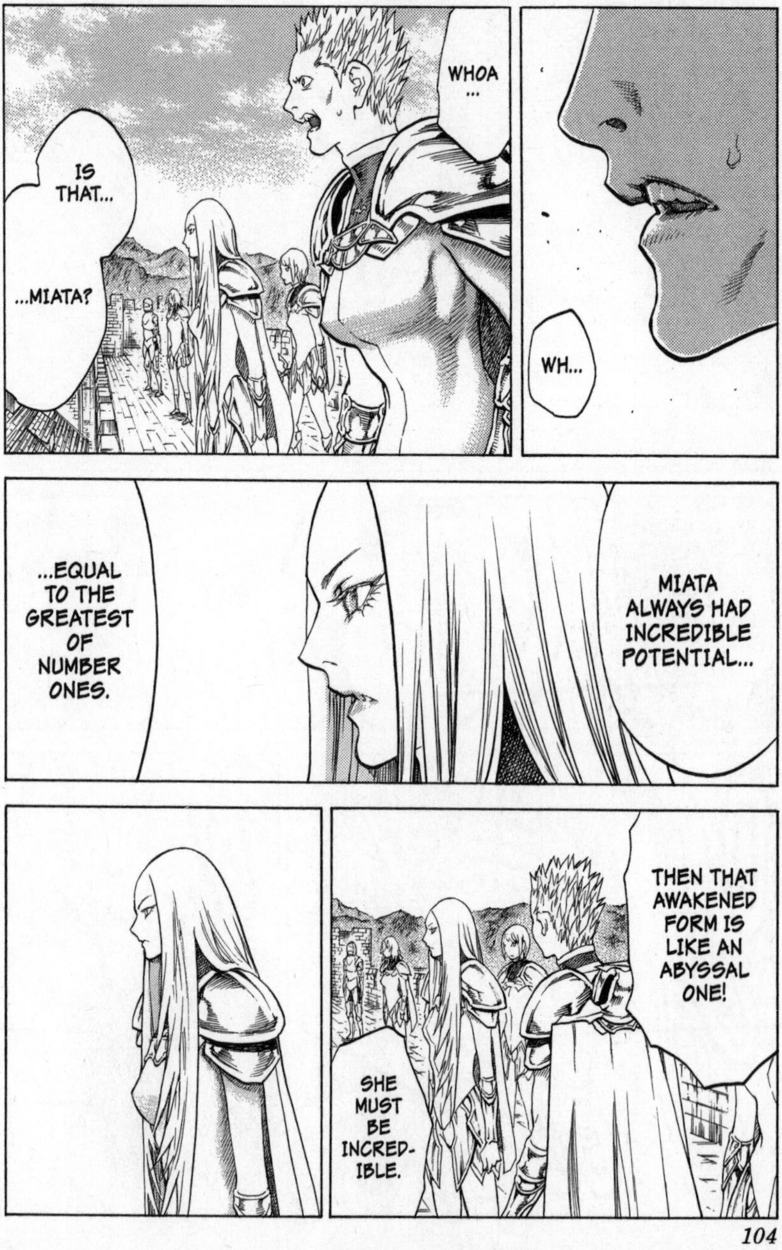
WH...
WHOA ...
IS THAT...
...MIATA?
MIATA ALWAYS HAD INCREDIBLE POTENTIAL...
...EQUAL TO THE GREATEST OF NUMBER ONES.
THEN THAT AWAKENED FORM IS LIKE AN ABYSSAL ONE!
SHE MUST BE INCRED-IBLE.

READ THIS WAY

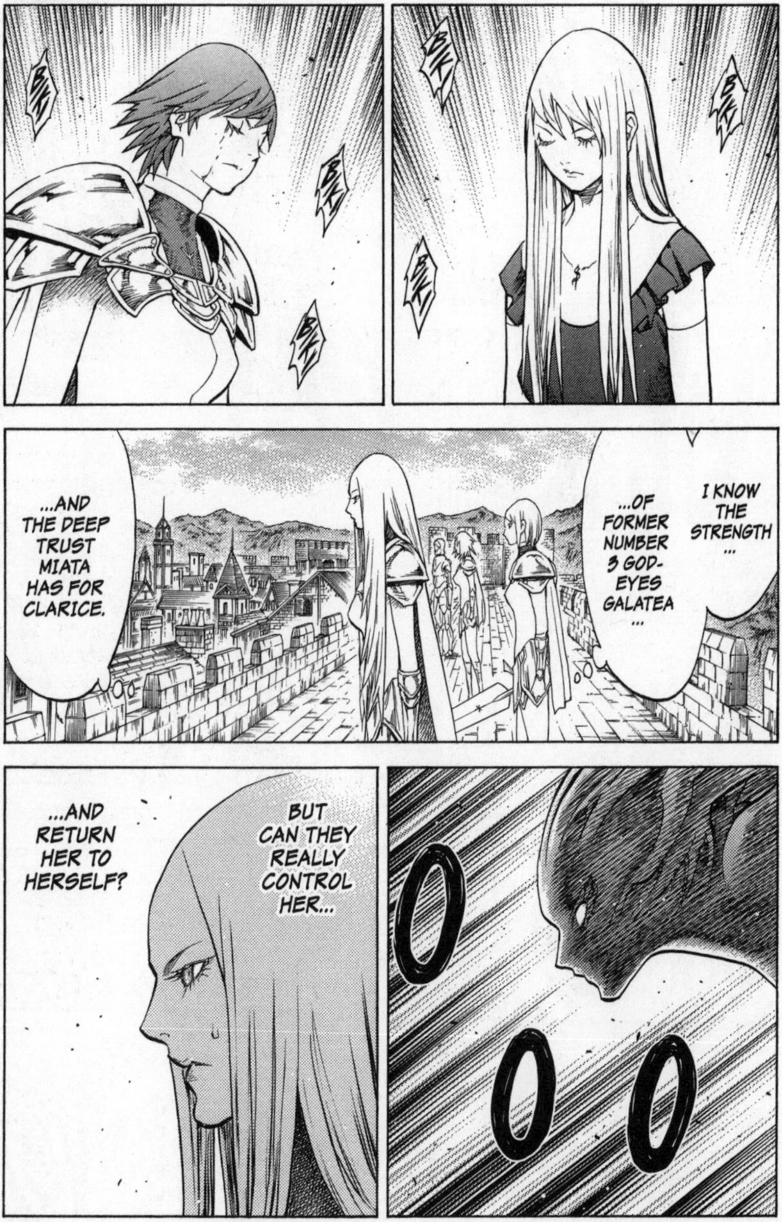

BIKI
BIKI
BIKI
BIKI
BIKI
BIKI
I KNOW THE STRENGTH ...
...OF FORMER NUMBER 3 GOD-EYES GALATEA ...
...AND THE DEEP TRUST MIATA HAS FOR CLARICE.
BUT CAN THEY REALLY CONTROL HER...
...AND RETURN HER TO HERSELF?

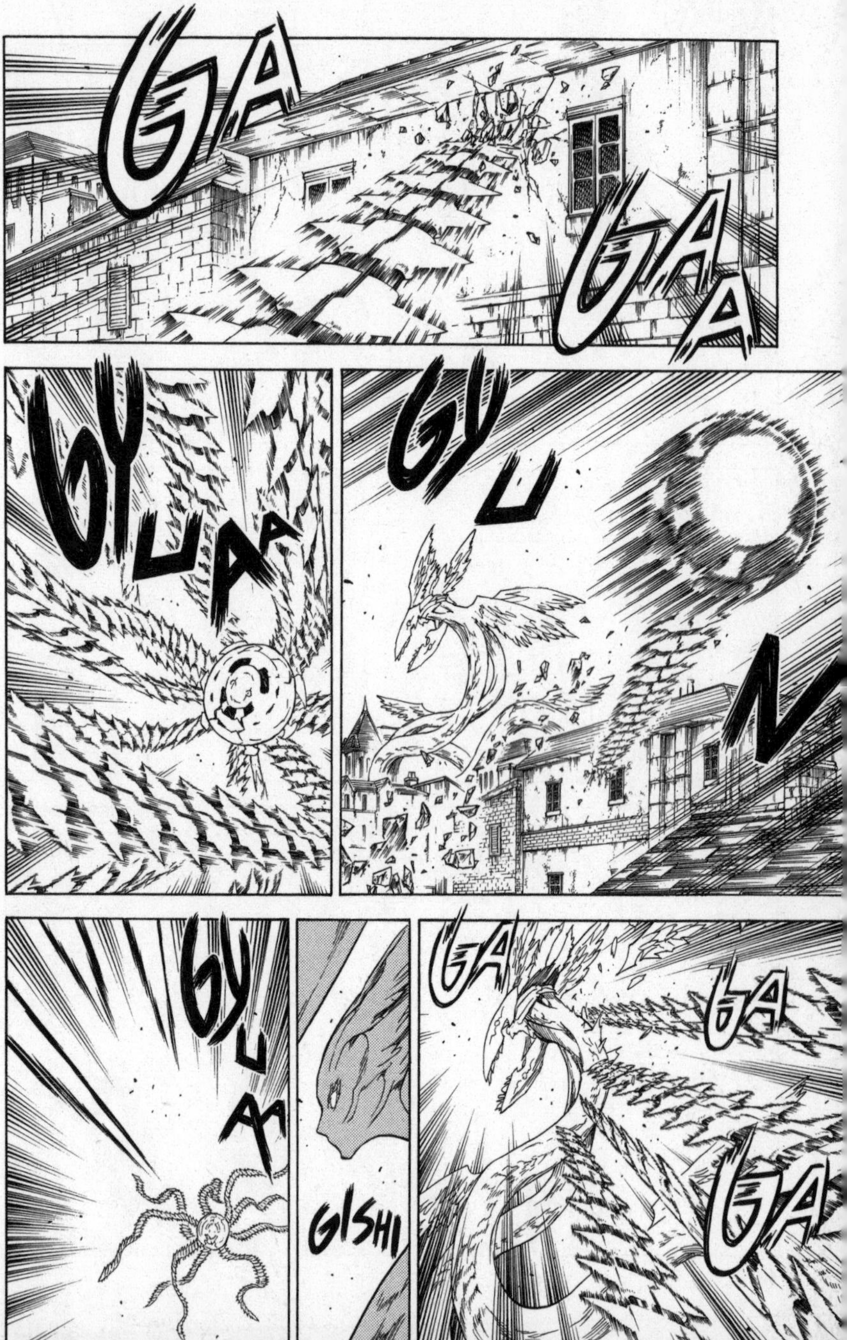
GA
GAAA
GYUN
GYUAA
GA
GA
GA
GISHI
GYUAA

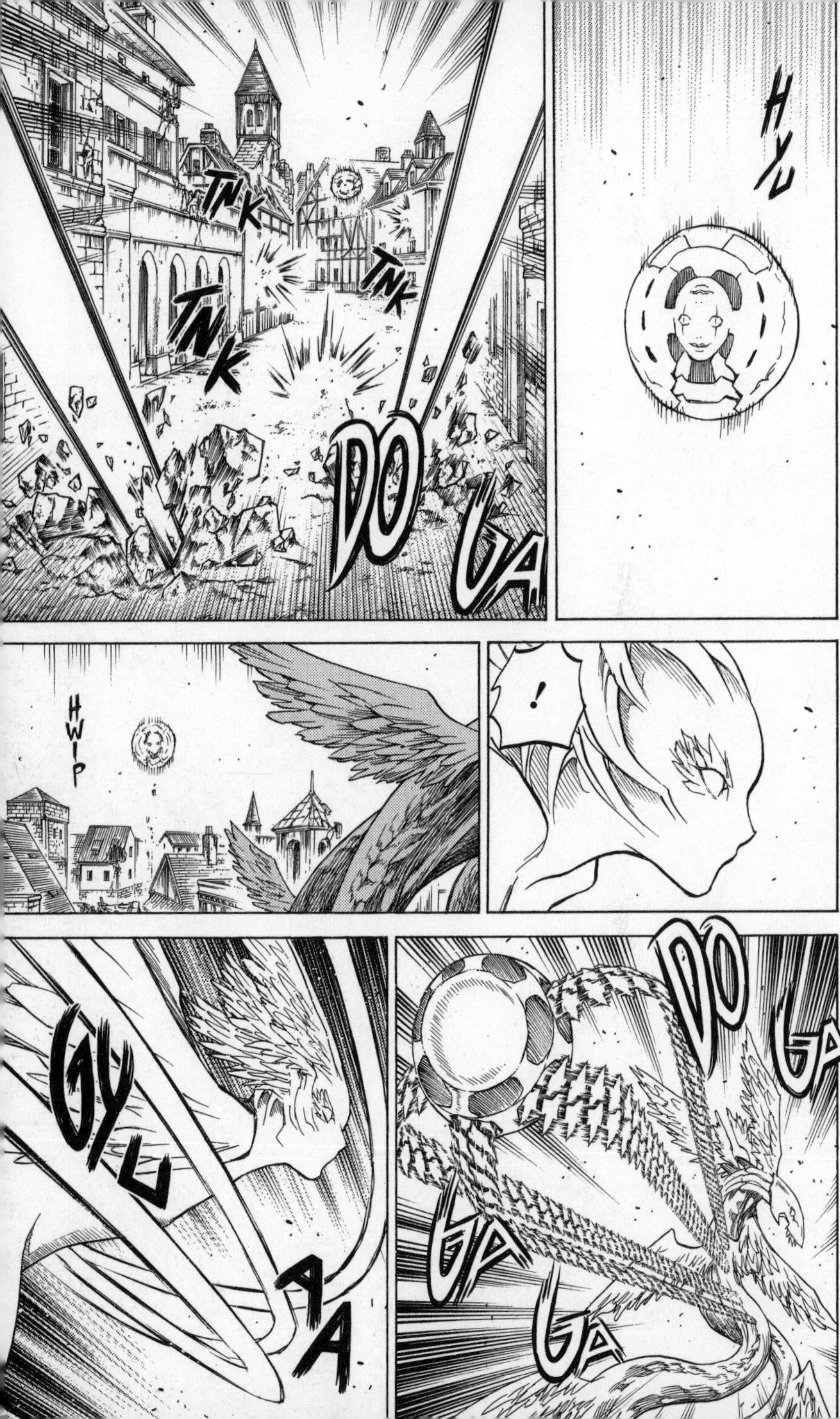
HYU
TNK
TNK
TNK
DOGA
!
HWIP
DOGA
GA
GA
GYU
AA

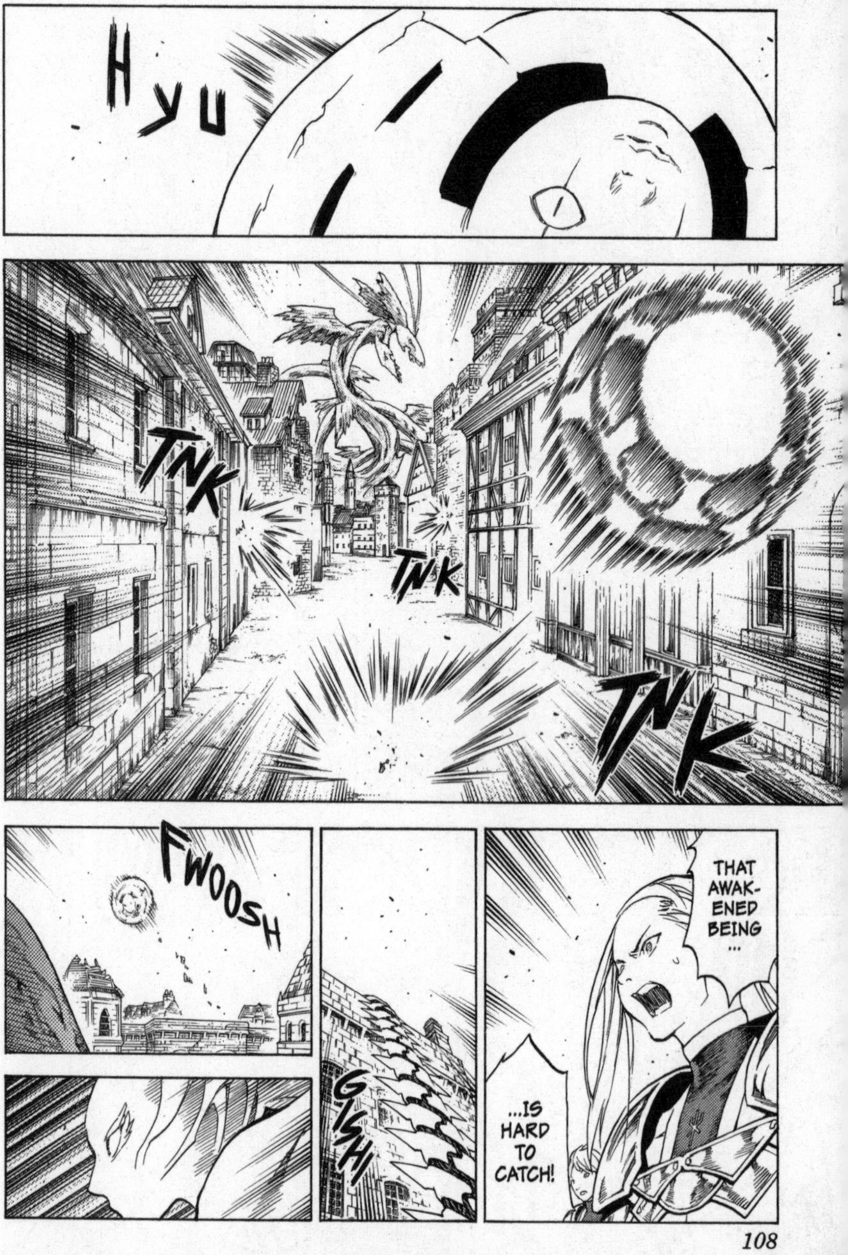
HYU
TNK
TNK
TNK
THAT AWAKENED BEING...
...IS HARD TO CATCH!
GISH
FWOOSH

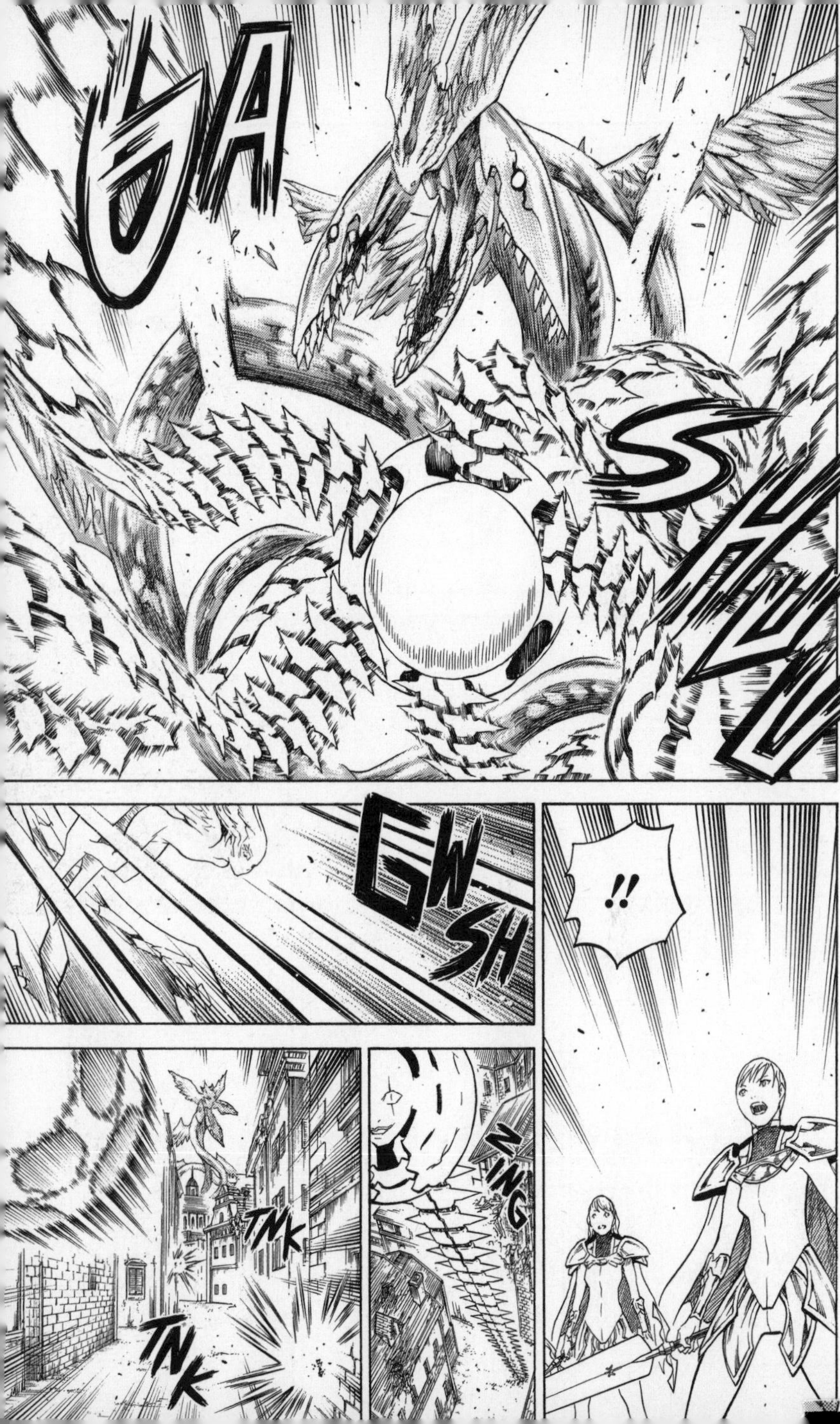
GA
SHUU
!!
GWSH
ZING
TNK
TNK

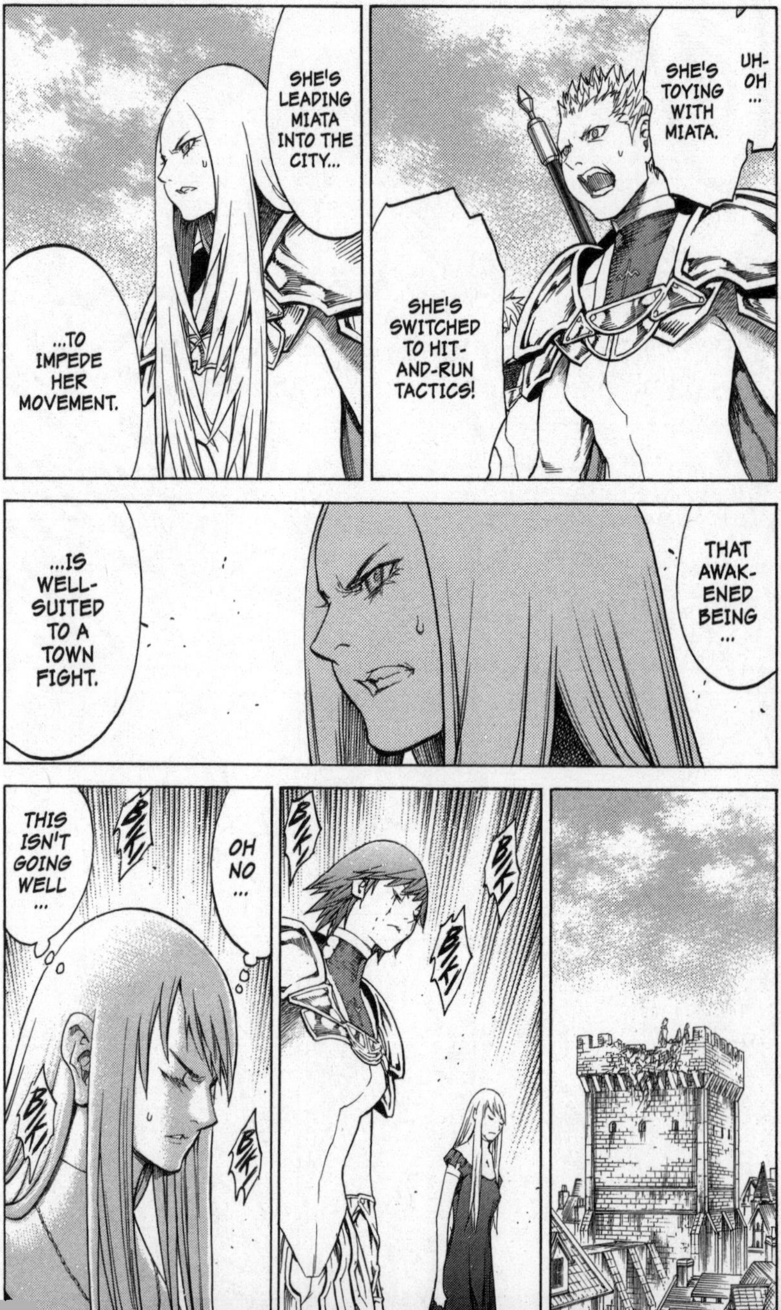
UH-OH ...
SHE'S TOYING WITH MIATA.
SHE'S SWITCHED TO HIT-AND-RUN TACTICS!
SHE'S LEADING MIATA INTO THE CITY...
...TO IMPEDE HER MOVEMENT.
THAT AWAKENED BEING ...
...IS WELL-SUITED TO A TOWN FIGHT.
BIKI
BIKI
BIKI
OH NO ...
THIS ISN'T GOING WELL ...
BIKI
BIKI
BIKI

READ THIS WAY

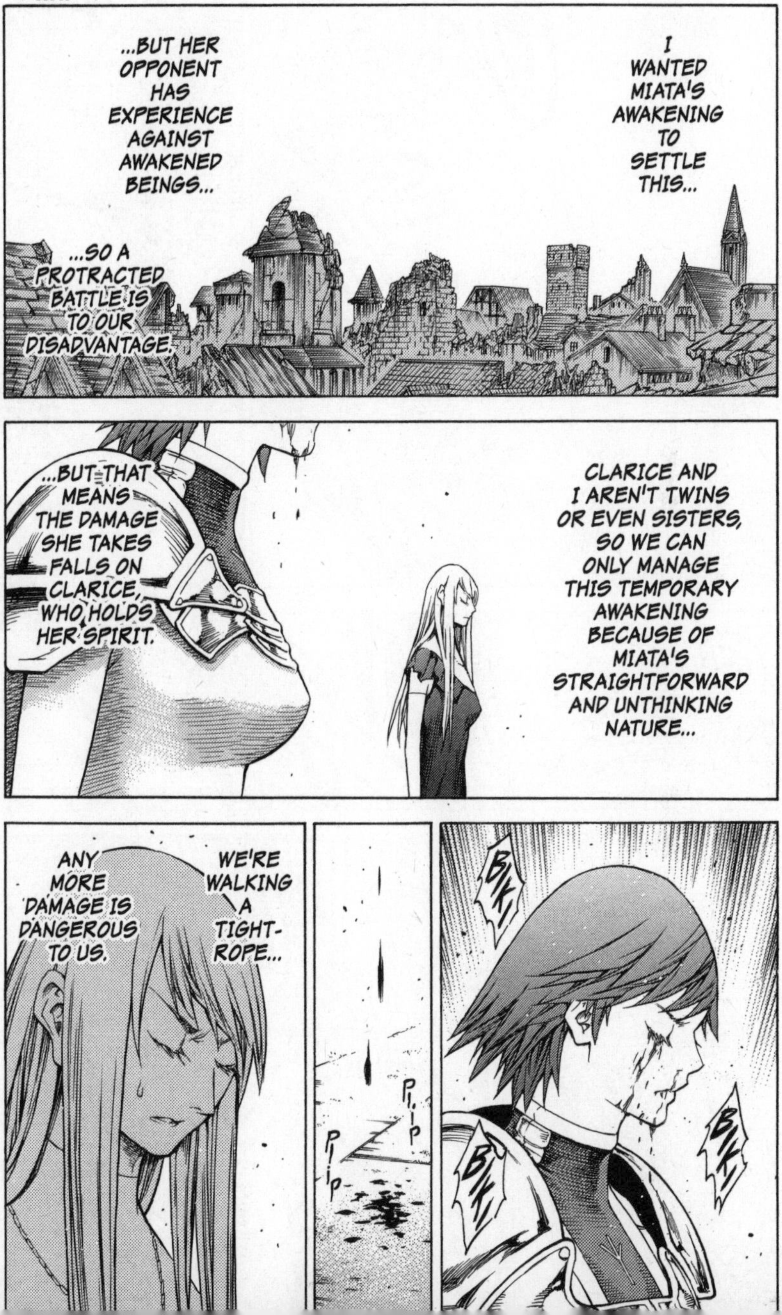
I WANTED MIATA'S AWAKENING TO SETTLE THIS...
...BUT HER OPPONENT HAS EXPERIENCE AGAINST AWAKENED BEINGS...
...SO A PROTRACTED BATTLE IS TO OUR DISADVANTAGE.
CLARICE AND I AREN'T TWINS OR EVEN SISTERS, SO WE CAN ONLY MANAGE THIS TEMPORARY AWAKENING BECAUSE OF MIATA'S STRAIGHTFORWARD AND UNTHINKING NATURE...
...BUT THAT MEANS THE DAMAGE SHE TAKES FALLS ON CLARICE, WHO HOLDS HER SPIRIT.
BIKI
BIKI
BIKI
PLIP
PLIP
WE'RE WALKING A TIGHT-ROPE...
ANY MORE DAMAGE IS DANGEROUS TO US.

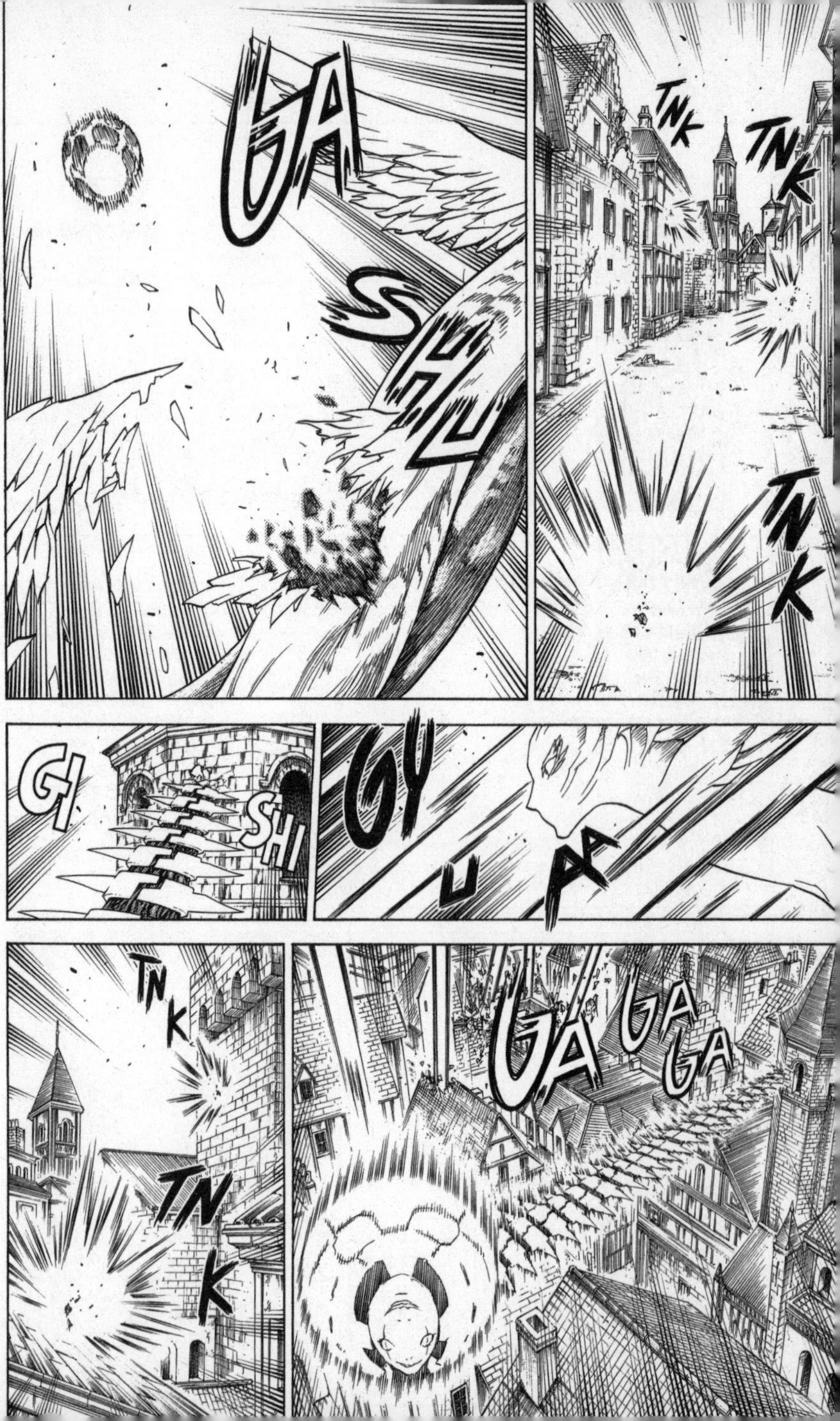
TNK
TNK
TNK
GA
SHU
GY
U
AA
GI
SHI
GA
GA
GA
TNK
TNK

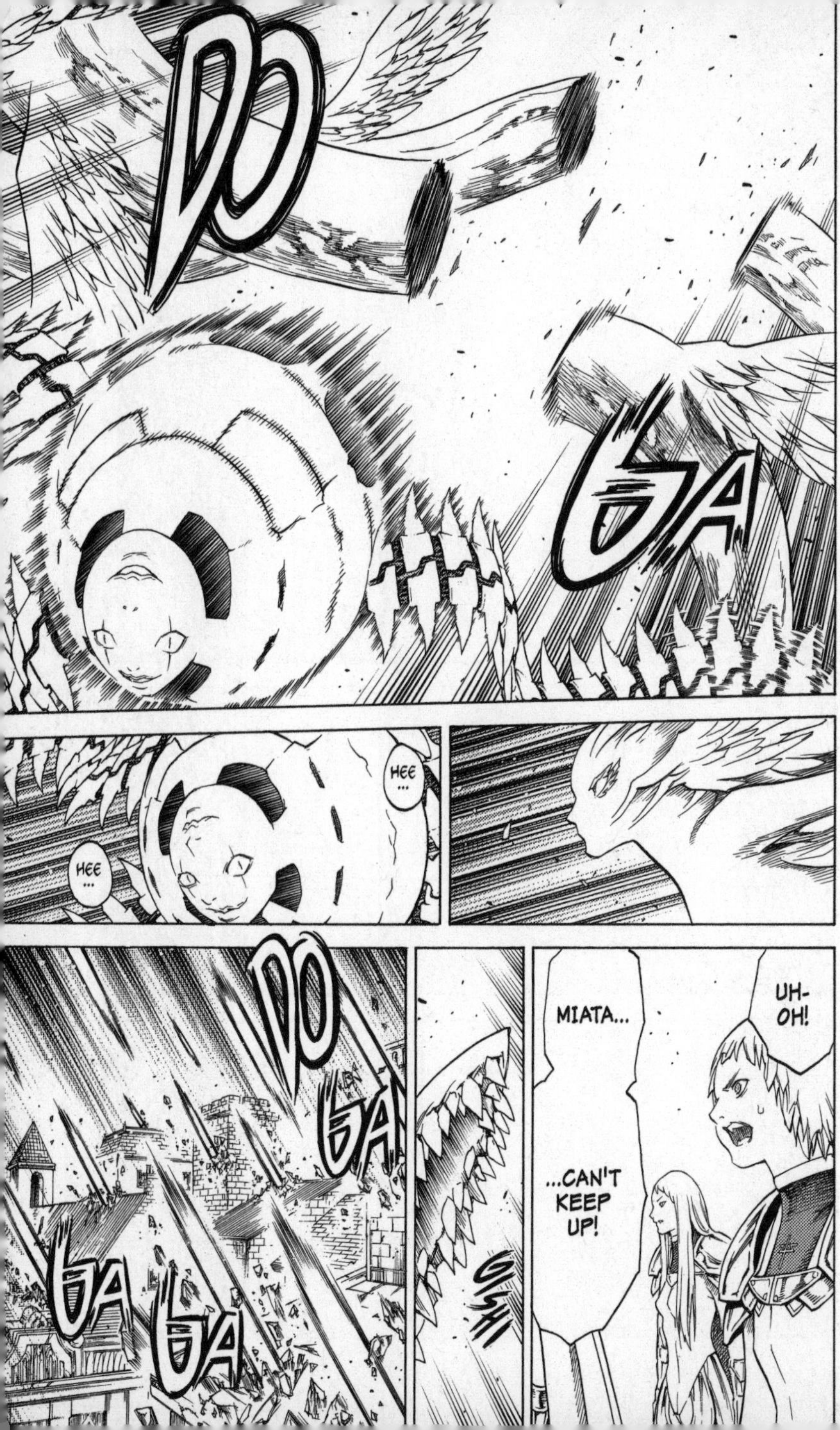
DO
GA
HEE...
HEE...
UH-OH!
MIATA...
...CAN'T KEEP UP!
GOSHI
DO
GA
GA
GA
GA

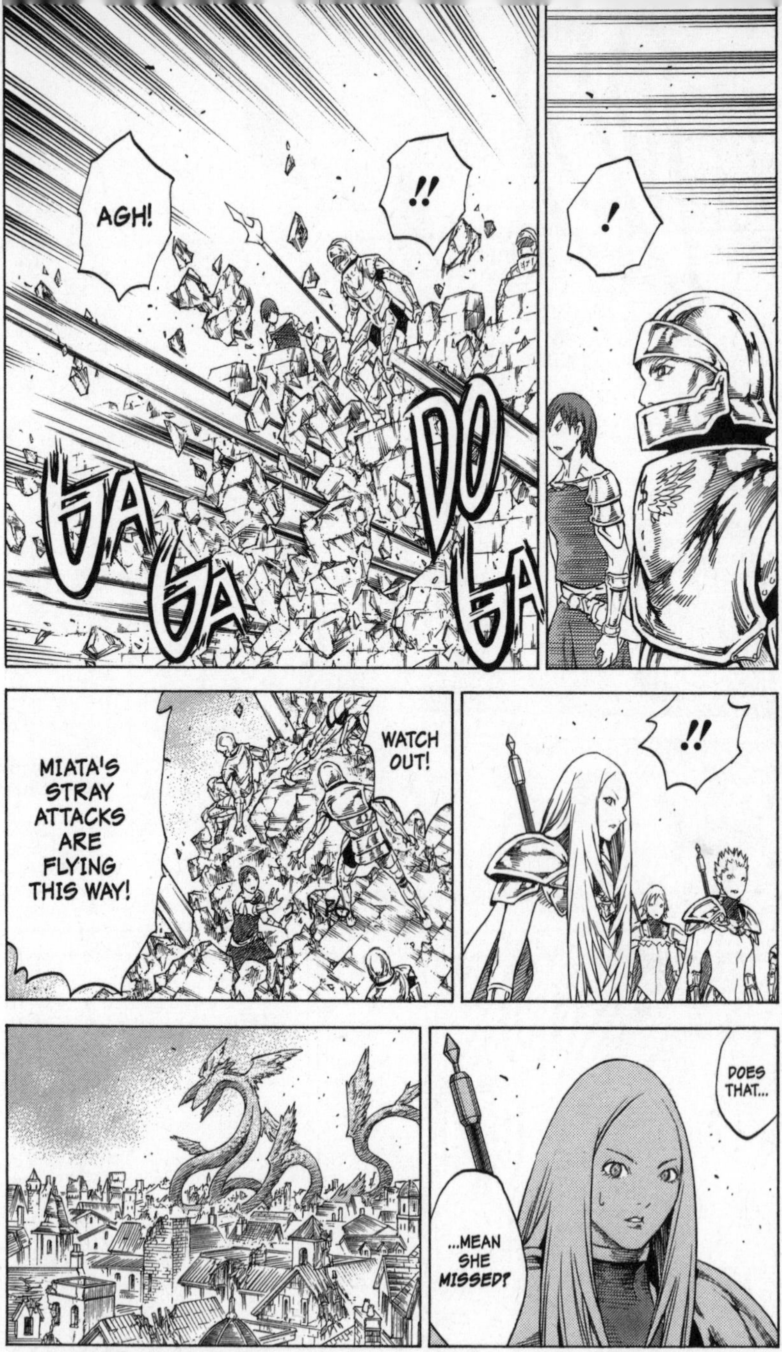
!
!!
AGH!
DO
GA
GA
GA
!!
WATCH OUT!
MIATA'S STRAY ATTACKS ARE FLYING THIS WAY!
DOES THAT...
...MEAN SHE MISSED?

READ THIS WAY

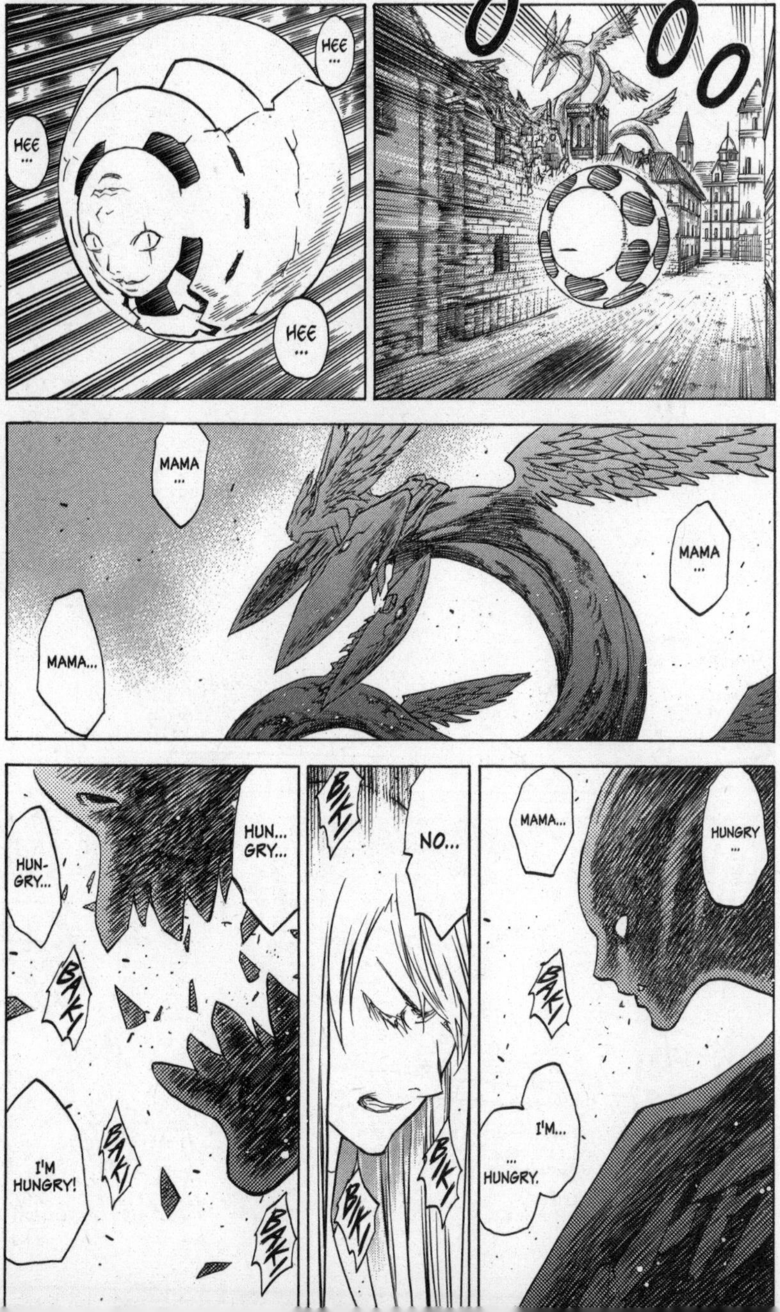
OOOO
HEE...
HEE...
HEE...
MAMA...
MAMA...
MAMA...
HUNGRY...
MAMA...
BAKI
I'M...
...HUNGRY.
BIKI
NO...
BIKI
BIKI
HUN... GRY...
HUN-GRY...
BAKI
BAKI
I'M HUNGRY!
BAKI

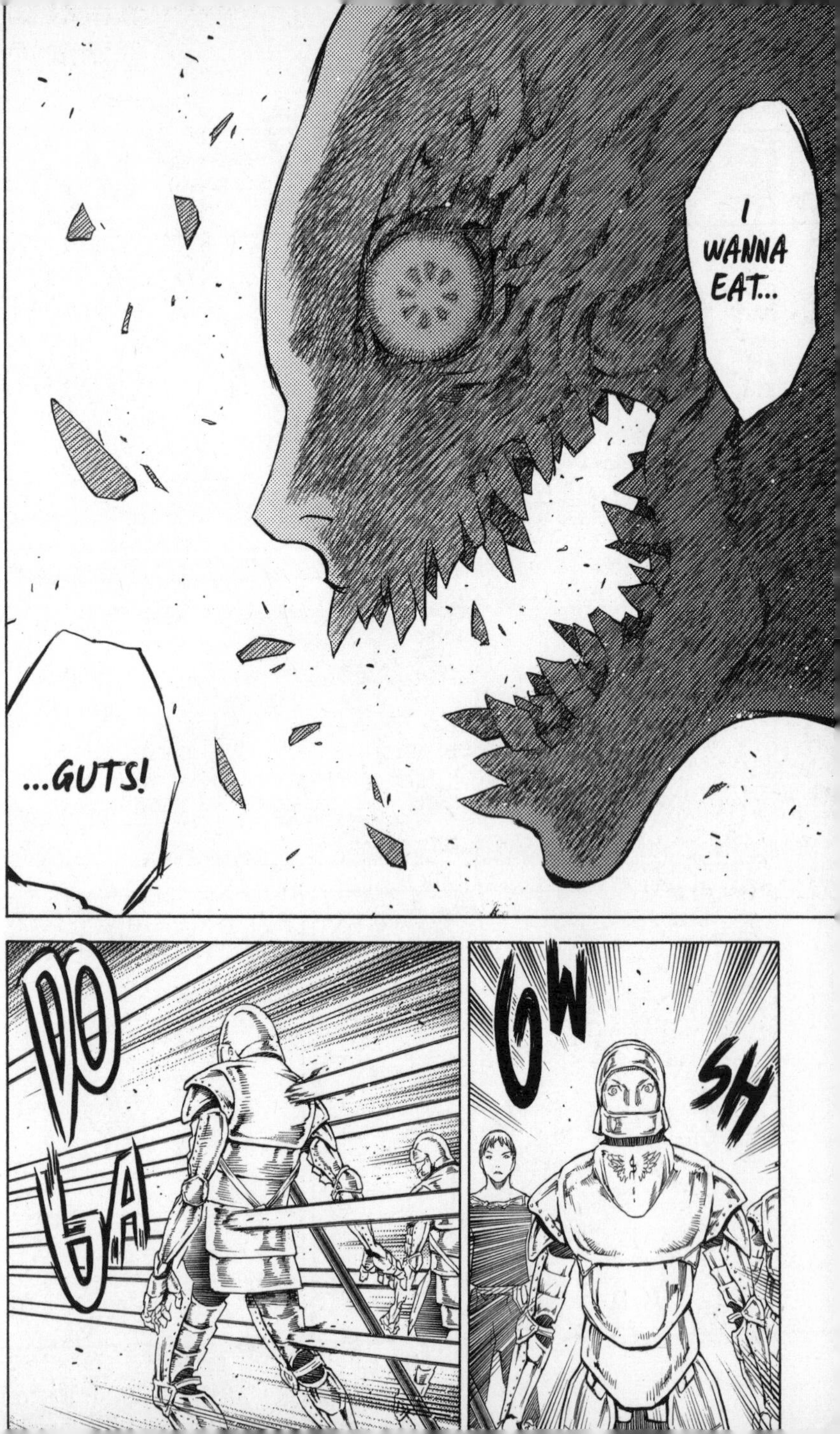
I WANNA EAT...
...GUTS!
GWSH
DOGA

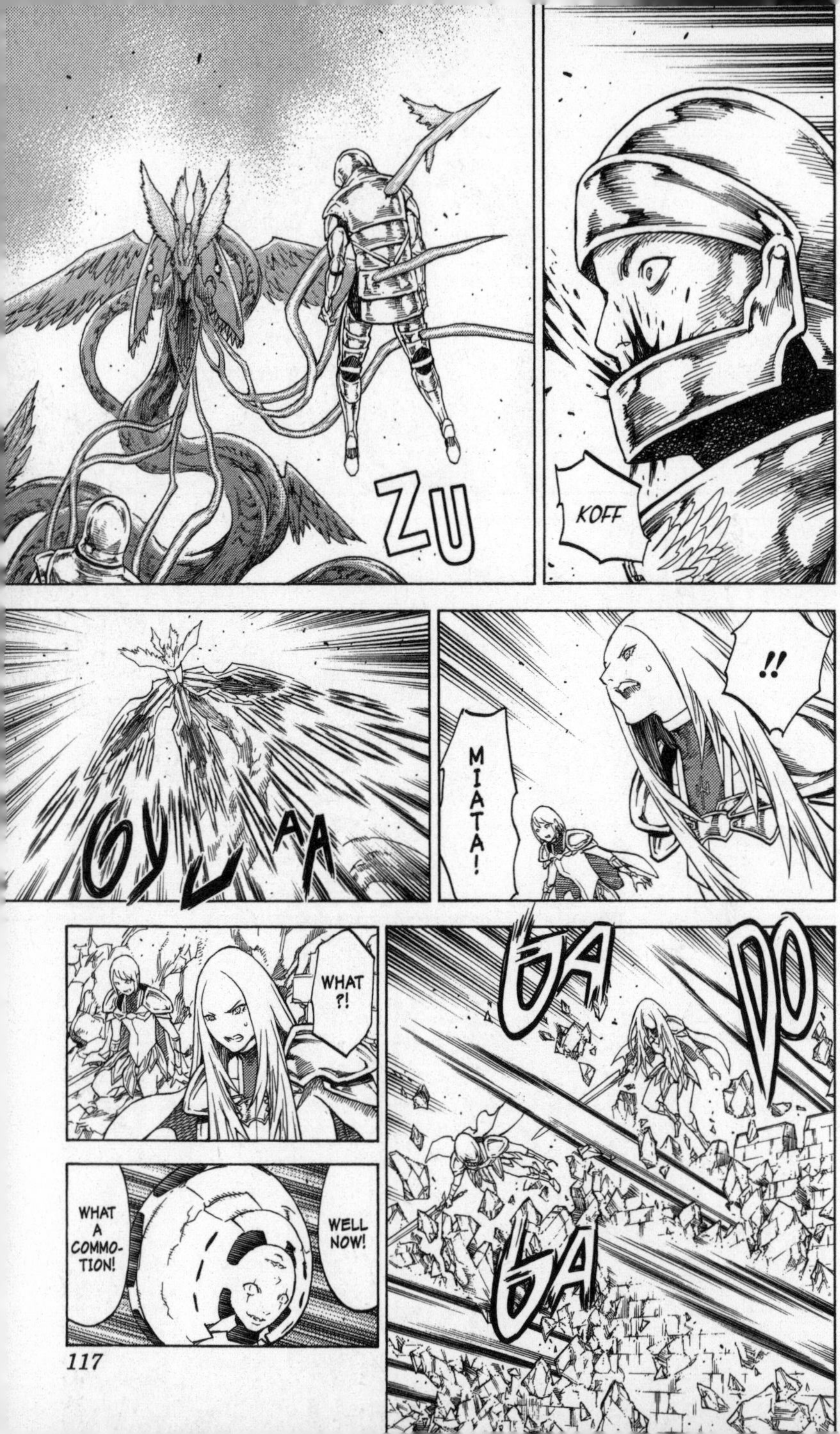
KOFF
ZU
!!
MIATA!
GYUAA
DO
GA
GA
WHAT ?!
WELL NOW!
WHAT A COMMOTION!

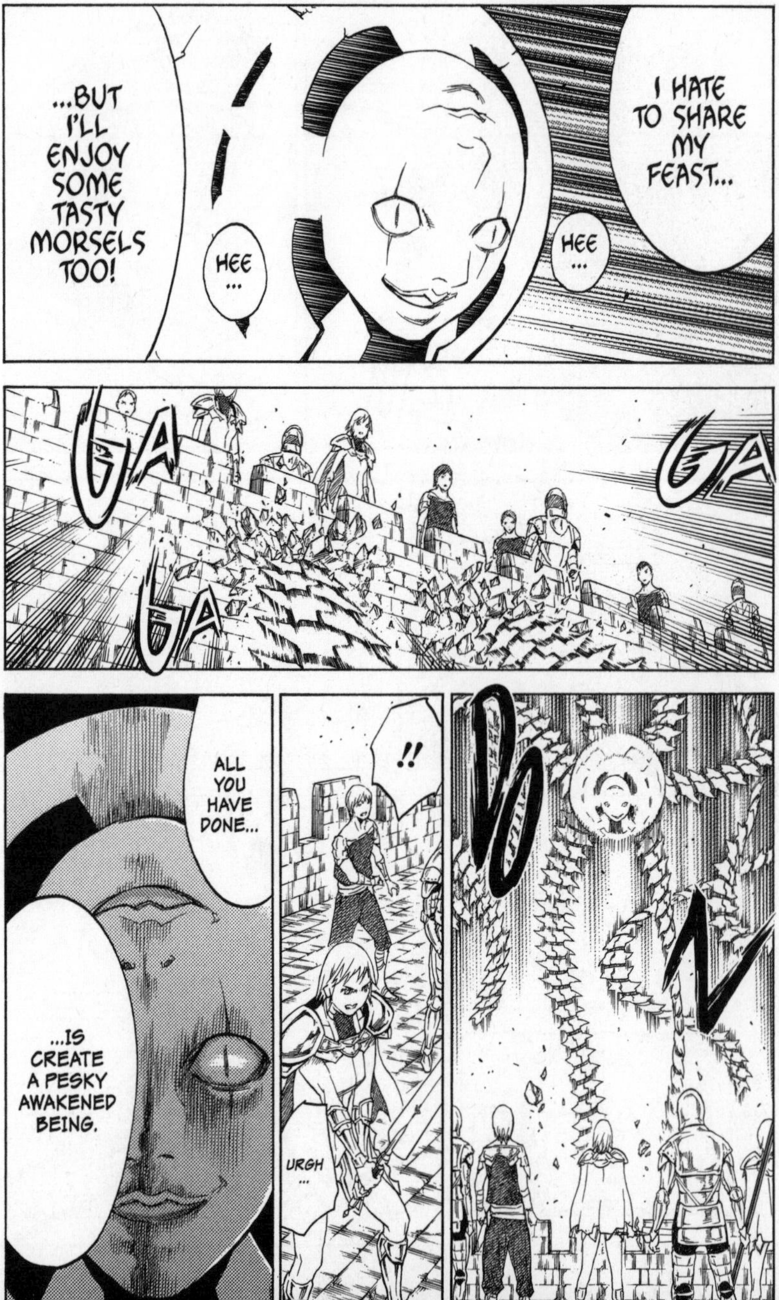
I HATE TO SHARE MY FEAST...
HEE ...
HEE ...
...BUT I'LL ENJOY SOME TASTY MORSELS TOO!
GA
GA
GA
!!
ALL YOU HAVE DONE...
URGH ...
...IS CREATE A PESKY AWAKENED BEING.

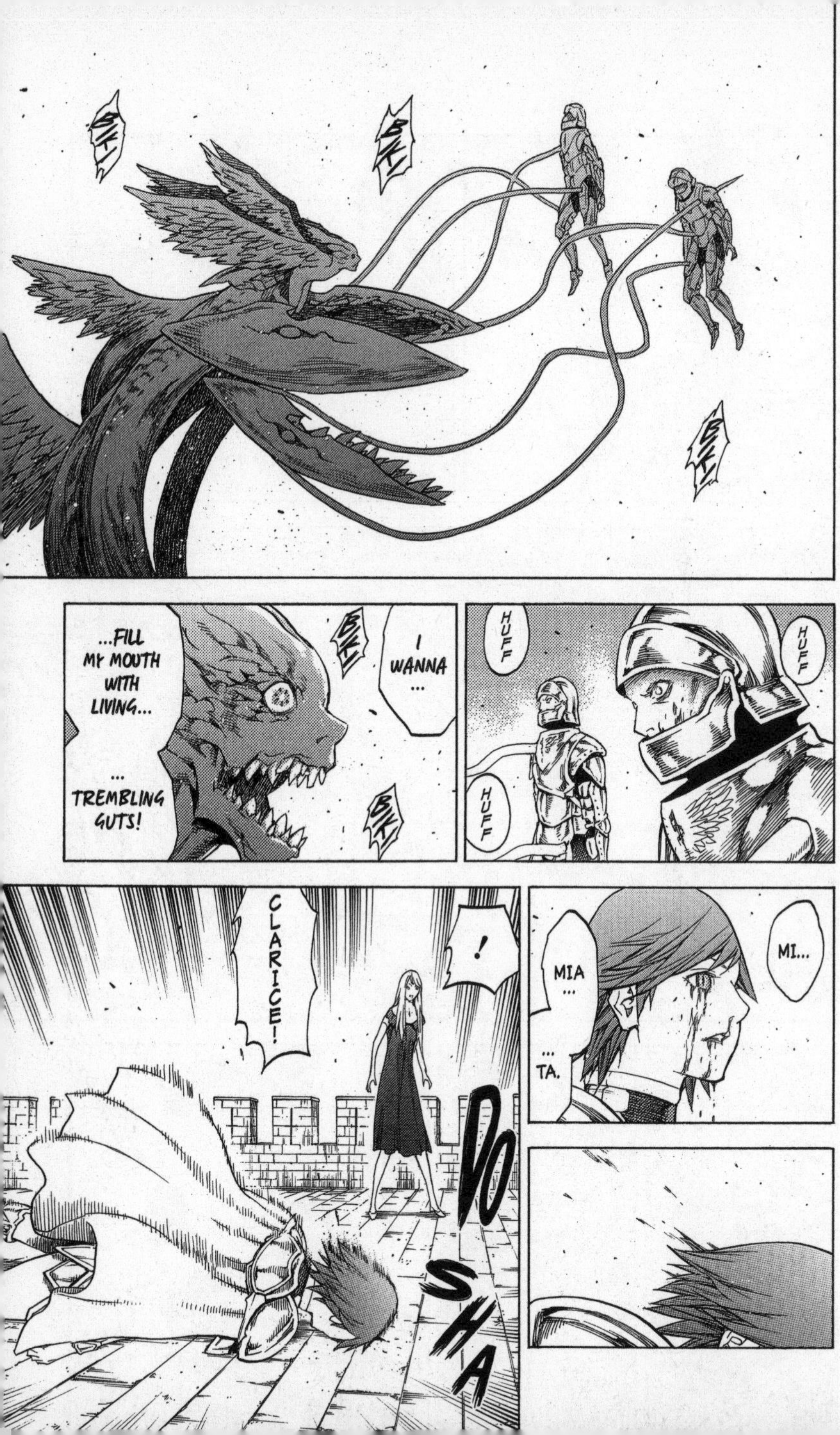

BIKI
BIKI
BIKI
HUFF
HUFF
HUFF
I WANNA ...
BIKI
...FILL MY MOUTH WITH LIVING...
... TREMBLING GUTS!
BIKI
MI...
MIA ...
... TA.
!
CLARICE!
DOSHA

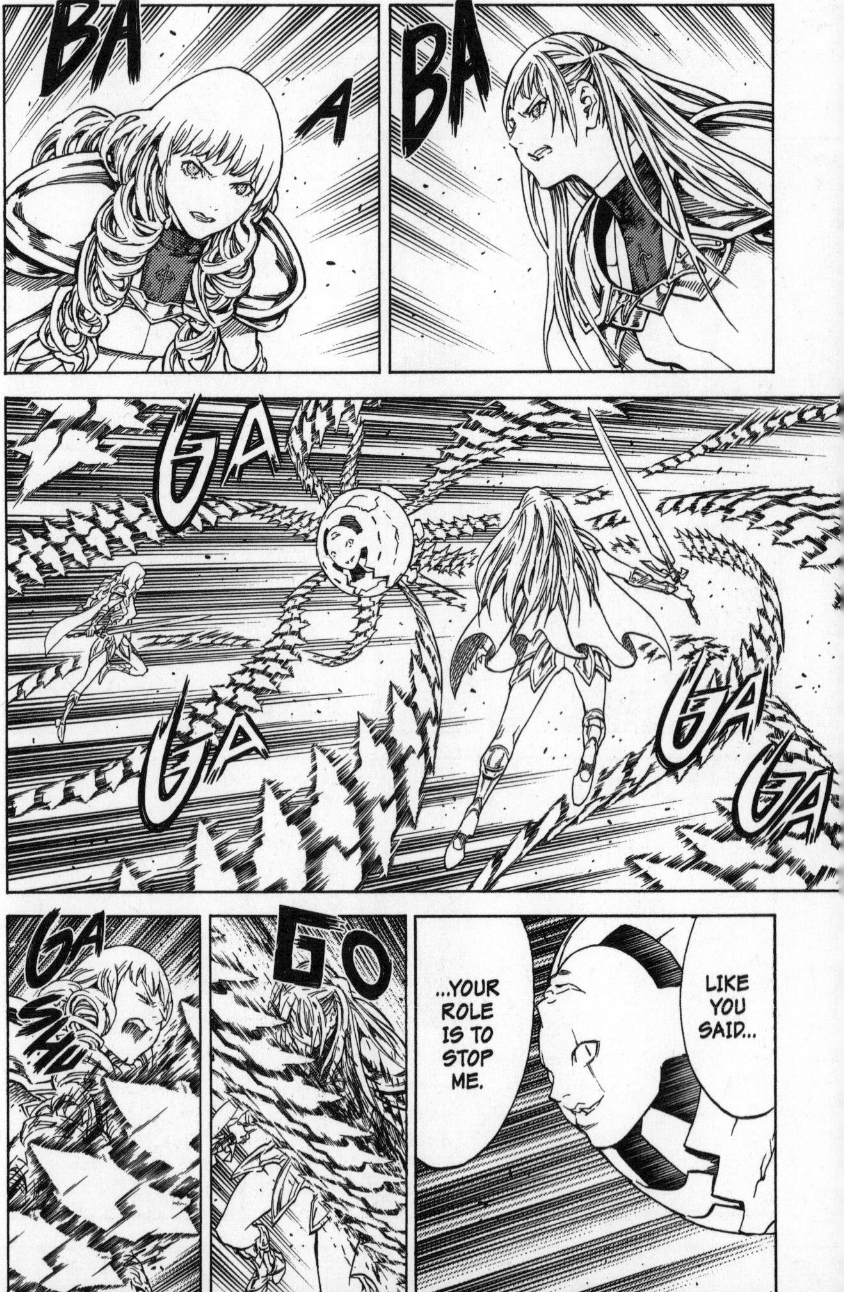
BA
BA
A
GA
GA
GA
GA
LIKE YOU SAID...
...YOUR ROLE IS TO STOP ME.
GO
GA
SHU

BUT YOU'VE FINISHED THAT...

...SO YOUR TIME HERE IS THROUGH!

IF THIS...

...KEEPS UP...

ARGH!

BIKI

BIKI

BIKI

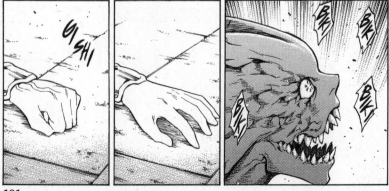

GISHI

BIKI

BIKI

BIKI

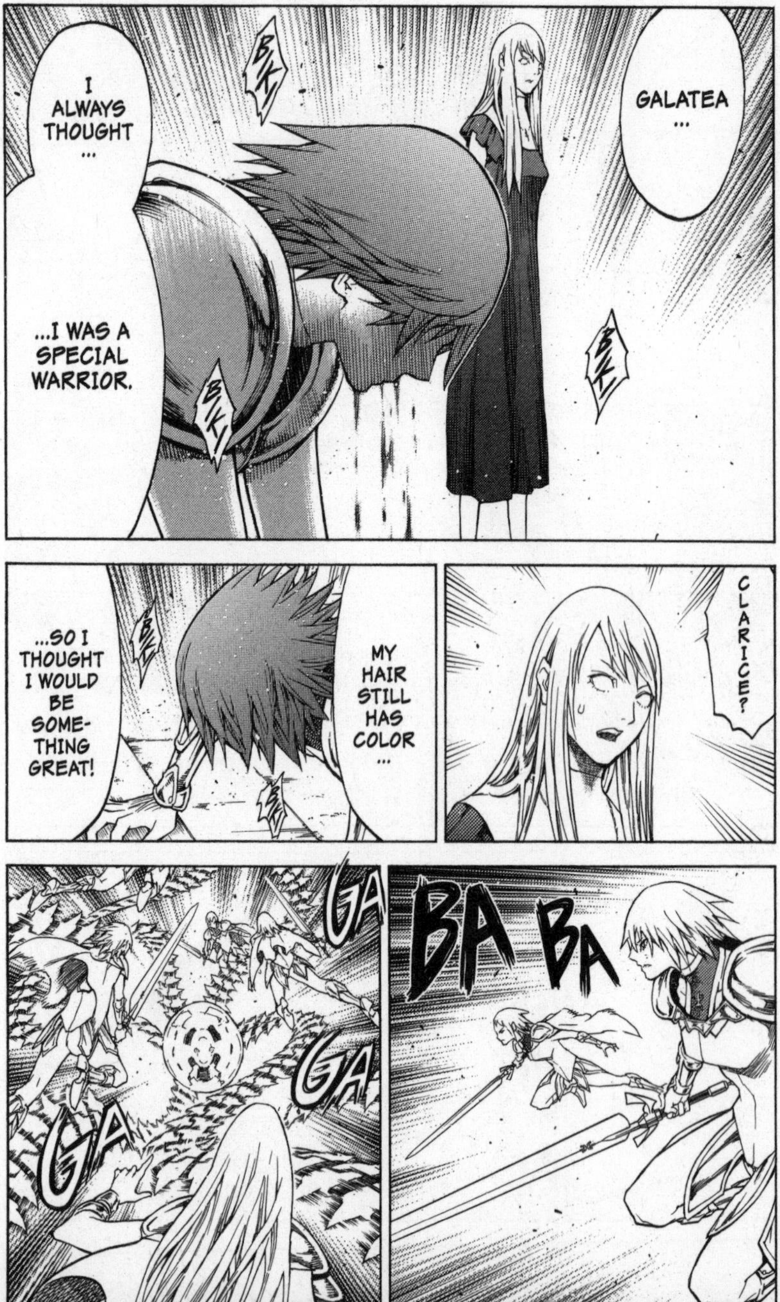
GALATEA ...
BIKI
BIKI
I ALWAYS THOUGHT ...
...I WAS A SPECIAL WARRIOR.
BIKI
CLARICE?
MY HAIR STILL HAS COLOR ...
BIKI
...SO I THOUGHT I WOULD BE SOME-THING GREAT!
BIKI
BA BA
GA
GA
GA

READ THIS WAY

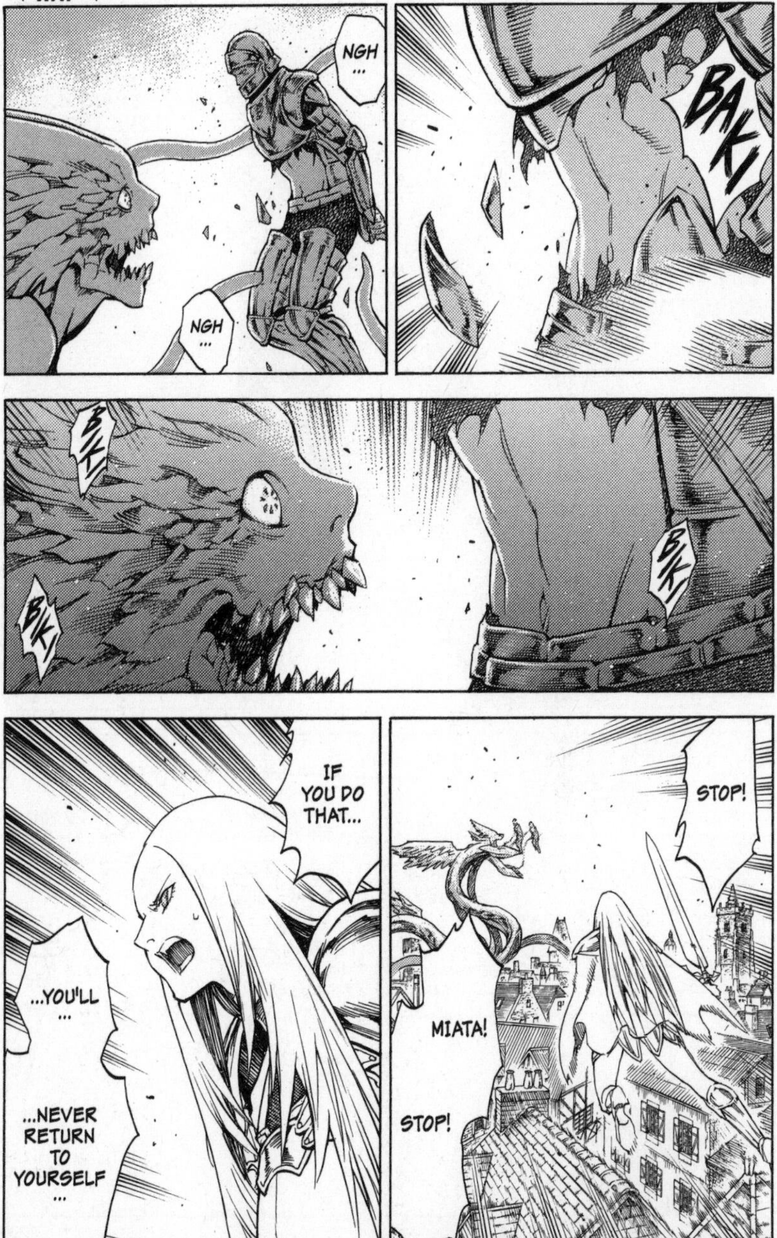

BAKI
NGH ...
NGH ...
BIKI
BIKI
BIKI
STOP!
MIATA!
STOP!
IF YOU DO THAT...
...YOU'LL ...
...NEVER RETURN TO YOURSELF ...

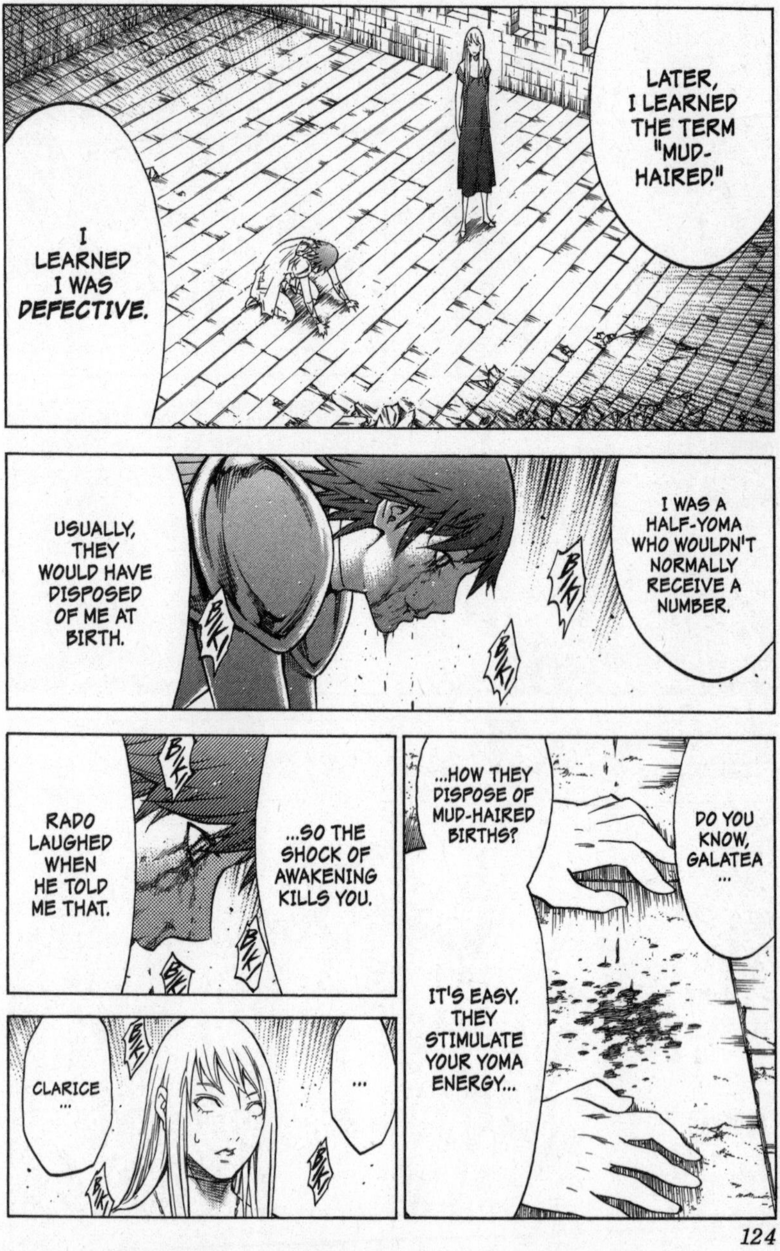
LATER, I LEARNED THE TERM "MUD-HAIRED."
I LEARNED I WAS DEFECTIVE.
I WAS A HALF-YOMA WHO WOULDN'T NORMALLY RECEIVE A NUMBER.
BIKI
BIKI
BIKI
USUALLY, THEY WOULD HAVE DISPOSED OF ME AT BIRTH.
DO YOU KNOW, GALATEA ...
...HOW THEY DISPOSE OF MUD-HAIRED BIRTHS?
IT'S EASY. THEY STIMULATE YOUR YOMA ENERGY...
BIKI
...SO THE SHOCK OF AWAKENING KILLS YOU.
RADO LAUGHED WHEN HE TOLD ME THAT.
BIKI
BIKI
...
BIKI
CLARICE ...
BIKI
BIKI

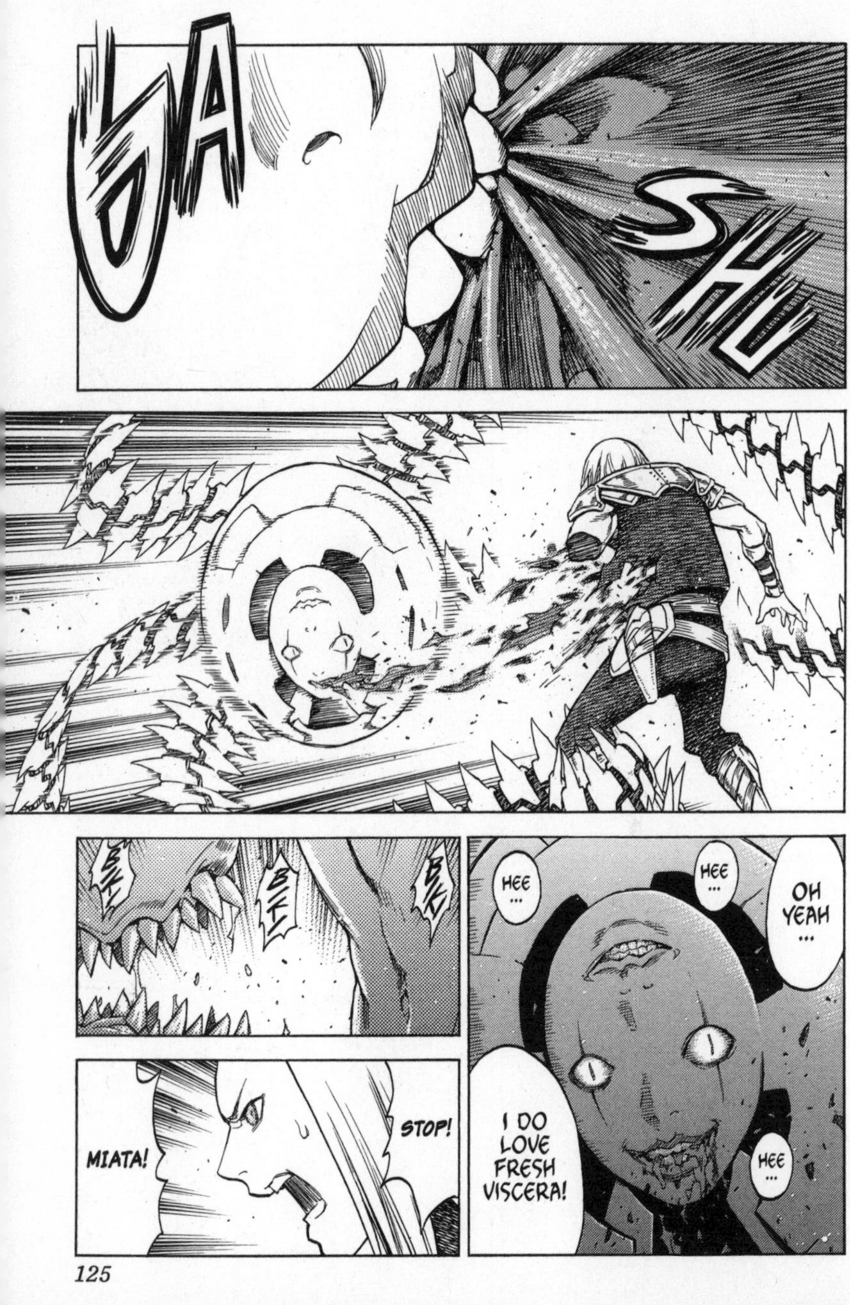
SA
SHU
OH YEAH ...
HEE ...
HEE ...
I DO LOVE FRESH VISCERA!
HEE ...
BKI
BKI
BKI
STOP!
MIATA!

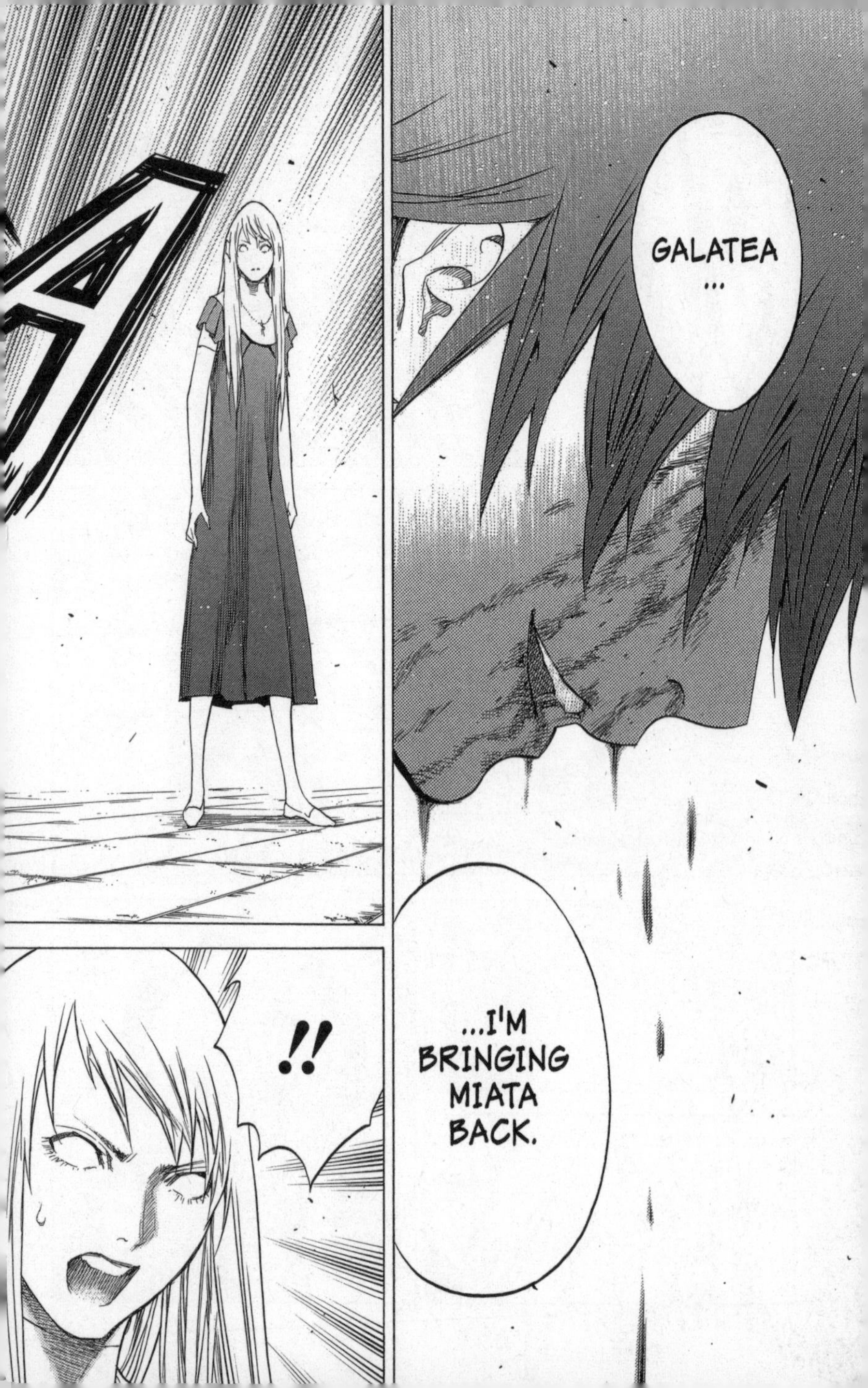
GALATEA ...
...I'M BRINGING MIATA BACK.
!!

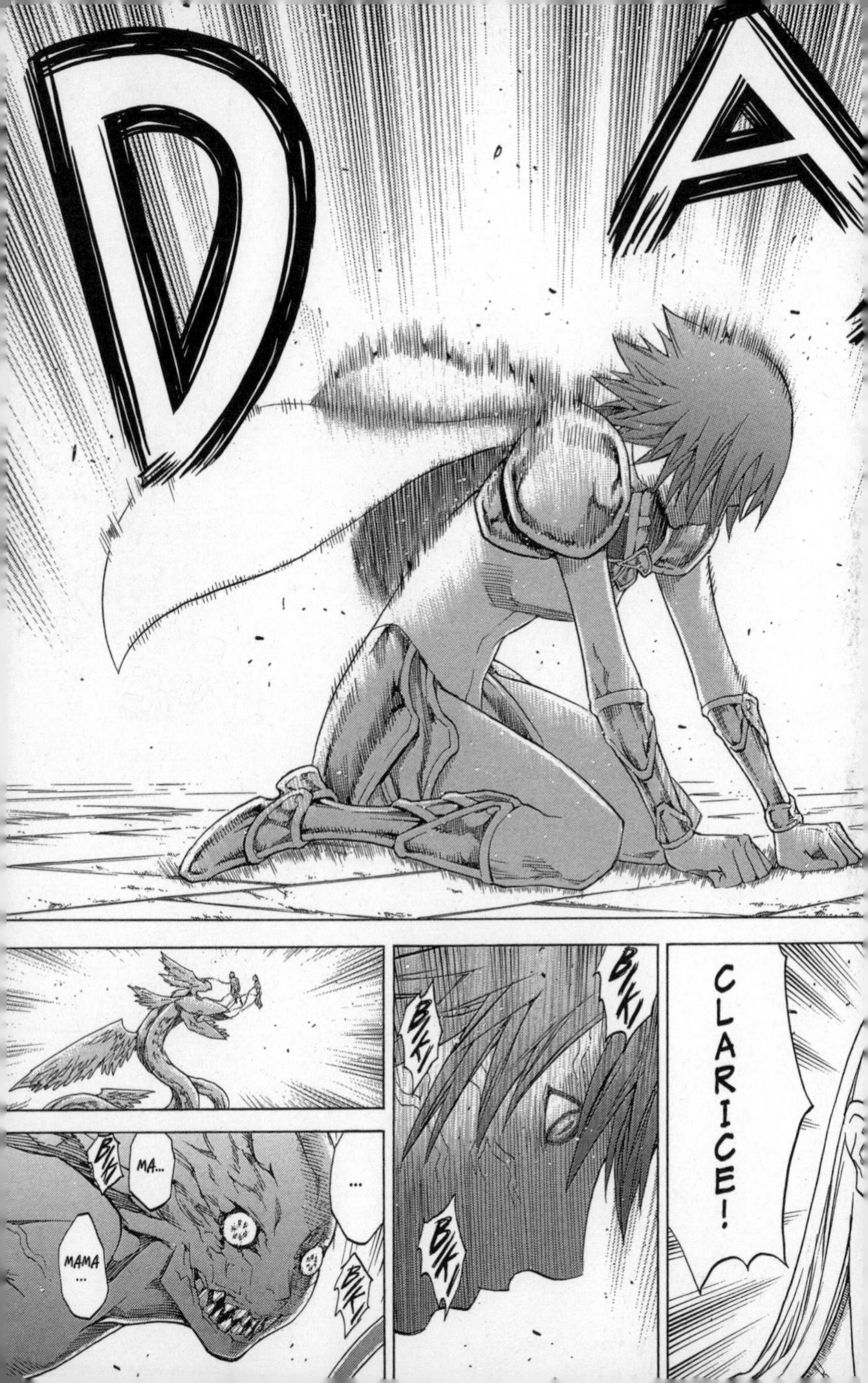
DA
CLARICE!
BIKI
BIKI
BIKI
...
MA...
BIKI
BIKI
MAMA ...

クレイモア
Claymore

Scene 142: Sword of the Dark Deep, Part 4

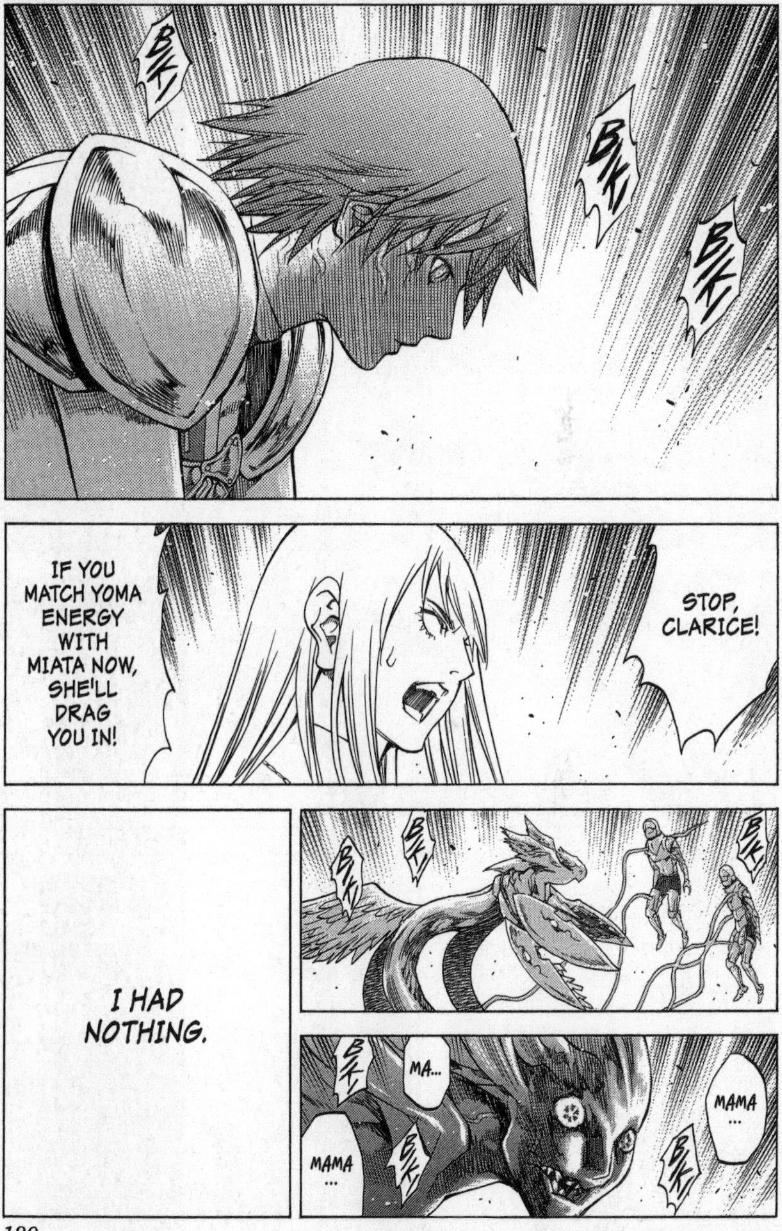
BIKI
BIKI
BIKI
STOP, CLARICE!
IF YOU MATCH YOMA ENERGY WITH MIATA NOW, SHE'LL DRAG YOU IN!
BIKI
BIKI
BIKI
MAMA...
MA...
BIKI
BIKI
BIKI
MAMA...
I HAD NOTHING.

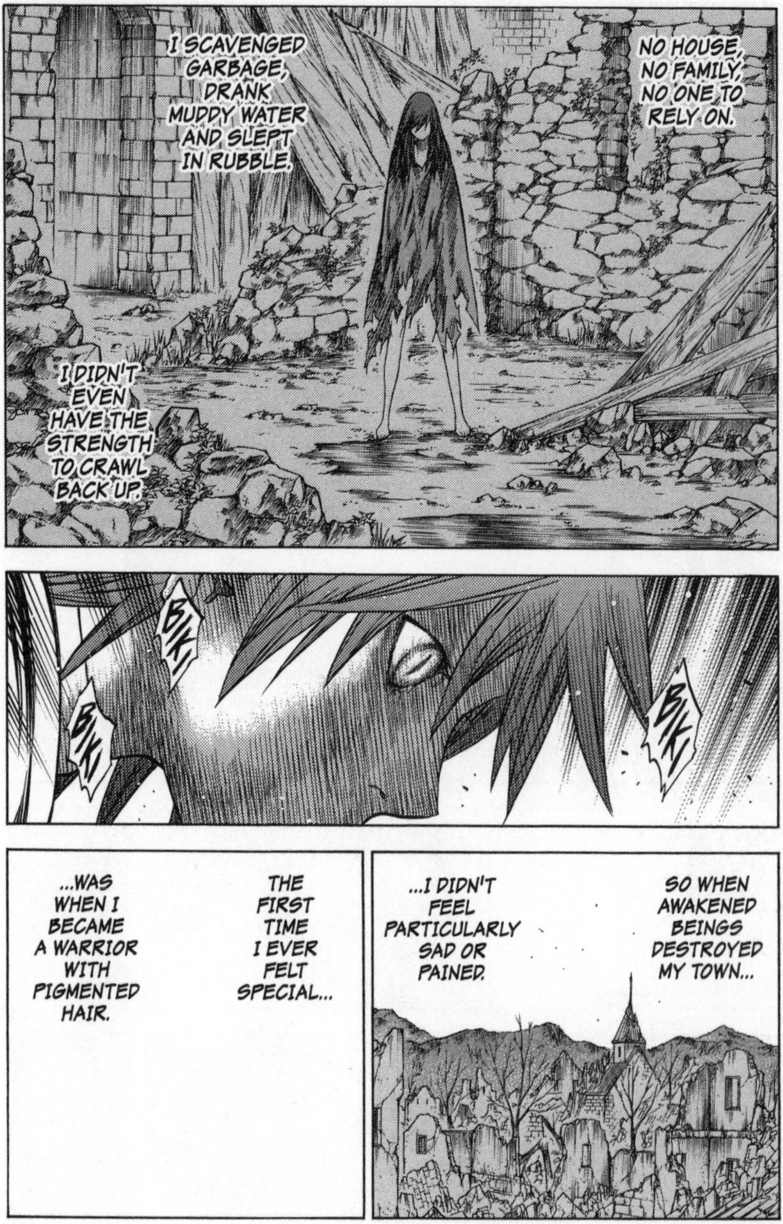
NO HOUSE, NO FAMILY, NO ONE TO RELY ON.
I SCAVENGED GARBAGE, DRANK MUDDY WATER AND SLEPT IN RUBBLE.
I DIDN'T EVEN HAVE THE STRENGTH TO CRAWL BACK UP.
BIKI
BIKI
BIKI
SO WHEN AWAKENED BEINGS DESTROYED MY TOWN...
...I DIDN'T FEEL PARTICULARLY SAD OR PAINED.
THE FIRST TIME I EVER FELT SPECIAL...
...WAS WHEN I BECAME A WARRIOR WITH PIGMENTED HAIR.

READ THIS WAY

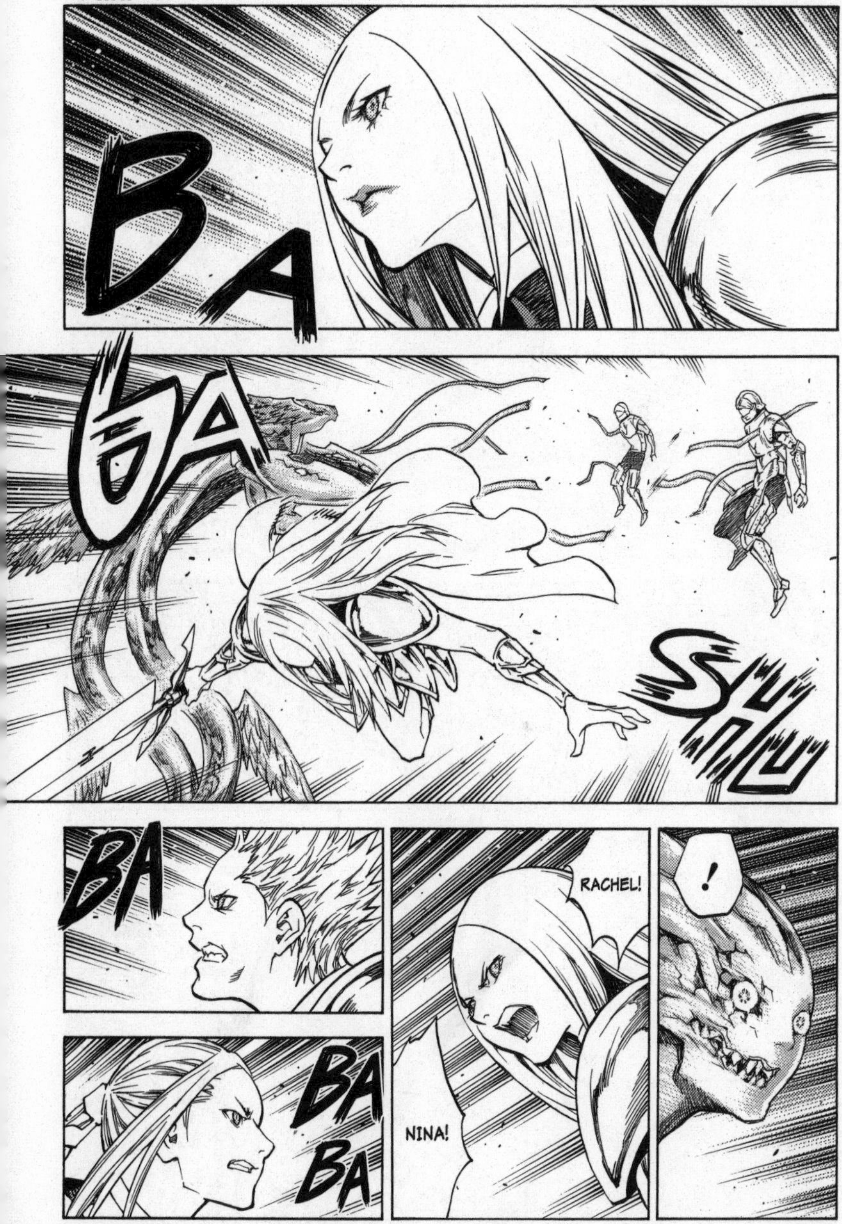

BA
BA
SHU
!
RACHEL!
NINA!
BA
BA
BA
BA

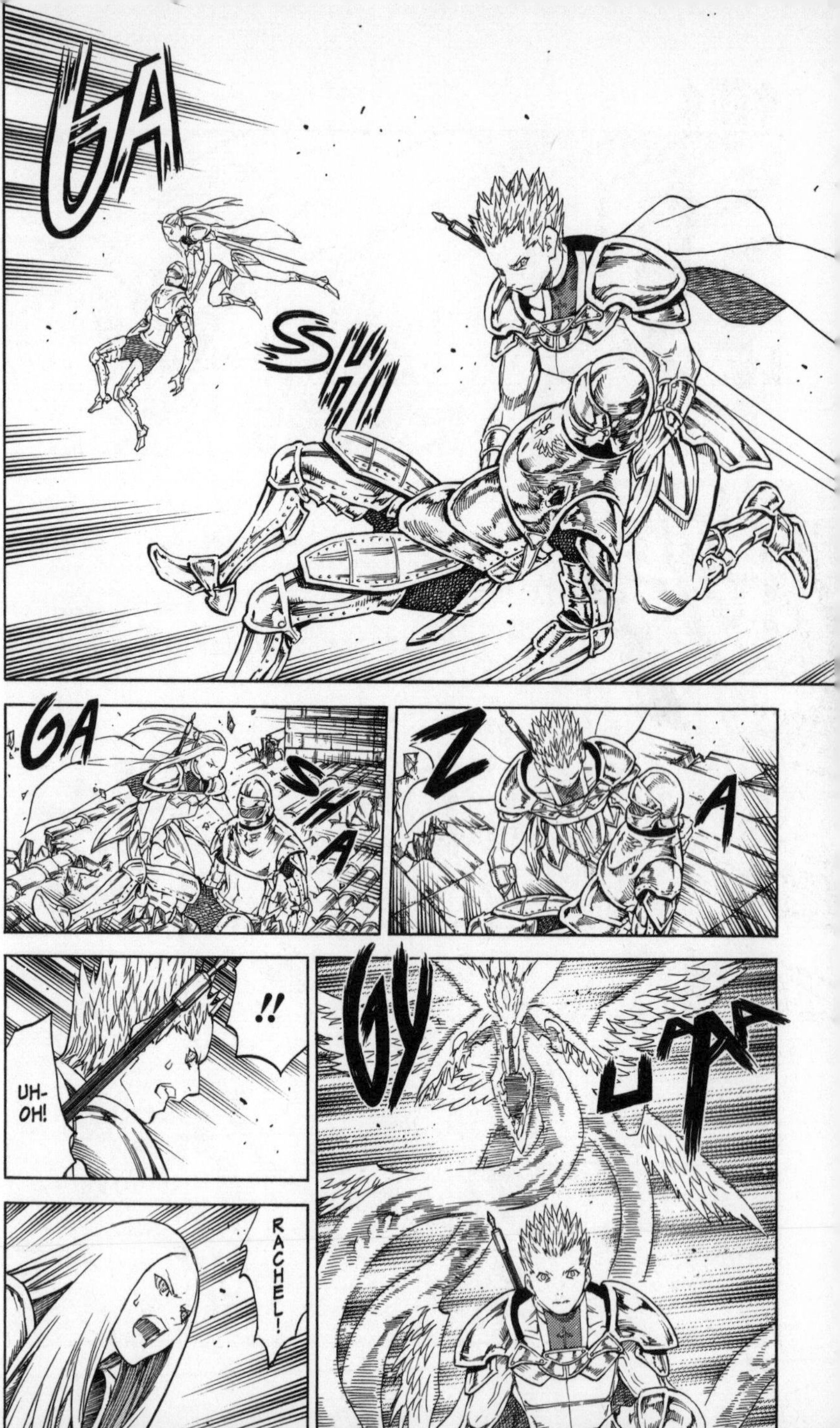
GA
SSHU
Z
A
GA
SHA
GY
UAAA
!!
UH-OH!
RACHEL!

READ THIS WAY

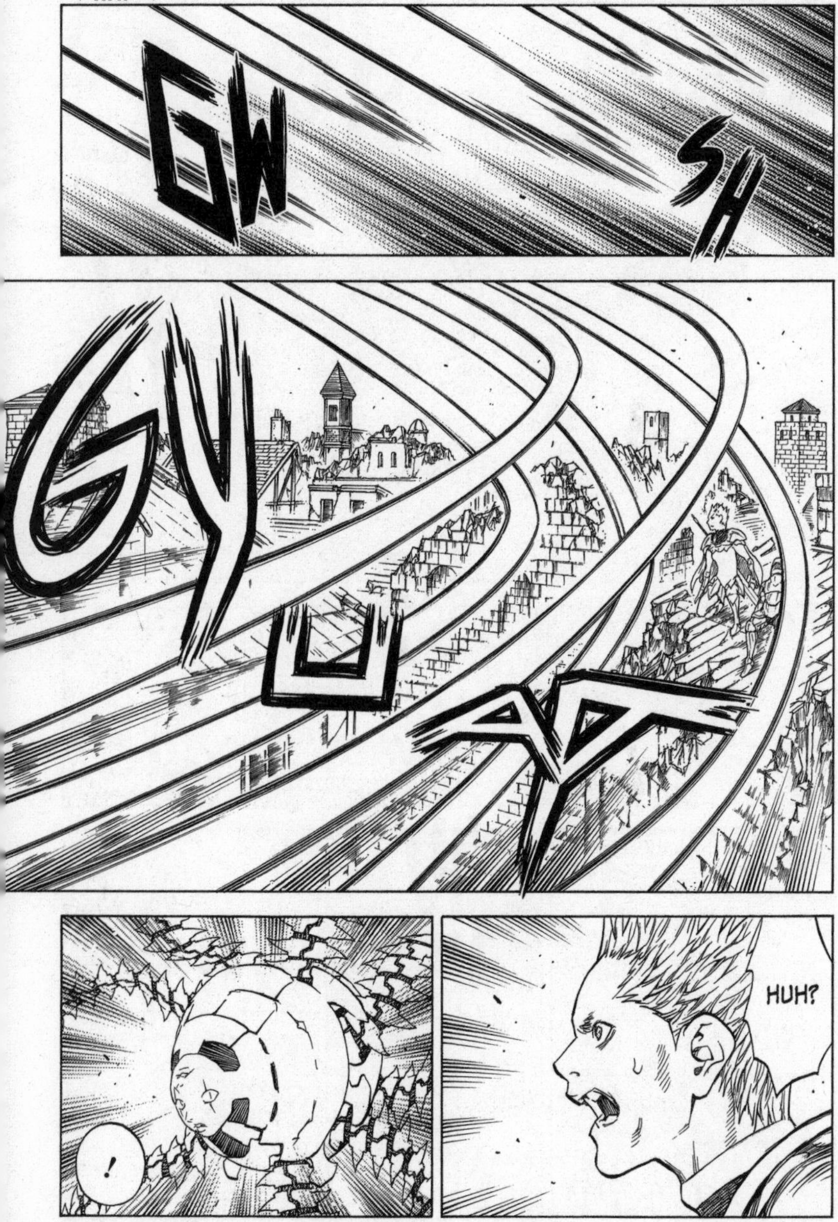
GWSH
GYUAA
HUH?
!

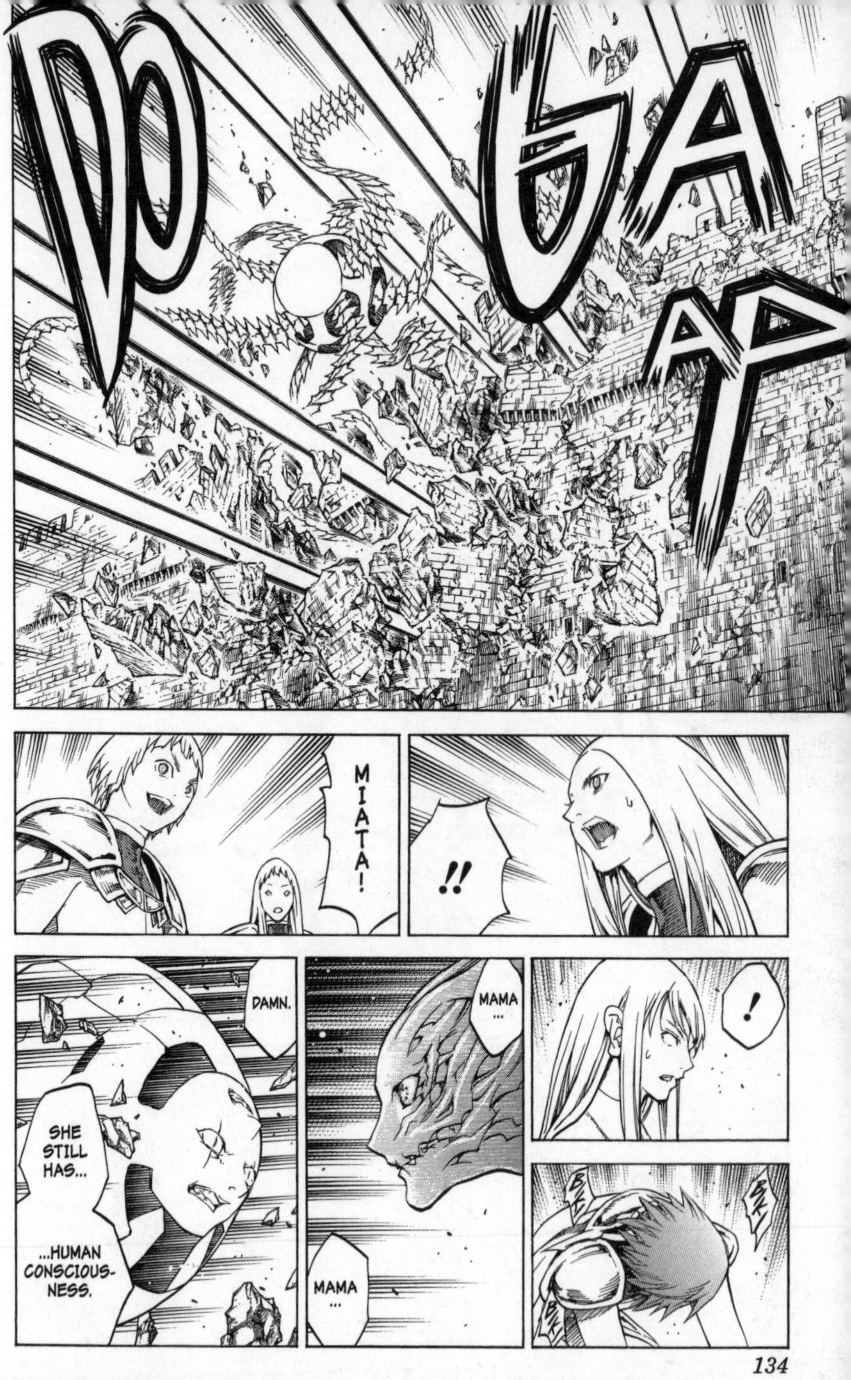

DOGAAP
!!
MIATA!
!
MAMA...
MAMA...
DAMN.
SHE STILL HAS...
...HUMAN CONSCIOUS-NESS.

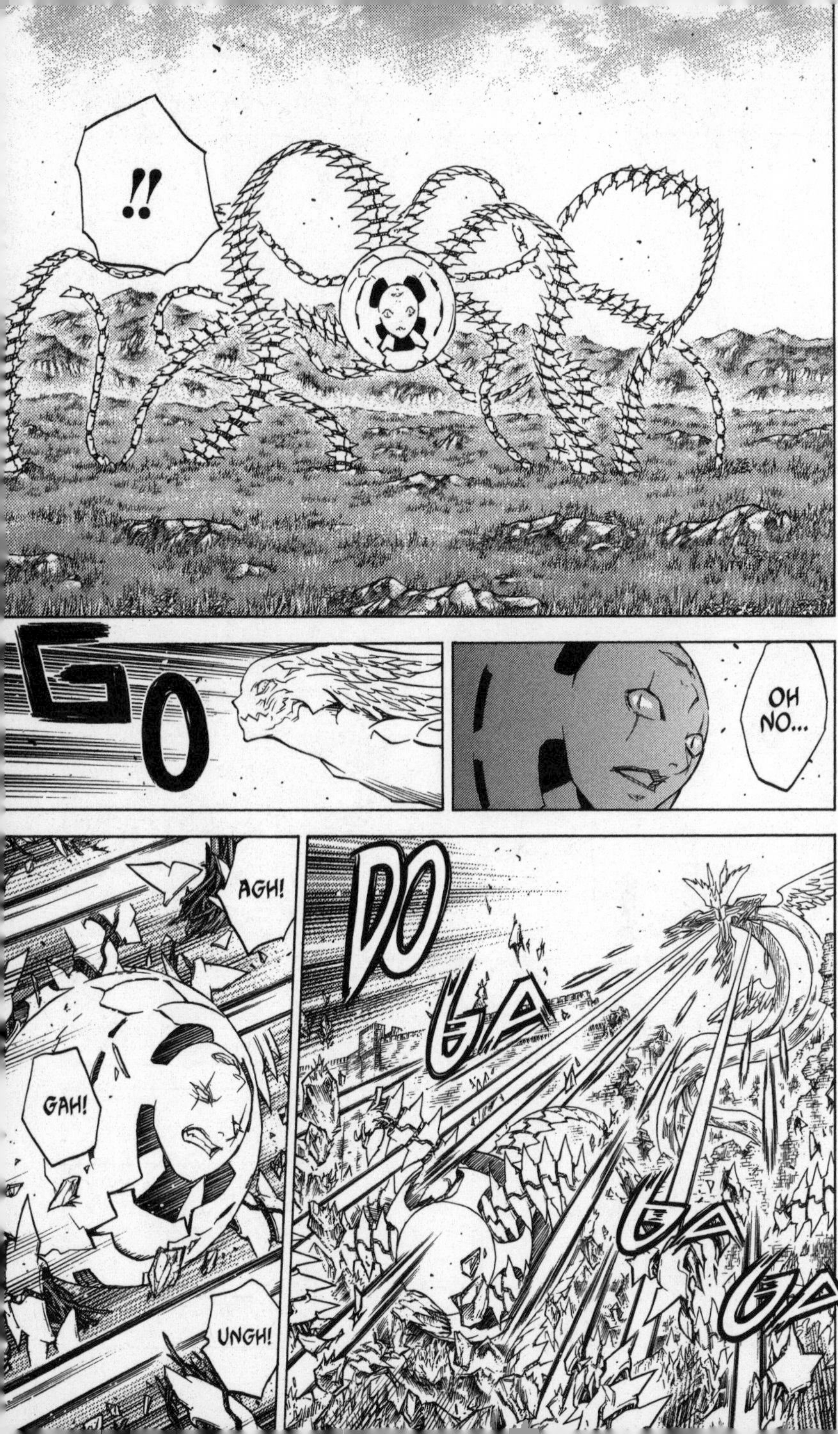
!!
OH NO...
GO
DO
GA
GA
GA
AGH!
GAH!
UNGH!

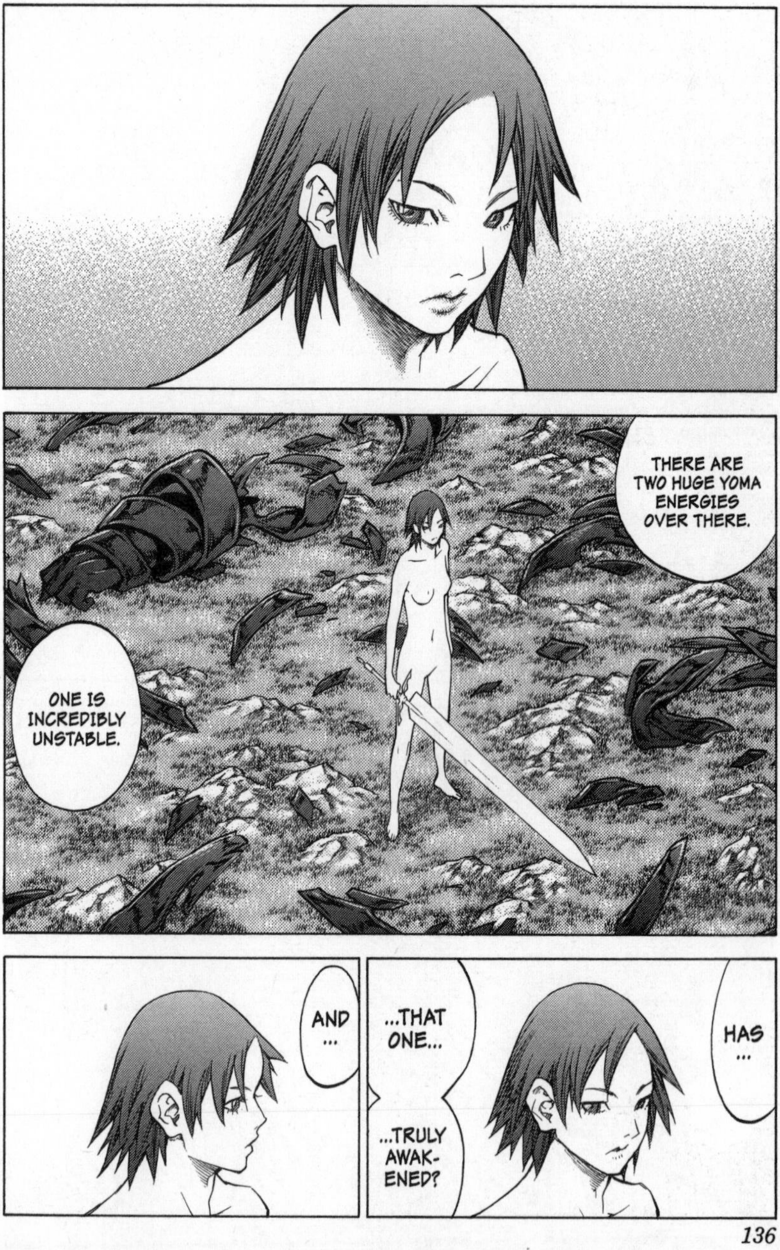
THERE ARE TWO HUGE YOMA ENERGIES OVER THERE.
ONE IS INCREDIBLY UNSTABLE.
HAS ...
...THAT ONE...
...TRULY AWAK-ENED?
AND ...

READ THIS WAY

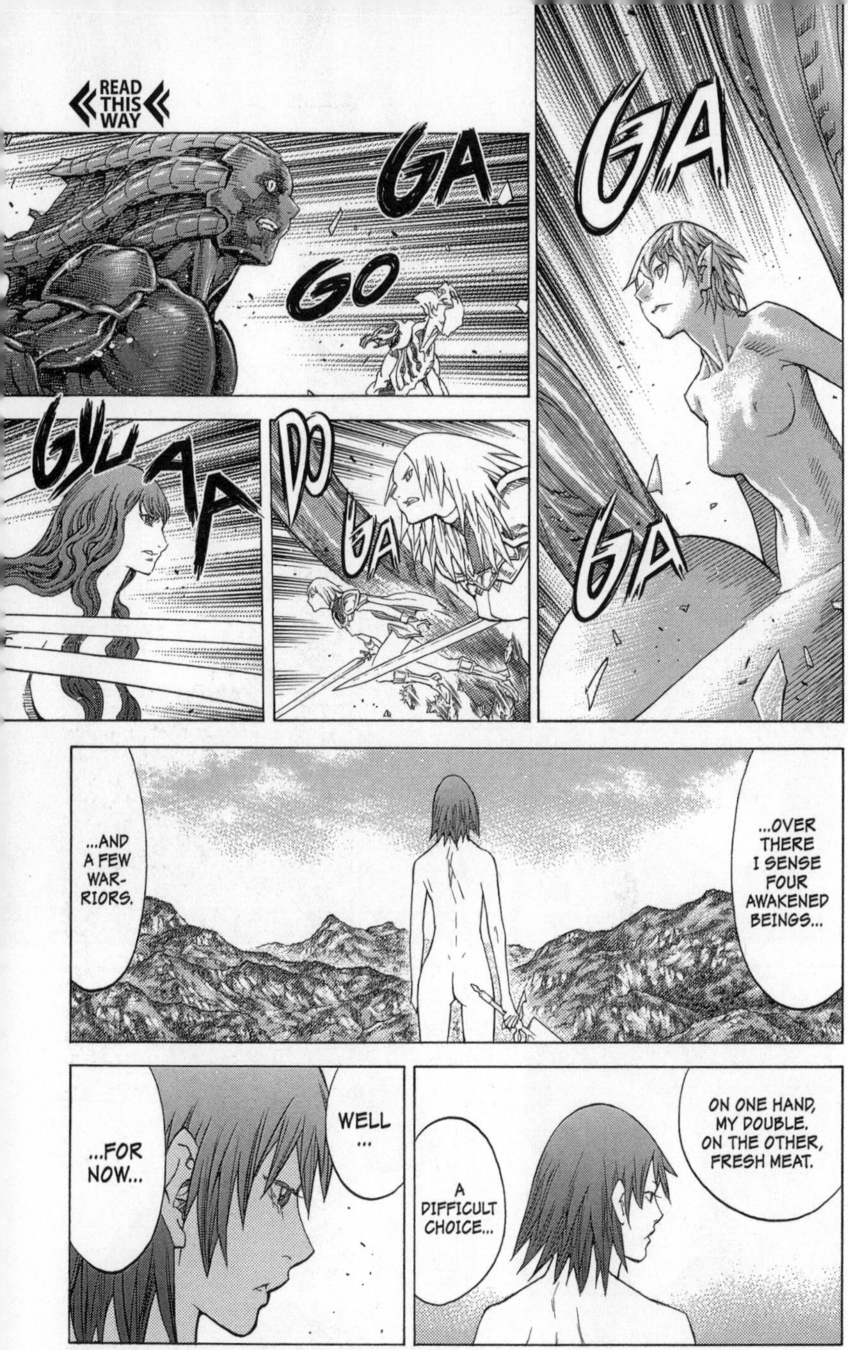
GA
GA
GA
GO
DO
GA
GYUAA
...OVER THERE I SENSE FOUR AWAKENED BEINGS...
...AND A FEW WARRIORS.
ON ONE HAND, MY DOUBLE. ON THE OTHER, FRESH MEAT.
A DIFFICULT CHOICE...
WELL ...
...FOR NOW...

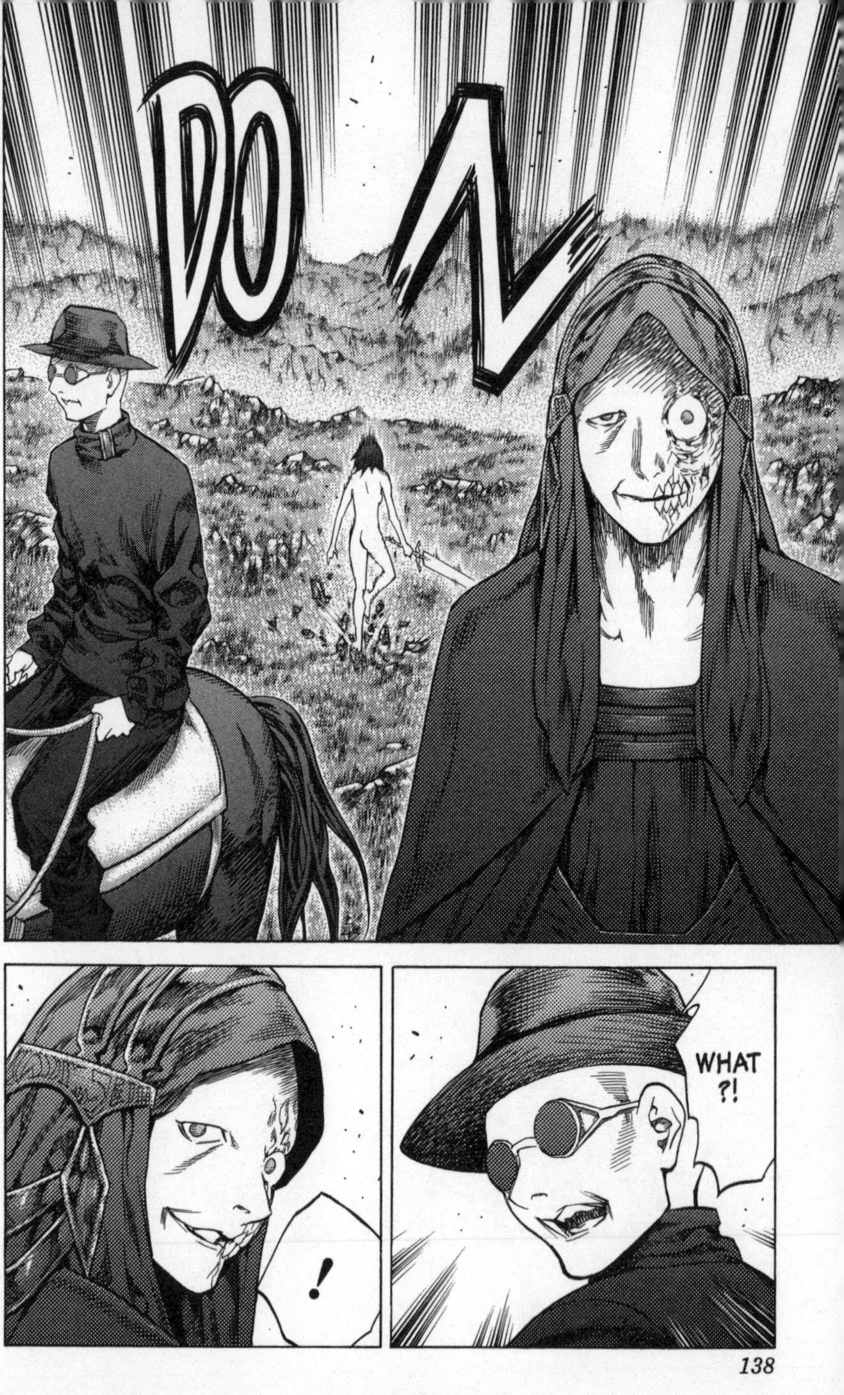
DO N
WHAT ?!
!

READ THIS WAY

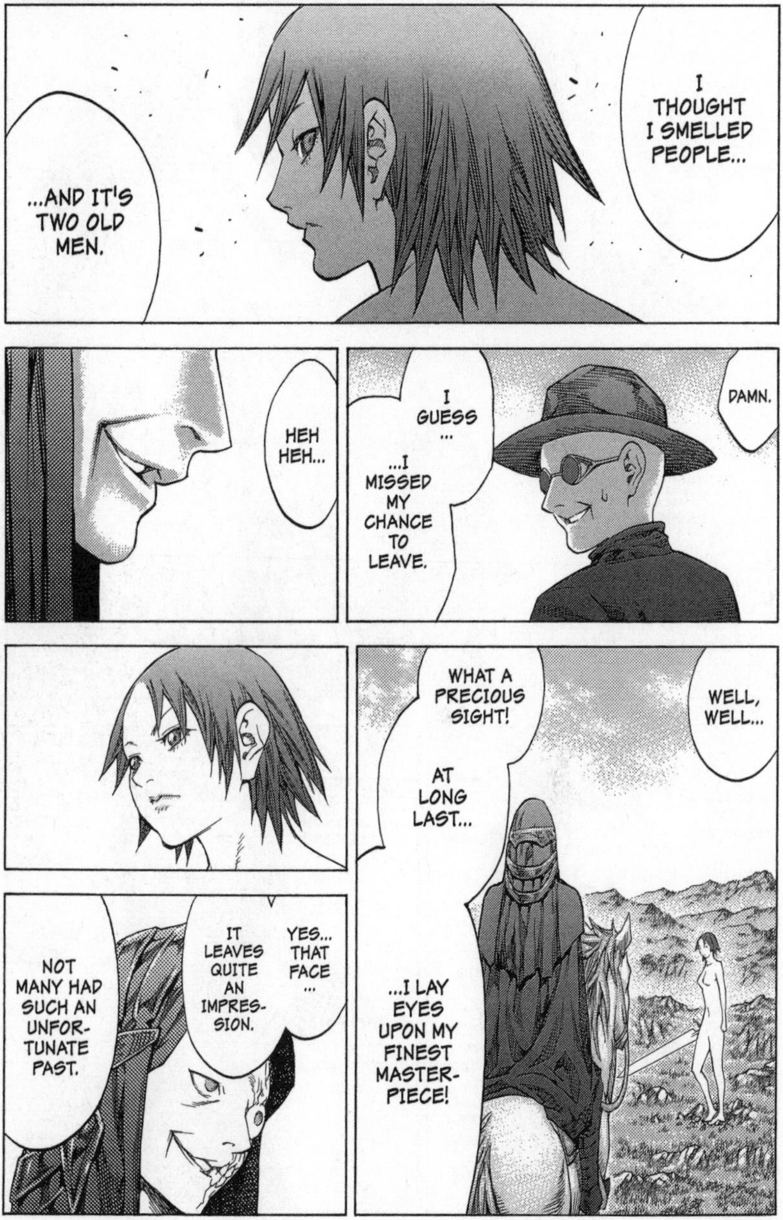

I THOUGHT I SMELLED PEOPLE...
...AND IT'S TWO OLD MEN.
DAMN.
I GUESS ...
...I MISSED MY CHANCE TO LEAVE.
HEH HEH...
WELL, WELL...
WHAT A PRECIOUS SIGHT!
AT LONG LAST...
...I LAY EYES UPON MY FINEST MASTERPIECE!
YES... THAT FACE ...
IT LEAVES QUITE AN IMPRESSION.
NOT MANY HAD SUCH AN UNFORTUNATE PAST.

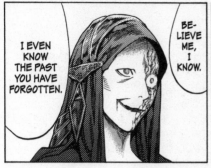

WHAT ...
...DO YOU KNOW ABOUT ME?
BE-LIEVE ME, I KNOW.
I EVEN KNOW THE PAST YOU HAVE FORGOTTEN.
INSPIRED BY THE STRONG WARRIOR YOU BECAME...
...WE SUBJECTED OTHER WARRIOR CANDIDATES TO SIMILAR TREATMENT...
...BUT IT NEVER WORKED AS WELL.
I SUPPOSE THAT'S BECAUSE ...
...IN ADDITION TO EXTREME DURESS...
...YOU TOOK THE FINAL STEP OF YOUR OWN WILL.
WHAT?
WHAT ARE YOU TALKING ABOUT?
I'M TALKING ABOUT **AFTER** YOU KILLED THE YOMA...
...WHO REPLACED YOUR FATHER.

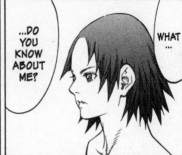

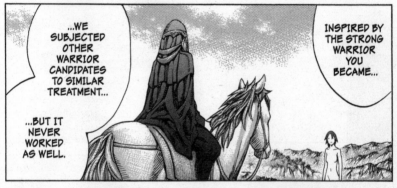

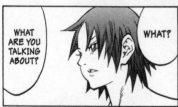

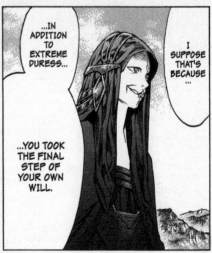

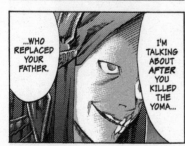

READ THIS WAY

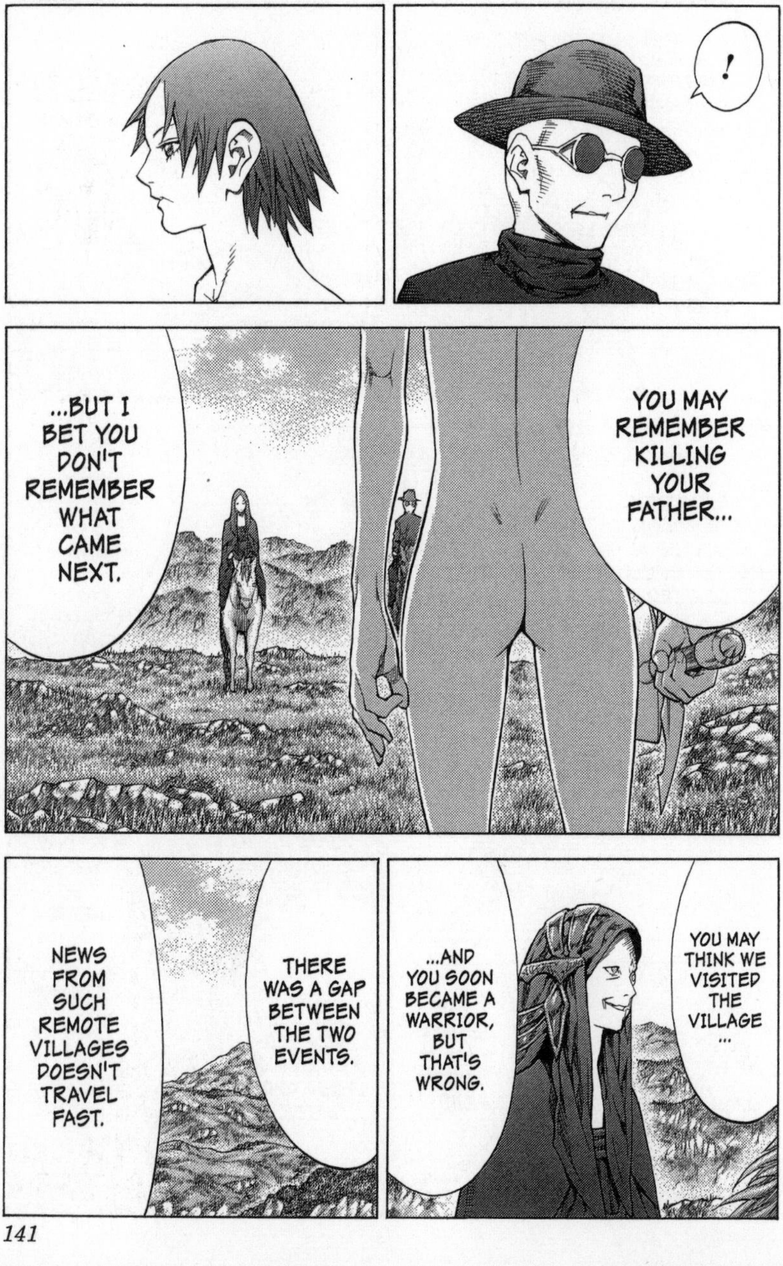
!
YOU MAY REMEMBER KILLING YOUR FATHER...
...BUT I BET YOU DON'T REMEMBER WHAT CAME NEXT.
YOU MAY THINK WE VISITED THE VILLAGE ...
...AND YOU SOON BECAME A WARRIOR, BUT THAT'S WRONG.
THERE WAS A GAP BETWEEN THE TWO EVENTS.
NEWS FROM SUCH REMOTE VILLAGES DOESN'T TRAVEL FAST.

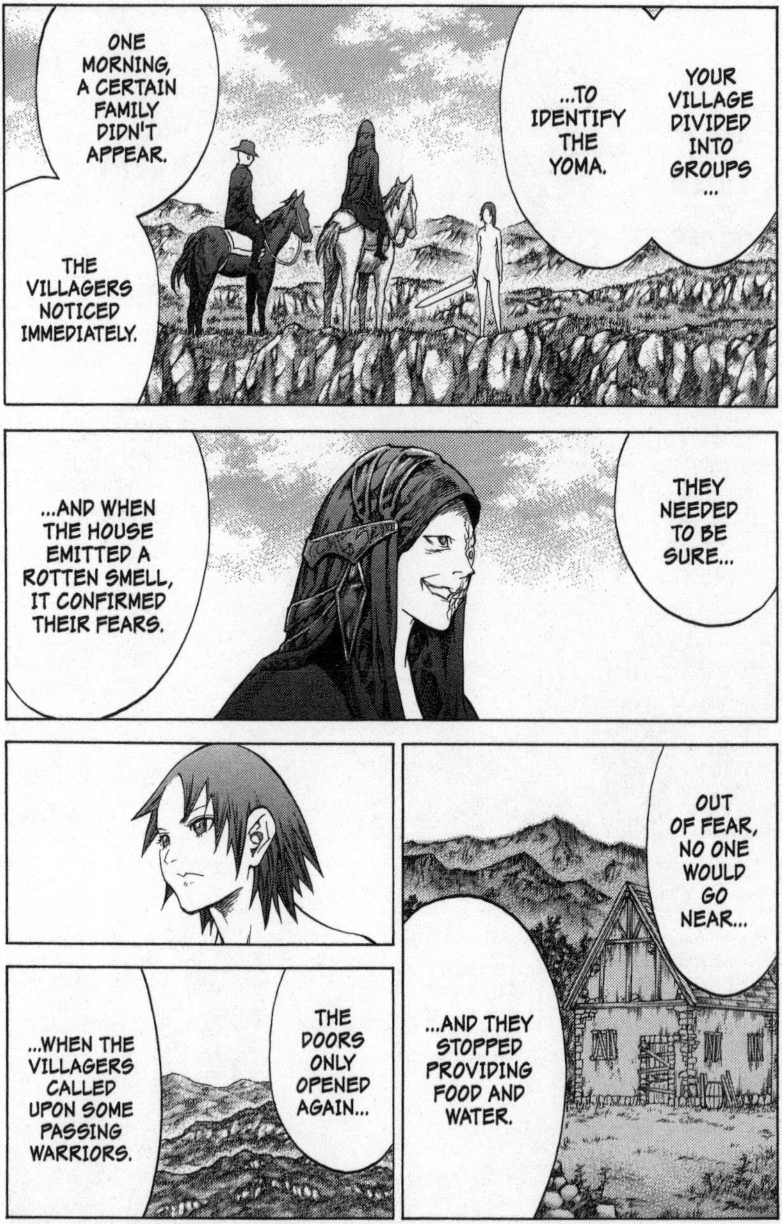
YOUR VILLAGE DIVIDED INTO GROUPS...
...TO IDENTIFY THE YOMA.
ONE MORNING, A CERTAIN FAMILY DIDN'T APPEAR.
THE VILLAGERS NOTICED IMMEDIATELY.
THEY NEEDED TO BE SURE...
...AND WHEN THE HOUSE EMITTED A ROTTEN SMELL, IT CONFIRMED THEIR FEARS.
OUT OF FEAR, NO ONE WOULD GO NEAR...
...AND THEY STOPPED PROVIDING FOOD AND WATER.
THE DOORS ONLY OPENED AGAIN...
...WHEN THE VILLAGERS CALLED UPON SOME PASSING WARRIORS.

READ THIS WAY

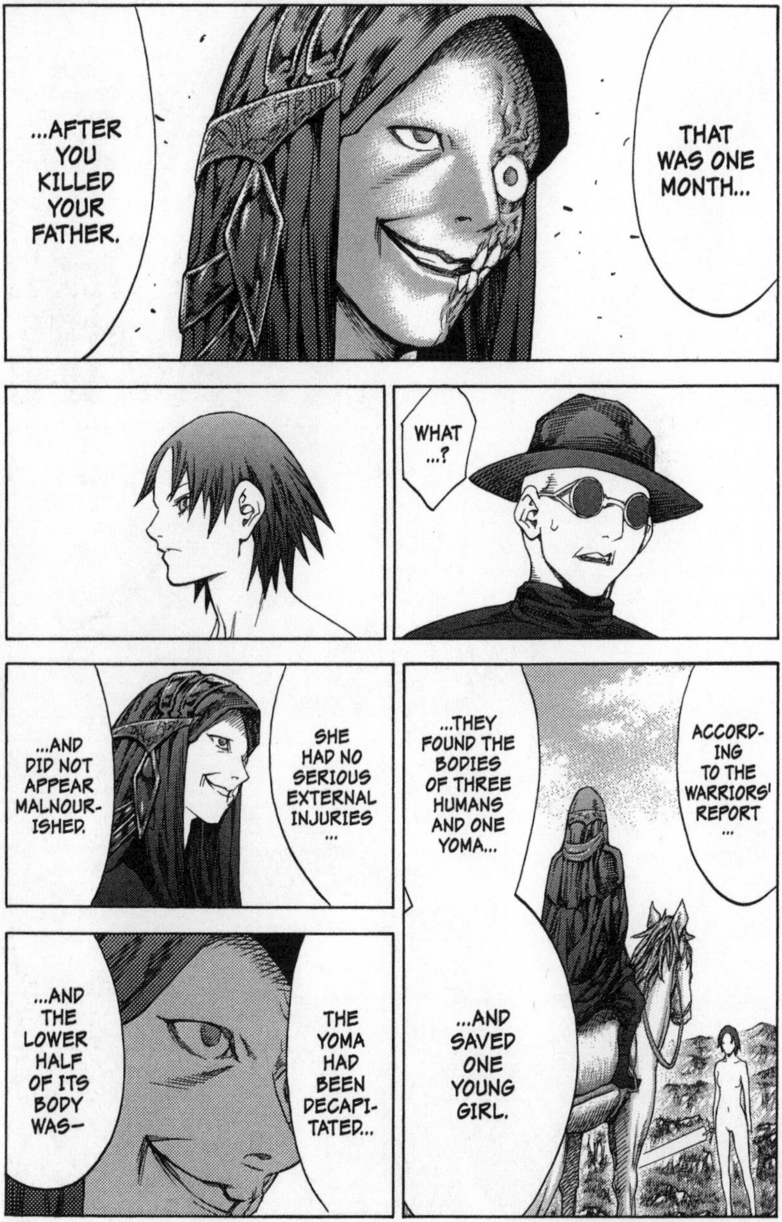
THAT WAS ONE MONTH...
...AFTER YOU KILLED YOUR FATHER.
WHAT ...?
ACCORD-ING TO THE WARRIORS' REPORT ...
...THEY FOUND THE BODIES OF THREE HUMANS AND ONE YOMA...
...AND SAVED ONE YOUNG GIRL.
SHE HAD NO SERIOUS EXTERNAL INJURIES ...
...AND DID NOT APPEAR MALNOUR-ISHED.
THE YOMA HAD BEEN DECAPI-TATED...
...AND THE LOWER HALF OF ITS BODY WAS—

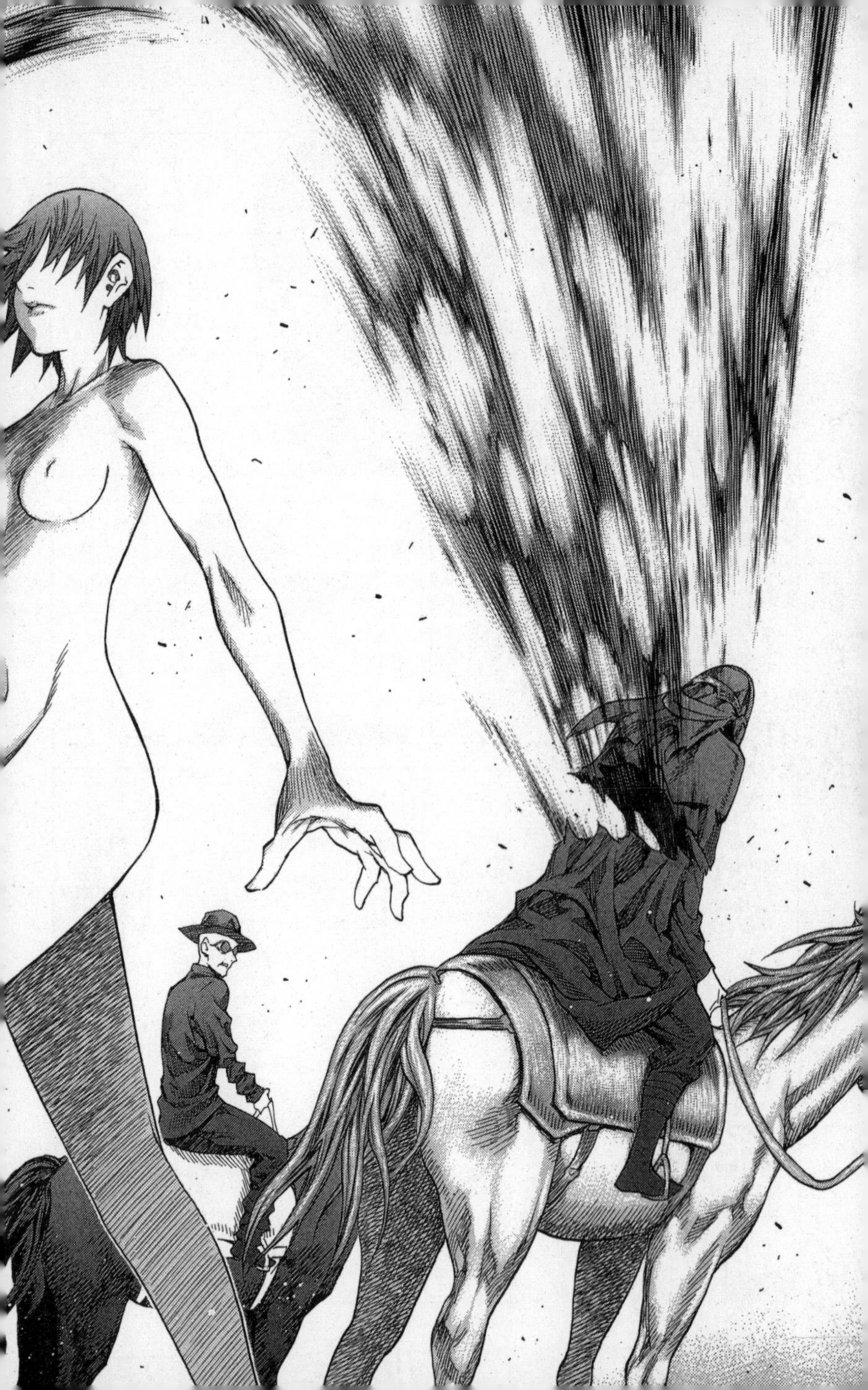

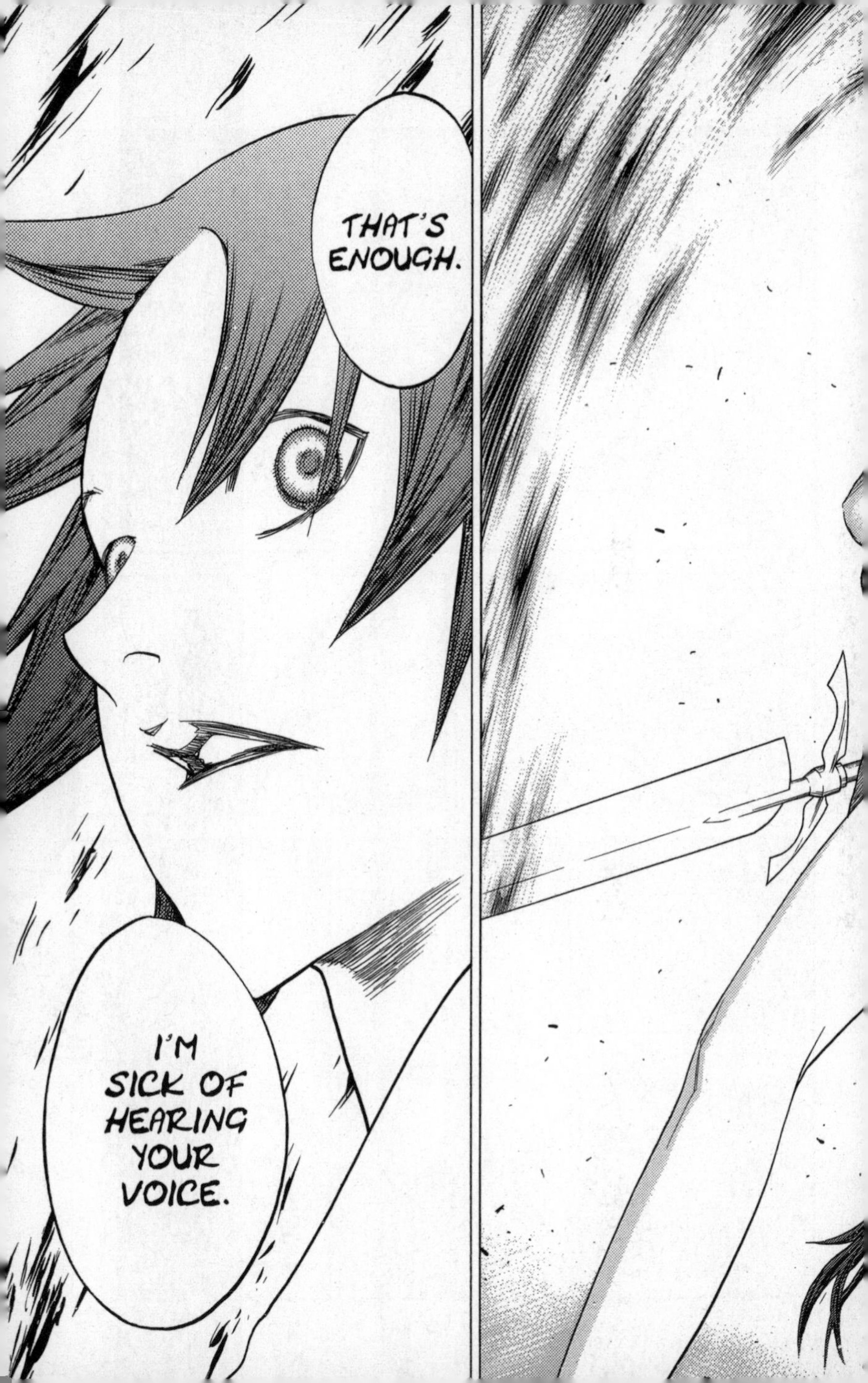
THAT'S ENOUGH.
I'M SICK OF HEARING YOUR VOICE.

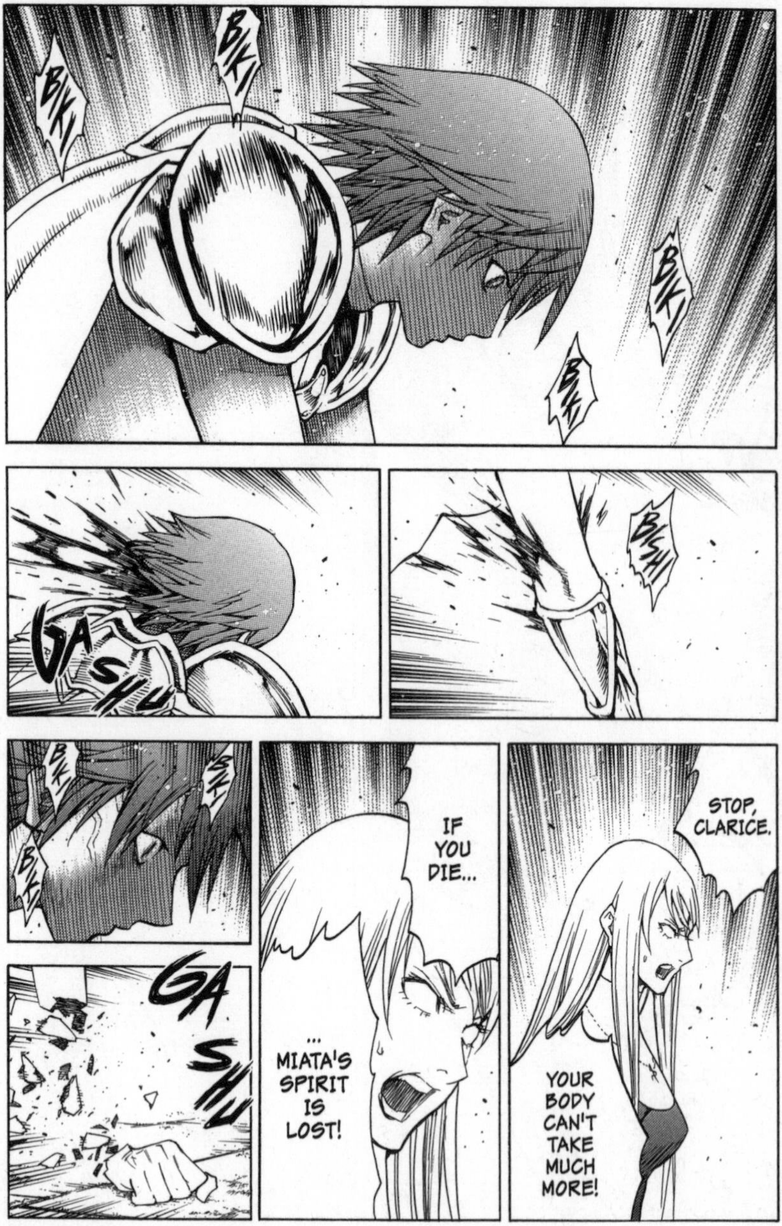
BIKI
BIKI
BIKI
BIKI
BISH
GASHU
STOP, CLARICE.
YOUR BODY CAN'T TAKE MUCH MORE!
IF YOU DIE...
...MIATA'S SPIRIT IS LOST!
BIKI
BIKI
BIKI
GASHU

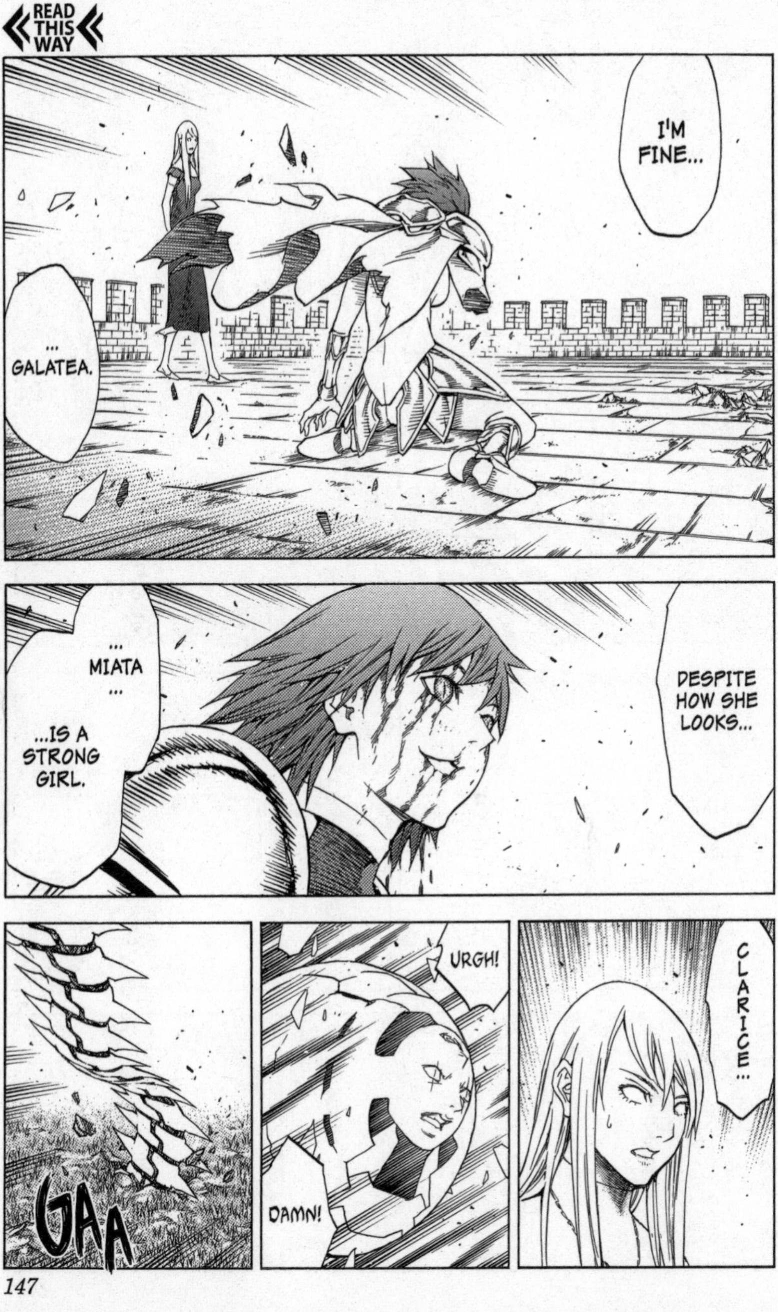
READ THIS WAY
I'M FINE...
... GALATEA.
DESPITE HOW SHE LOOKS...
... MIATA ...
...IS A STRONG GIRL.
CLARICE...
URGH!
DAMN!
GAA

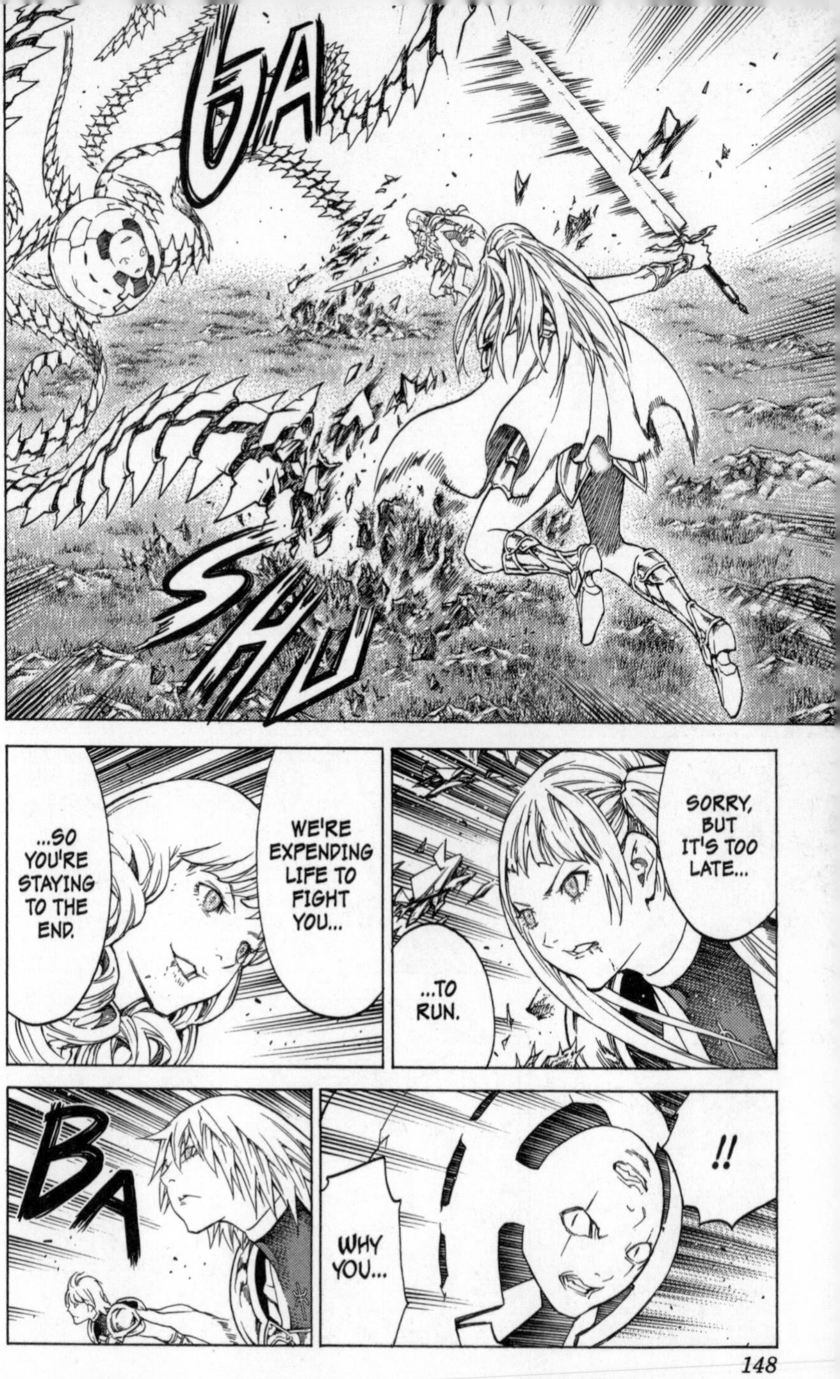
BA
SHU
SORRY, BUT IT'S TOO LATE...
...TO RUN.
WE'RE EXPENDING LIFE TO FIGHT YOU...
...SO YOU'RE STAYING TO THE END.
!!
WHY YOU...
BA

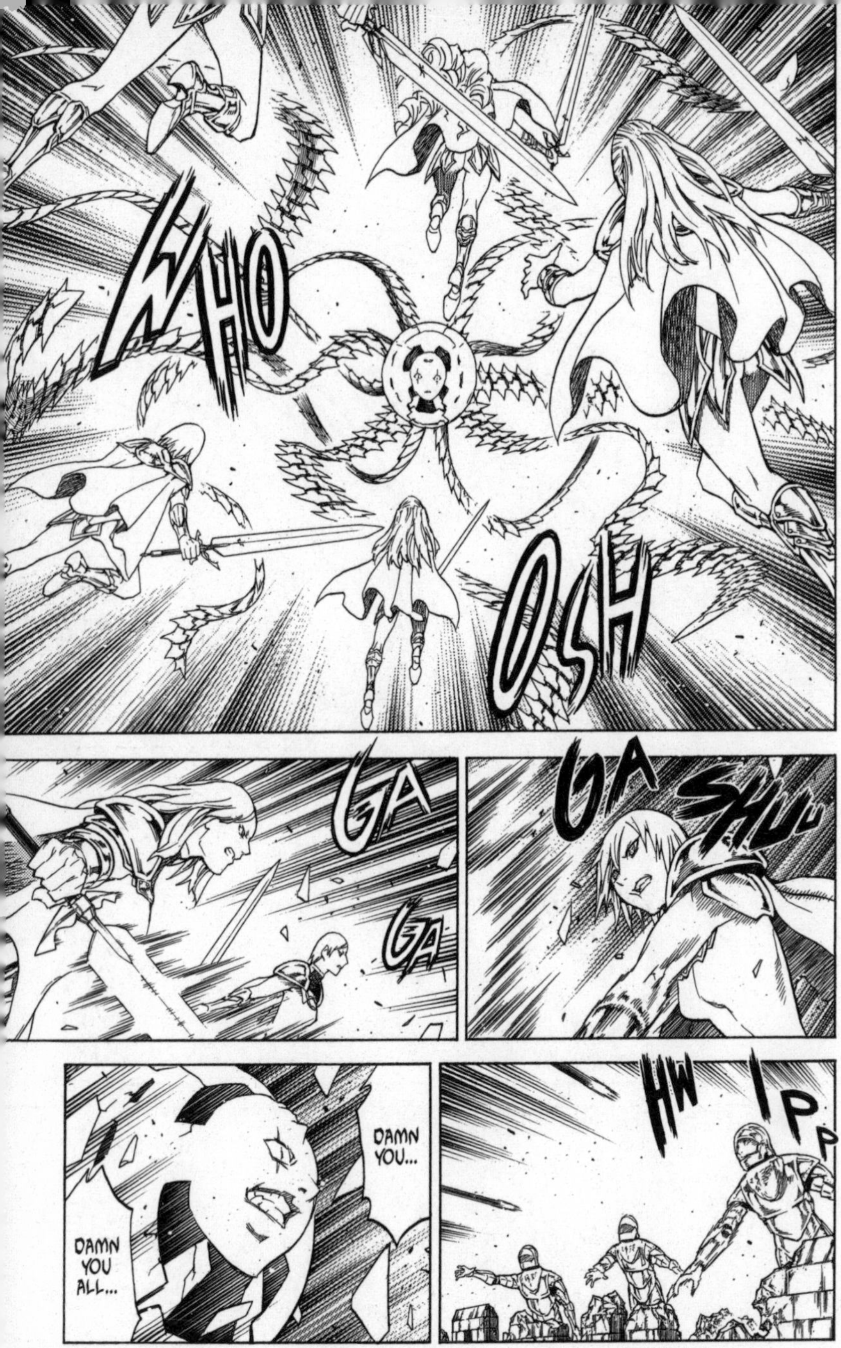
WHO
OSH
GA
SHU
GA
GA
HW
IPP
DAMN YOU...
DAMN YOU ALL...

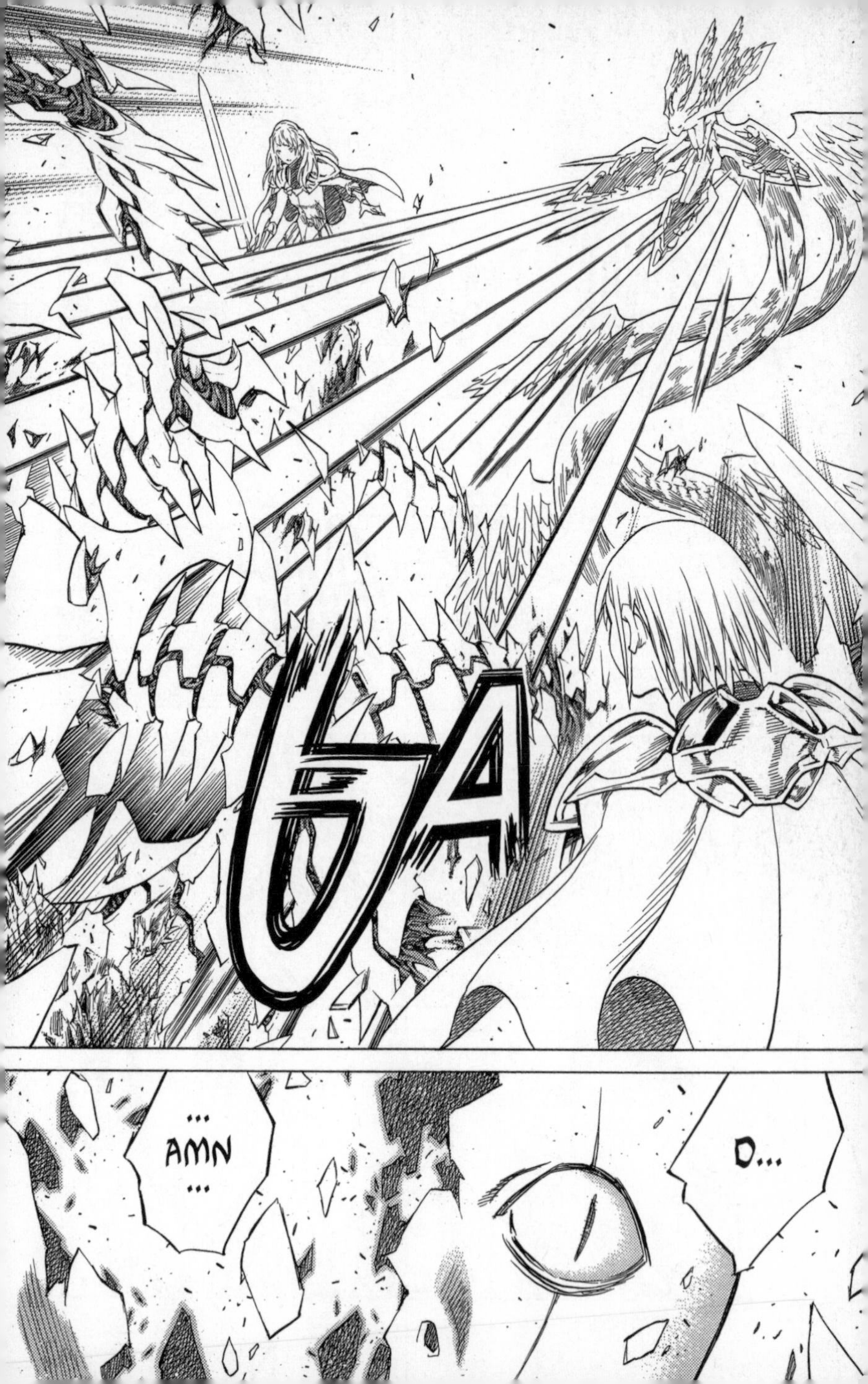
GA
D...
...
AMN
...

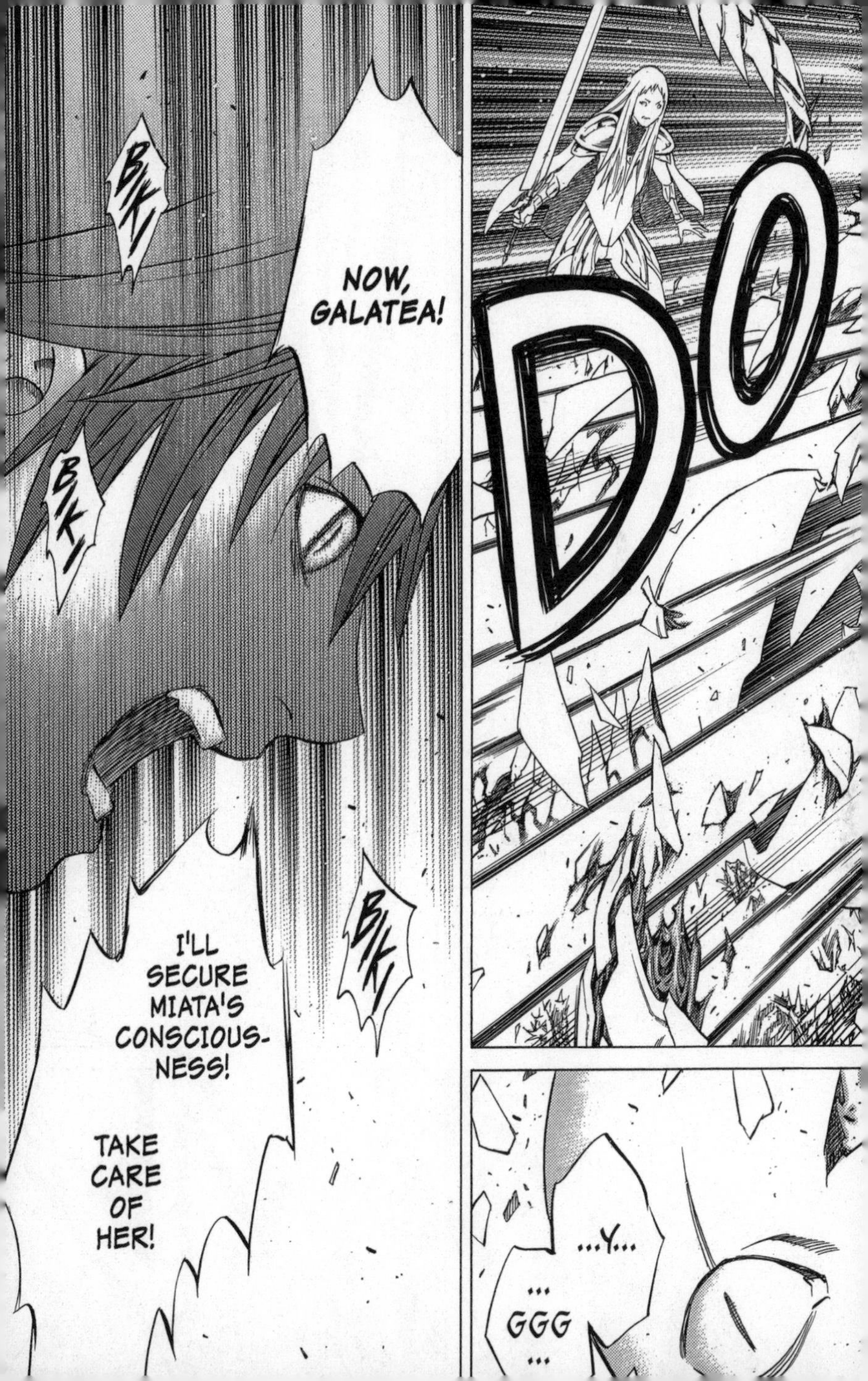
DO
...Y...
...
GGG
...
BIKI
NOW, GALATEA!
BIKI
BIKI
I'LL SECURE MIATA'S CONSCIOUS-NESS!
TAKE CARE OF HER!

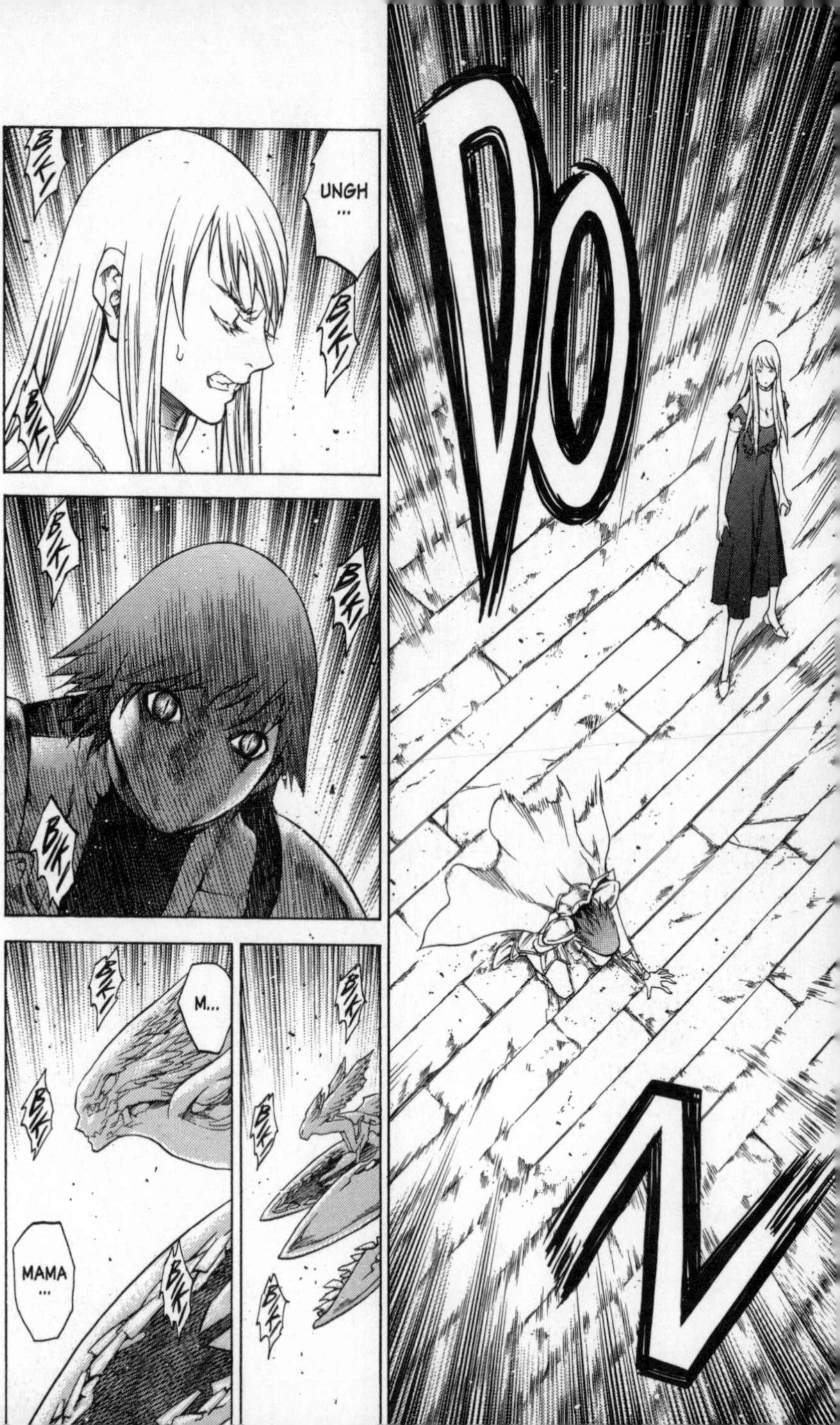
DO
N
BIKI
UNGH ...
BIKI
BIKI
BIKI
BIKI
BIKI
BIKI
BIKI
BIKI
BIKI
M...
BIKI
MAMA ...
BIKI

READ THIS WAY

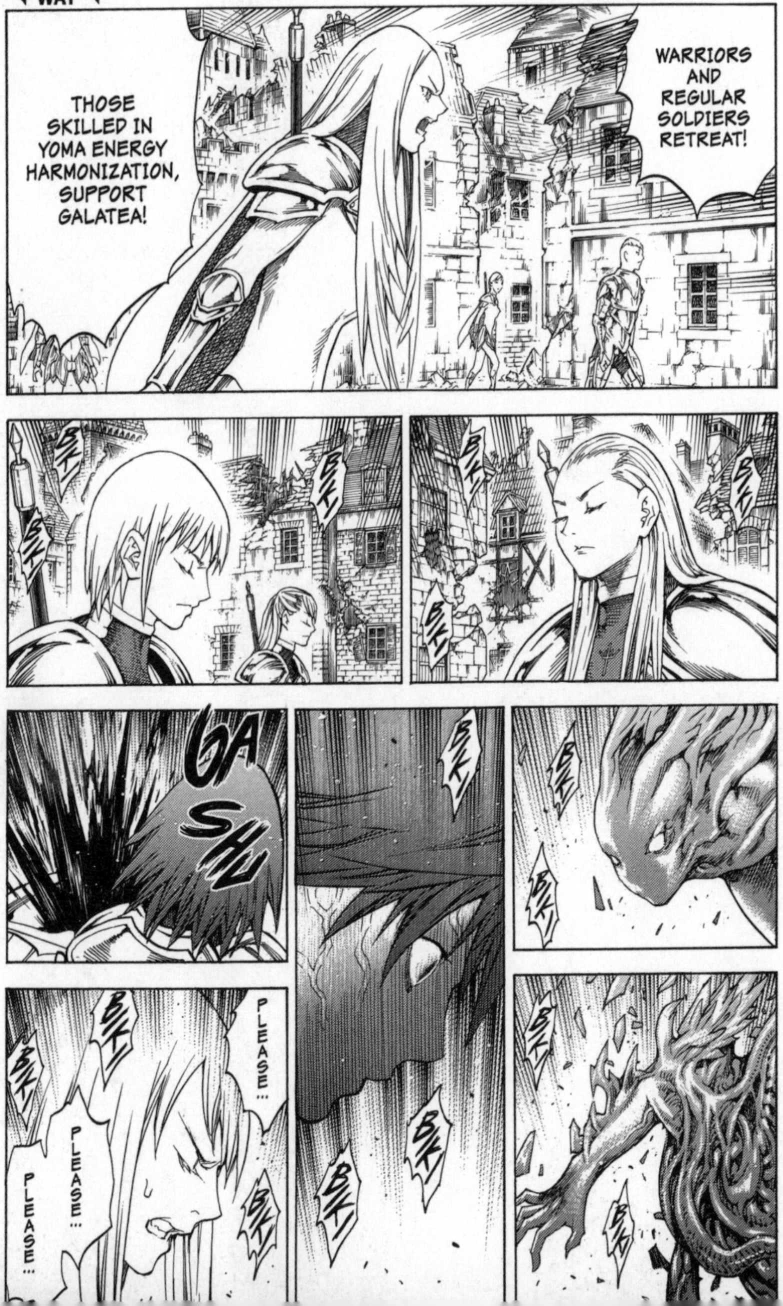
WARRIORS AND REGULAR SOLDIERS RETREAT!
THOSE SKILLED IN YOMA ENERGY HARMONIZATION, SUPPORT GALATEA!
BKI
BKI
BKI
BKI
BKI
BKI
BKI
BKI
BKI
BKI
BKI
BKI
BKI
BKI
GASHU
BKI
BKI
PLEASE...
PLEASE...
PLEASE...
BKI

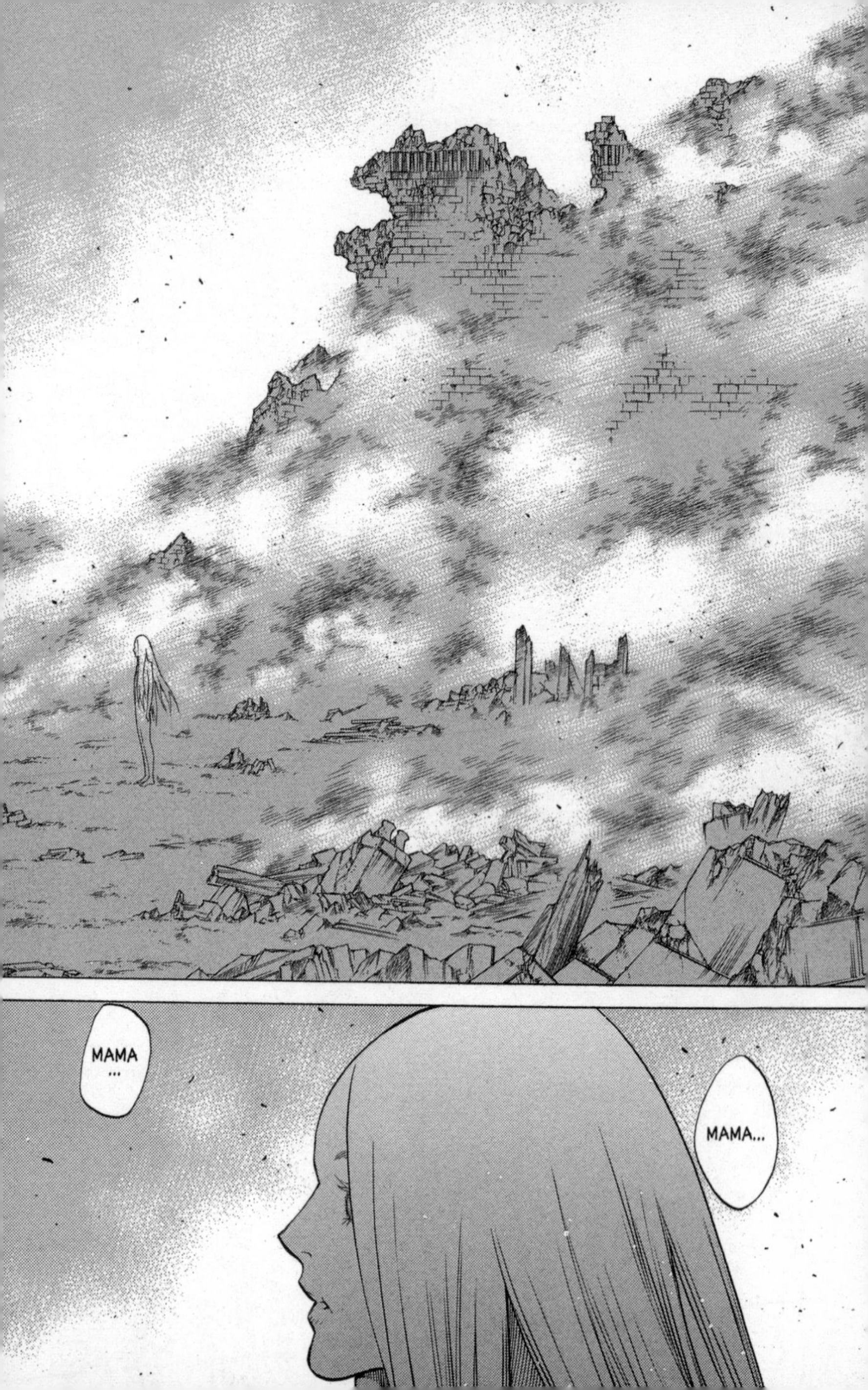
MAMA...
MAMA ...

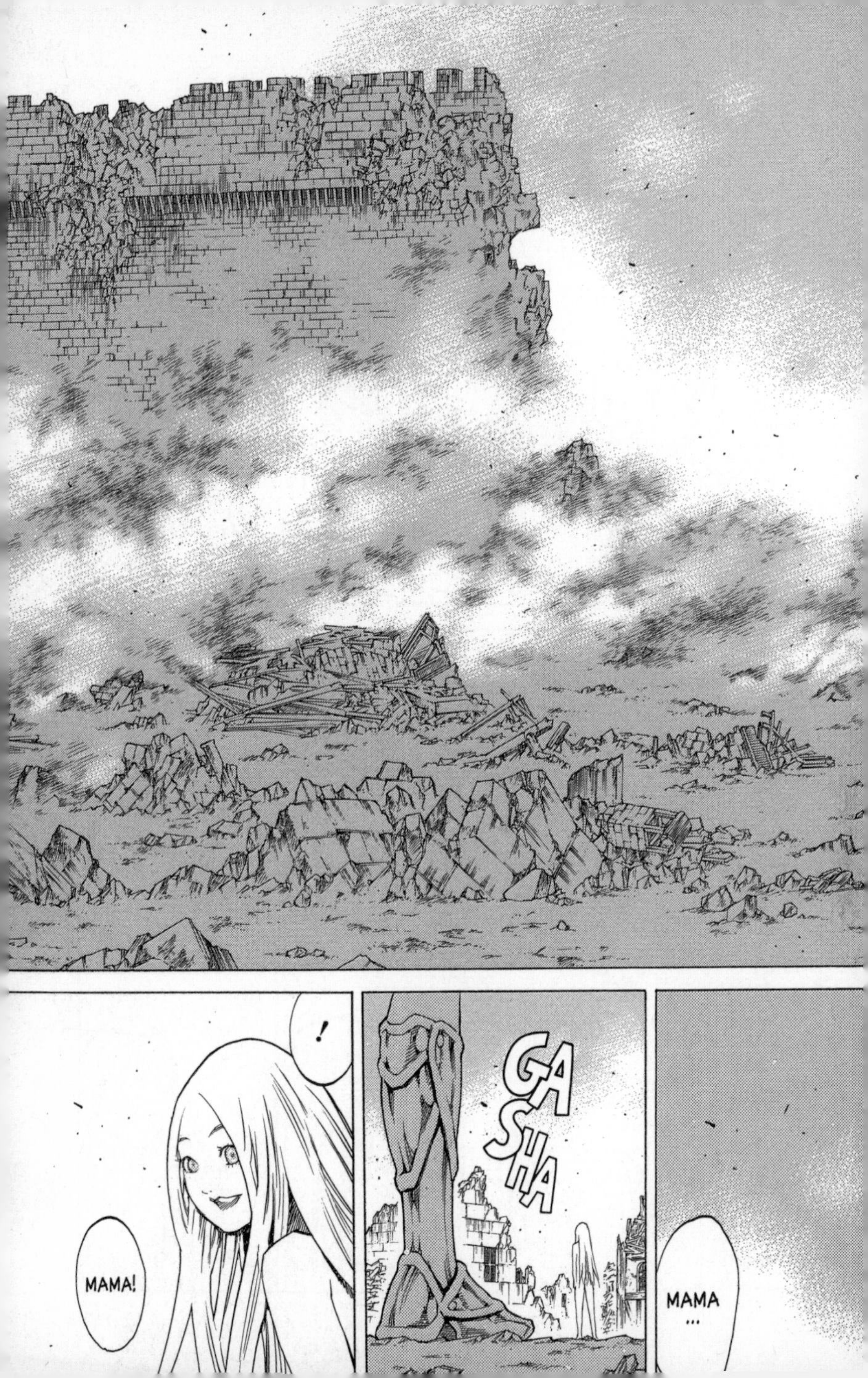
MAMA
...
GASHA
!
MAMA!

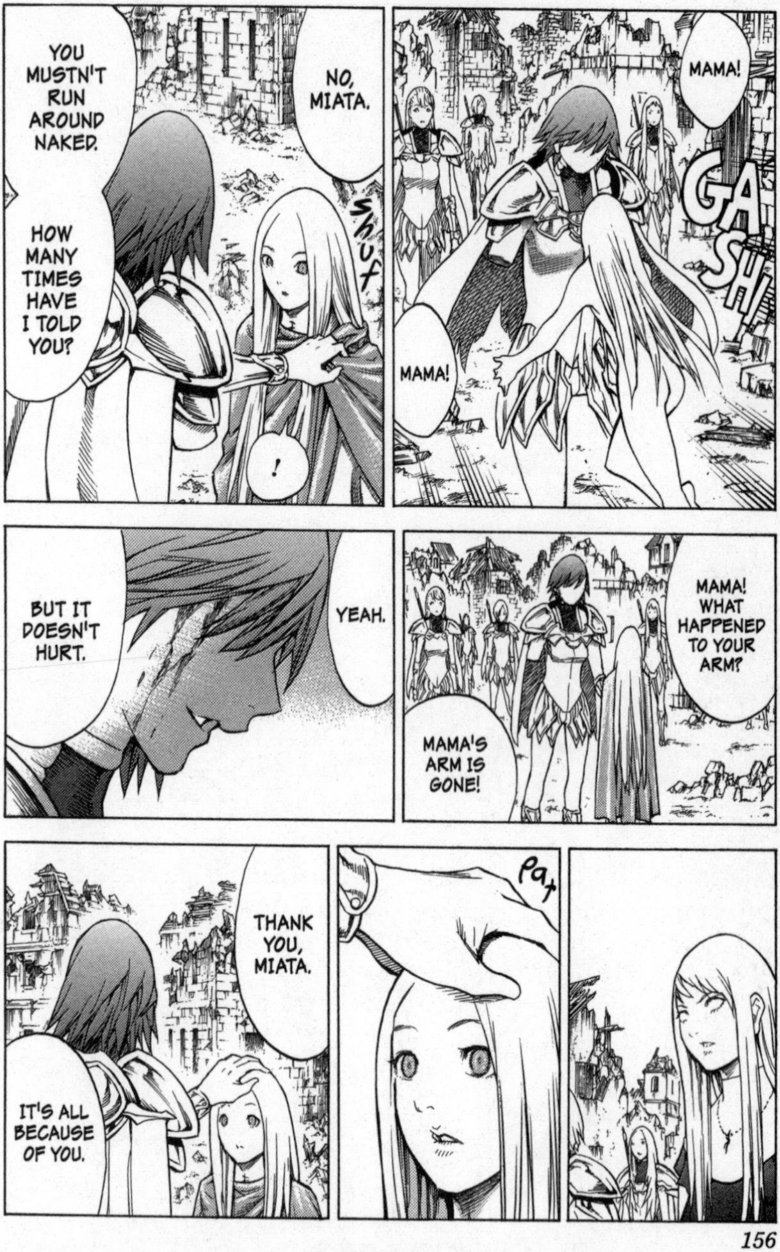
MAMA!
GASHI
MAMA!
NO, MIATA.
SHUF
YOU MUSTN'T RUN AROUND NAKED.
HOW MANY TIMES HAVE I TOLD YOU?
!
MAMA! WHAT HAPPENED TO YOUR ARM?
MAMA'S ARM IS GONE!
YEAH.
BUT IT DOESN'T HURT.
PAT
THANK YOU, MIATA.
IT'S ALL BECAUSE OF YOU.

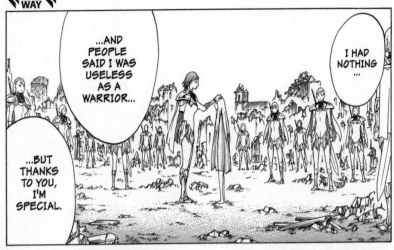

READ THIS WAY

I HAD NOTHING ...
...AND PEOPLE SAID I WAS USELESS AS A WARRIOR...
...BUT THANKS TO YOU, I'M SPECIAL.
MAMA ?
YOU'RE A STRONG GIRL.
YOU'LL BE FINE.
YOU CAN MAKE IT ALONE.
NOW CLOSE YOUR EYES.
I'M GOING TO DO MAGIC ON YOU.
MAGIC?
IT WILL MAKE YOU STRONGER ...
...NOW AND FOR-EVER.
I LOVE YOU, MIATA.

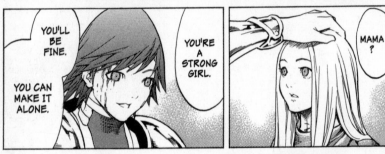

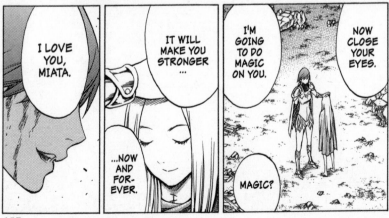

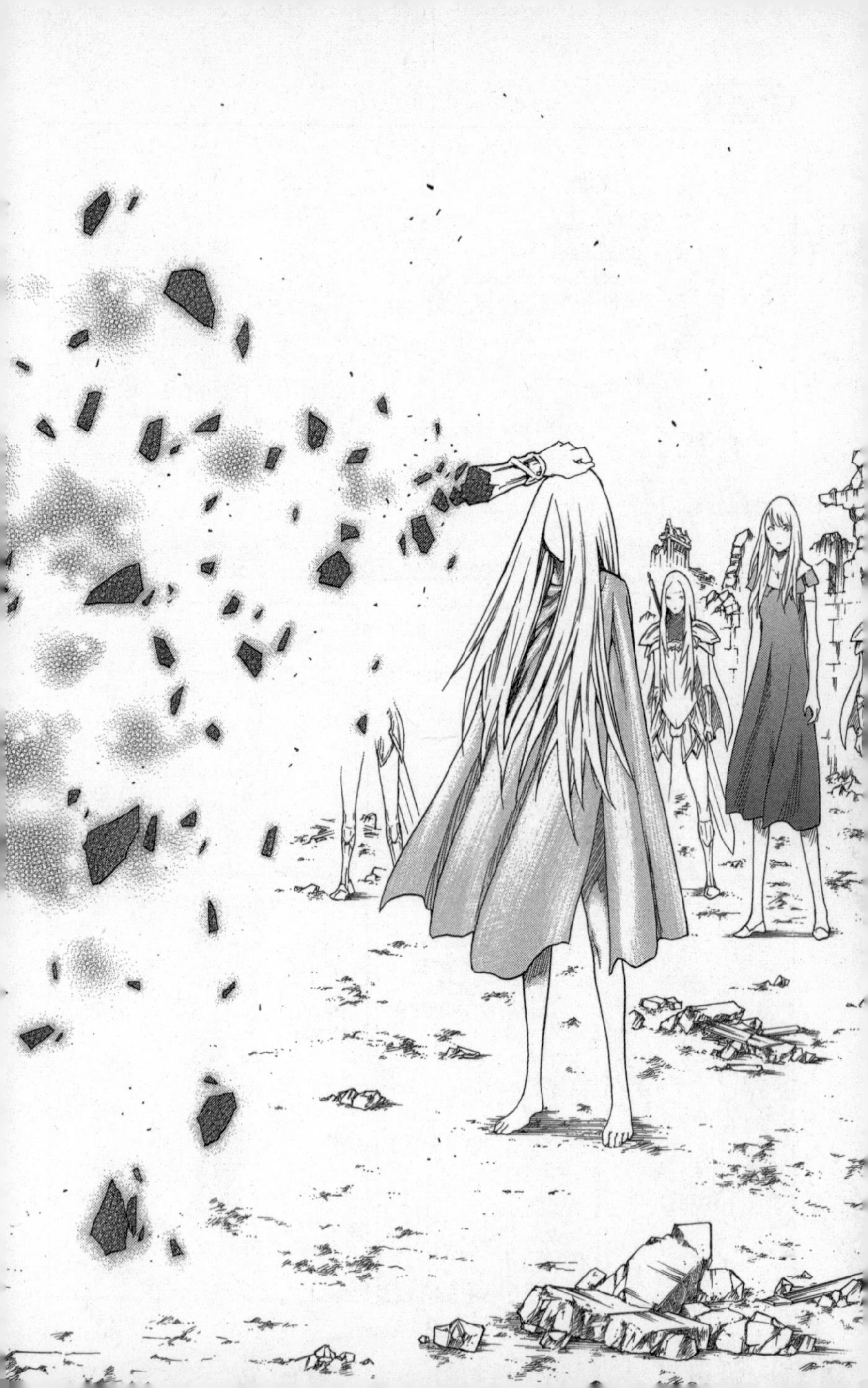

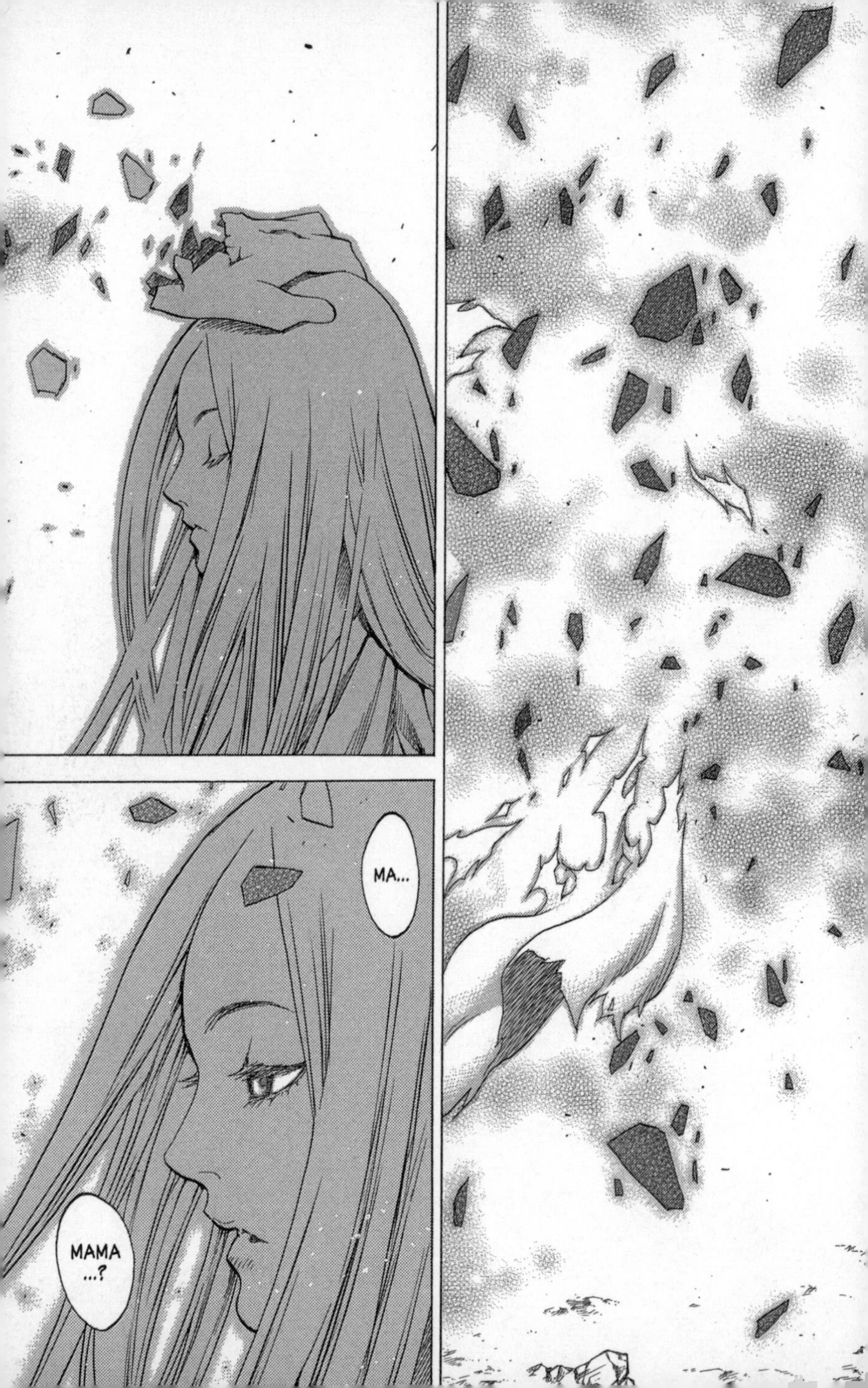
MA...
MAMA ...?

クレイモア
Claymore

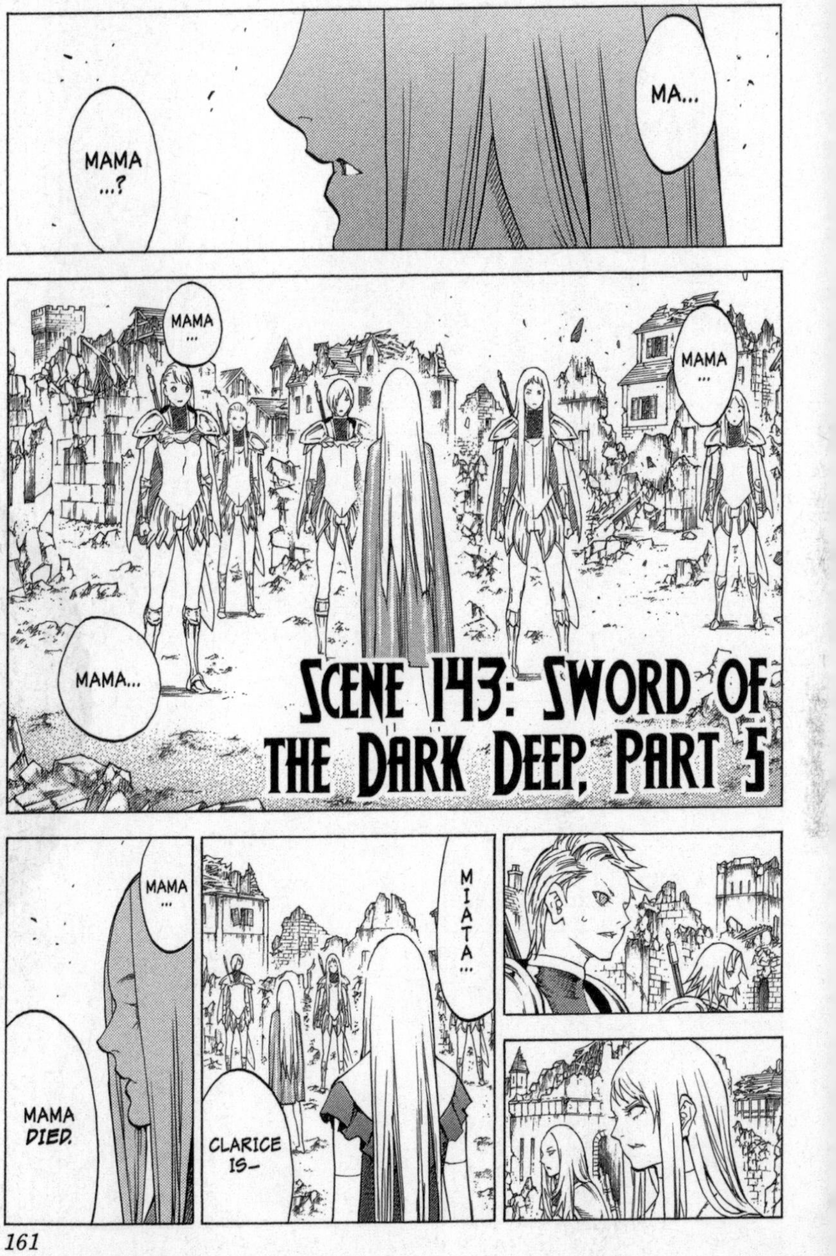
MA...
MAMA ...?
MAMA ...
MAMA ...
MAMA...
SCENE 143: SWORD OF THE DARK DEEP, PART 5
MIATA...
CLARICE IS—
MAMA ...
MAMA DIED.

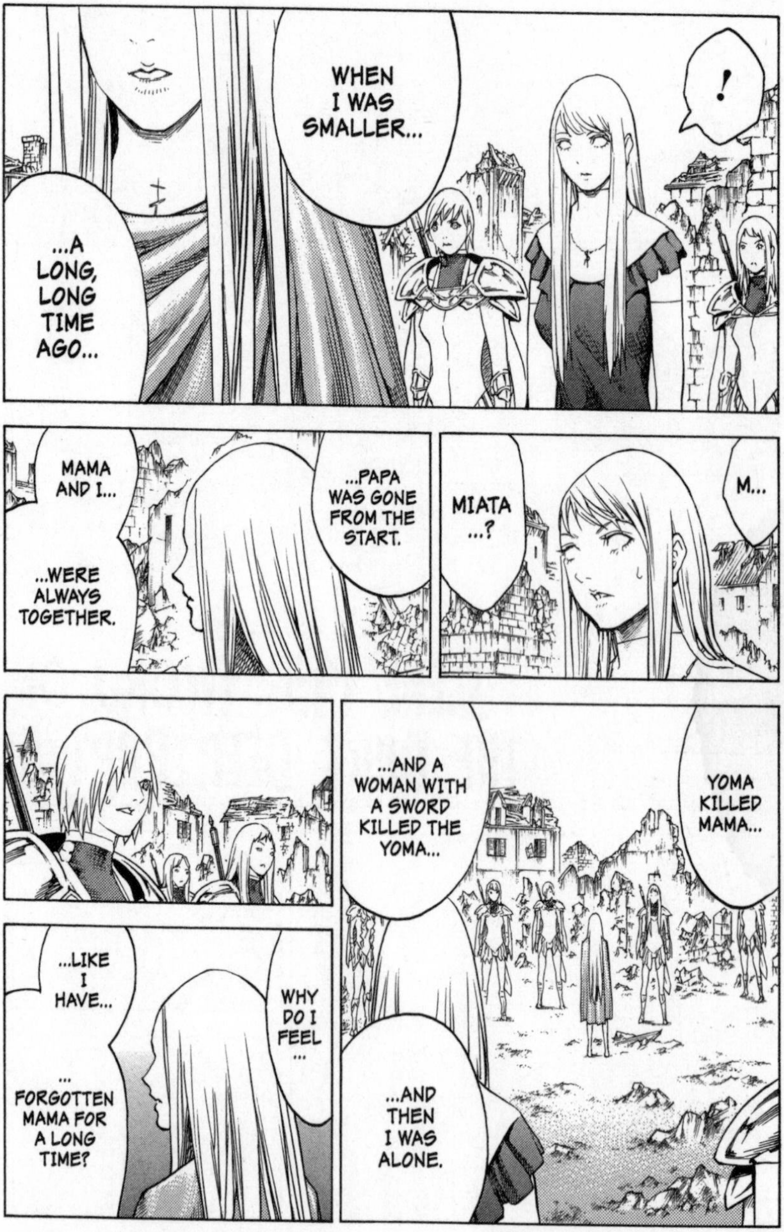
!
WHEN I WAS SMALLER...
...A LONG, LONG TIME AGO...
M...
MIATA ...?
...PAPA WAS GONE FROM THE START.
MAMA AND I...
...WERE ALWAYS TOGETHER.
YOMA KILLED MAMA...
...AND A WOMAN WITH A SWORD KILLED THE YOMA...
...AND THEN I WAS ALONE.
WHY DO I FEEL ...
...LIKE I HAVE...
... FORGOTTEN MAMA FOR A LONG TIME?

READ THIS WAY

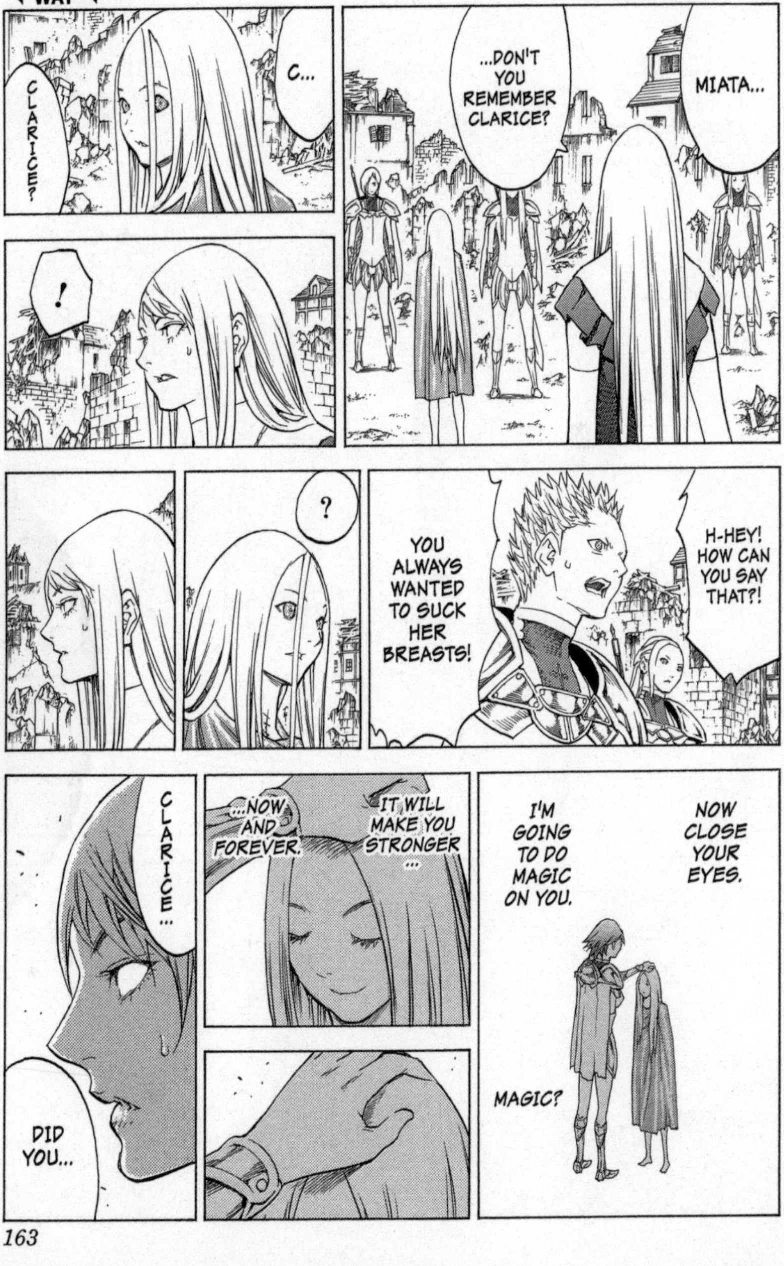

MIATA...
...DON'T YOU REMEMBER CLARICE?
C...
CLARICE?
!
H-HEY! HOW CAN YOU SAY THAT?!
YOU ALWAYS WANTED TO SUCK HER BREASTS!
?
NOW CLOSE YOUR EYES.
I'M GOING TO DO MAGIC ON YOU.
MAGIC?
IT WILL MAKE YOU STRONGER...
...NOW AND FOREVER.
CLARICE...
DID YOU...

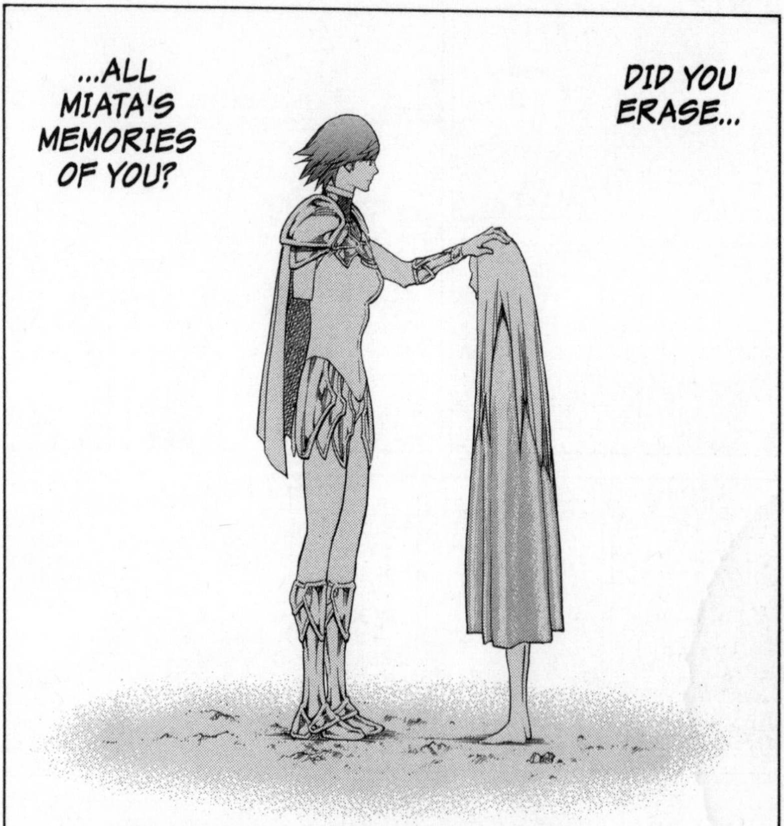
DID YOU ERASE...
...ALL MIATA'S MEMORIES OF YOU?

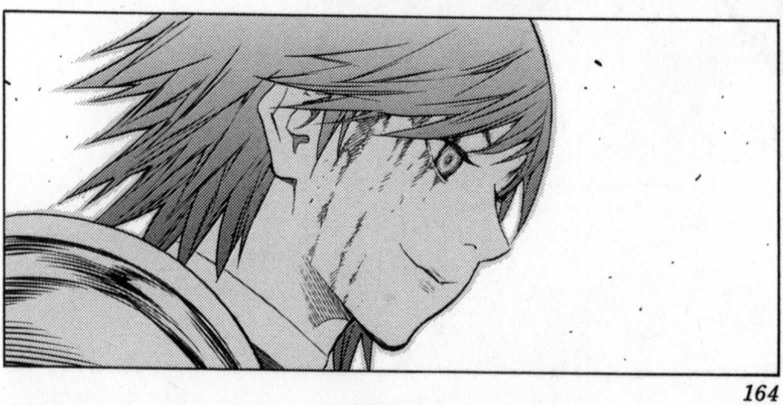

READ THIS WAY

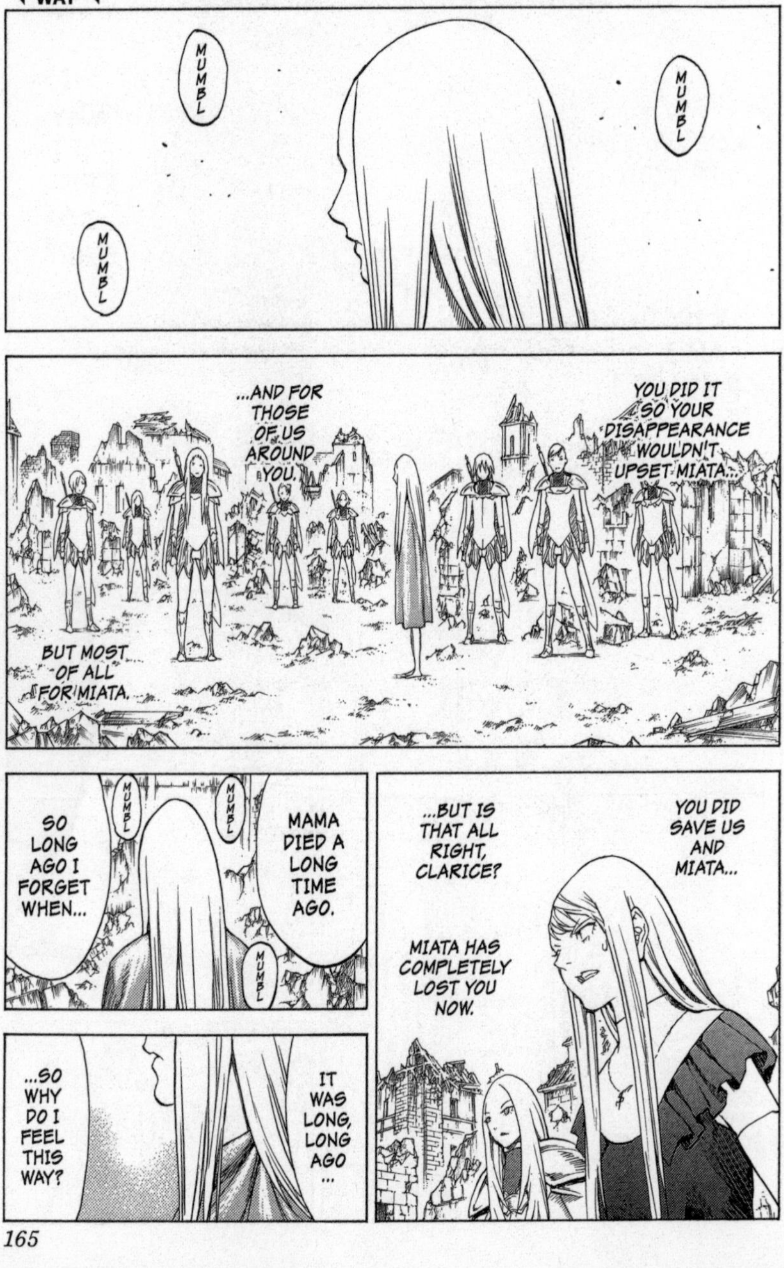
MUMBL
MUMBL
MUMBL
YOU DID IT SO YOUR DISAPPEARANCE WOULDN'T UPSET MIATA...
...AND FOR THOSE OF US AROUND YOU.
BUT MOST OF ALL FOR MIATA.
YOU DID SAVE US AND MIATA...
...BUT IS THAT ALL RIGHT, CLARICE?
MIATA HAS COMPLETELY LOST YOU NOW.
MUMBL
MAMA DIED A LONG TIME AGO.
MUMBL
SO LONG AGO I FORGET WHEN...
MUMBL
IT WAS LONG, LONG AGO...
...SO WHY DO I FEEL THIS WAY?

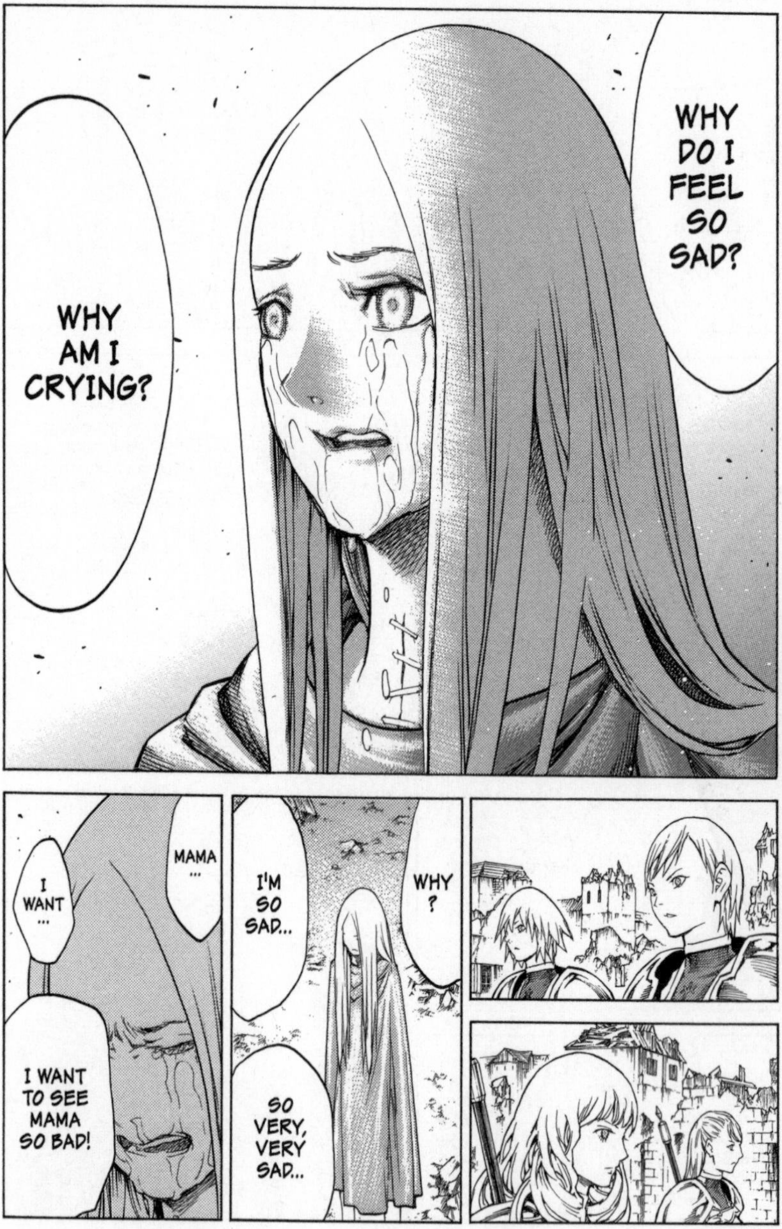
WHY DO I FEEL SO SAD?
WHY AM I CRYING?
WHY?
I'M SO SAD...
SO VERY, VERY SAD...
MAMA...
I WANT...
I WANT TO SEE MAMA SO BAD!

READ THIS WAY

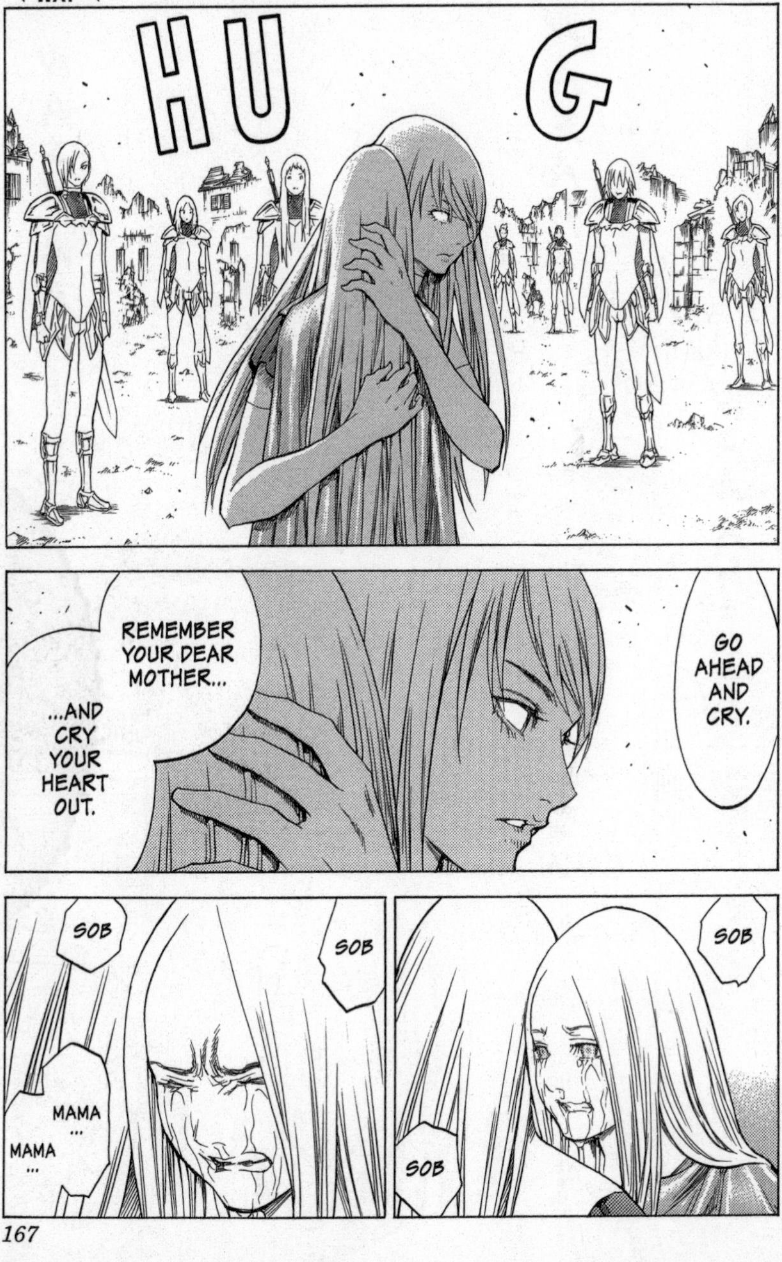
HUG
GO AHEAD AND CRY.
REMEMBER YOUR DEAR MOTHER...
...AND CRY YOUR HEART OUT.
SOB
SOB
SOB
SOB
MAMA ...
MAMA ...

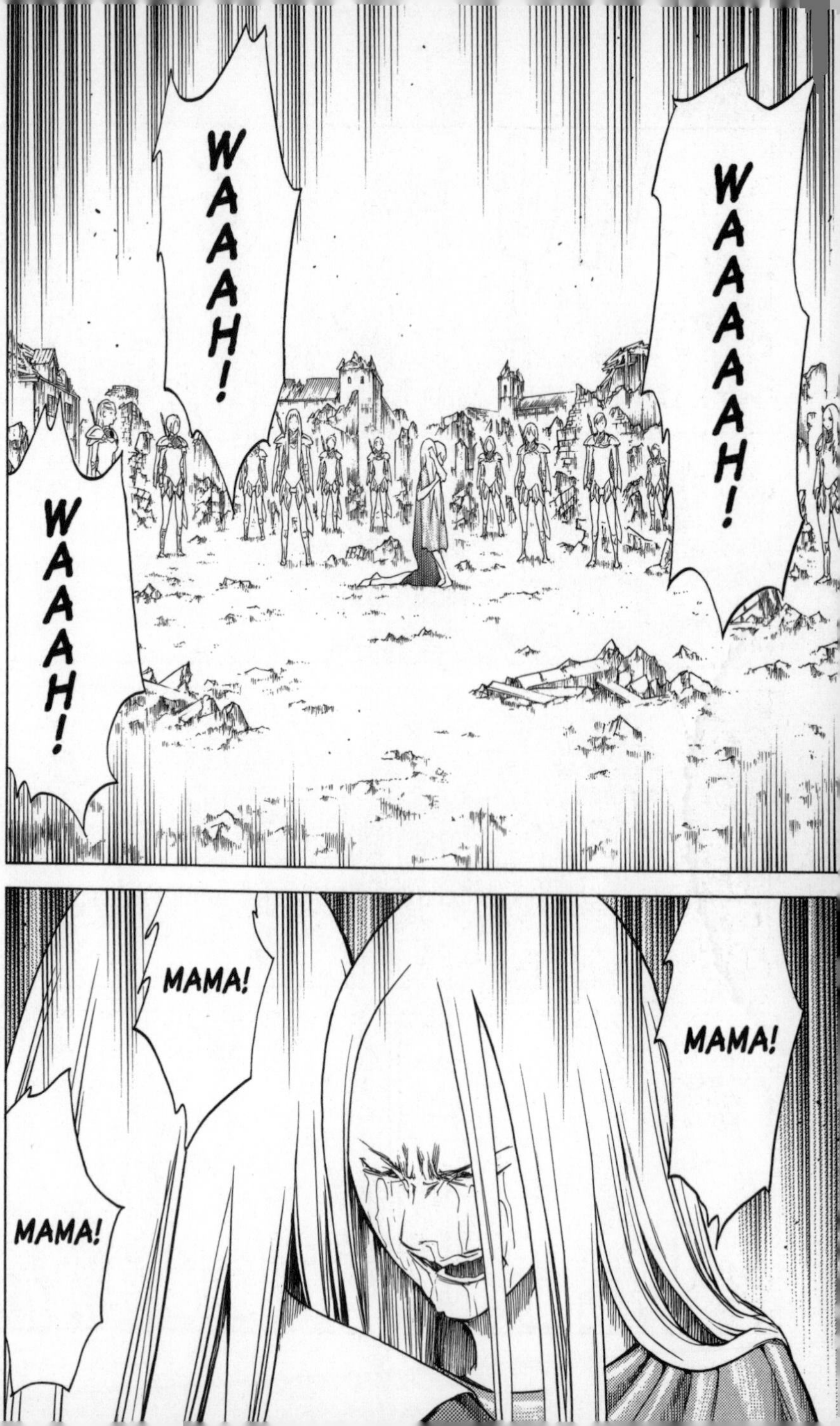
WAAAAAH!
WAAAH!
WAAAH!
MAMA!
MAMA!
MAMA!

READ THIS WAY

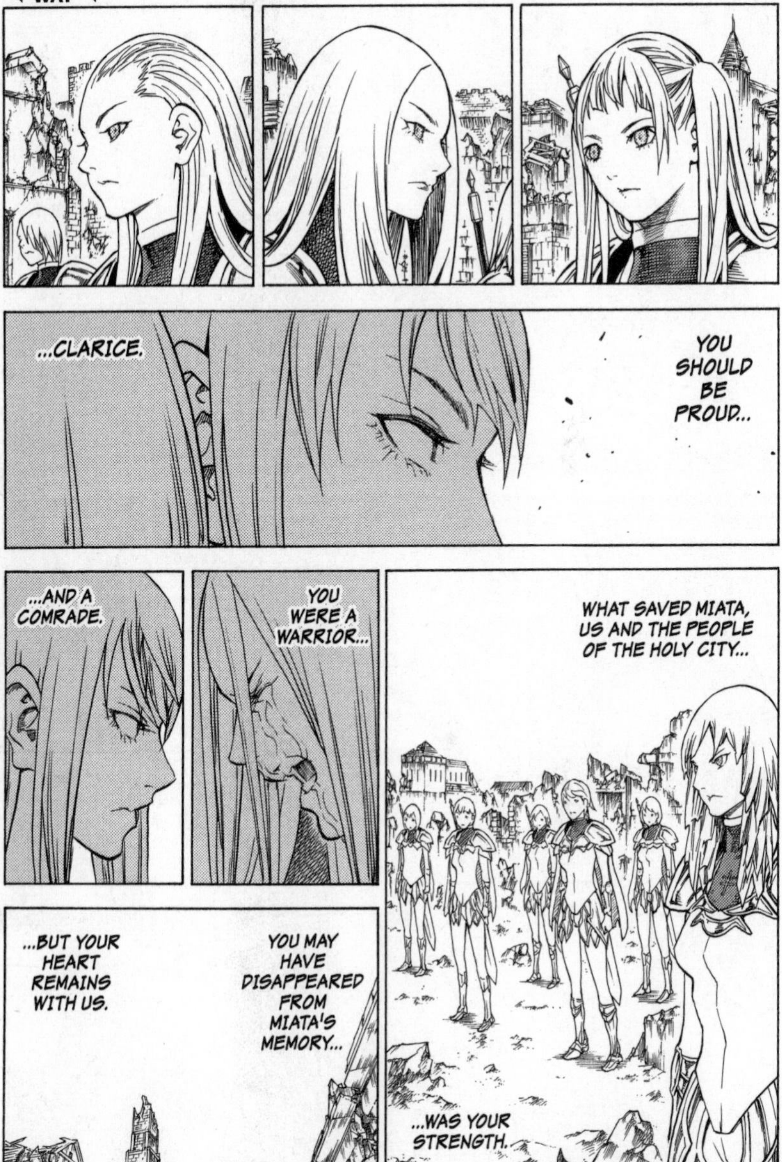
YOU SHOULD BE PROUD...
...CLARICE.
WHAT SAVED MIATA, US AND THE PEOPLE OF THE HOLY CITY...
...WAS YOUR STRENGTH.
YOU WERE A WARRIOR...
...AND A COMRADE.
YOU MAY HAVE DISAPPEARED FROM MIATA'S MEMORY...
...BUT YOUR HEART REMAINS WITH US.

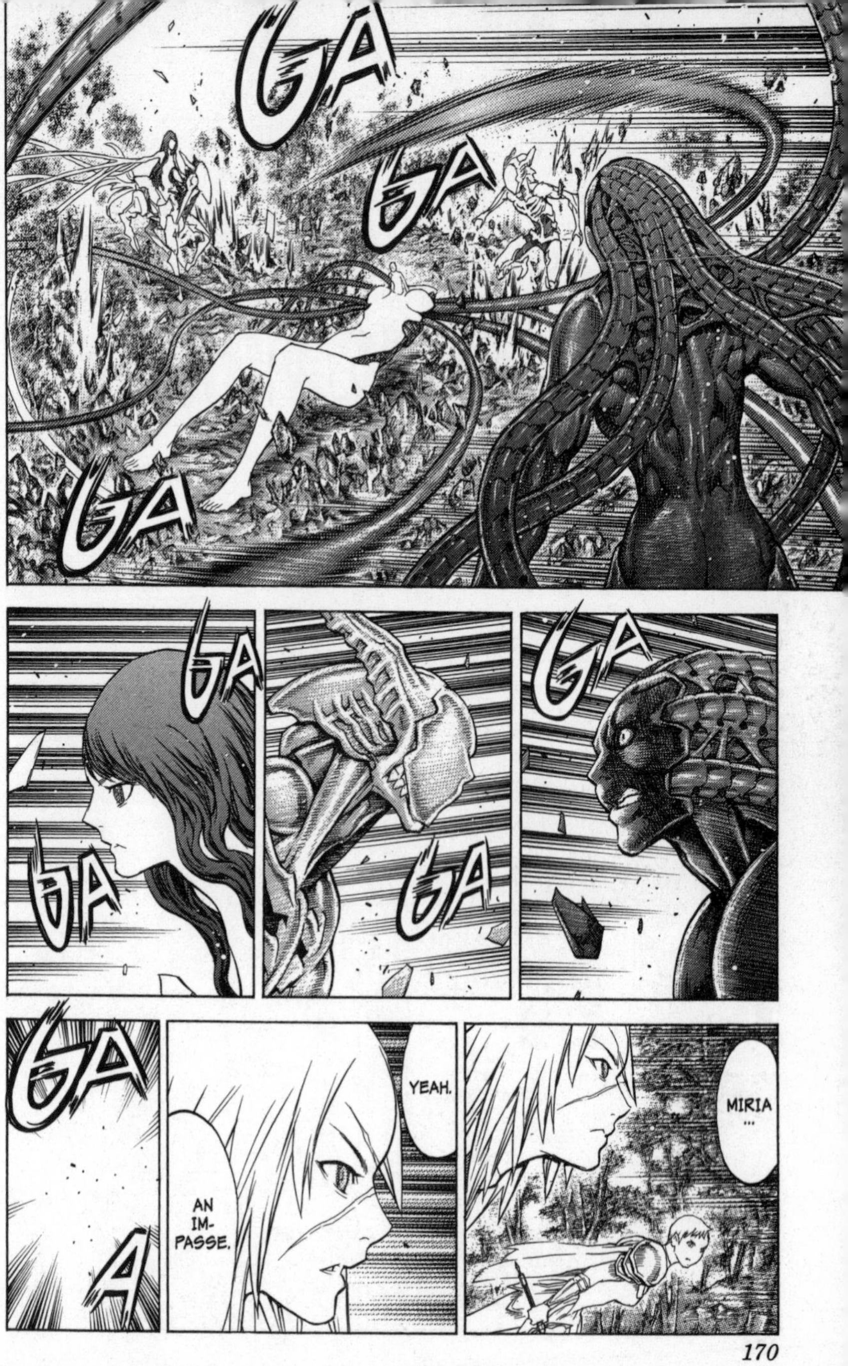
GA
GA
GA
GA
GA
GA
GA
GA
MIRIA ...
YEAH.
AN IM-PASSE.
GA
A

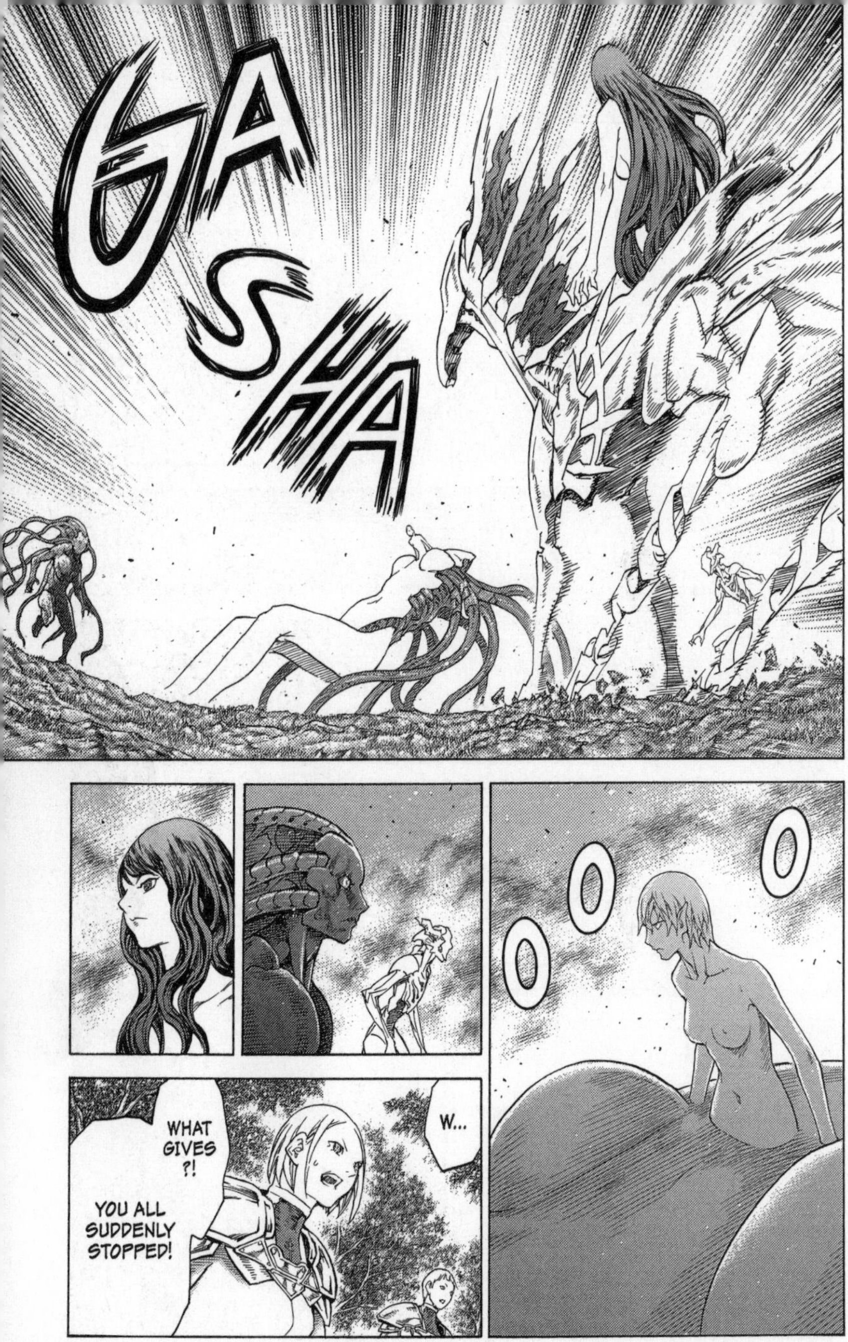
GASHA
OOOO
W...
WHAT GIVES ?!
YOU ALL SUDDENLY STOPPED!

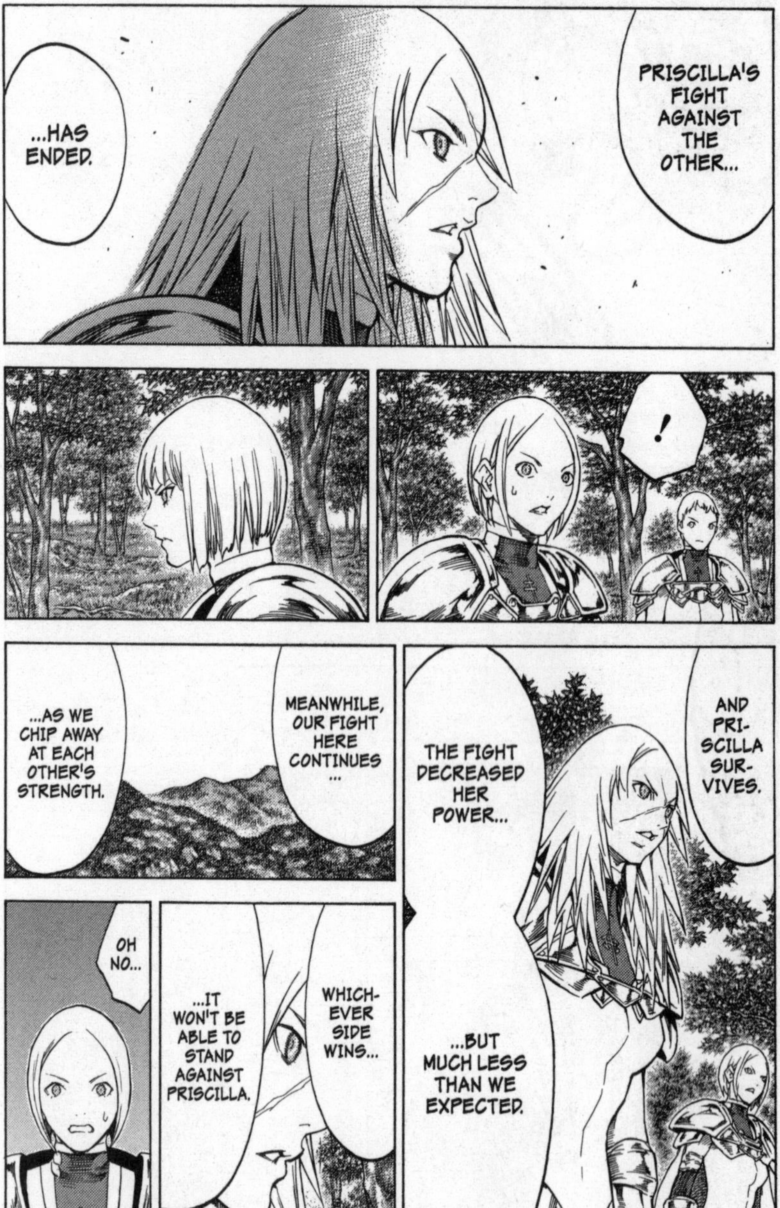
PRISCILLA'S FIGHT AGAINST THE OTHER...
...HAS ENDED.
!
AND PRISCILLA SURVIVES.
THE FIGHT DECREASED HER POWER...
...BUT MUCH LESS THAN WE EXPECTED.
MEANWHILE, OUR FIGHT HERE CONTINUES...
...AS WE CHIP AWAY AT EACH OTHER'S STRENGTH.
WHICHEVER SIDE WINS...
...IT WON'T BE ABLE TO STAND AGAINST PRISCILLA.
OH NO...

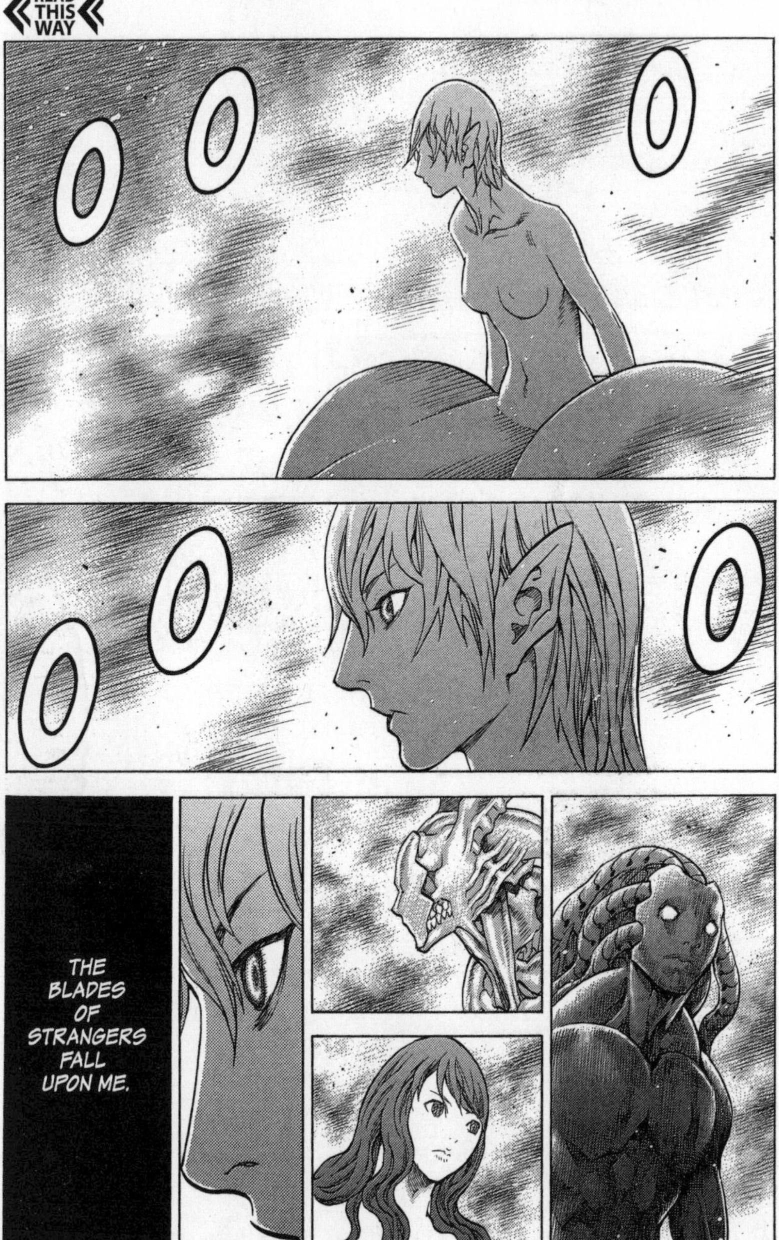
READ THIS WAY
O
O
O
O
O
O
THE BLADES OF STRANGERS FALL UPON ME.

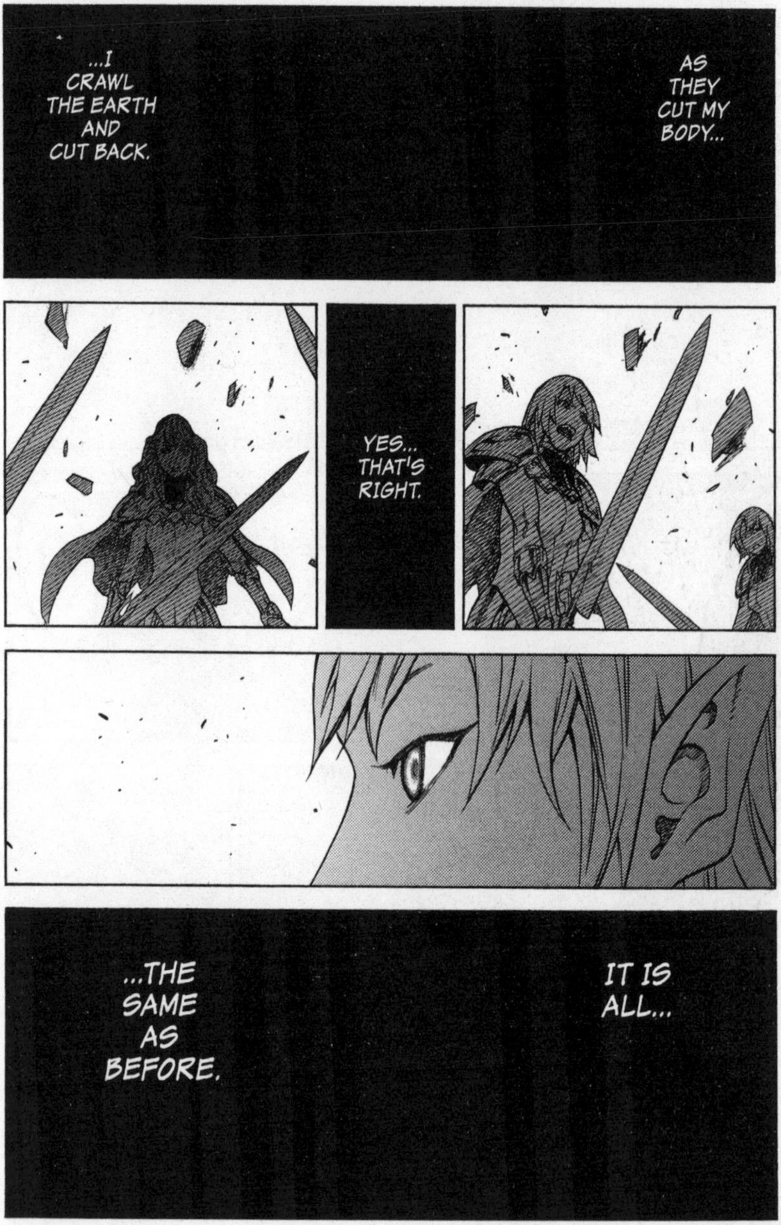
AS THEY CUT MY BODY...
...I CRAWL THE EARTH AND CUT BACK.
YES... THAT'S RIGHT.
IT IS ALL...
...THE SAME AS BEFORE.

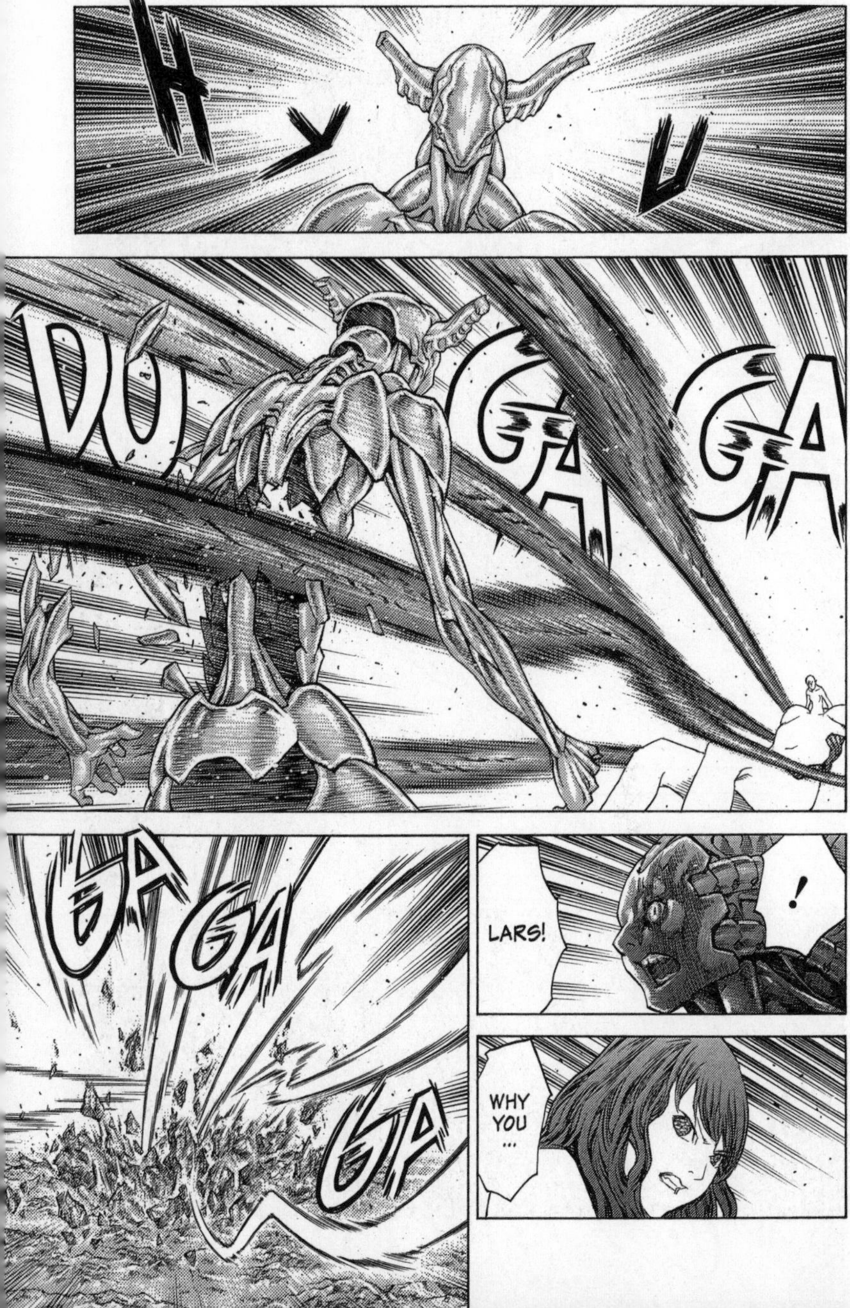
HyU
DO GA GA
!
LARS!
WHY YOU ...
GA GA GA

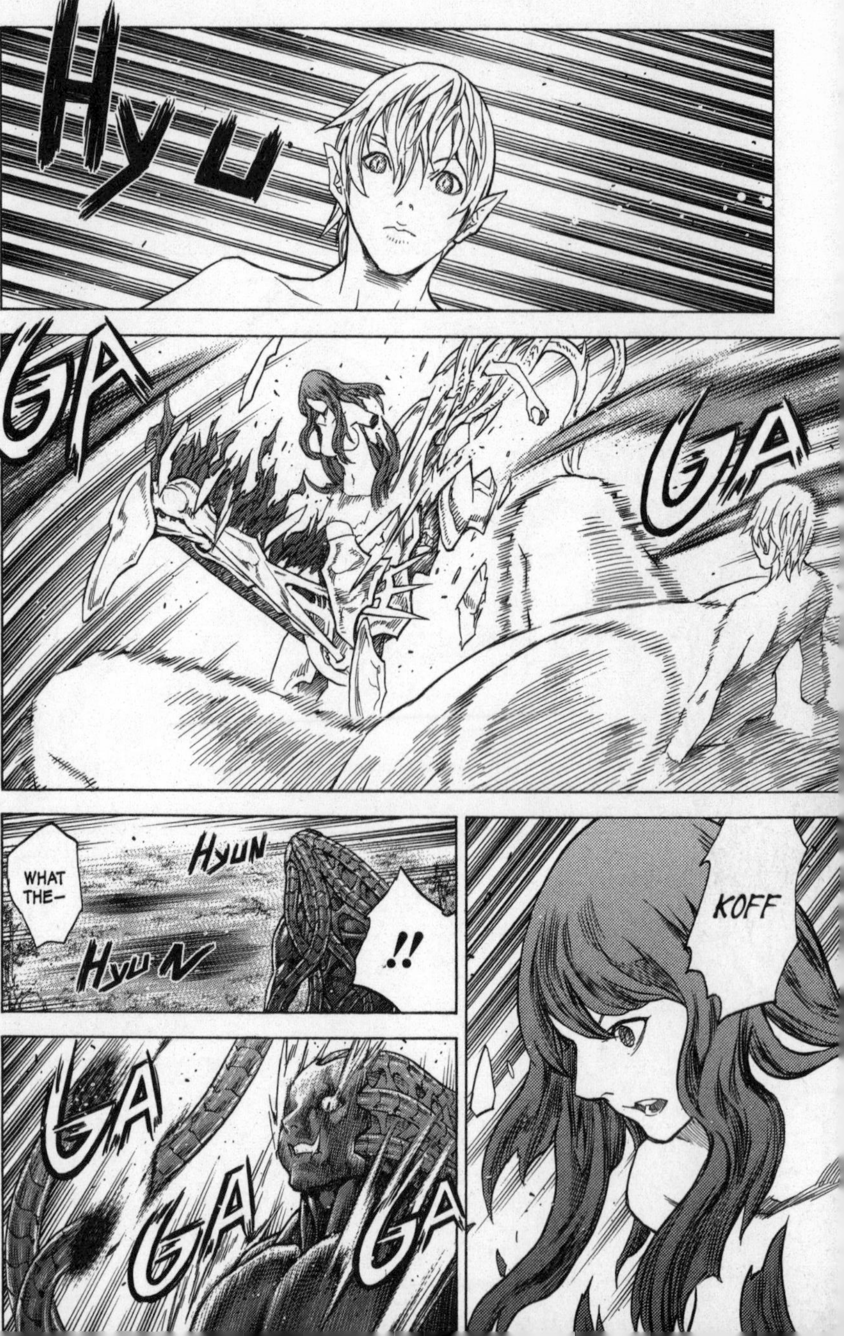
HYU
GA
GA
KOFF
HYUN
WHAT THE—
!!
HYUN
GA
GA
GA

READ THIS WAY

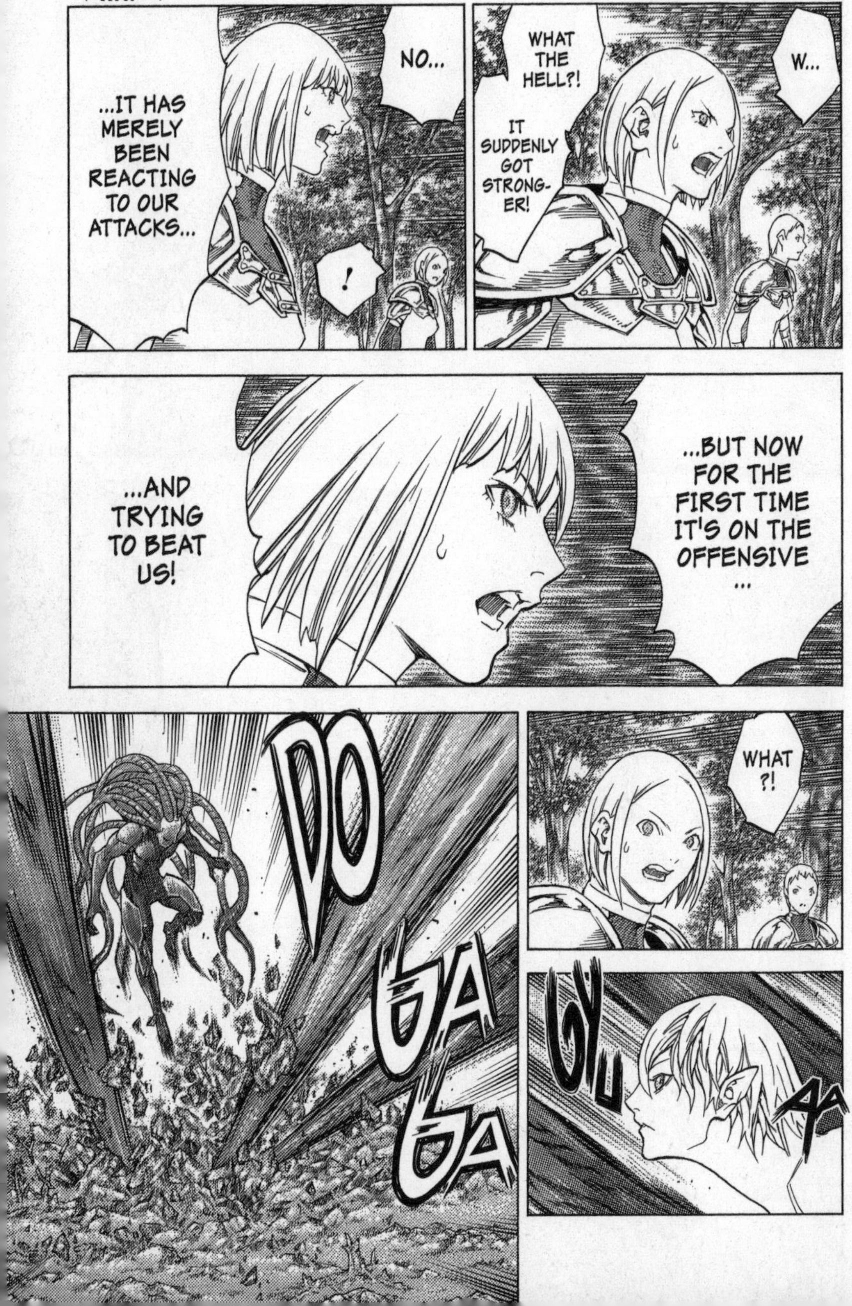
W...
WHAT THE HELL?!
IT SUDDENLY GOT STRONG-ER!
NO...
...IT HAS MERELY BEEN REACTING TO OUR ATTACKS...
!
...BUT NOW FOR THE FIRST TIME IT'S ON THE OFFENSIVE ...
...AND TRYING TO BEAT US!
WHAT ?!
GYU
AA
DO
GA
GA

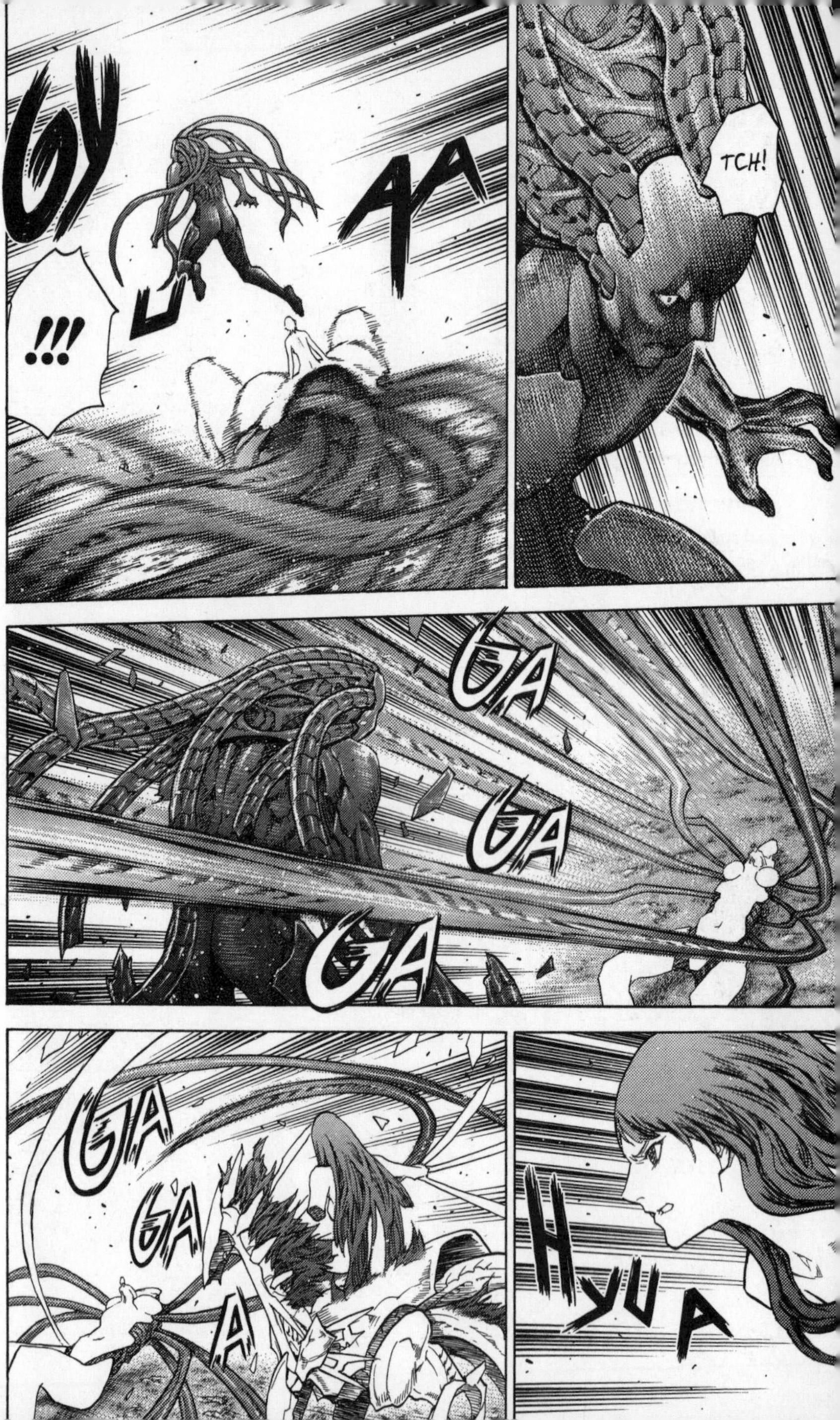
TCH!
GYUAA
!!!
GA
GA
GA
HYUA
GA
GA
A

READ THIS WAY

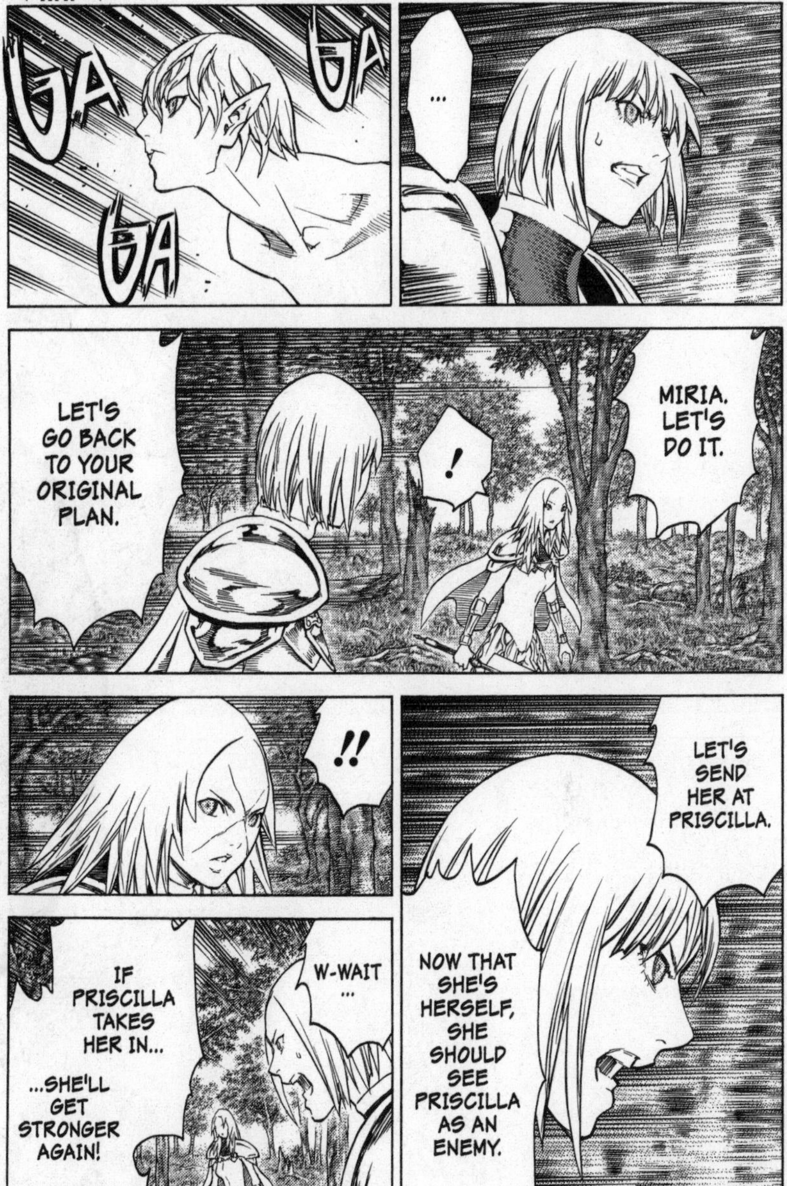

...
GA
GA
GA
MIRIA. LET'S DO IT.
!
LET'S GO BACK TO YOUR ORIGINAL PLAN.
LET'S SEND HER AT PRISCILLA.
NOW THAT SHE'S HERSELF, SHE SHOULD SEE PRISCILLA AS AN ENEMY.
!!
W-WAIT ...
IF PRISCILLA TAKES HER IN...
...SHE'LL GET STRONGER AGAIN!

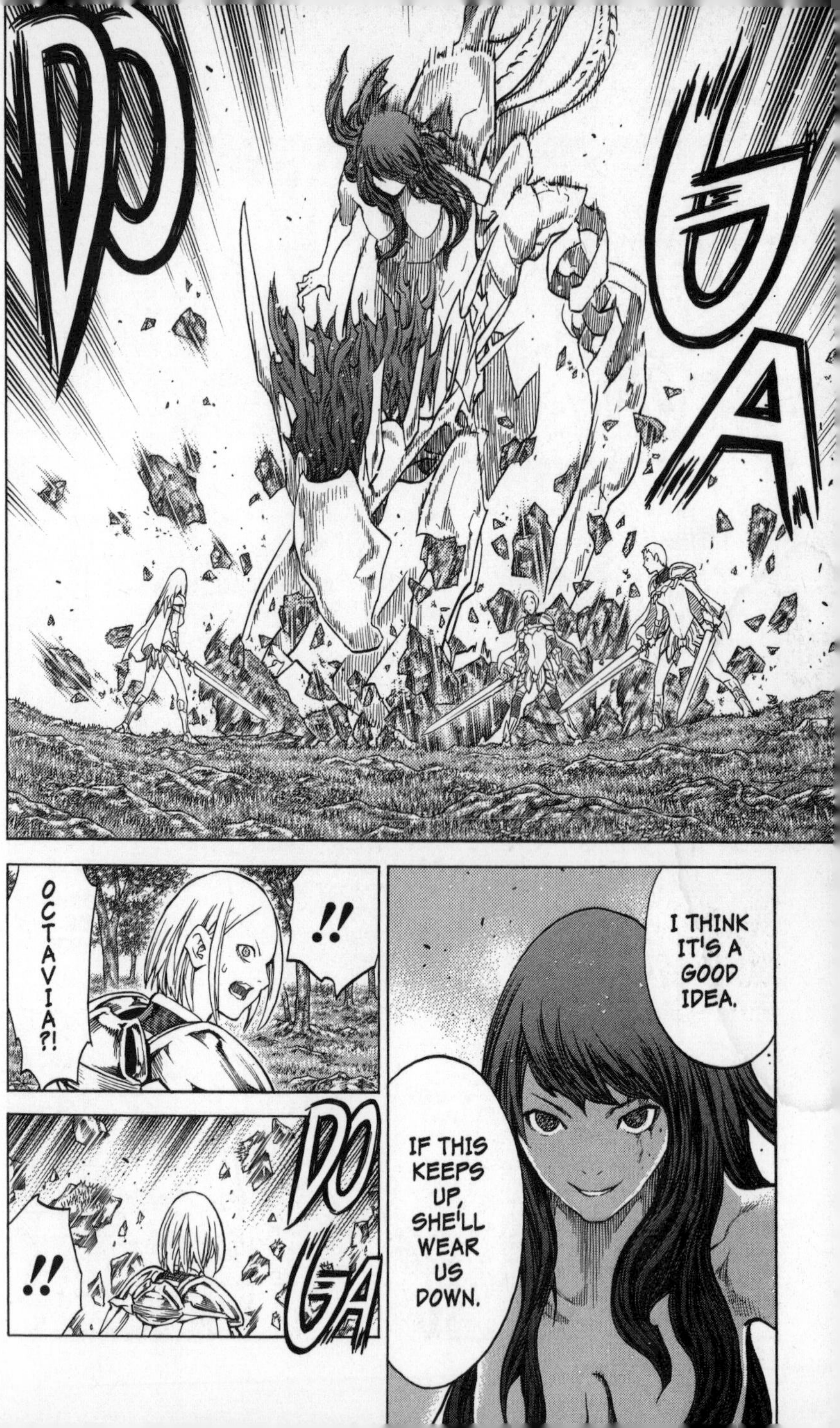
DOGA
I THINK IT'S A GOOD IDEA.
IF THIS KEEPS UP, SHE'LL WEAR US DOWN.
!!
OCTAVIA?!
DOGA
!!

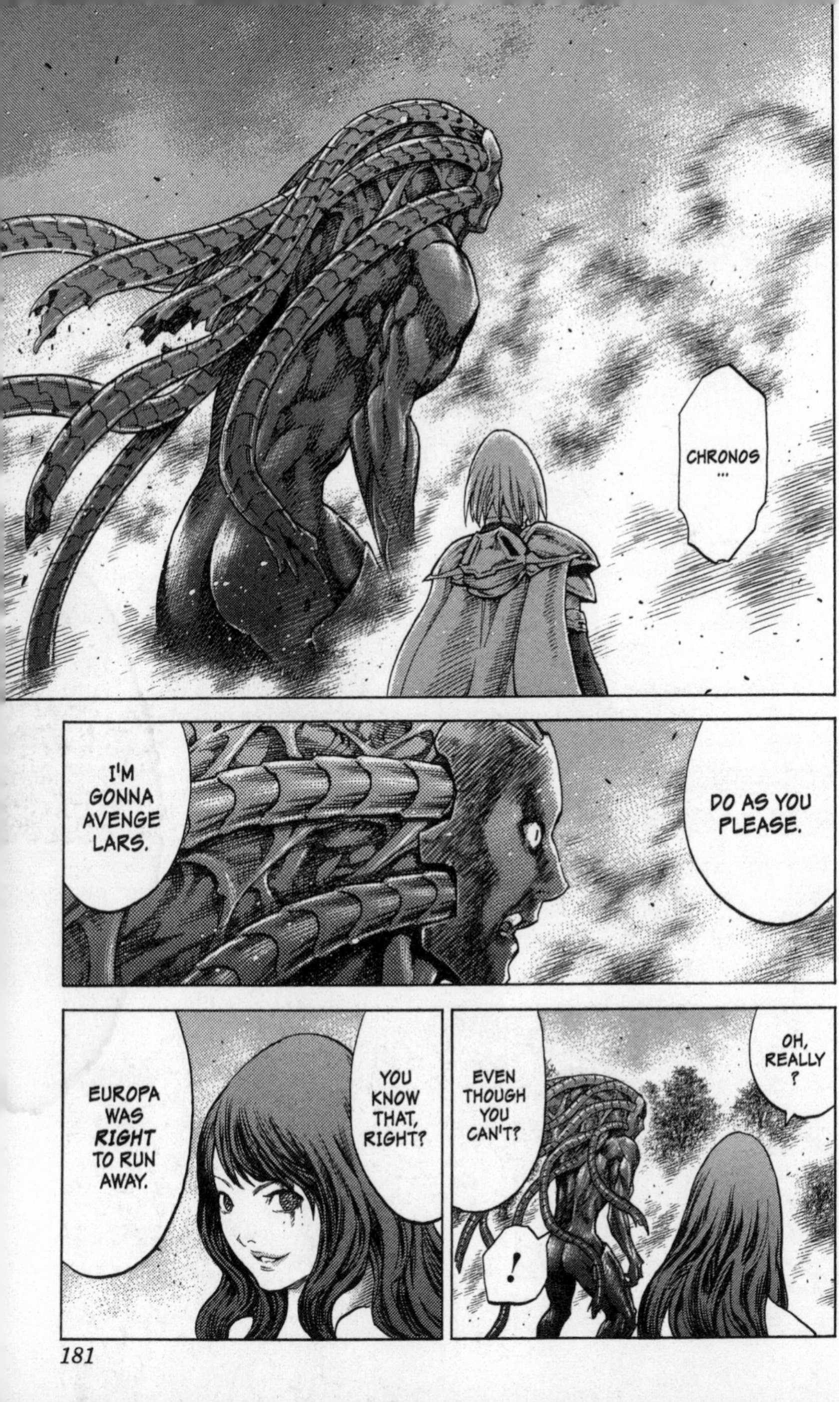
CHRONOS ...
DO AS YOU PLEASE.
I'M GONNA AVENGE LARS.
OH, REALLY?
!
EVEN THOUGH YOU CAN'T?
YOU KNOW THAT, RIGHT?
EUROPA WAS RIGHT TO RUN AWAY.

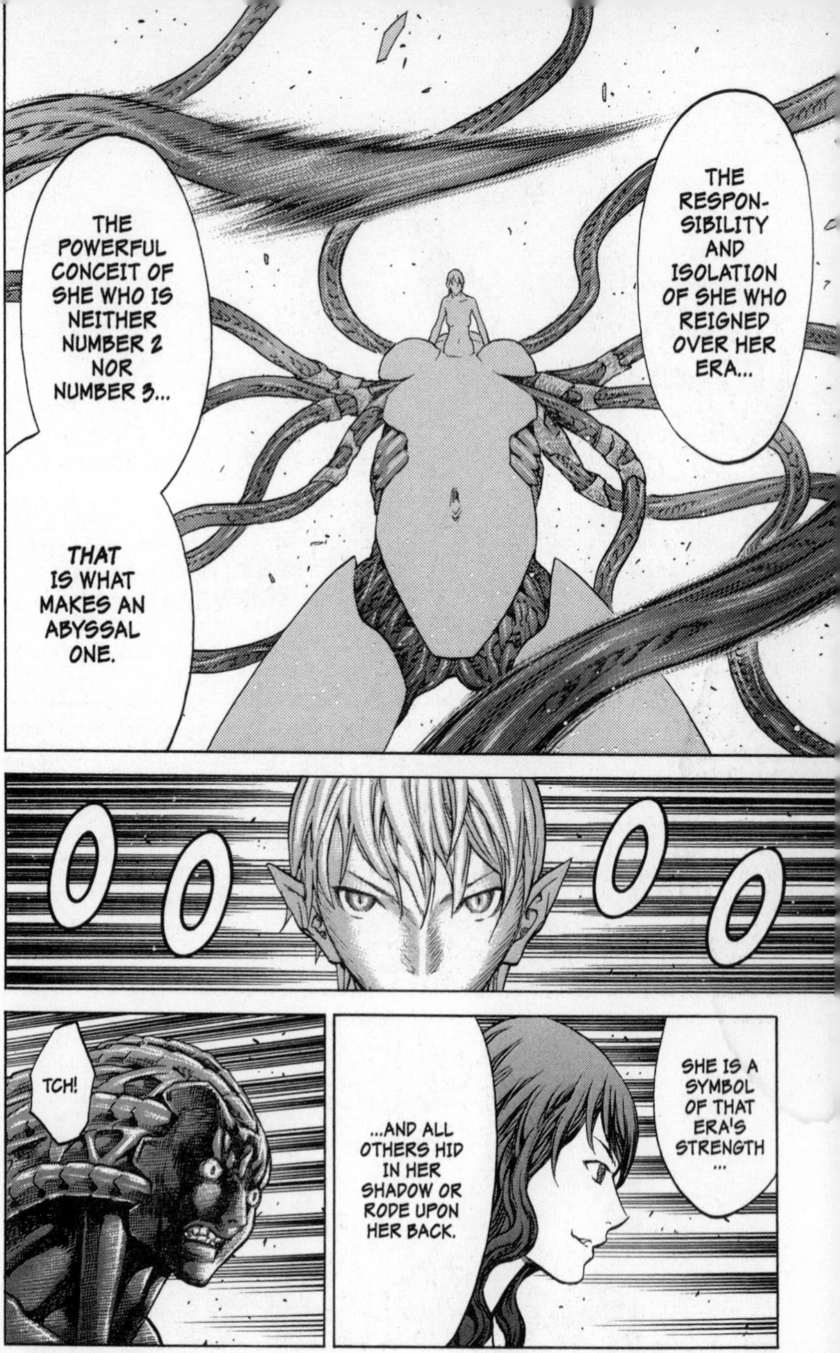
THE RESPON-SIBILITY AND ISOLATION OF SHE WHO REIGNED OVER HER ERA...
THE POWERFUL CONCEIT OF SHE WHO IS NEITHER NUMBER 2 NOR NUMBER 3...
THAT IS WHAT MAKES AN ABYSSAL ONE.
SHE IS A SYMBOL OF THAT ERA'S STRENGTH...
...AND ALL OTHERS HID IN HER SHADOW OR RODE UPON HER BACK.
TCH!

READ THIS WAY

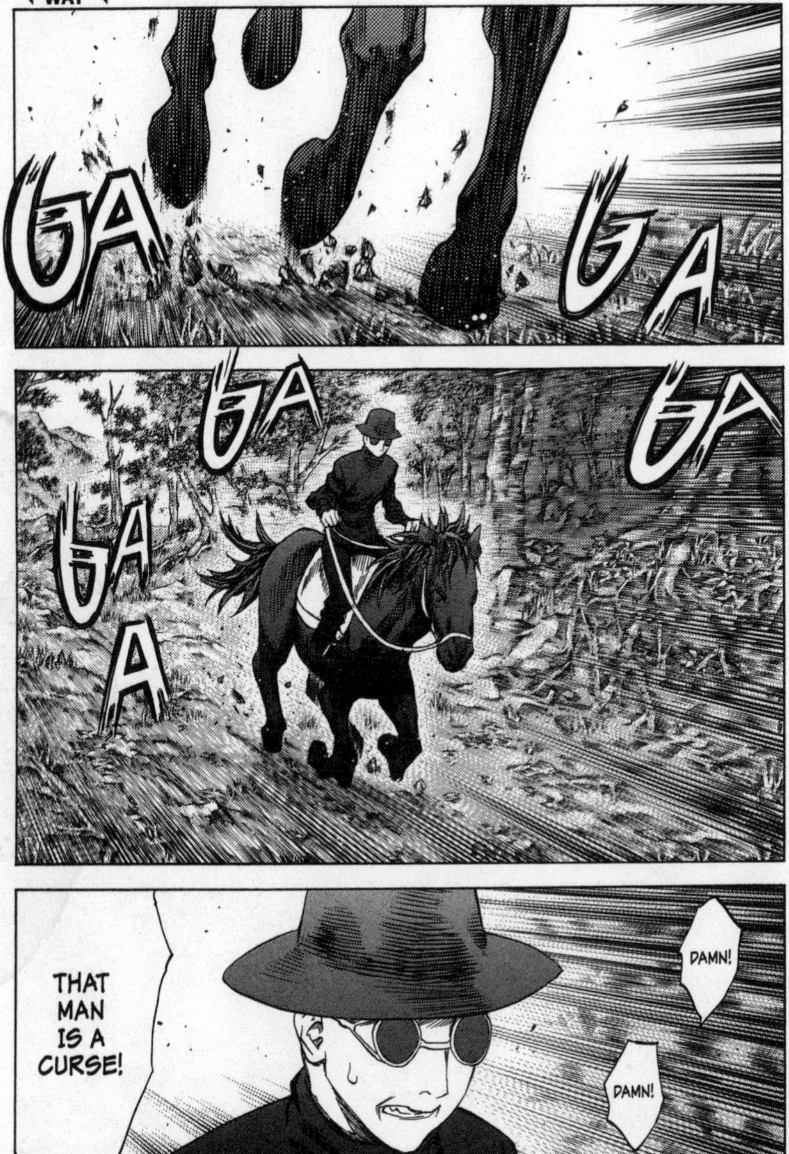
GA
GA
GA
GA
GA
GA
A
DAMN!
DAMN!
THAT MAN IS A CURSE!

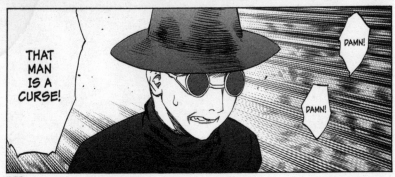

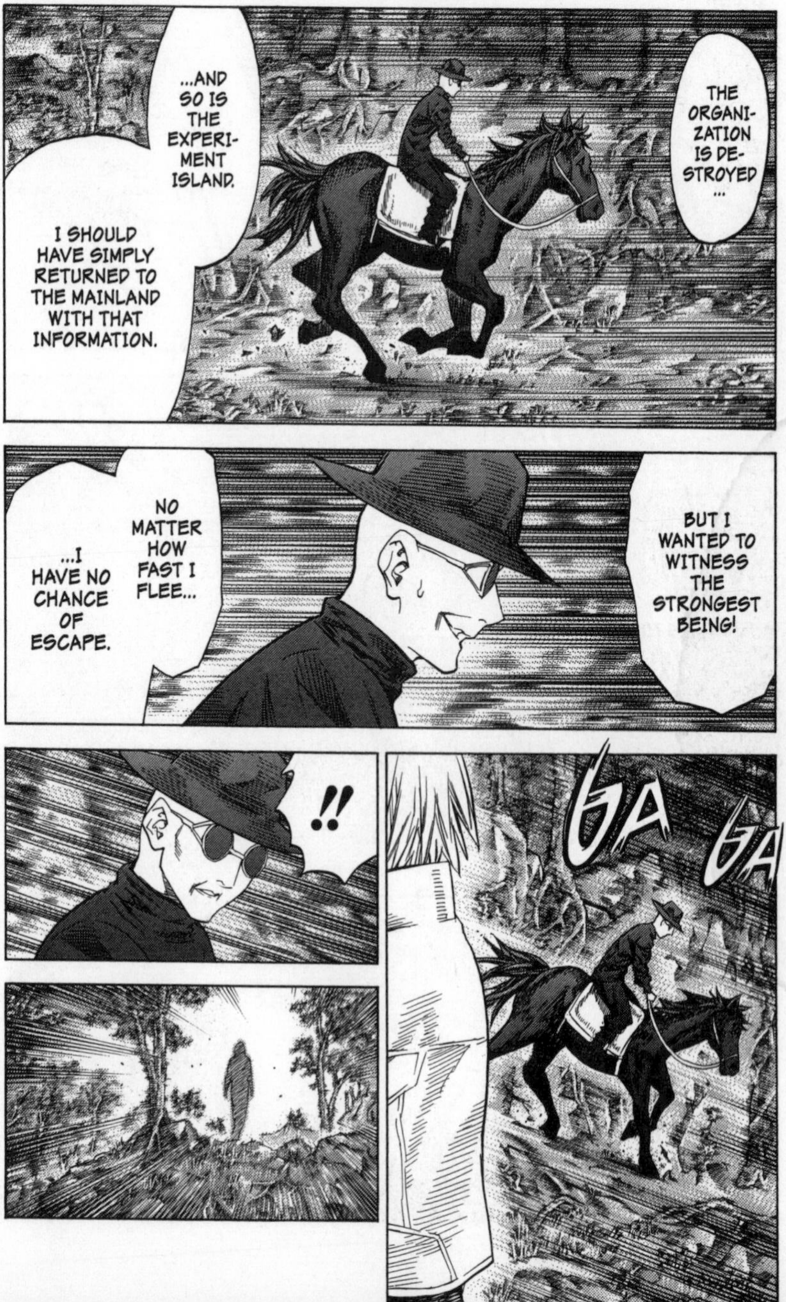
THE ORGANI-ZATION IS DE-STROYED ...
...AND SO IS THE EXPERI-MENT ISLAND.
I SHOULD HAVE SIMPLY RETURNED TO THE MAINLAND WITH THAT INFORMATION.
BUT I WANTED TO WITNESS THE STRONGEST BEING!
NO MATTER HOW FAST I FLEE...
...I HAVE NO CHANCE OF ESCAPE.
GA GA
!!

READ THIS WAY

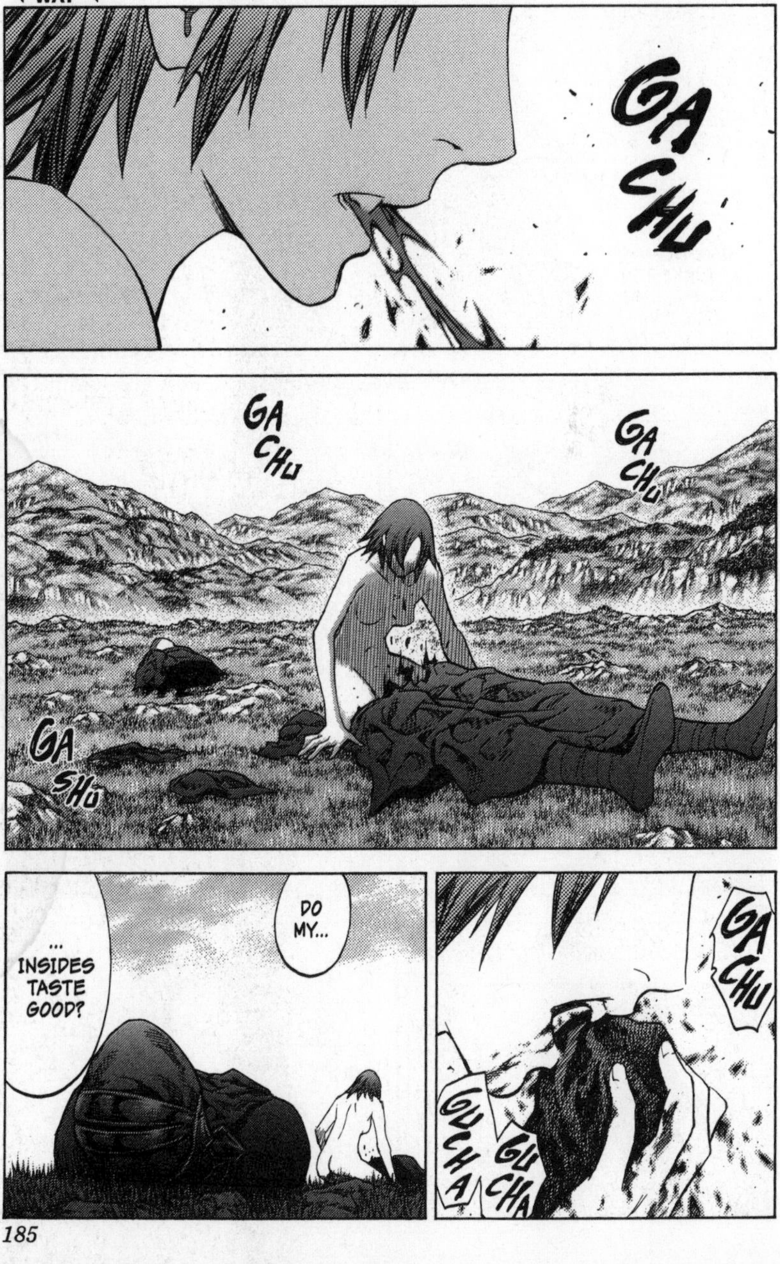

GACHU
GACHU
GACHU
GASHU
GACHU
GUCHA GUCHA
GUCHA
DO MY...
... INSIDES TASTE GOOD?

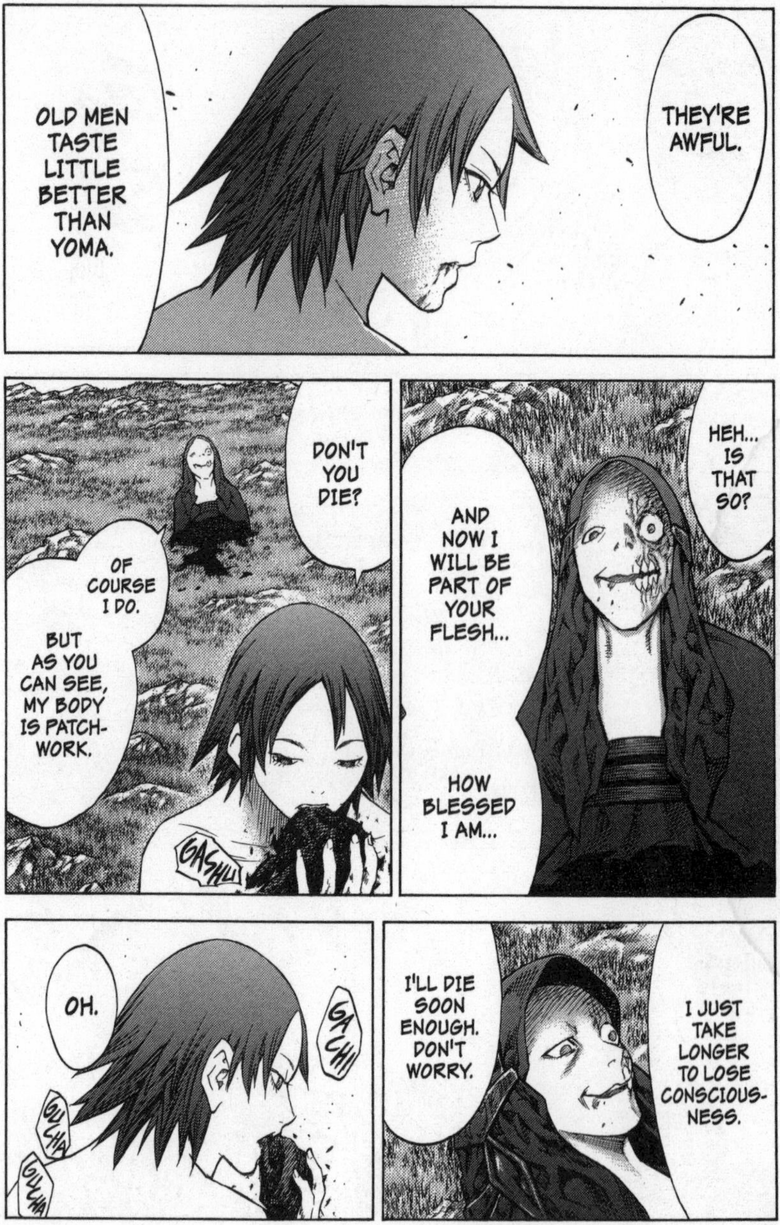
THEY'RE AWFUL.
OLD MEN TASTE LITTLE BETTER THAN YOMA.
HEH... IS THAT SO?
AND NOW I WILL BE PART OF YOUR FLESH...
HOW BLESSED I AM...
DON'T YOU DIE?
OF COURSE I DO.
BUT AS YOU CAN SEE, MY BODY IS PATCH-WORK.
GASHU
I JUST TAKE LONGER TO LOSE CONSCIOUS-NESS.
I'LL DIE SOON ENOUGH. DON'T WORRY.
GACHI
OH.
GUCHA
GUCHA

READ THIS WAY

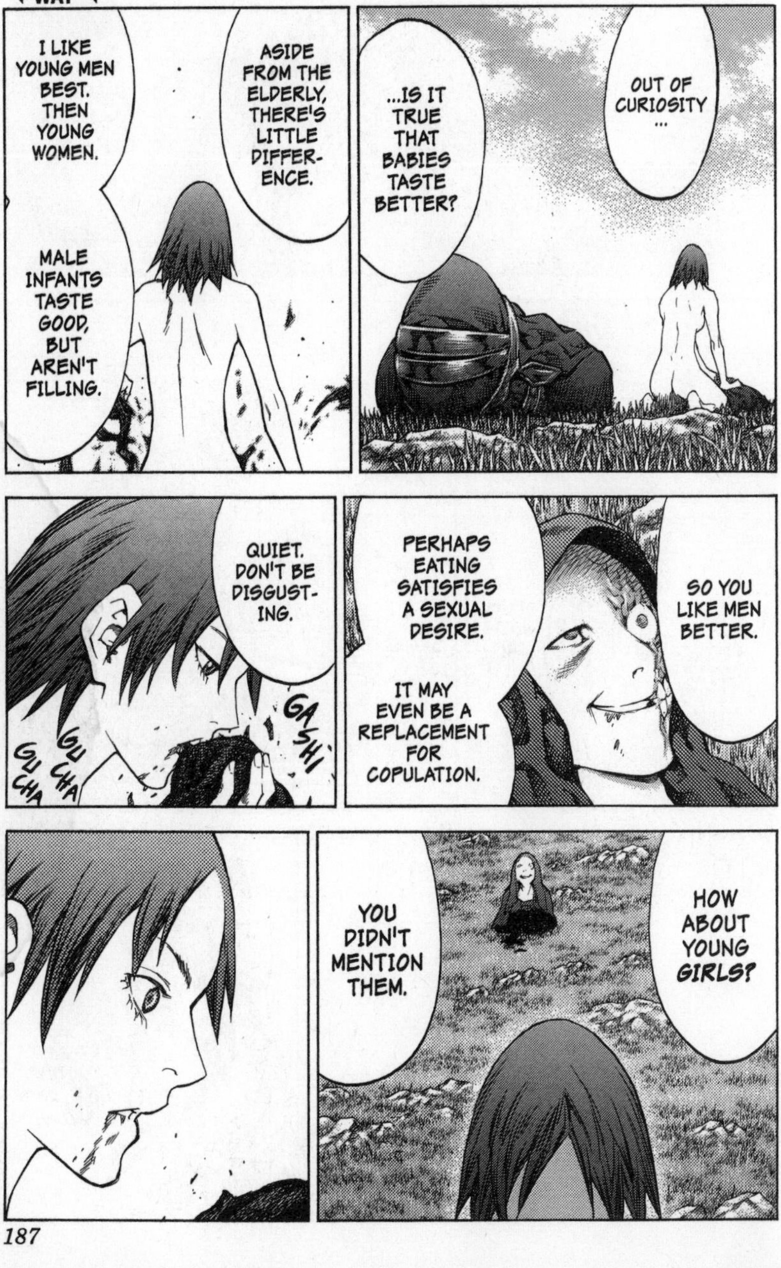

OUT OF CURIOSITY ...
...IS IT TRUE THAT BABIES TASTE BETTER?
ASIDE FROM THE ELDERLY, THERE'S LITTLE DIFFER-ENCE.
I LIKE YOUNG MEN BEST. THEN YOUNG WOMEN.
MALE INFANTS TASTE GOOD, BUT AREN'T FILLING.
SO YOU LIKE MEN BETTER.
PERHAPS EATING SATISFIES A SEXUAL DESIRE.
IT MAY EVEN BE A REPLACEMENT FOR COPULATION.
QUIET. DON'T BE DISGUST-ING.
GASHI
GUCHA
GUCHA
HOW ABOUT YOUNG GIRLS?
YOU DIDN'T MENTION THEM.

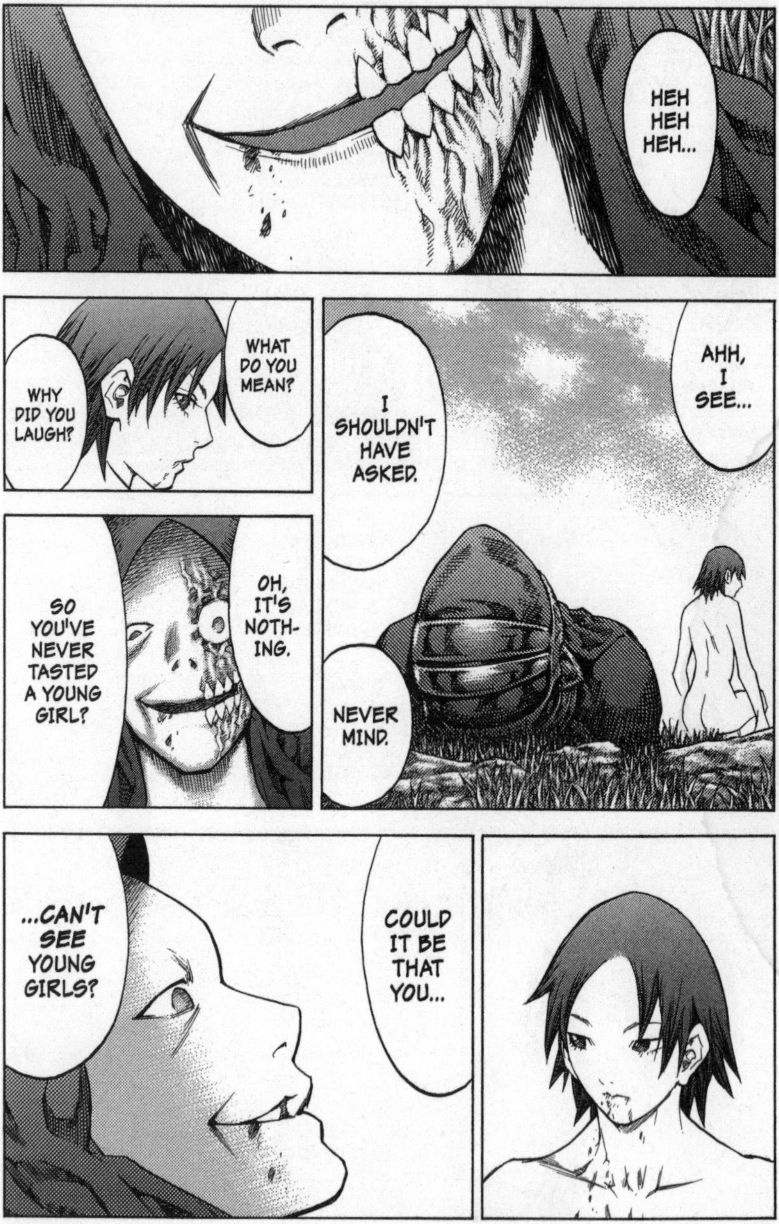
HEH HEH HEH...
AHH, I SEE...
I SHOULDN'T HAVE ASKED.
NEVER MIND.
WHAT DO YOU MEAN?
WHY DID YOU LAUGH?
OH, IT'S NOTH-ING.
SO YOU'VE NEVER TASTED A YOUNG GIRL?
COULD IT BE THAT YOU...
...CAN'T SEE YOUNG GIRLS?

READ THIS WAY

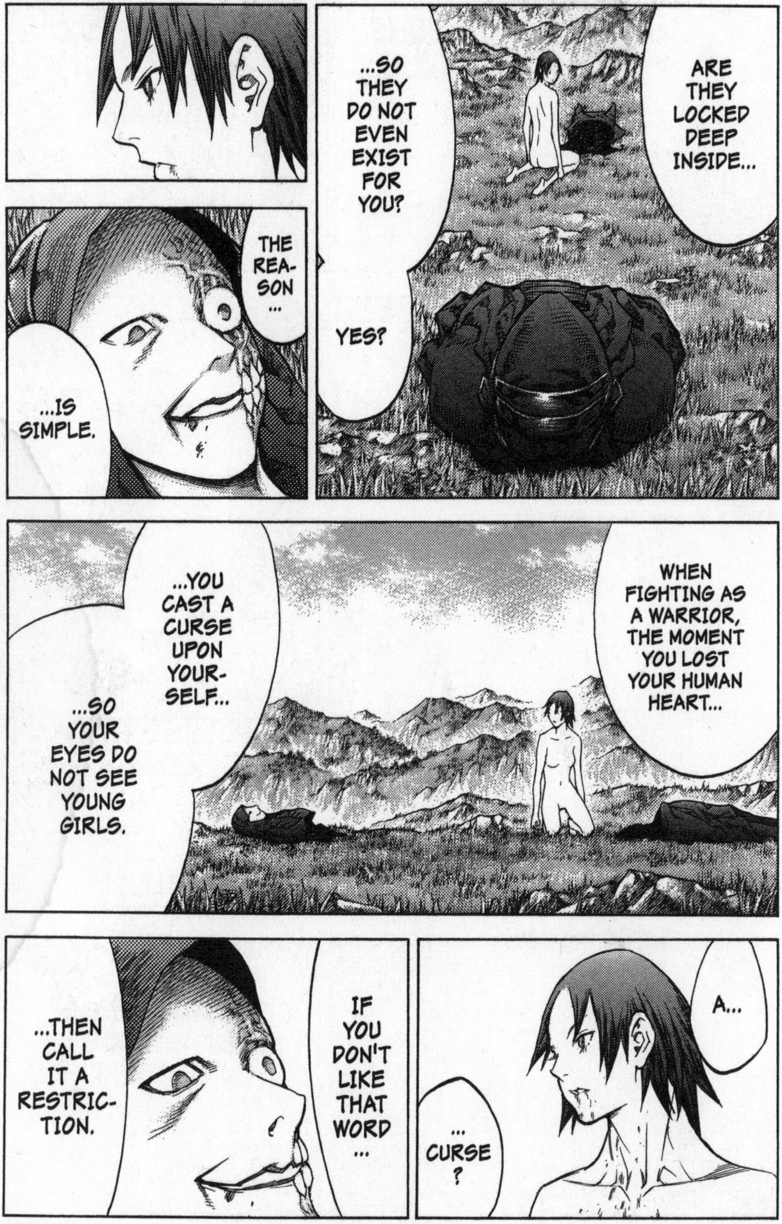
ARE THEY LOCKED DEEP INSIDE...
...SO THEY DO NOT EVEN EXIST FOR YOU?
YES?
THE REASON...
...IS SIMPLE.
WHEN FIGHTING AS A WARRIOR, THE MOMENT YOU LOST YOUR HUMAN HEART...
...YOU CAST A CURSE UPON YOURSELF...
...SO YOUR EYES DO NOT SEE YOUNG GIRLS.
A...
...CURSE?
IF YOU DON'T LIKE THAT WORD...
...THEN CALL IT A RESTRICTION.

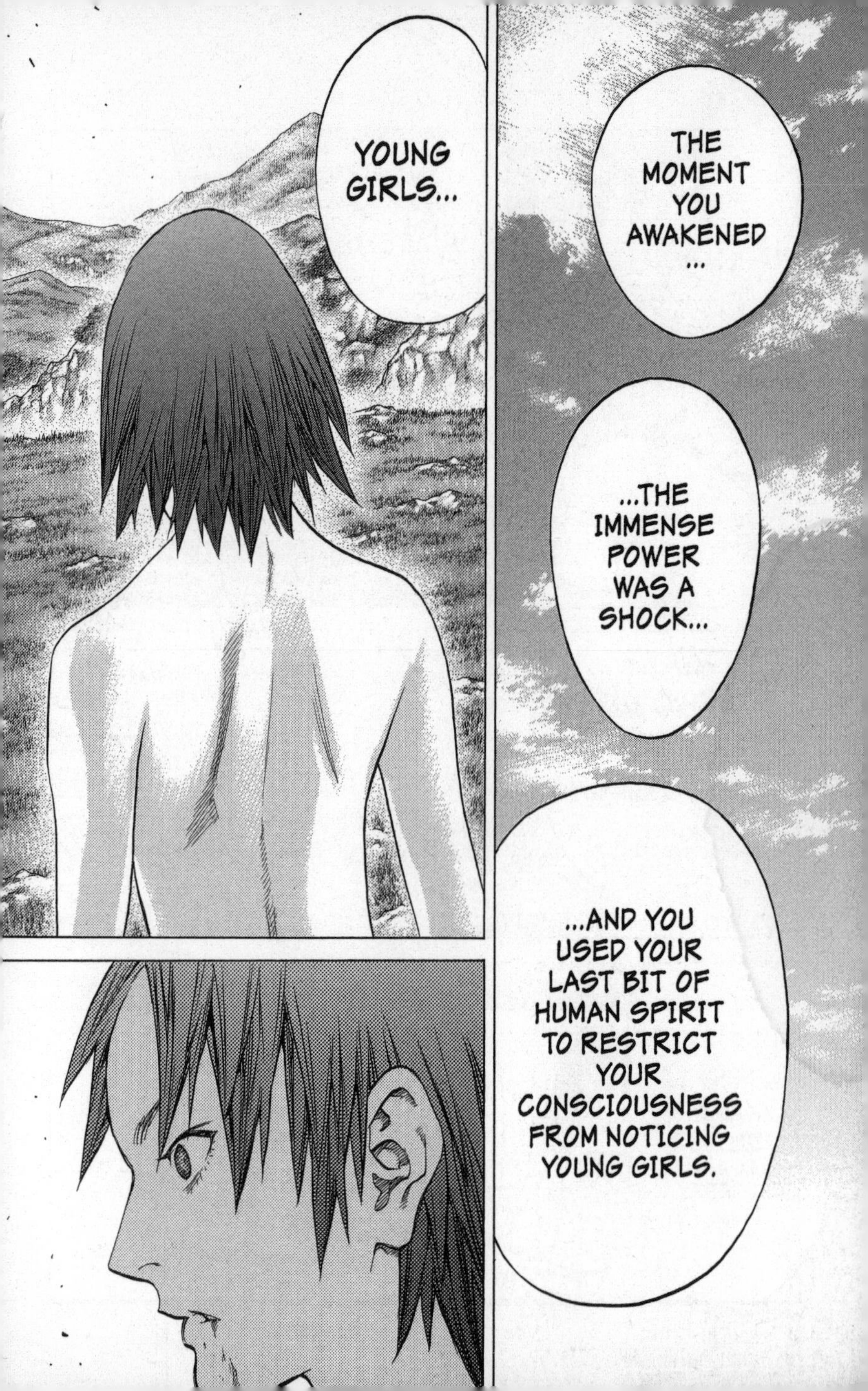
THE MOMENT YOU AWAKENED...
...THE IMMENSE POWER WAS A SHOCK...
...AND YOU USED YOUR LAST BIT OF HUMAN SPIRIT TO RESTRICT YOUR CONSCIOUSNESS FROM NOTICING YOUNG GIRLS.
YOUNG GIRLS...

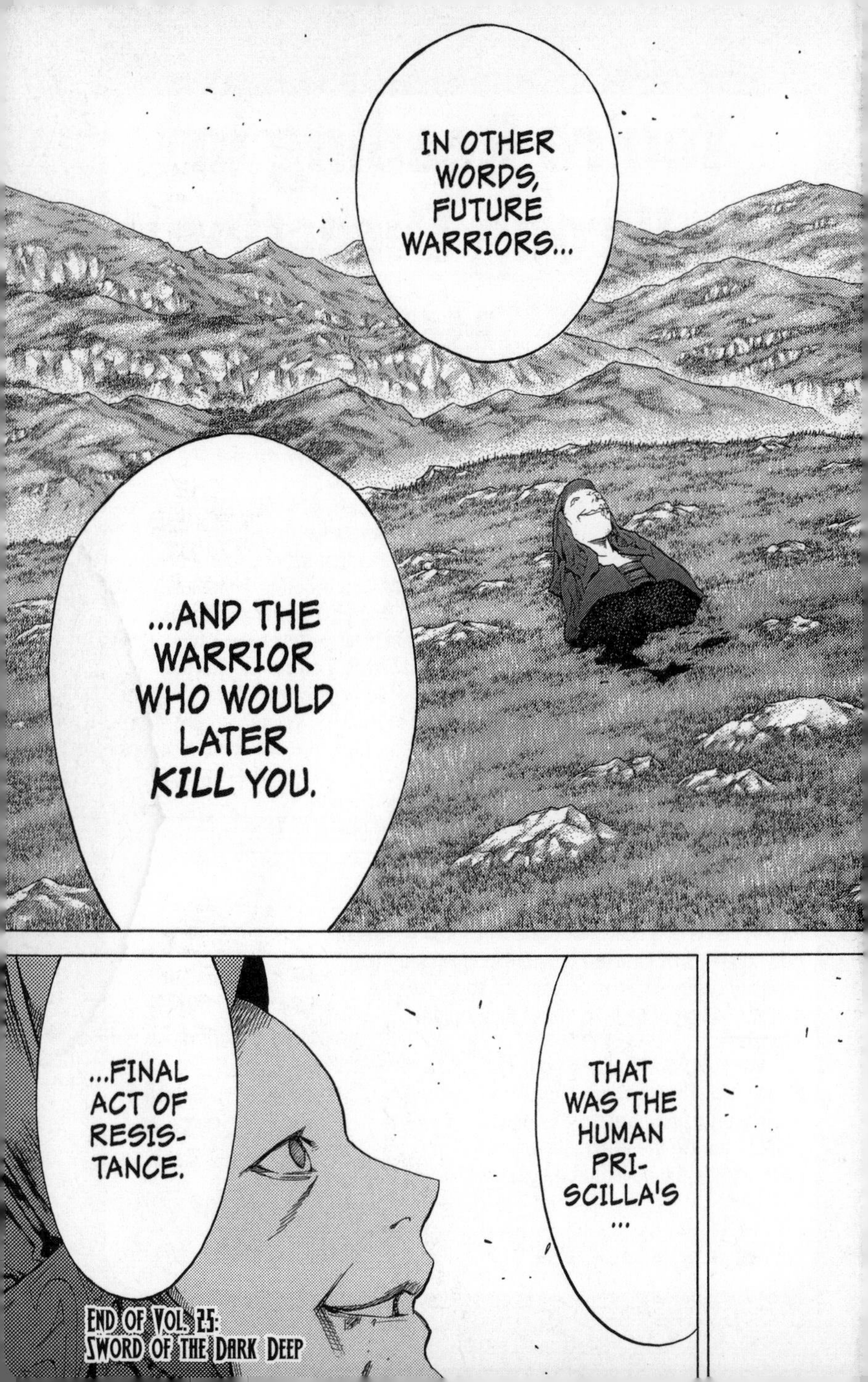
IN OTHER WORDS, FUTURE WARRIORS...
...AND THE WARRIOR WHO WOULD LATER KILL YOU.
THAT WAS THE HUMAN PRI-SCILLA'S ...
...FINAL ACT OF RESIS-TANCE.
END OF VOL. 25: SWORD OF THE DARK DEEP

You're Reading in the Wrong Direction!!

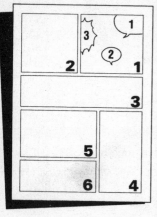

Whoops! Guess what? You're starting at the wrong end of the comic!

…It's true! In keeping with the original Japanese format, **Claymore** is meant to be read from right to left, starting in the upper-right corner.

Unlike English, which is read from left to right, Japanese is read from right to left, meaning that action, sound effects and word-balloon order are completely reversed… something which can make readers unfamiliar with Japanese feel pretty backwards themselves. For this reason, manga or Japanese comics published in the U.S. in English have sometimes been published "flopped"—that is, printed in exact reverse order, as though seen from the other side of a mirror.

By flopping pages, U.S. publishers can avoid confusing readers, but the compromise is not without its downside. For one thing, a character in a flopped manga series who once wore in the original Japanese version a T-shirt emblazoned with "M A Y" (as in "the merry month of") now wears one which reads "Y A M"! Additionally, many manga creators in Japan are themselves unhappy with the process, as some feel the mirror-imaging of their art skews their original intentions.

We are proud to bring you Norihiro Yagi's **Claymore** in the original unflopped format. For now, though, turn to the other side of the book and let the adventure begin…!

—Editor